D•N•ANGEL

BY YUKIRU SUGISAKI

VOLUME 8

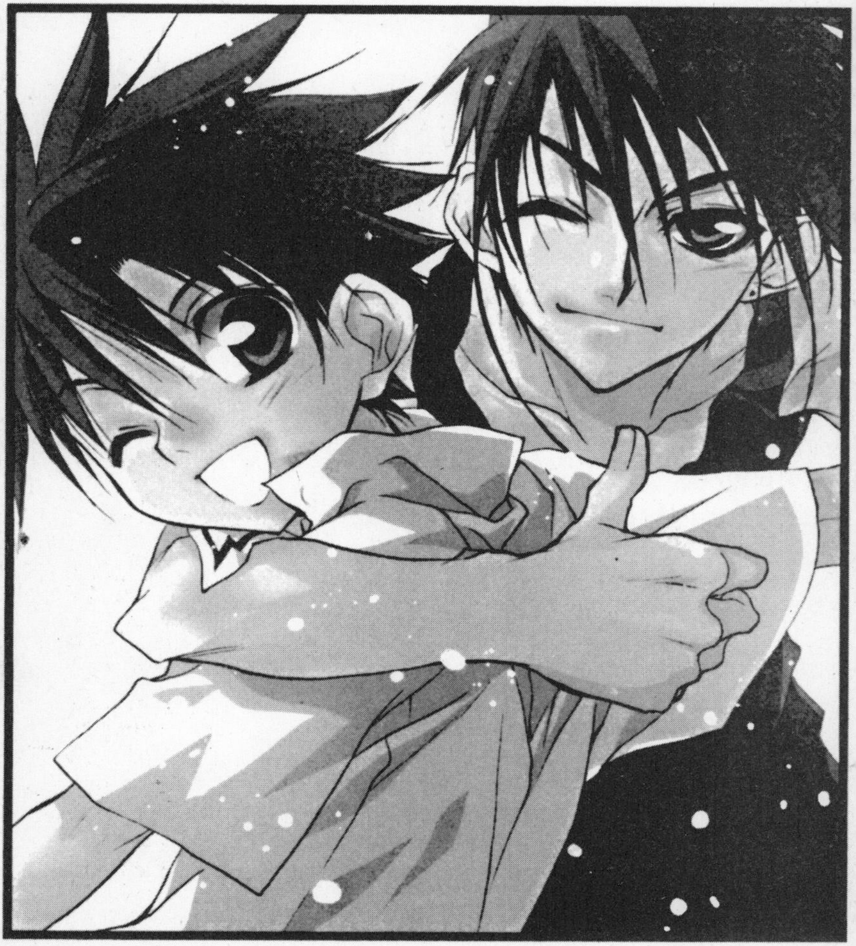

& STORY

Daisuke and Riku have finally resolved their relationship and are happily in love...but the connection between Dark and Satoshi is not so straightforward. When Dark and Daisuke went on their latest mission to steal the Toki no Byoushin, or the "Second Hand of Time," it somehow came to life and captured Daisuke, pulling him into a world it created inside his own painting! Dark followed him into the painting with Riku in an attempt to save him, but failed, and was forced to return to the real world. Now, Dark can't stop feeling that Daisuke is in terrible danger as long as he remains inside the mysterious world of snow...

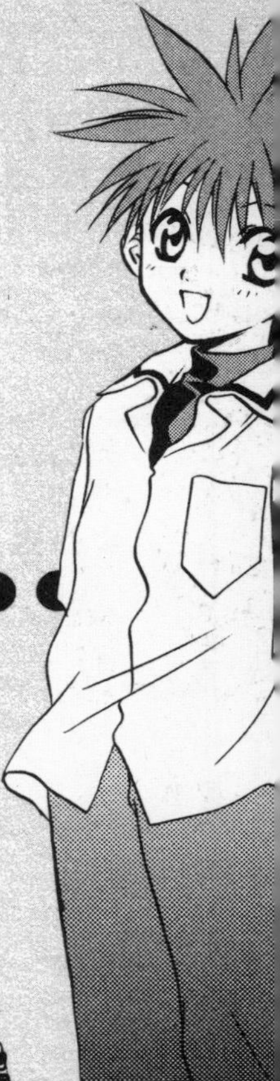

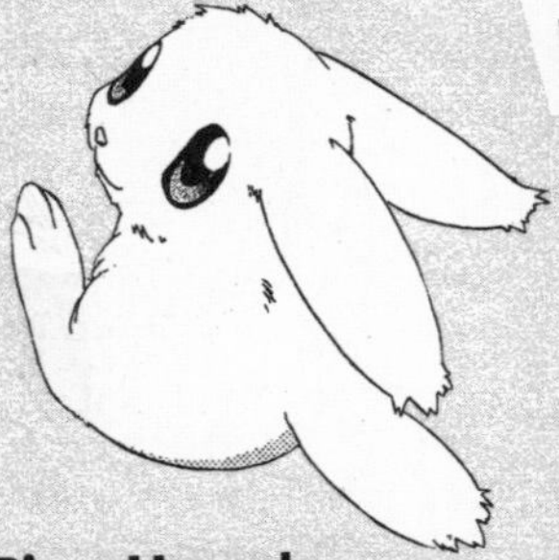

Wiz

A mysterious animal who acts as Dark's familiar, and who can transform into many things, including Dark's black wings. He can also transform himself into Dark or Daisuke.

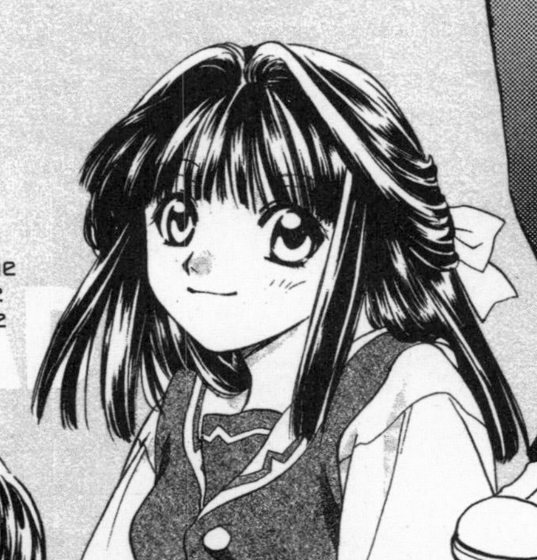

Risa Harada (younger sister)

Daisuke's first crush. Daisuke confessed his love to her...but she rejected him. She's been in love with Dark since the first time she saw him on TV.

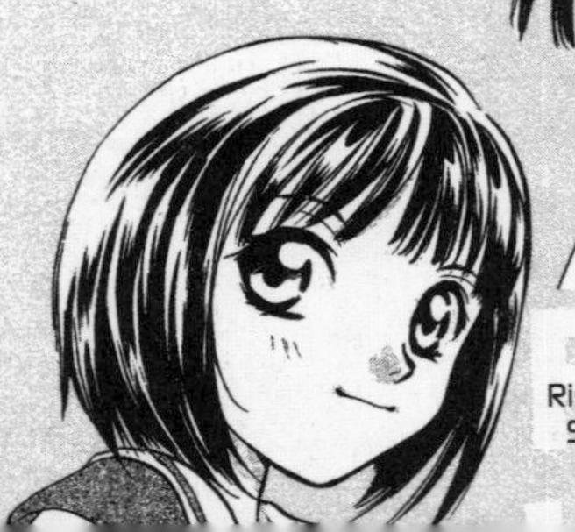

Riku Harada (older sister)

Risa's identical twin sister. She and Daisuke have fallen for each other.

Daisuke Niwa

A 14-year-old student at Azumano Middle School. He has a unique genetic condition that causes him to transform into the infamous Phantom Thief Dark whenever he has romantic feelings.

CHARACTERS

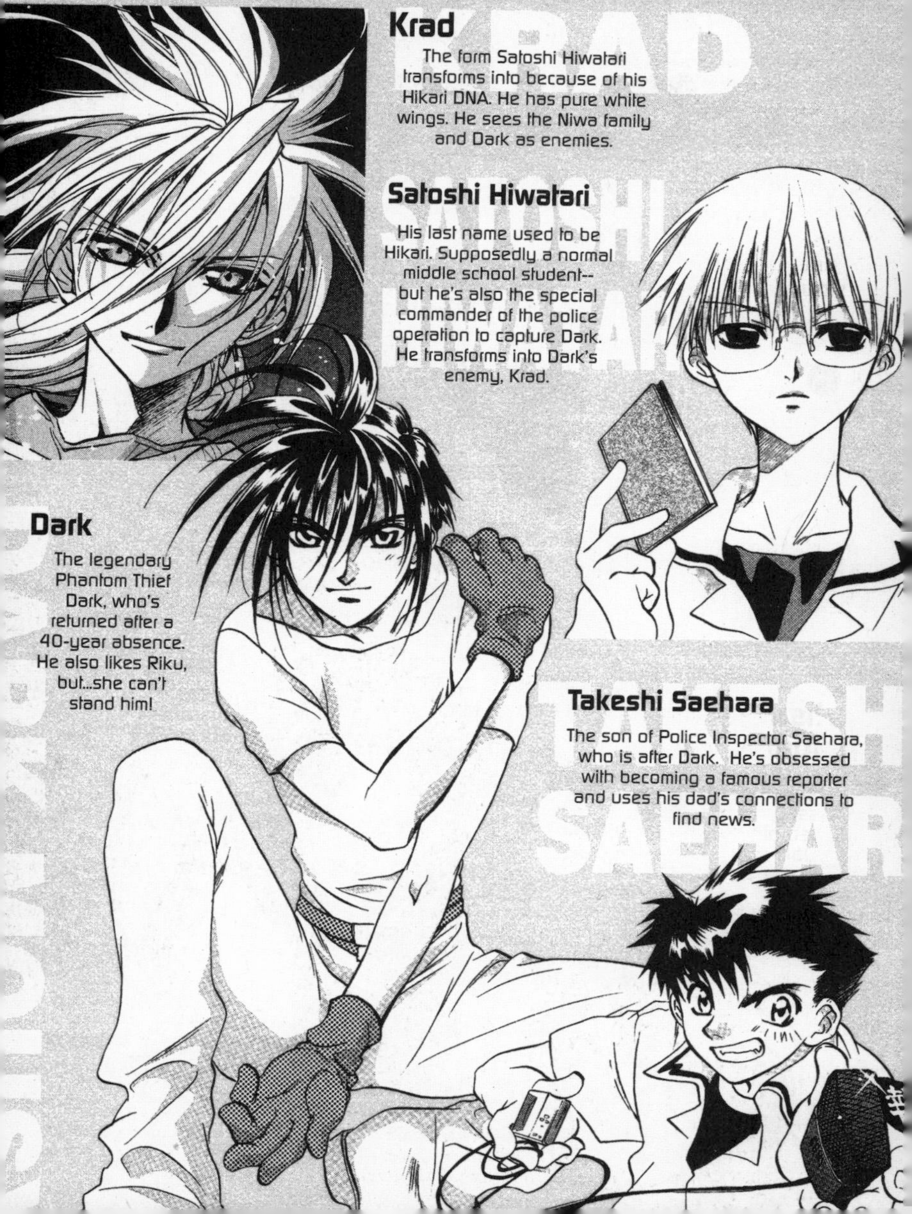

Krad

The form Satoshi Hiwatari transforms into because of his Hikari DNA. He has pure white wings. He sees the Niwa family and Dark as enemies.

Satoshi Hiwatari

His last name used to be Hikari. Supposedly a normal middle school student--but he's also the special commander of the police operation to capture Dark. He transforms into Dark's enemy, Krad.

Dark

The legendary Phantom Thief Dark, who's returned after a 40-year absence. He also likes Riku, but...she can't stand him!

Takeshi Saehara

The son of Police Inspector Saehara, who is after Dark. He's obsessed with becoming a famous reporter and uses his dad's connections to find news.

D•N•ANGEL Vol. 8
Created by Yukiru Sugisaki

Translation - Alethea and Athena Nibley
English Adaptation - Sarah Dyer
Copy Editor - Peter Ahlstrom
Retouch and Lettering - Samantha Yamanaka
Production Artist - Vicente Rivera, Jr.
Cover Design - Thea Willis

Editor - Bryce P. Coleman
Digital Imaging Manager - Chris Buford
Pre-Press Manager - Antonio DePietro
Production Managers - Jennifer Miller and Mutsumi Miyazaki
Art Director - Matt Alford
Managing Editor - Jill Freshney
VP of Production - Ron Klamert
Editor-in-Chief - Mike Kiley
President and C.O.O. - John Parker
Publisher and C.E.O. - Stuart Levy

A  Manga

TOKYOPOP Inc.
5900 Wilshire Blvd. Suite 2000
Los Angeles, CA 90036

E-mail: info@TOKYOPOP.com
Come visit us online at www.TOKYOPOP.com

ISBN: 1-59182-957-7

First TOKYOPOP printing: June 2005
10 9 8 7 6 5 4 3
Printed in the USA

D·N·ANGEL

Volume 8

By

Yukiru Sugisaki

TOKYOPOP®

HAMBURG // LONDON // LOS ANGELES // TOKYO

CONTENTS

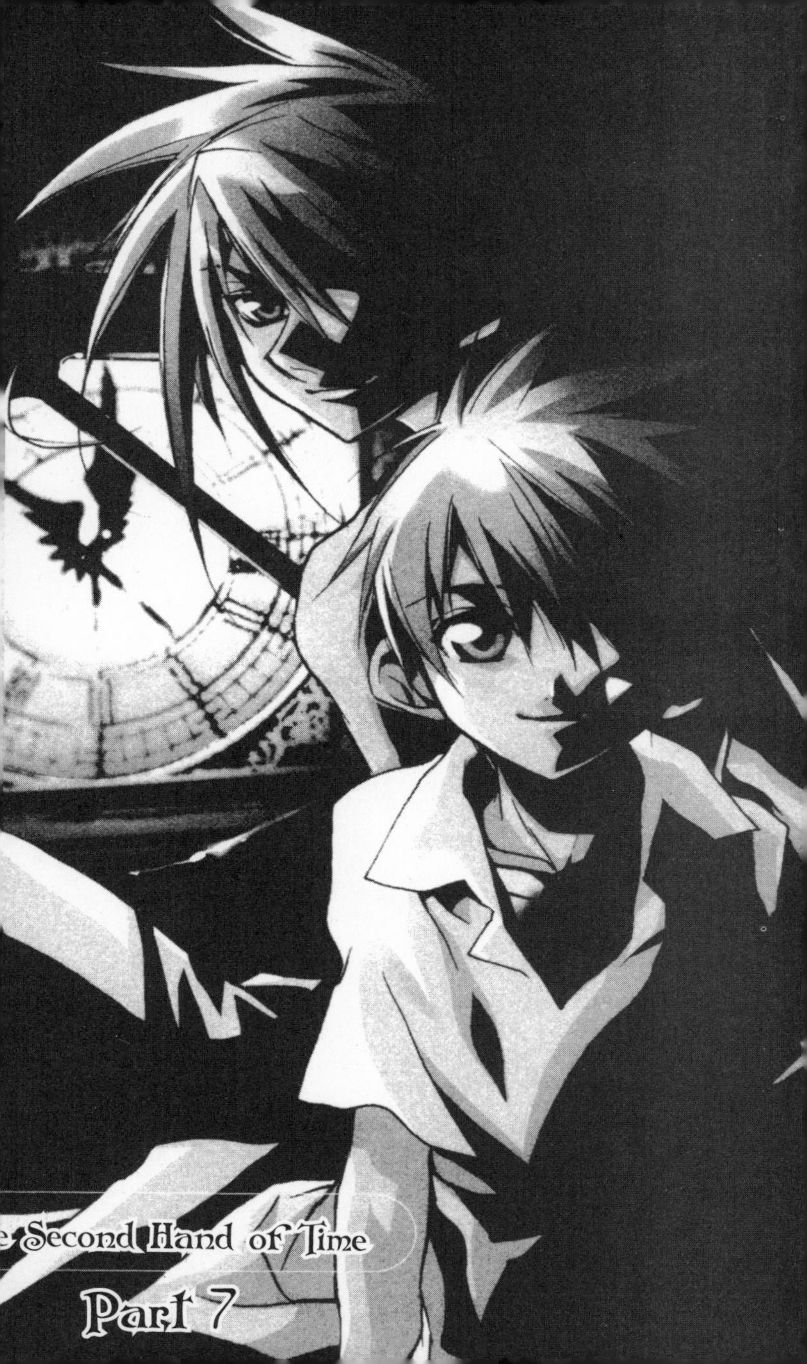
e Second Hand of Time
Part 7

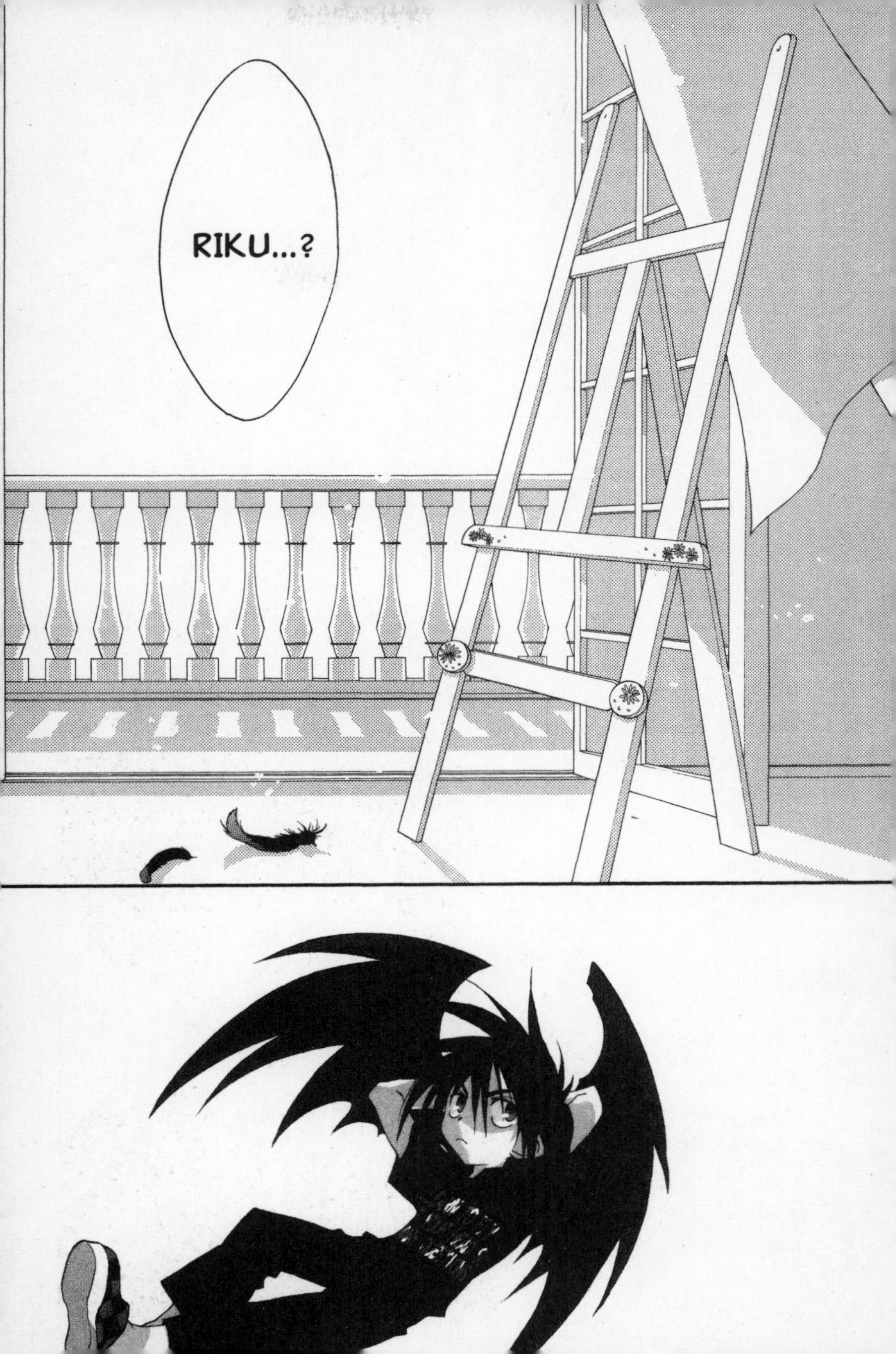
RIKU...?

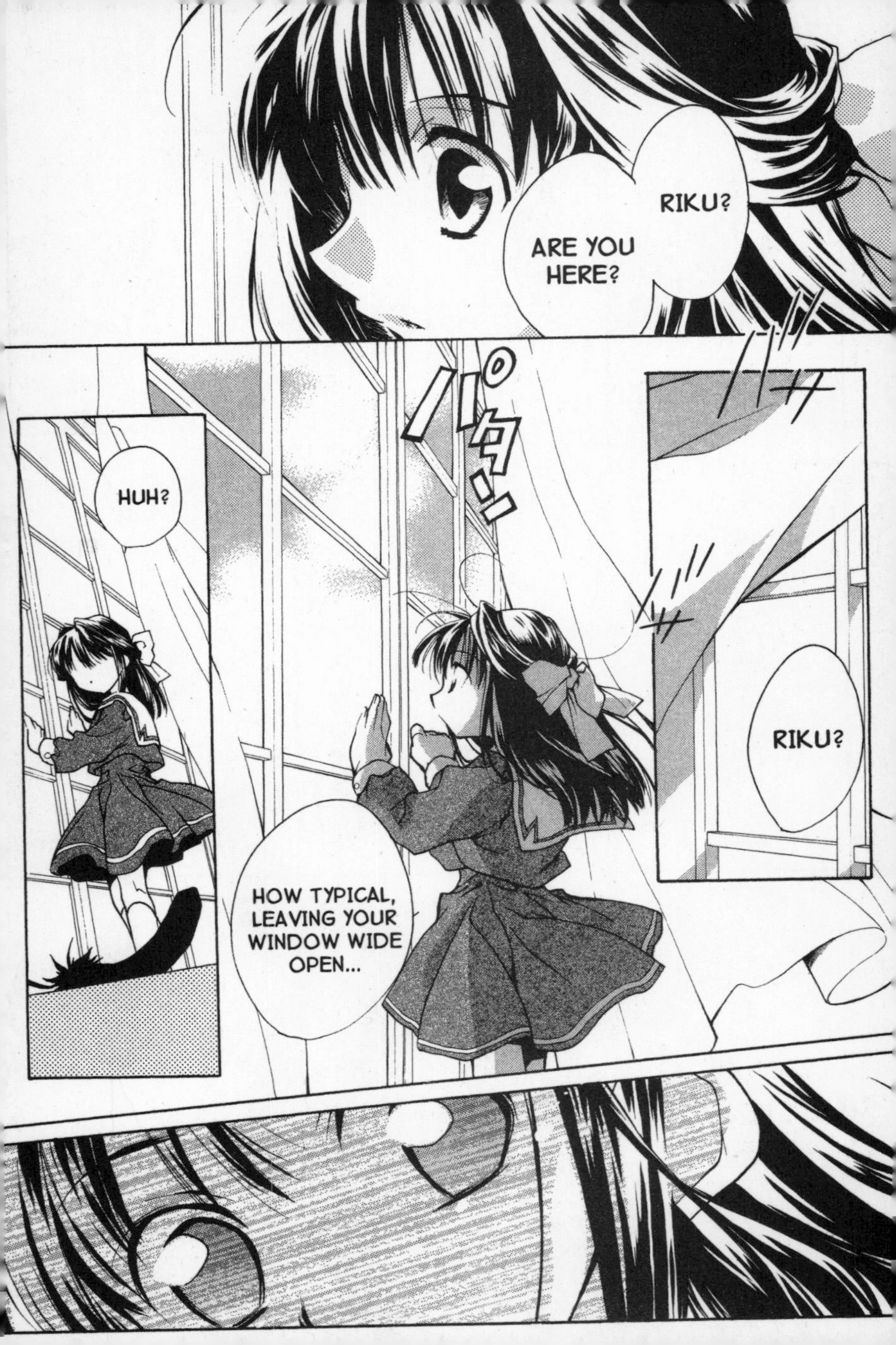
RIKU?
ARE YOU HERE?
RIKU?
パタン
HOW TYPICAL, LEAVING YOUR WINDOW WIDE OPEN...
HUH?

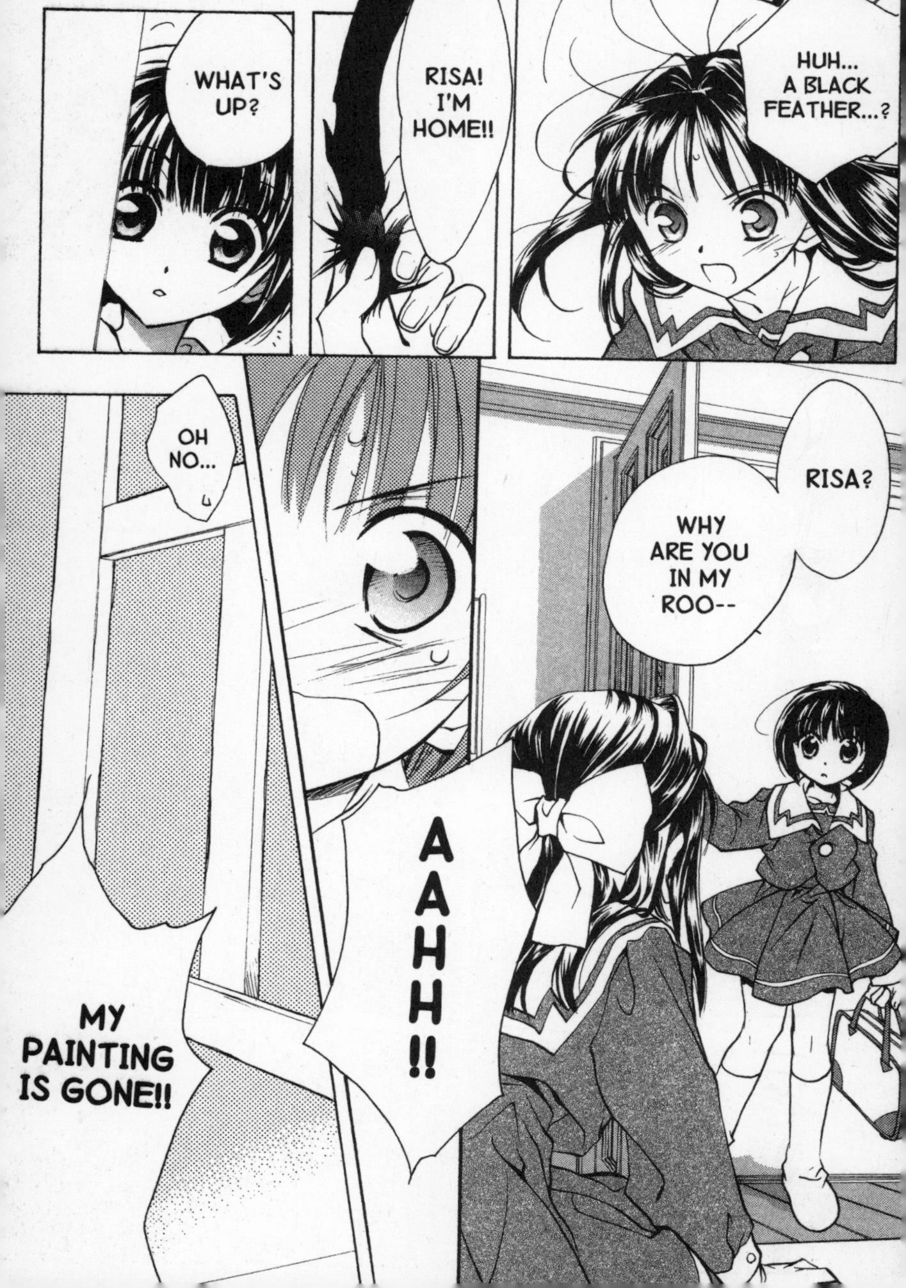
HUH... A BLACK FEATHER...?
RISA! I'M HOME!!
WHAT'S UP?
RISA?
WHY ARE YOU IN MY ROO--
OH NO...
AAHH!!
MY PAINTING IS GONE!!

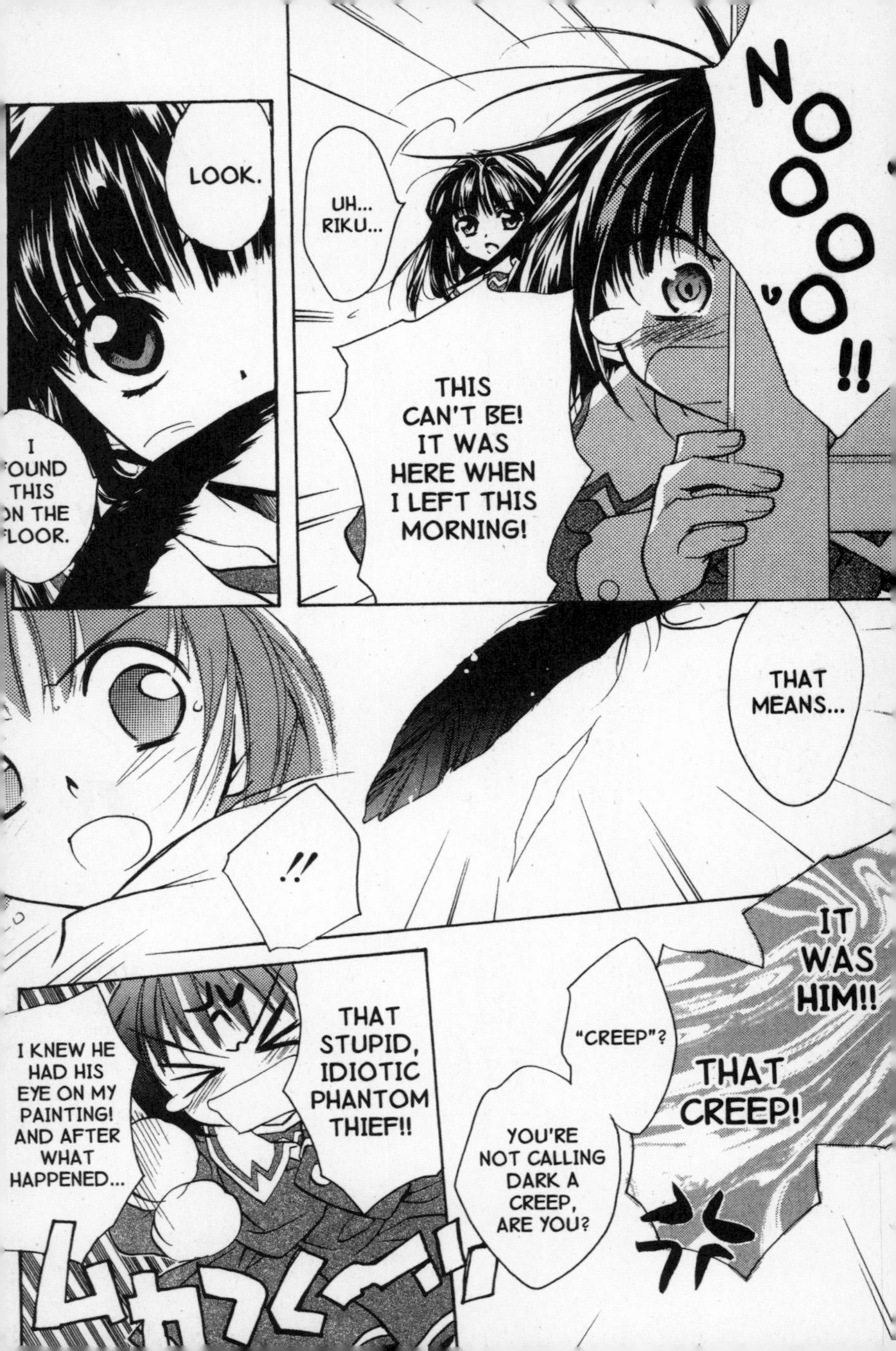
NOOOO!!
UH... RIKU...
THIS CAN'T BE! IT WAS HERE WHEN I LEFT THIS MORNING!
LOOK.
I FOUND THIS ON THE FLOOR.
THAT MEANS...
!!
IT WAS HIM!!
THAT CREEP!
"CREEP"?
YOU'RE NOT CALLING DARK A CREEP, ARE YOU?
THAT STUPID, IDIOTIC PHANTOM THIEF!!
I KNEW HE HAD HIS EYE ON MY PAINTING! AND AFTER WHAT HAPPENED...

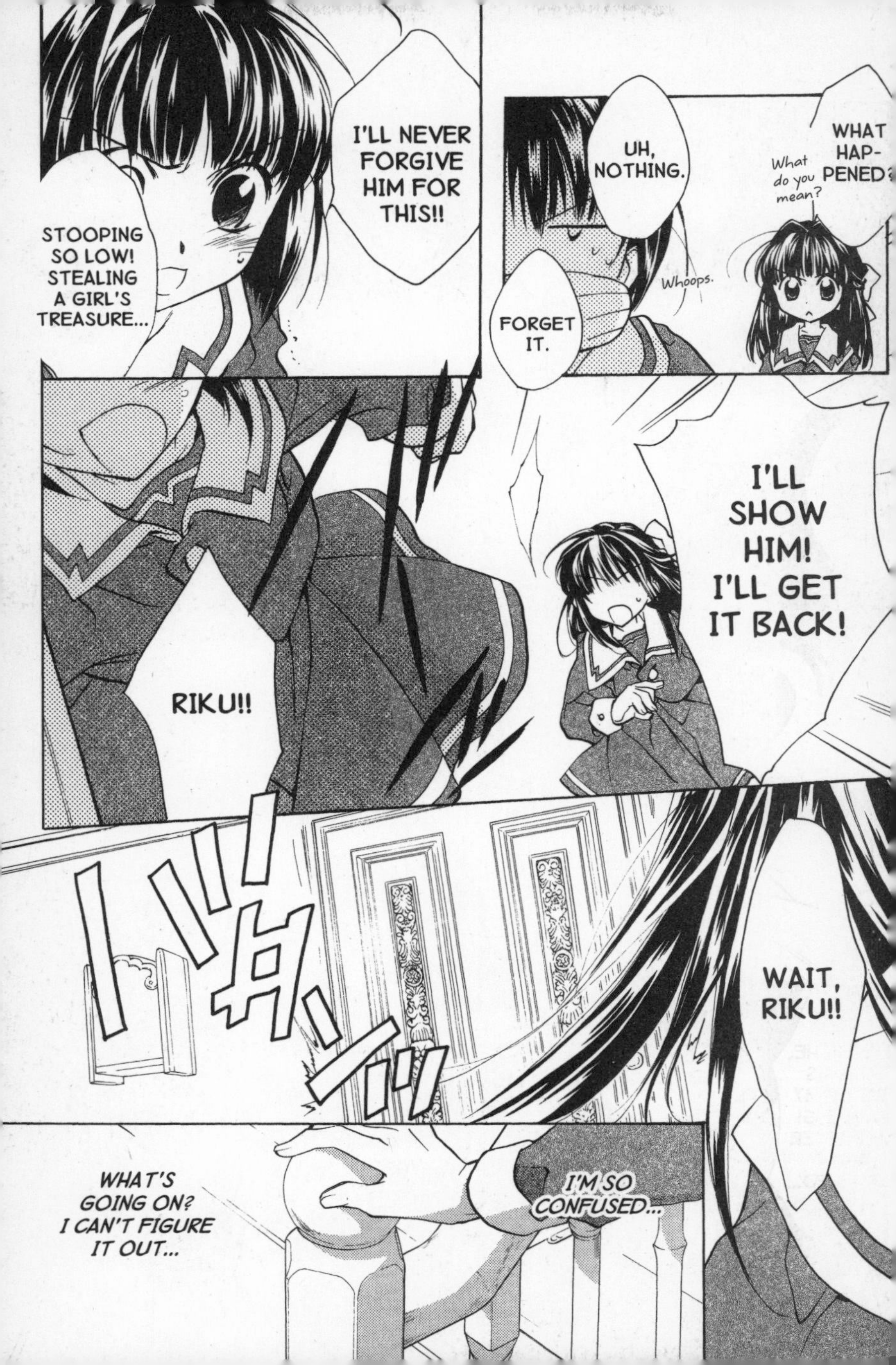
WHAT HAP-PENED?
What do you mean?
UH, NOTHING.
Whoops.
FORGET IT.
I'LL NEVER FORGIVE HIM FOR THIS!!
STOOPING SO LOW! STEALING A GIRL'S TREASURE...
I'LL SHOW HIM! I'LL GET IT BACK!
RIKU!!
WAIT, RIKU!!
ドタッ
I'M SO CONFUSED...
WHAT'S GOING ON? I CAN'T FIGURE IT OUT...

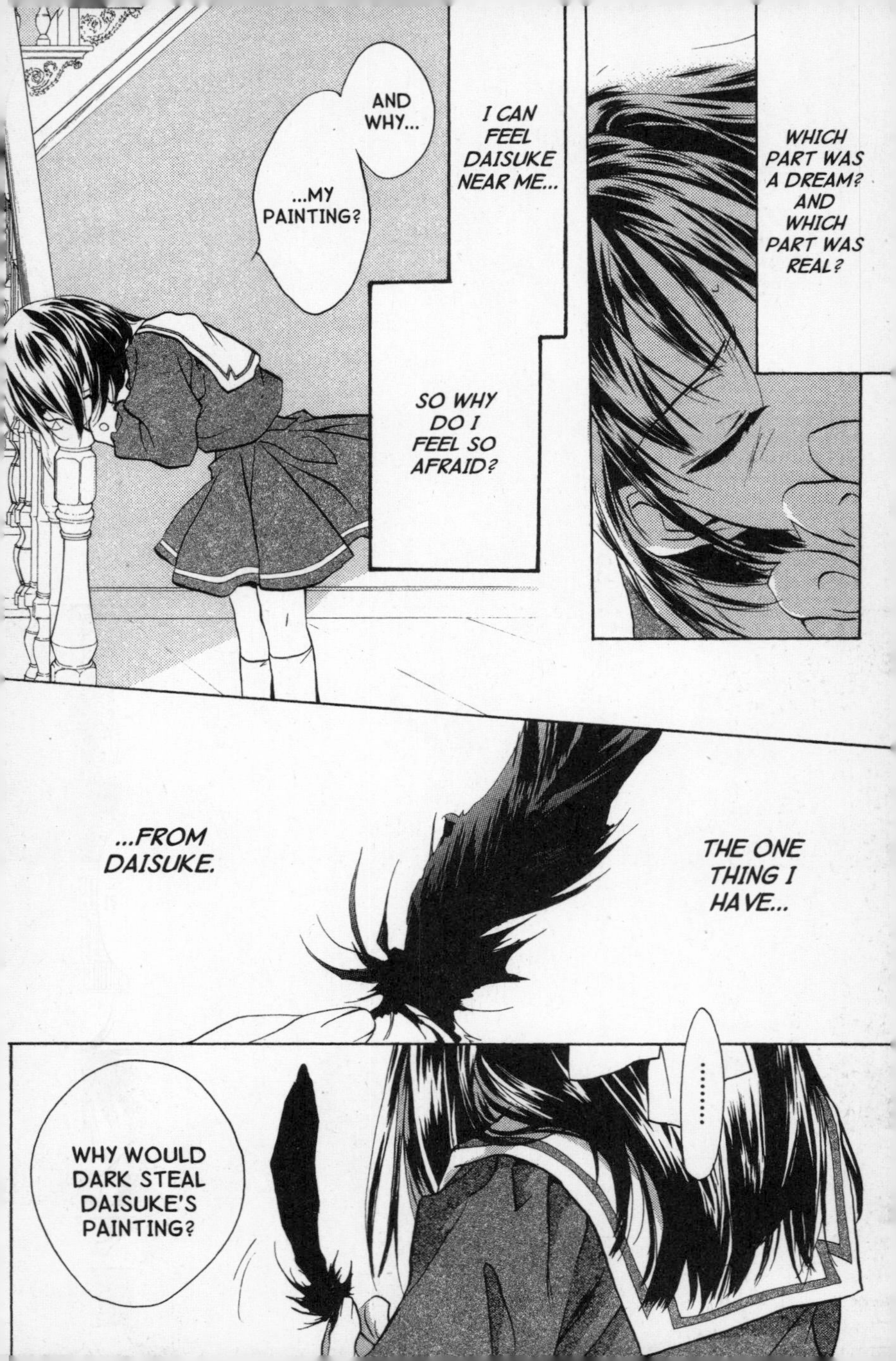
WHICH PART WAS A DREAM? AND WHICH PART WAS REAL?
I CAN FEEL DAISUKE NEAR ME...
SO WHY DO I FEEL SO AFRAID?
AND WHY...
...MY PAINTING?
THE ONE THING I HAVE...
...FROM DAISUKE.
......
WHY WOULD DARK STEAL DAISUKE'S PAINTING?

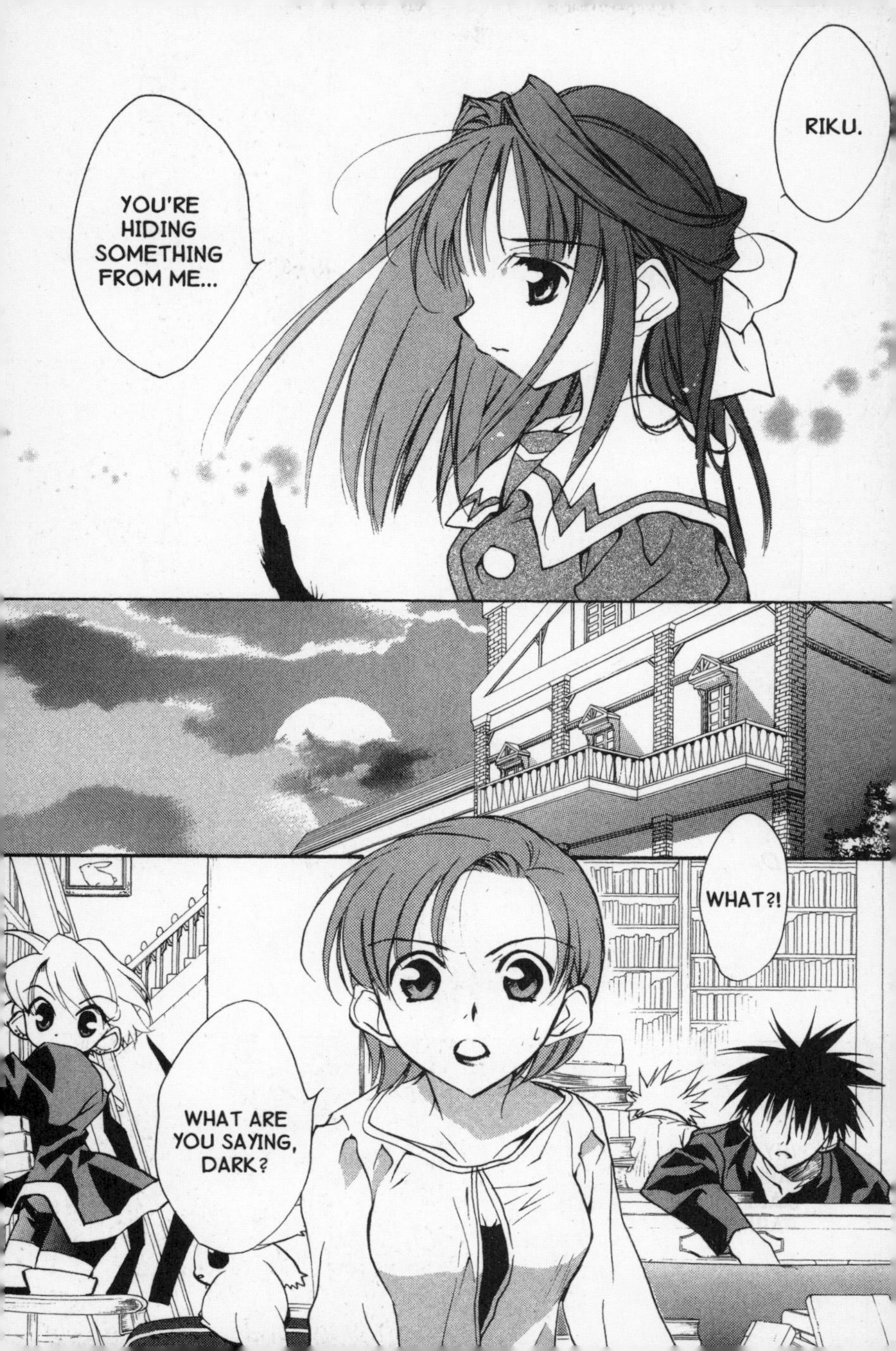
RIKU.
YOU'RE HIDING SOMETHING FROM ME...
WHAT?!
WHAT ARE YOU SAYING, DARK?

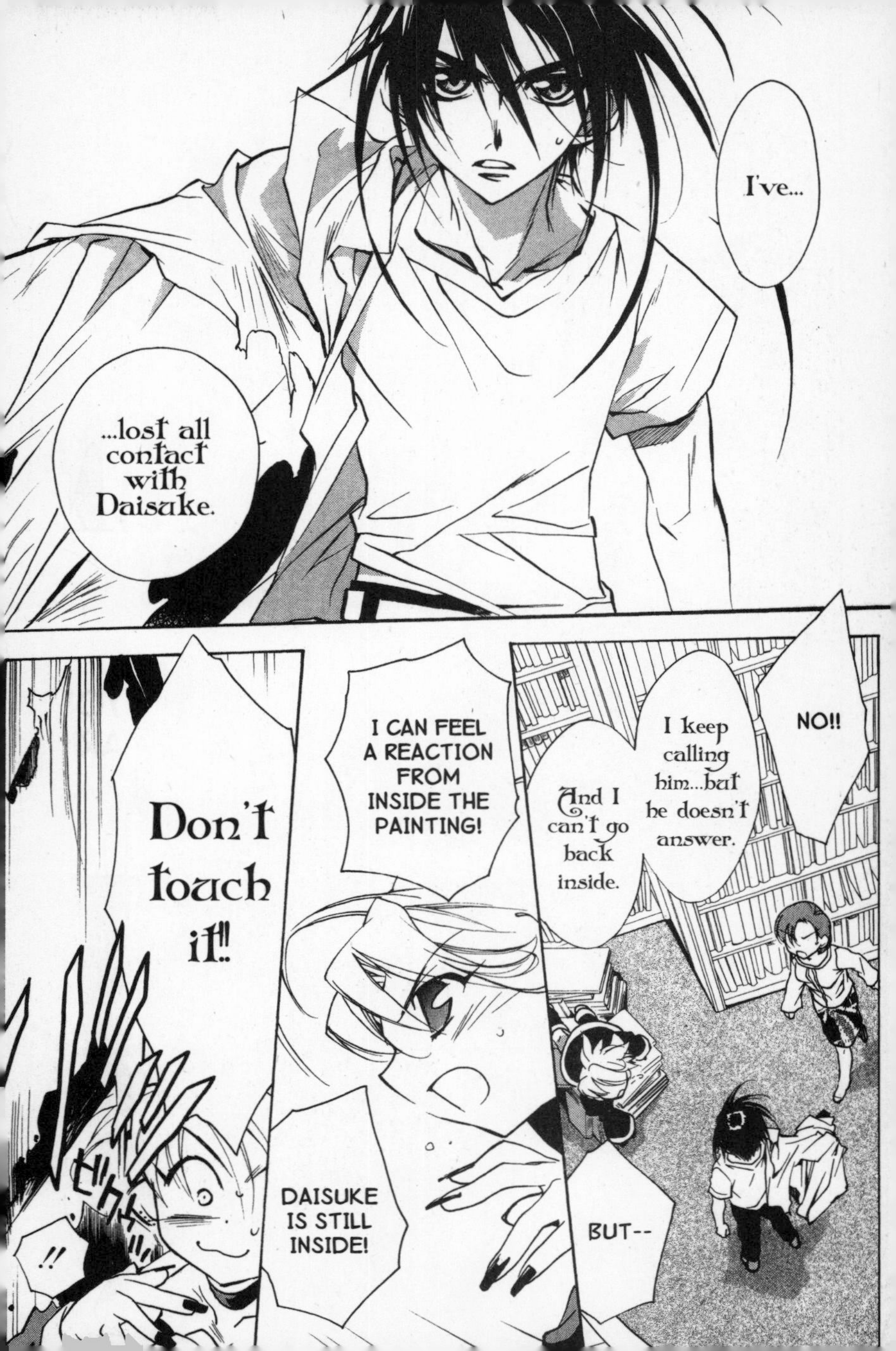
I've...
...lost all contact with Daisuke.
NO!!
I keep calling him...but he doesn't answer.
And I can't go back inside.
BUT--
I CAN FEEL A REACTION FROM INSIDE THE PAINTING!
DAISUKE IS STILL INSIDE!
Don't touch it!!
!!

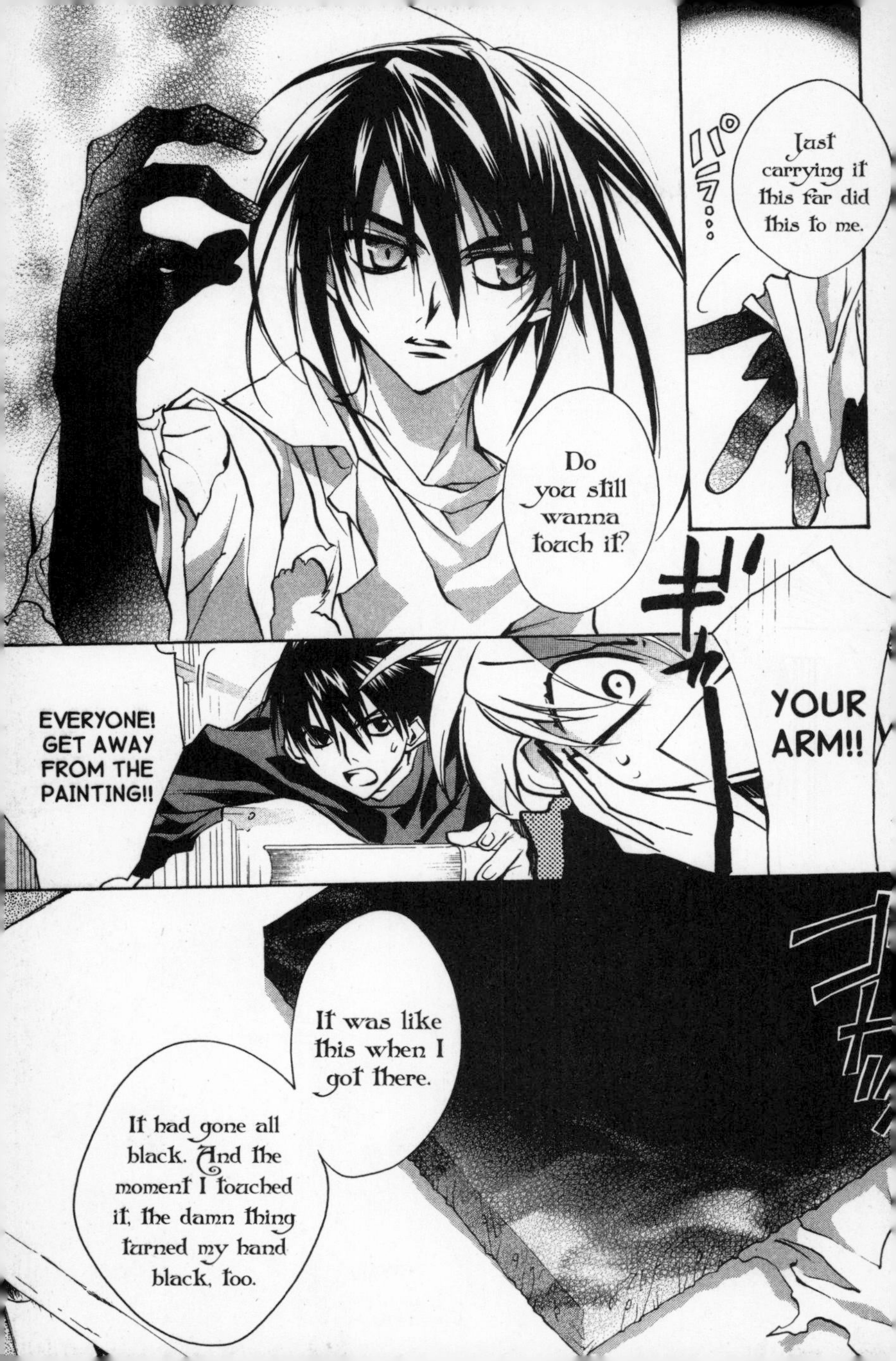
Just carrying it this far did this to me.
Do you still wanna touch it?
YOUR ARM!!
EVERYONE! GET AWAY FROM THE PAINTING!!
It was like this when I got there.
It had gone all black. And the moment I touched it, the damn thing turned my hand black, too.

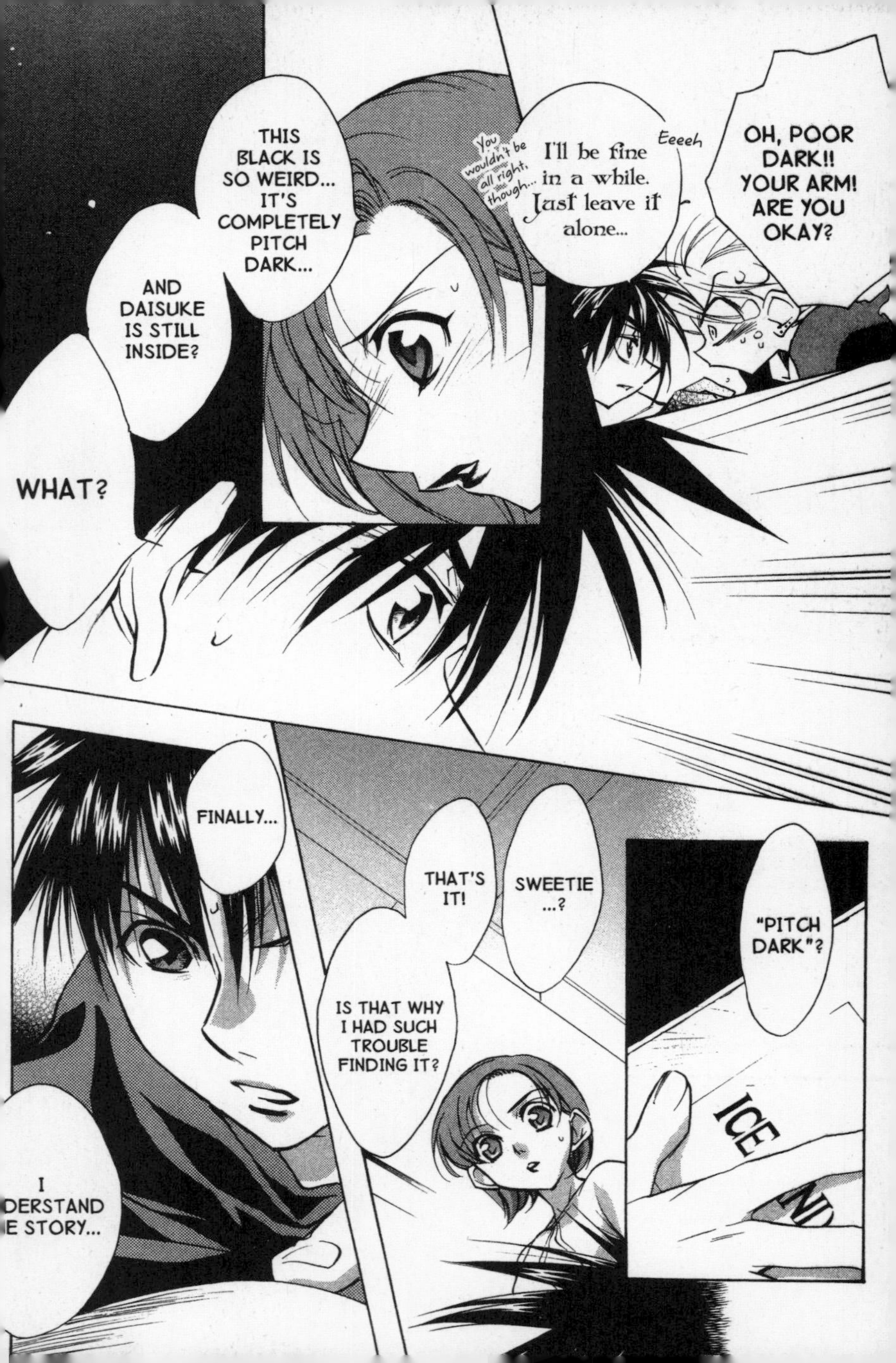
OH, POOR DARK!! YOUR ARM! ARE YOU OKAY?
Eeeeh
I'll be fine in a while. Just leave it alone...
You wouldn't be all right, though...
THIS BLACK IS SO WEIRD... IT'S COMPLETELY PITCH DARK...
AND DAISUKE IS STILL INSIDE?
WHAT?
"PITCH DARK"?
ICE
SWEETIE ...?
THAT'S IT!
IS THAT WHY I HAD SUCH TROUBLE FINDING IT?
FINALLY...
I DERSTAND E STORY...

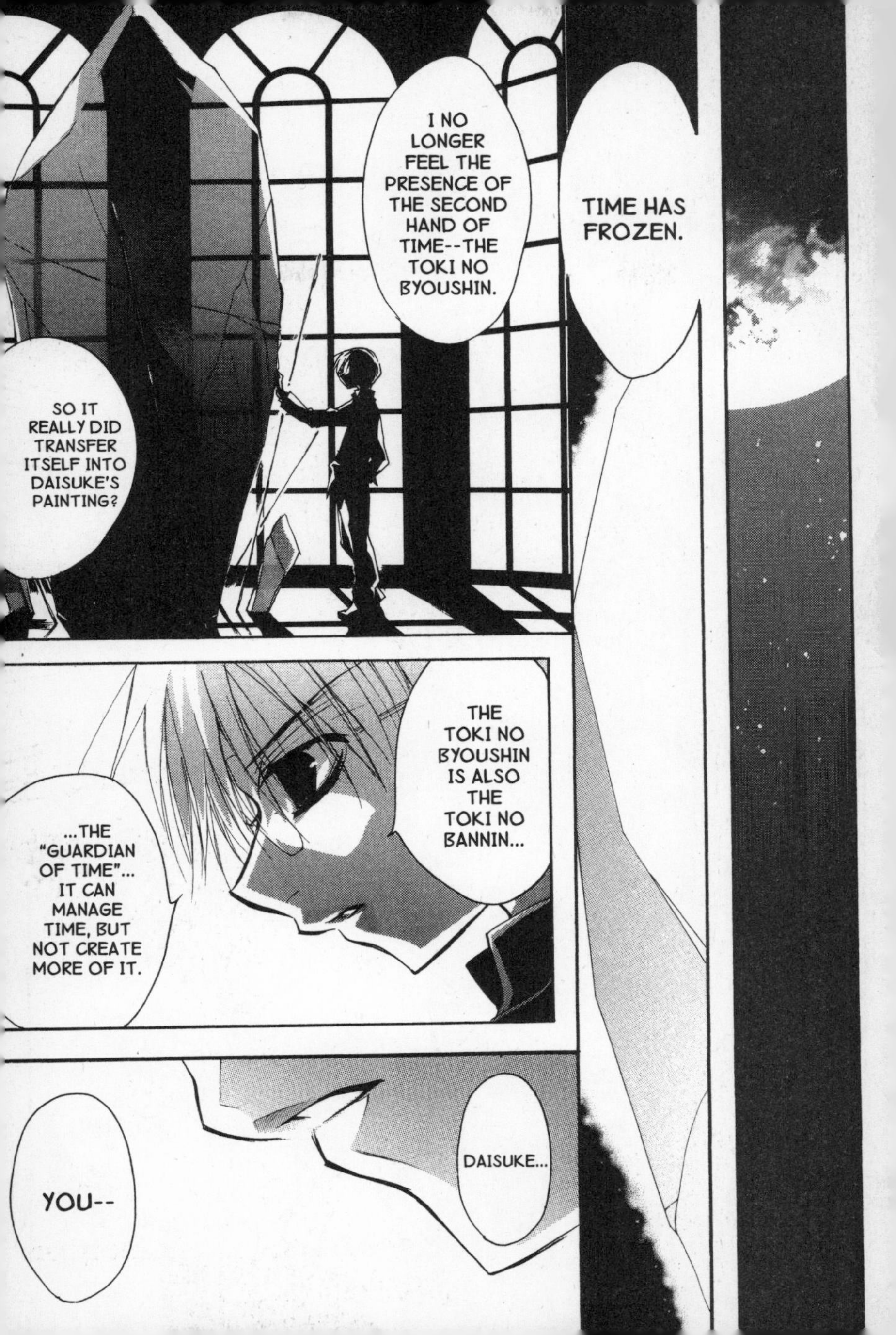
TIME HAS FROZEN.
I NO LONGER FEEL THE PRESENCE OF THE SECOND HAND OF TIME--THE TOKI NO BYOUSHIN.
SO IT REALLY DID TRANSFER ITSELF INTO DAISUKE'S PAINTING?
THE TOKI NO BYOUSHIN IS ALSO THE TOKI NO BANNIN...
...THE "GUARDIAN OF TIME"... IT CAN MANAGE TIME, BUT NOT CREATE MORE OF IT.
DAISUKE...
YOU--

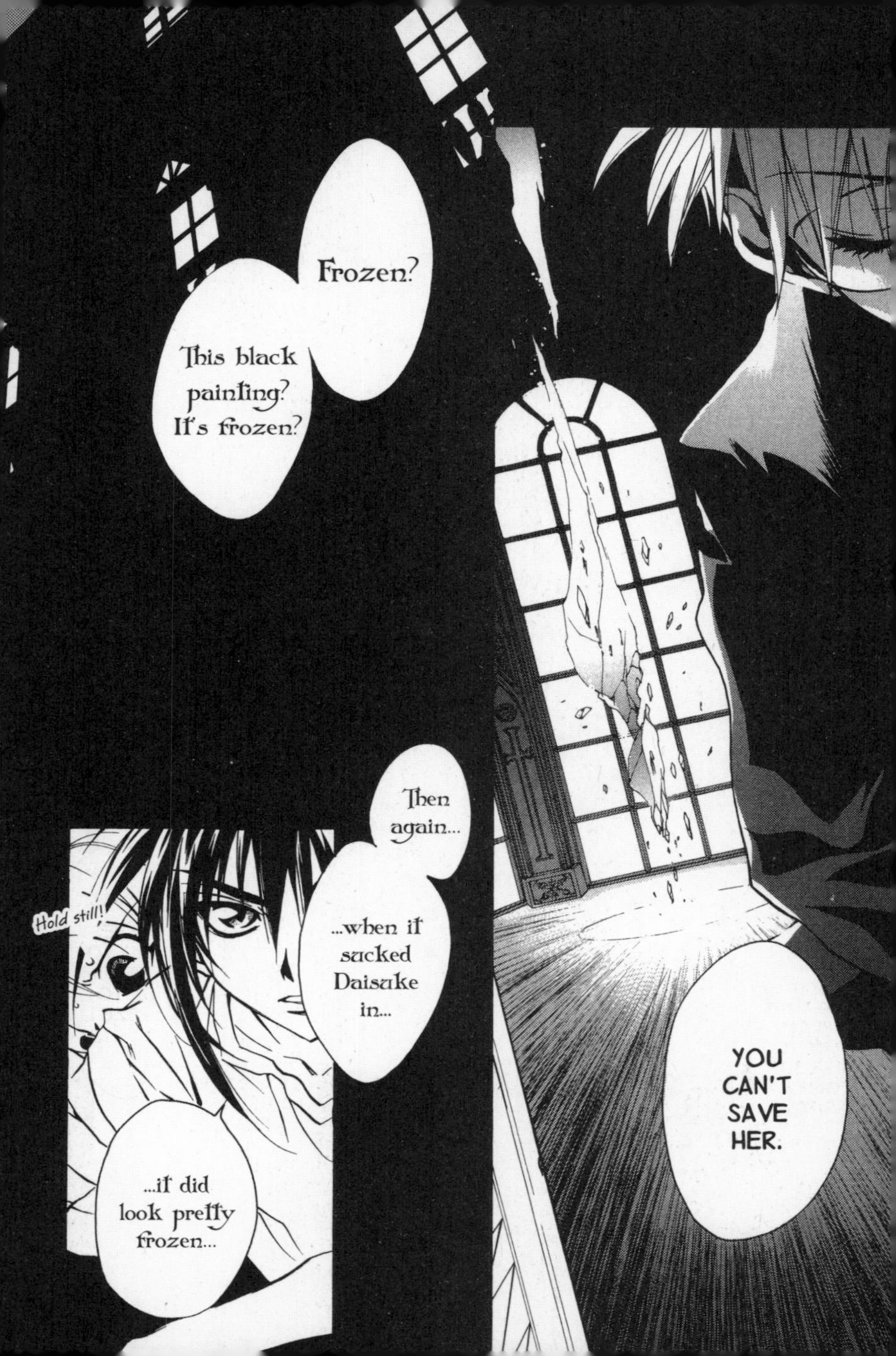
Frozen?
This black painting? It's frozen?
Then again...
...when it sucked Daisuke in...
Hold still!
...it did look pretty frozen...
YOU CAN'T SAVE HER.

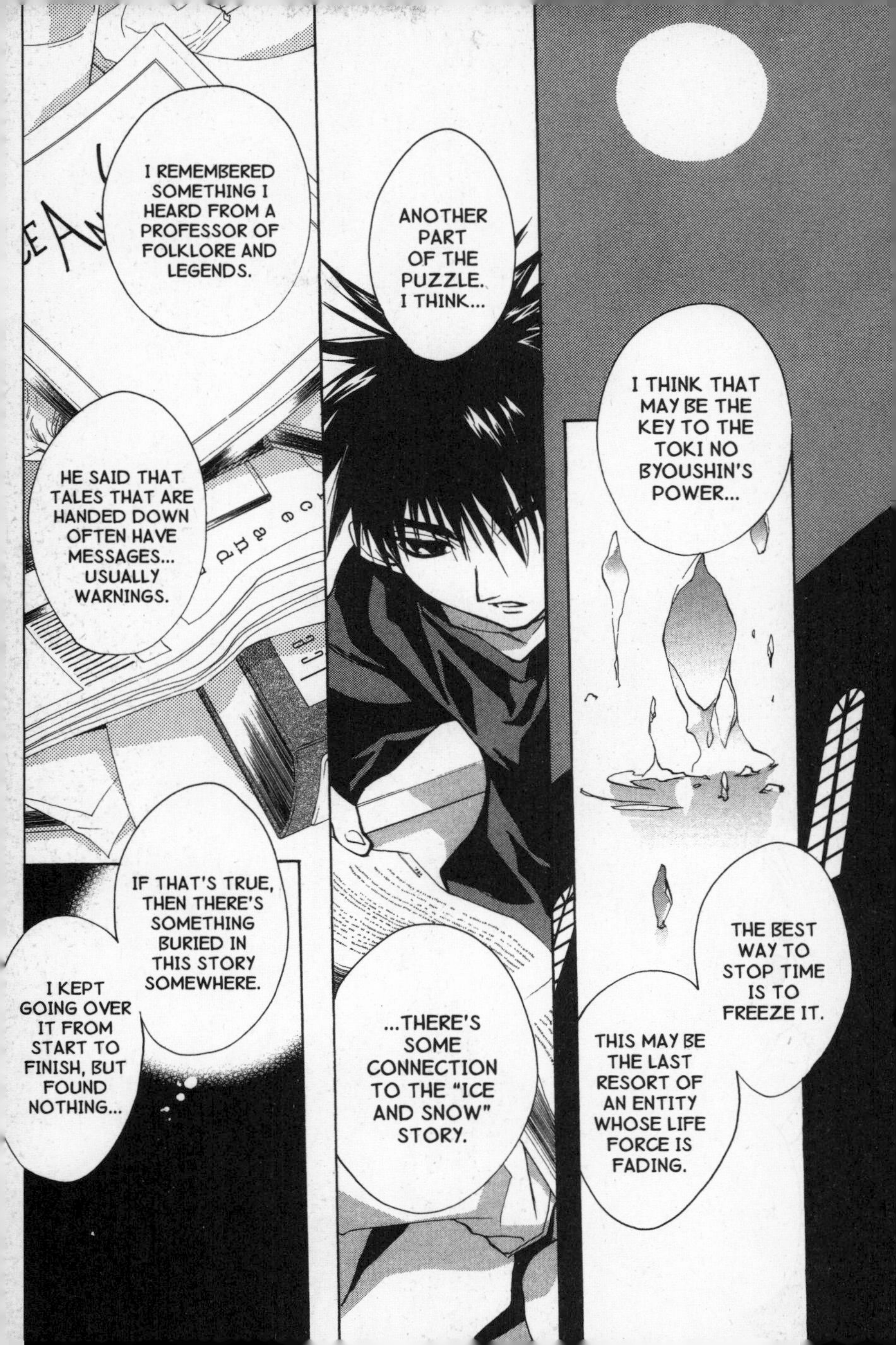
I THINK THAT MAY BE THE KEY TO THE TOKI NO BYOUSHIN'S POWER...
THE BEST WAY TO STOP TIME IS TO FREEZE IT.
THIS MAY BE THE LAST RESORT OF AN ENTITY WHOSE LIFE FORCE IS FADING.
ANOTHER PART OF THE PUZZLE. I THINK...
...THERE'S SOME CONNECTION TO THE "ICE AND SNOW" STORY.
I REMEMBERED SOMETHING I HEARD FROM A PROFESSOR OF FOLKLORE AND LEGENDS.
HE SAID THAT TALES THAT ARE HANDED DOWN OFTEN HAVE MESSAGES... USUALLY WARNINGS.
IF THAT'S TRUE, THEN THERE'S SOMETHING BURIED IN THIS STORY SOMEWHERE.
I KEPT GOING OVER IT FROM START TO FINISH, BUT FOUND NOTHING...

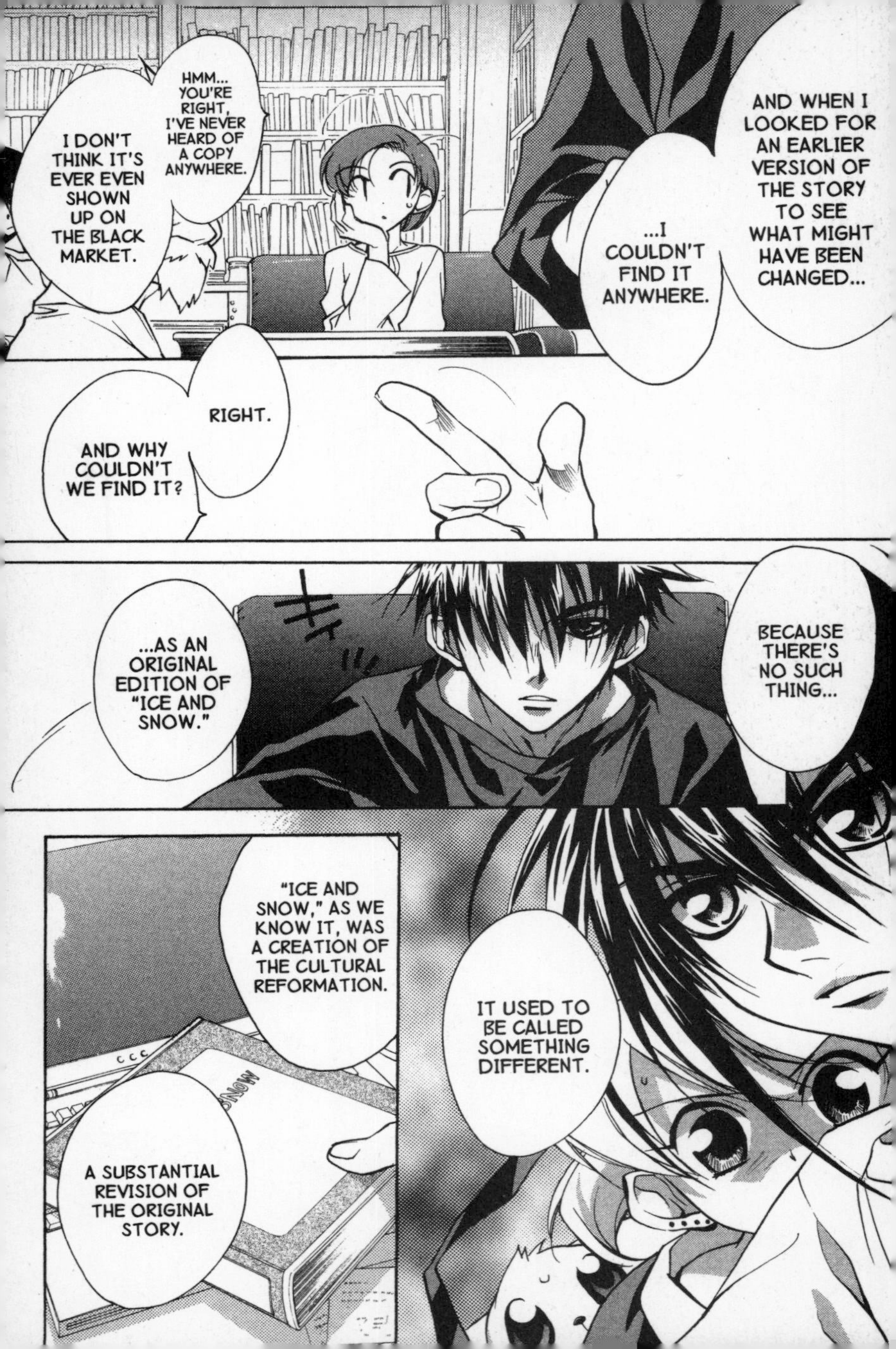

AND WHEN I LOOKED FOR AN EARLIER VERSION OF THE STORY TO SEE WHAT MIGHT HAVE BEEN CHANGED...
...I COULDN'T FIND IT ANYWHERE.
HMM... YOU'RE RIGHT, I'VE NEVER HEARD OF A COPY ANYWHERE.
I DON'T THINK IT'S EVER EVEN SHOWN UP ON THE BLACK MARKET.
RIGHT.
AND WHY COULDN'T WE FIND IT?
BECAUSE THERE'S NO SUCH THING...
...AS AN ORIGINAL EDITION OF "ICE AND SNOW."
"ICE AND SNOW," AS WE KNOW IT, WAS A CREATION OF THE CULTURAL REFORMATION.
A SUBSTANTIAL REVISION OF THE ORIGINAL STORY.
IT USED TO BE CALLED SOMETHING DIFFERENT.

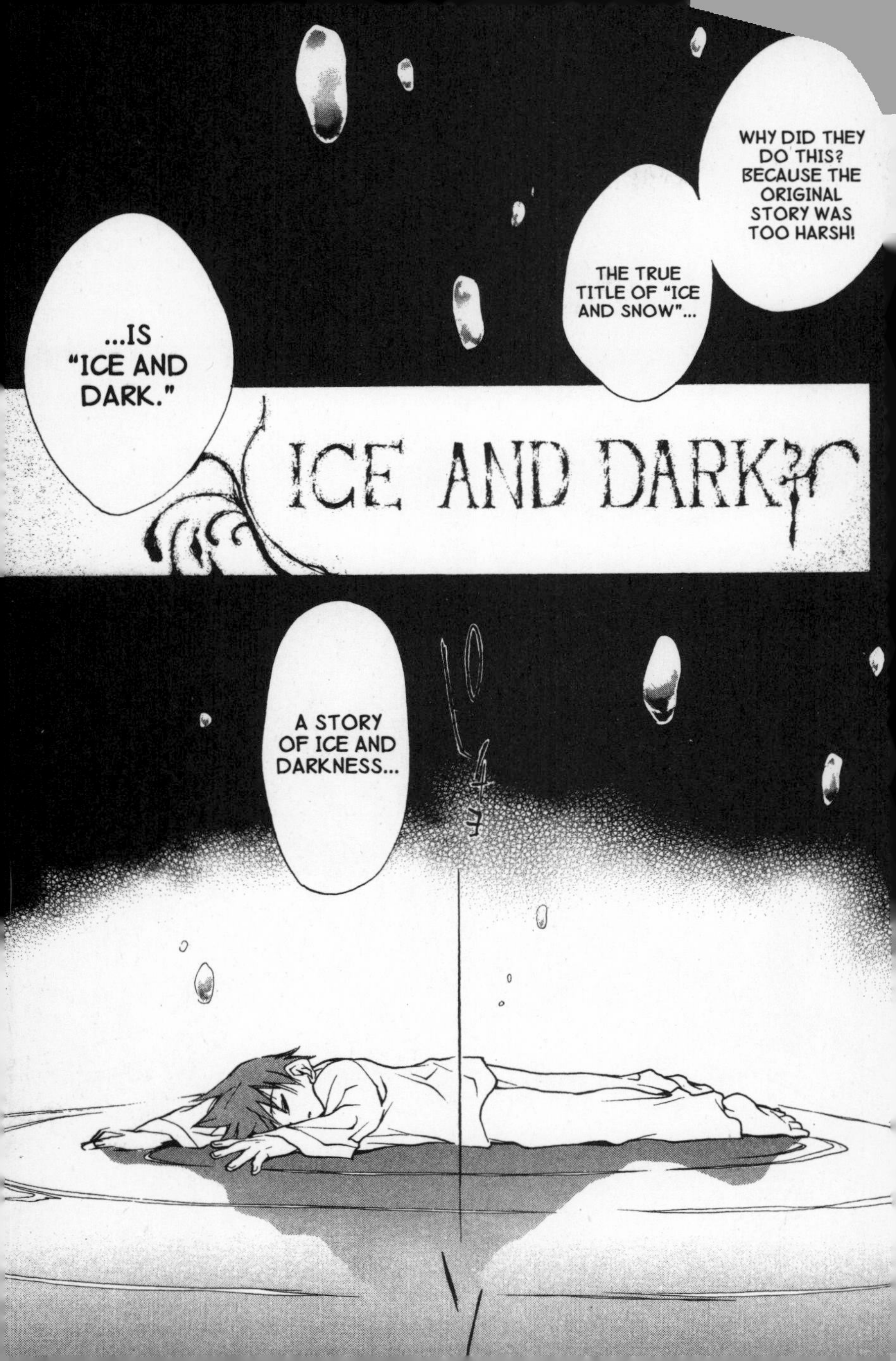
WHY DID THEY DO THIS? BECAUSE THE ORIGINAL STORY WAS TOO HARSH!
THE TRUE TITLE OF "ICE AND SNOW"...
...IS "ICE AND DARK."
ICE AND DARK
A STORY OF ICE AND DARKNESS...

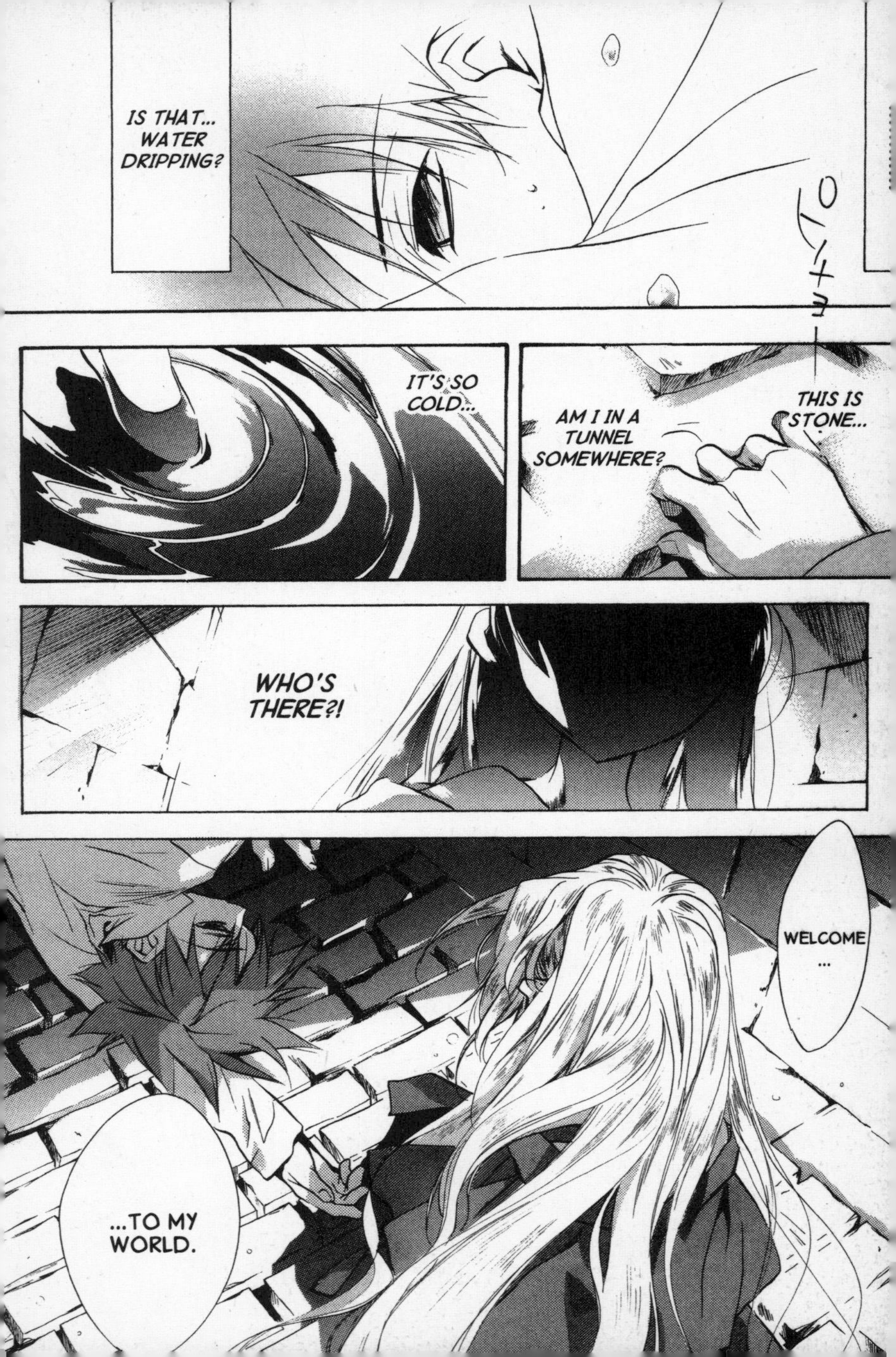
IS THAT... WATER DRIPPING?
THIS IS STONE...
AM I IN A TUNNEL SOMEWHERE?
IT'S SO COLD...
WHO'S THERE?!
WELCOME ...
...TO MY WORLD.

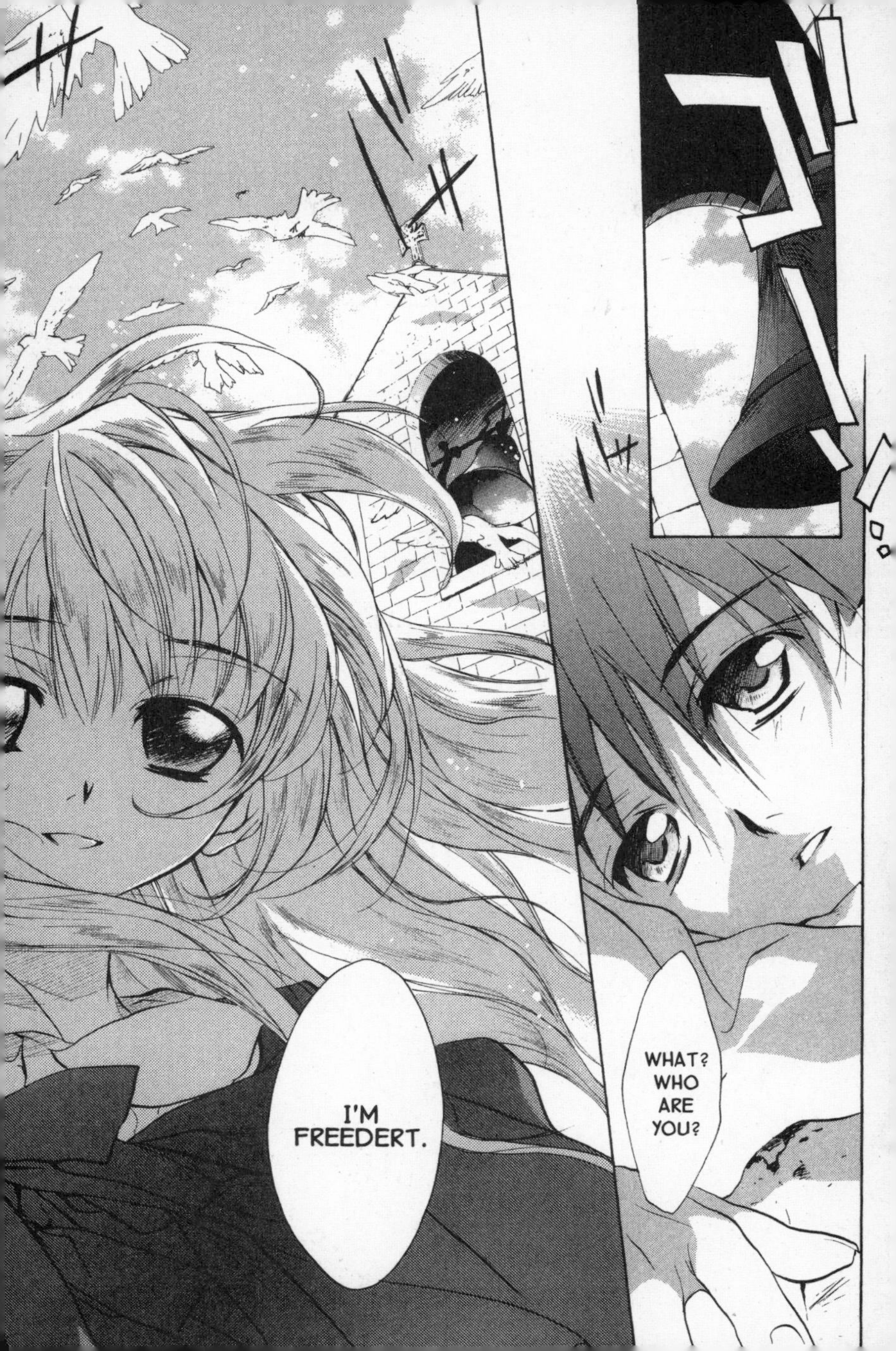
WHAT? WHO ARE YOU?
I'M FREEDERT.

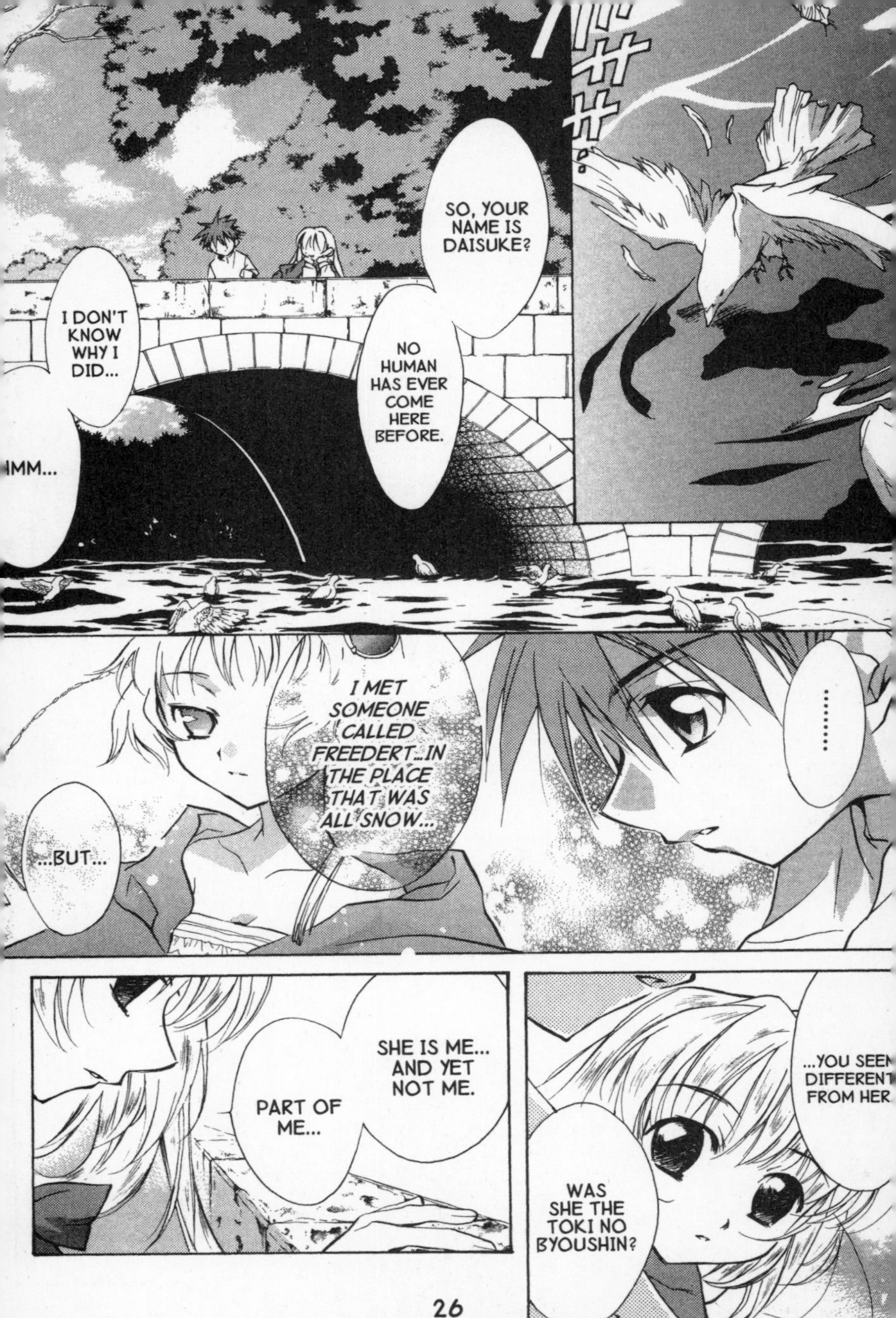
SO, YOUR NAME IS DAISUKE?
NO HUMAN HAS EVER COME HERE BEFORE.
I DON'T KNOW WHY I DID...
....
I MET SOMEONE CALLED FREEDERT...IN THE PLACE THAT WAS ALL SNOW...
...BUT...
...YOU SEEM DIFFERENT FROM HER.
WAS SHE THE TOKI NO BYOUSHIN?
SHE IS ME... AND YET NOT ME.
PART OF ME...

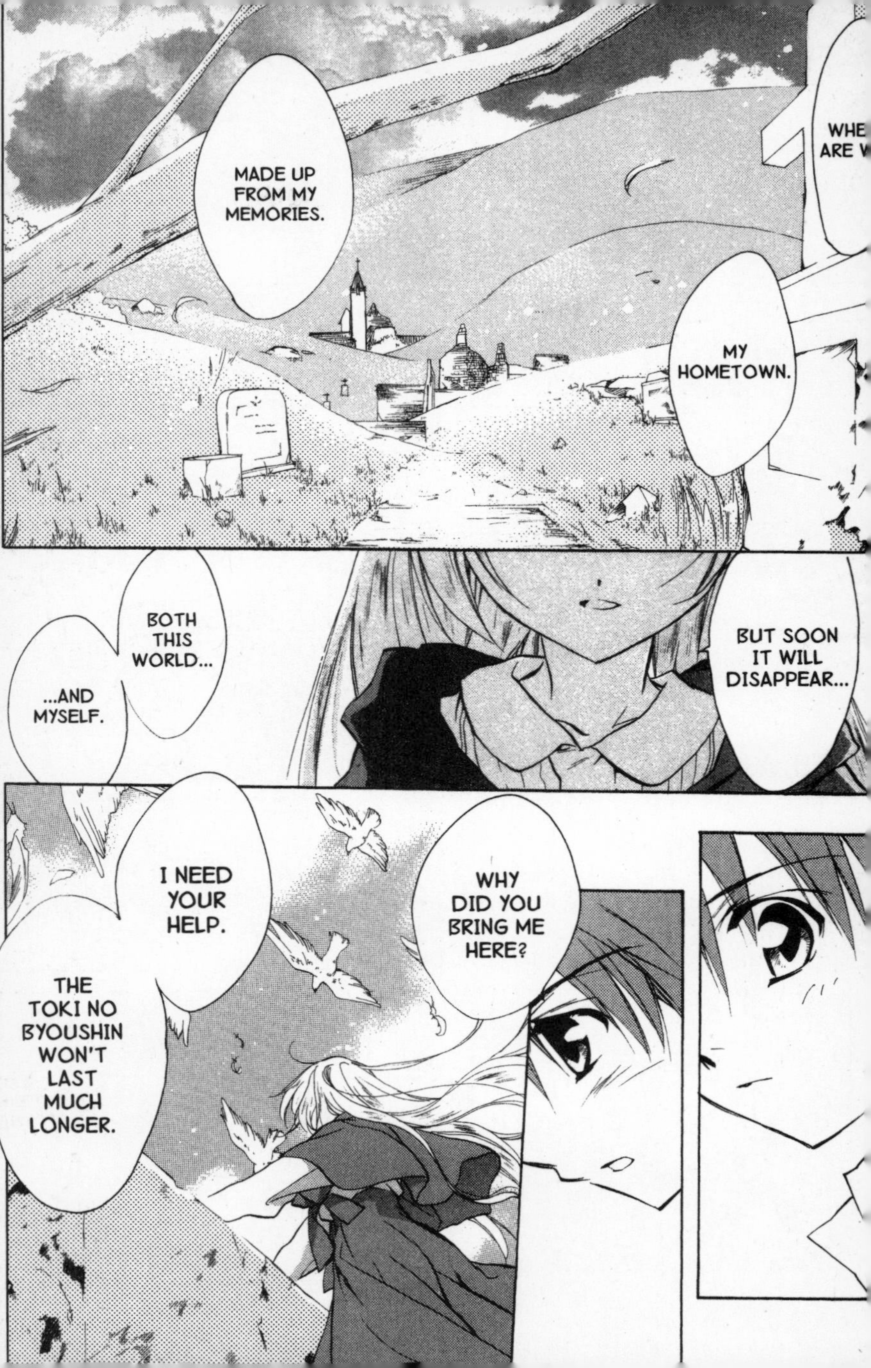
WHE ARE W
MY HOMETOWN.
MADE UP FROM MY MEMORIES.
BUT SOON IT WILL DISAPPEAR...
BOTH THIS WORLD...
...AND MYSELF.
WHY DID YOU BRING ME HERE?
I NEED YOUR HELP.
THE TOKI NO BYOUSHIN WON'T LAST MUCH LONGER.

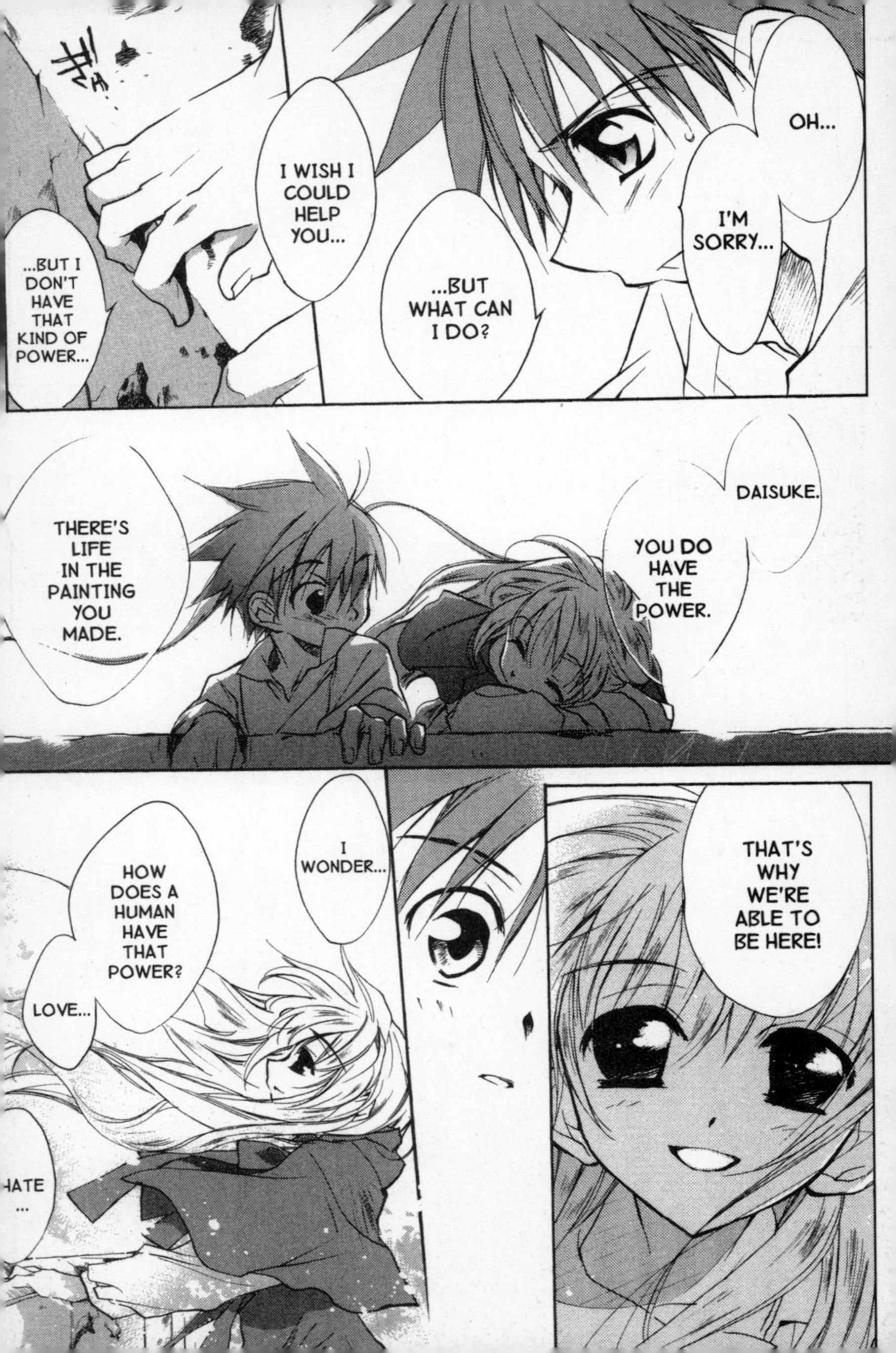
OH...
I'M SORRY...
...BUT WHAT CAN I DO?
I WISH I COULD HELP YOU...
...BUT I DON'T HAVE THAT KIND OF POWER...
DAISUKE.
YOU DO HAVE THE POWER.
THERE'S LIFE IN THE PAINTING YOU MADE.
THAT'S WHY WE'RE ABLE TO BE HERE!
I WONDER...
HOW DOES A HUMAN HAVE THAT POWER?
LOVE...
HATE ...

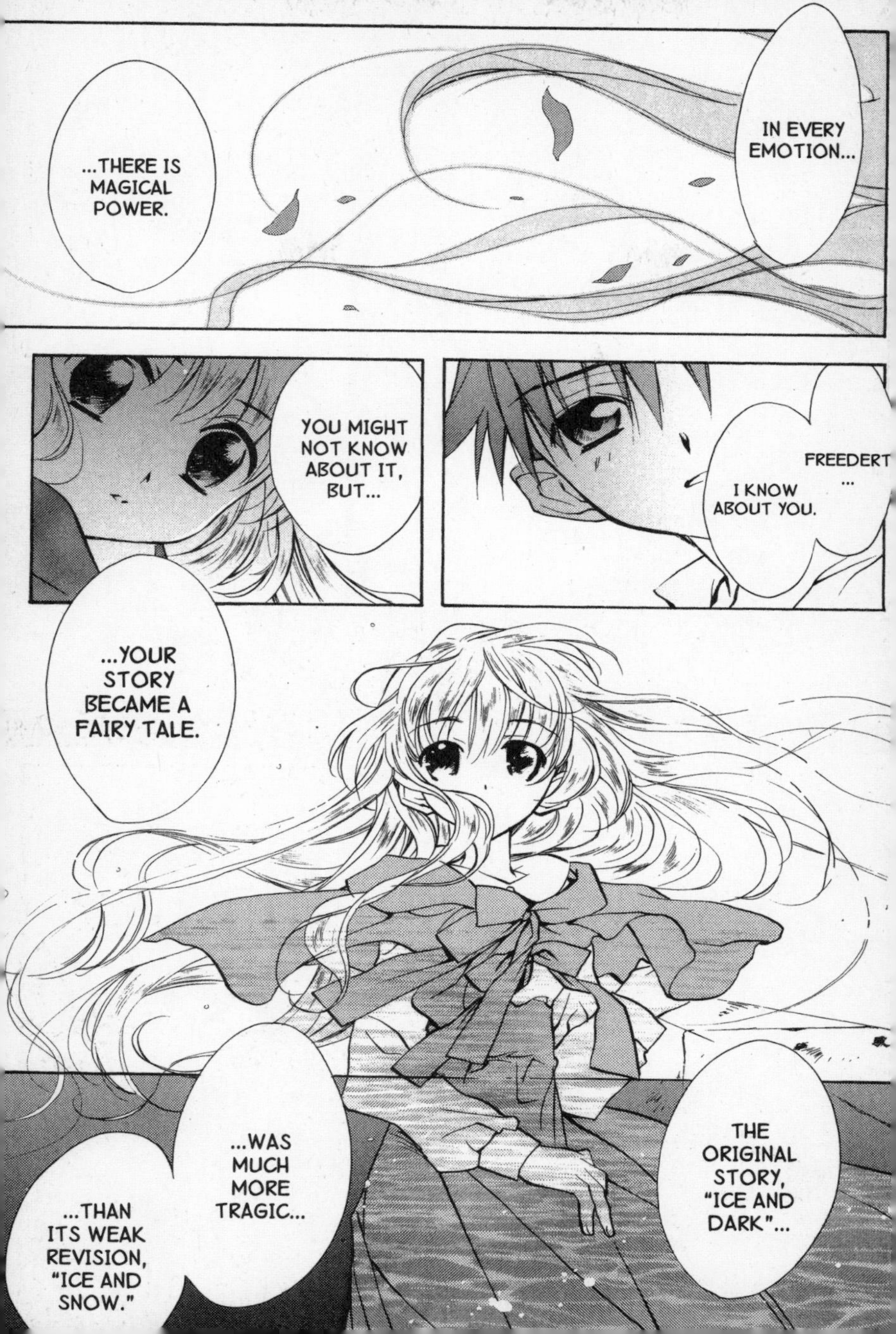

IN EVERY EMOTION...
...THERE IS MAGICAL POWER.
FREEDERT...
I KNOW ABOUT YOU.
YOU MIGHT NOT KNOW ABOUT IT, BUT...
...YOUR STORY BECAME A FAIRY TALE.
THE ORIGINAL STORY, "ICE AND DARK"...
...WAS MUCH MORE TRAGIC...
...THAN ITS WEAK REVISION, "ICE AND SNOW."

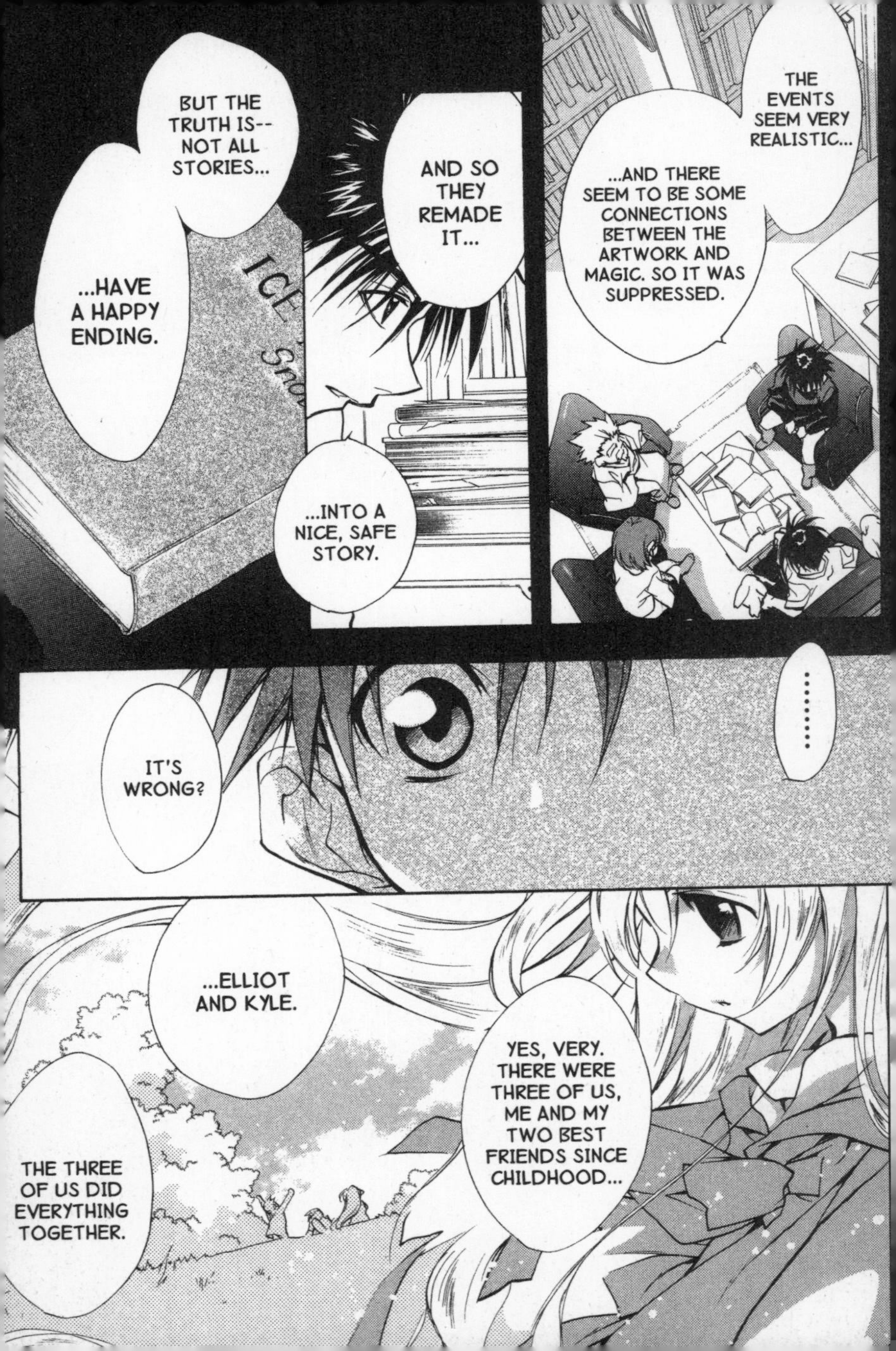
THE EVENTS SEEM VERY REALISTIC...
...AND THERE SEEM TO BE SOME CONNECTIONS BETWEEN THE ARTWORK AND MAGIC. SO IT WAS SUPPRESSED.
AND SO THEY REMADE IT...
...INTO A NICE, SAFE STORY.
BUT THE TRUTH IS-- NOT ALL STORIES...
...HAVE A HAPPY ENDING.
......
IT'S WRONG?
YES, VERY. THERE WERE THREE OF US, ME AND MY TWO BEST FRIENDS SINCE CHILDHOOD...
...ELLIOT AND KYLE.
THE THREE OF US DID EVERYTHING TOGETHER.

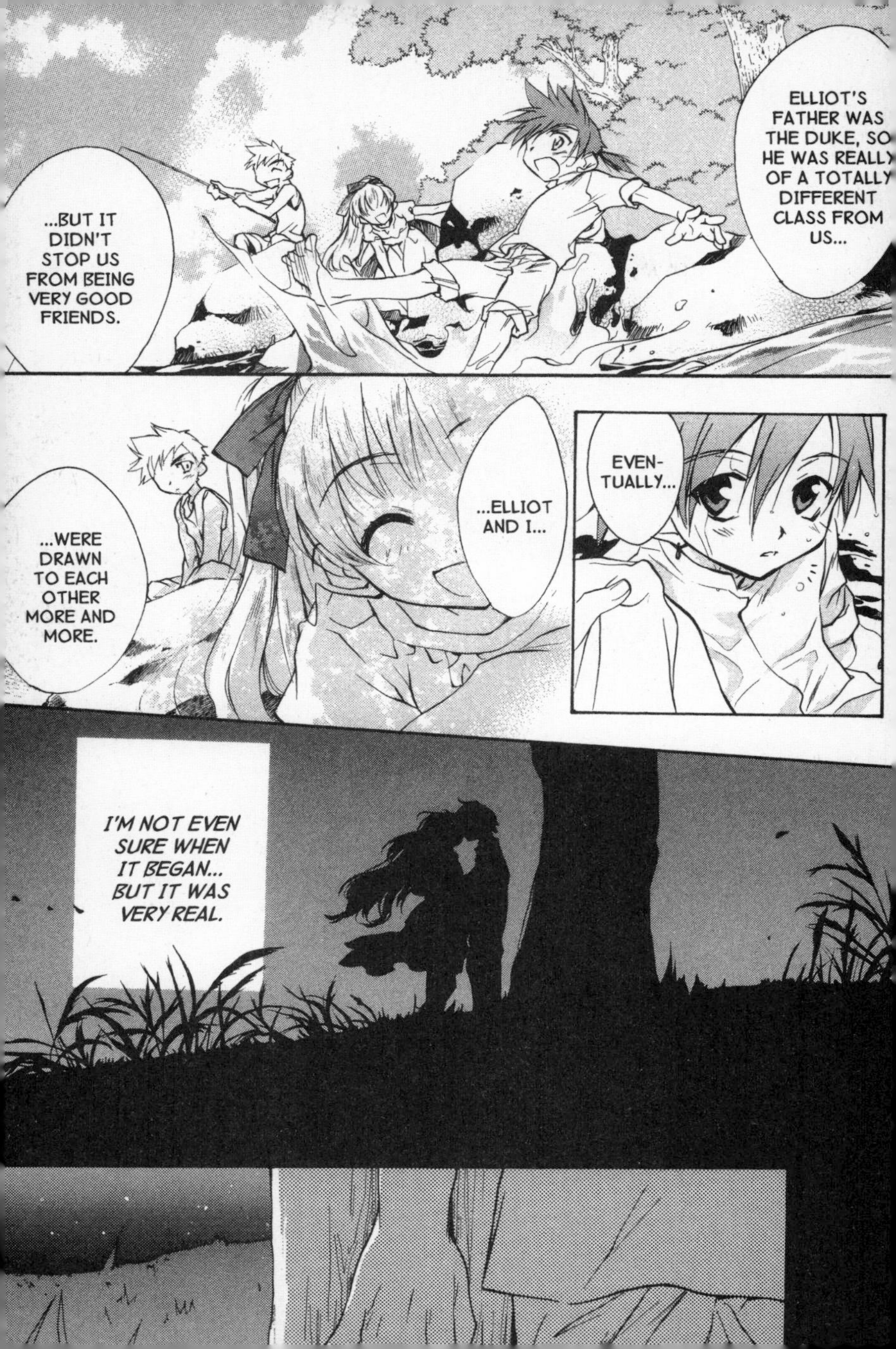
ELLIOT'S FATHER WAS THE DUKE, SO HE WAS REALLY OF A TOTALLY DIFFERENT CLASS FROM US...
...BUT IT DIDN'T STOP US FROM BEING VERY GOOD FRIENDS.
EVEN-TUALLY...
...ELLIOT AND I...
...WERE DRAWN TO EACH OTHER MORE AND MORE.
I'M NOT EVEN SURE WHEN IT BEGAN... BUT IT WAS VERY REAL.

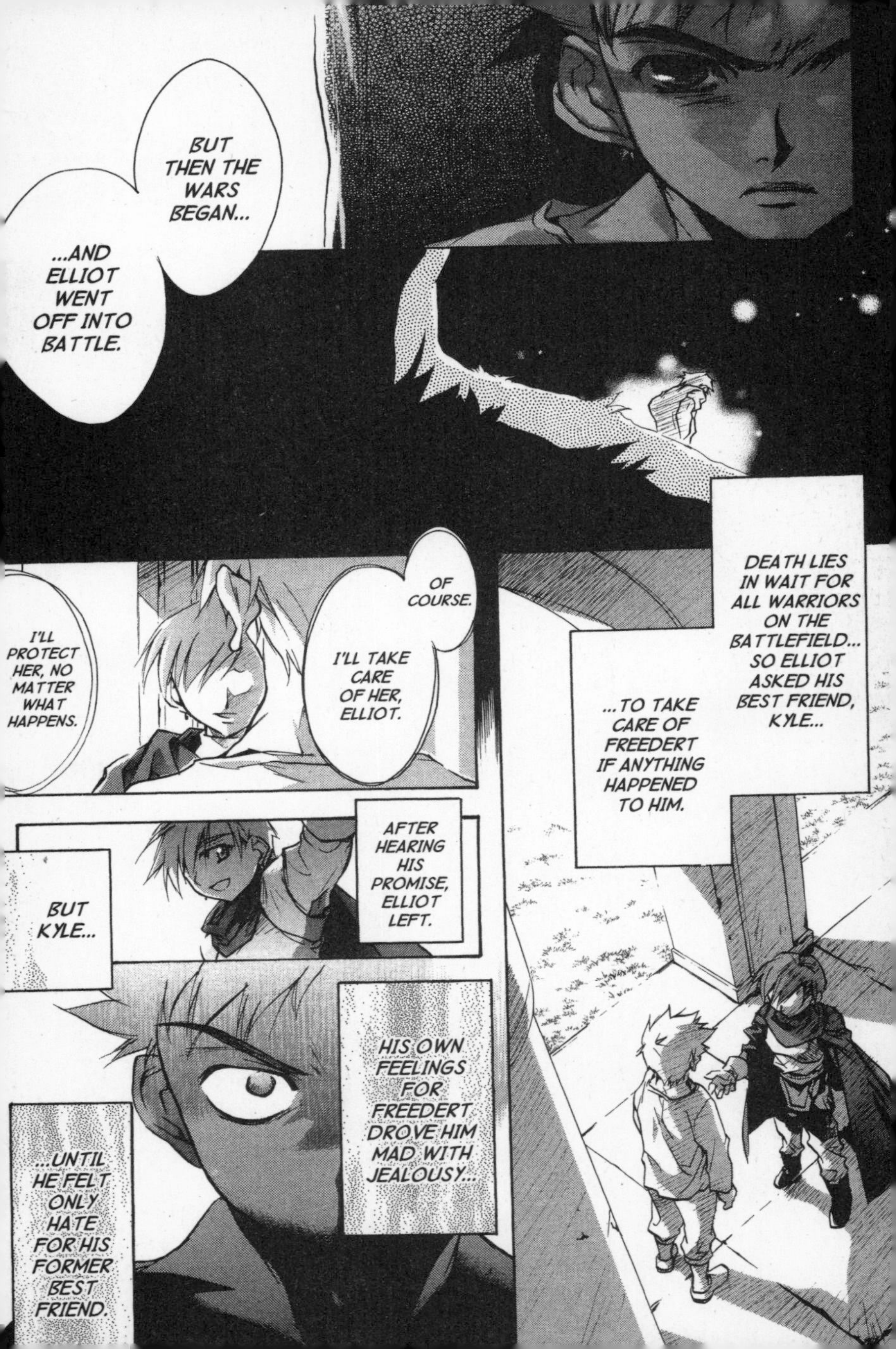
BUT THEN THE WARS BEGAN...
...AND ELLIOT WENT OFF INTO BATTLE.
DEATH LIES IN WAIT FOR ALL WARRIORS ON THE BATTLEFIELD... SO ELLIOT ASKED HIS BEST FRIEND, KYLE...
...TO TAKE CARE OF FREEDERT IF ANYTHING HAPPENED TO HIM.
OF COURSE.
I'LL TAKE CARE OF HER, ELLIOT.
I'LL PROTECT HER, NO MATTER WHAT HAPPENS.
AFTER HEARING HIS PROMISE, ELLIOT LEFT.
BUT KYLE...
HIS OWN FEELINGS FOR FREEDERT DROVE HIM MAD WITH JEALOUSY...
...UNTIL HE FELT ONLY HATE FOR HIS FORMER BEST FRIEND.

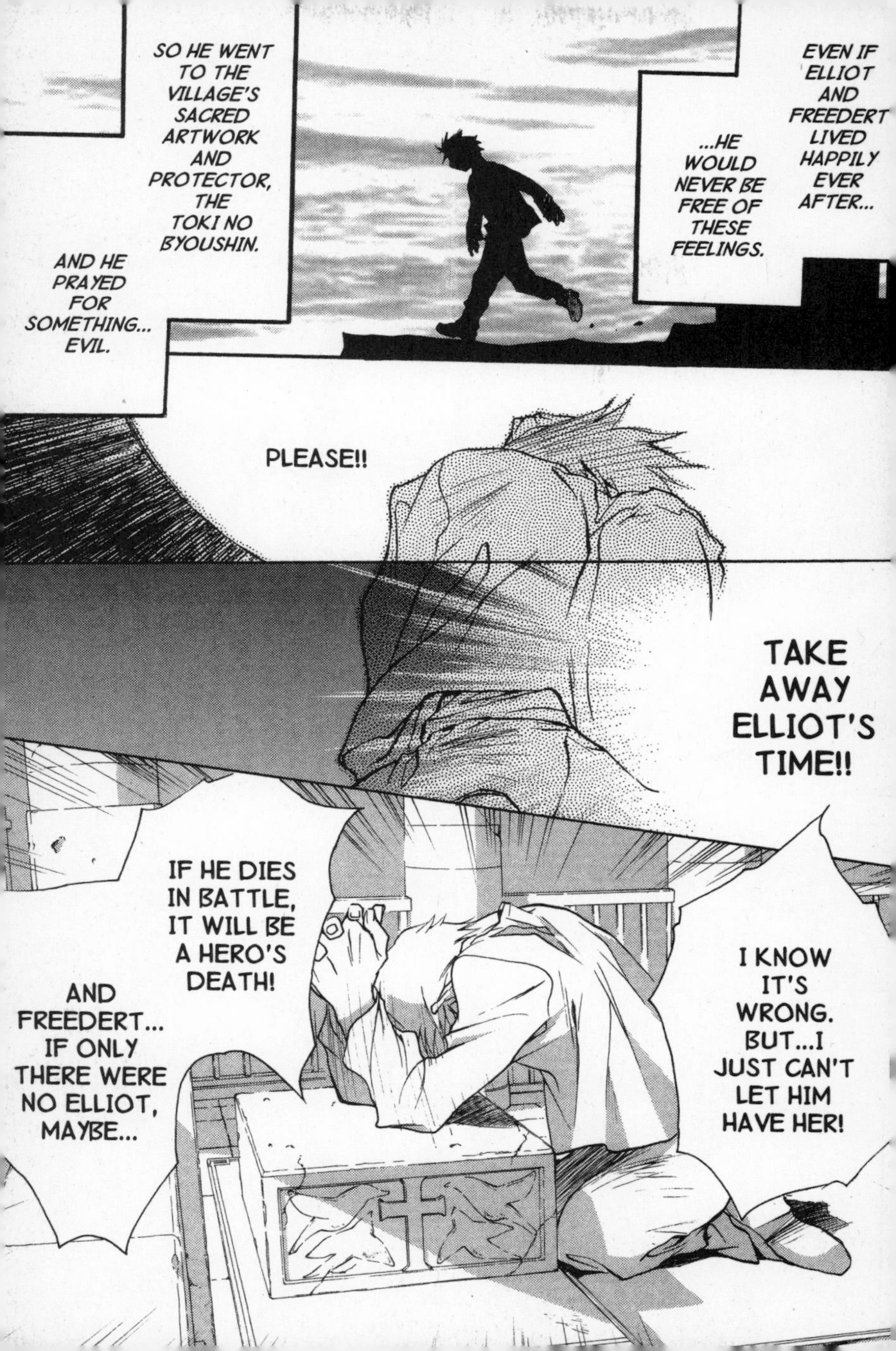
EVEN IF ELLIOT AND FREEDERT LIVED HAPPILY EVER AFTER...
...HE WOULD NEVER BE FREE OF THESE FEELINGS.
SO HE WENT TO THE VILLAGE'S SACRED ARTWORK AND PROTECTOR, THE TOKI NO BYOUSHIN.
AND HE PRAYED FOR SOMETHING... EVIL.
PLEASE!!
TAKE AWAY ELLIOT'S TIME!!
I KNOW IT'S WRONG. BUT...I JUST CAN'T LET HIM HAVE HER!
IF HE DIES IN BATTLE, IT WILL BE A HERO'S DEATH!
AND FREEDERT... IF ONLY THERE WERE NO ELLIOT, MAYBE...

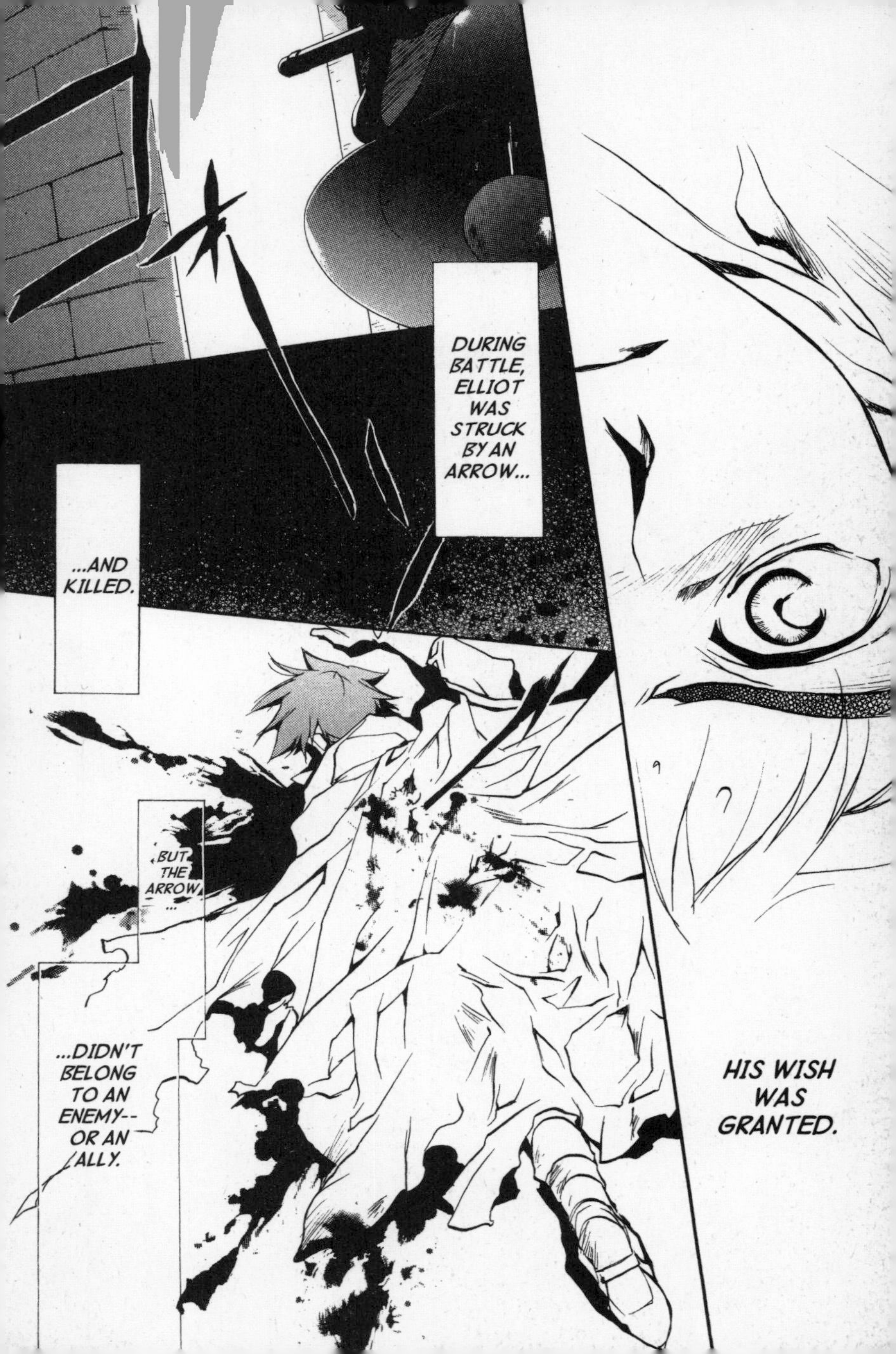
DURING BATTLE, ELLIOT WAS STRUCK BY AN ARROW...
...AND KILLED.
BUT THE ARROW...
...DIDN'T BELONG TO AN ENEMY--OR AN ALLY.
HIS WISH WAS GRANTED.

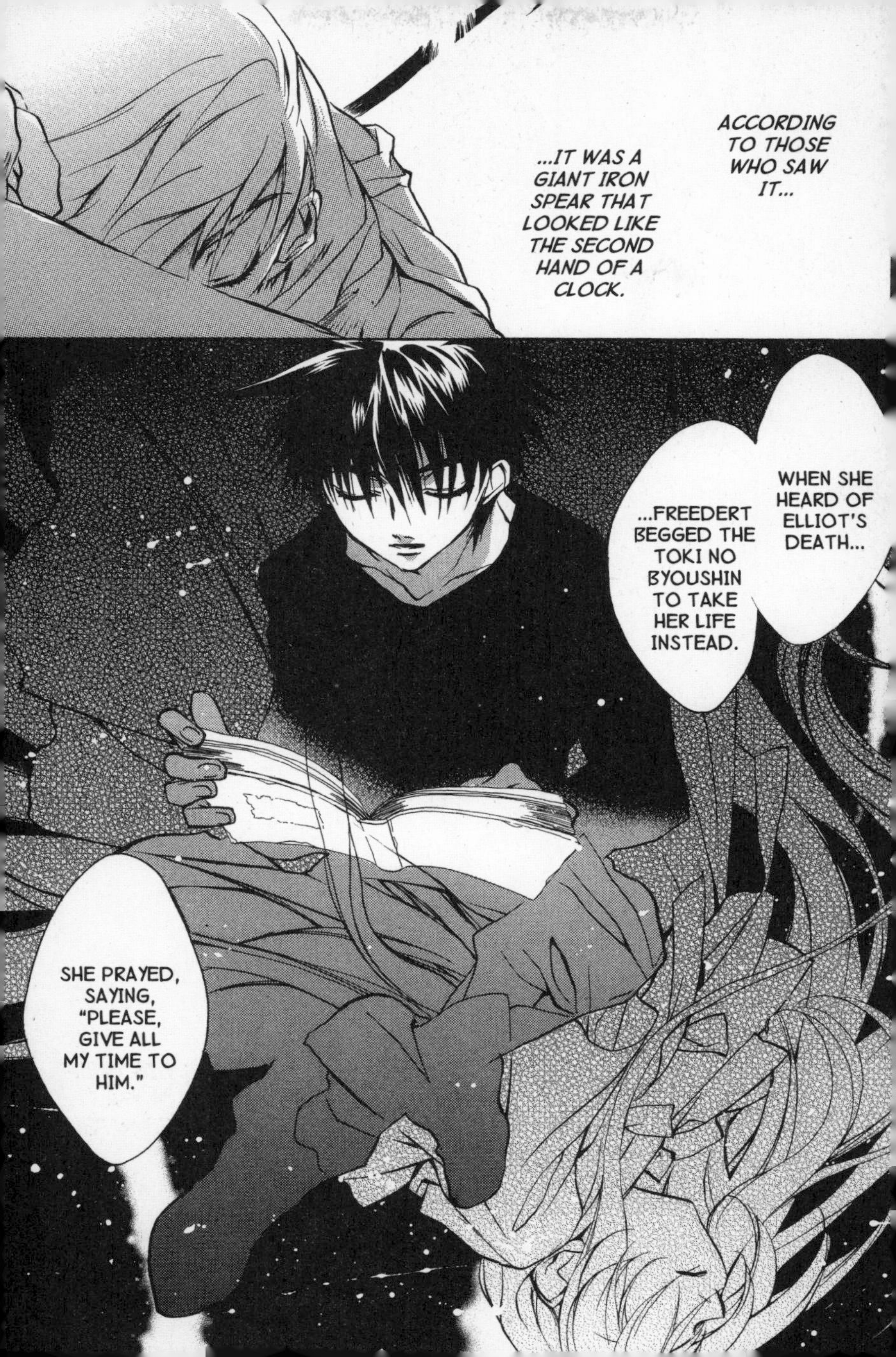
ACCORDING TO THOSE WHO SAW IT...
...IT WAS A GIANT IRON SPEAR THAT LOOKED LIKE THE SECOND HAND OF A CLOCK.
WHEN SHE HEARD OF ELLIOT'S DEATH...
...FREEDERT BEGGED THE TOKI NO BYOUSHIN TO TAKE HER LIFE INSTEAD.
SHE PRAYED, SAYING, "PLEASE, GIVE ALL MY TIME TO HIM."

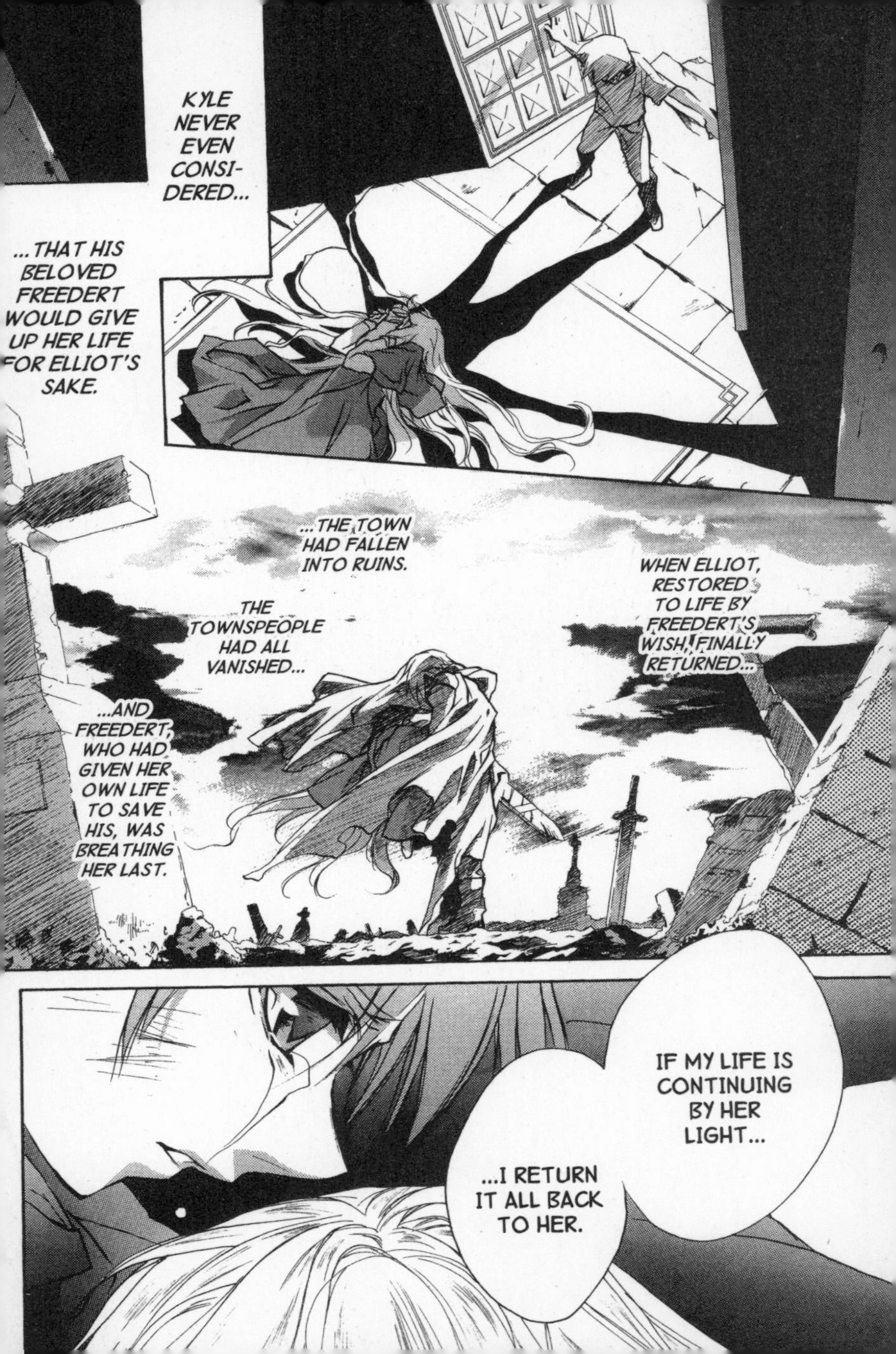
KYLE NEVER EVEN CONSI-DERED...
...THAT HIS BELOVED FREEDERT WOULD GIVE UP HER LIFE FOR ELLIOT'S SAKE.
WHEN ELLIOT, RESTORED TO LIFE BY FREEDERT'S WISH, FINALLY RETURNED...
...THE TOWN HAD FALLEN INTO RUINS.
THE TOWNSPEOPLE HAD ALL VANISHED...
...AND FREEDERT, WHO HAD GIVEN HER OWN LIFE TO SAVE HIS, WAS BREATHING HER LAST.
IF MY LIFE IS CONTINUING BY HER LIGHT...
...I RETURN IT ALL BACK TO HER.

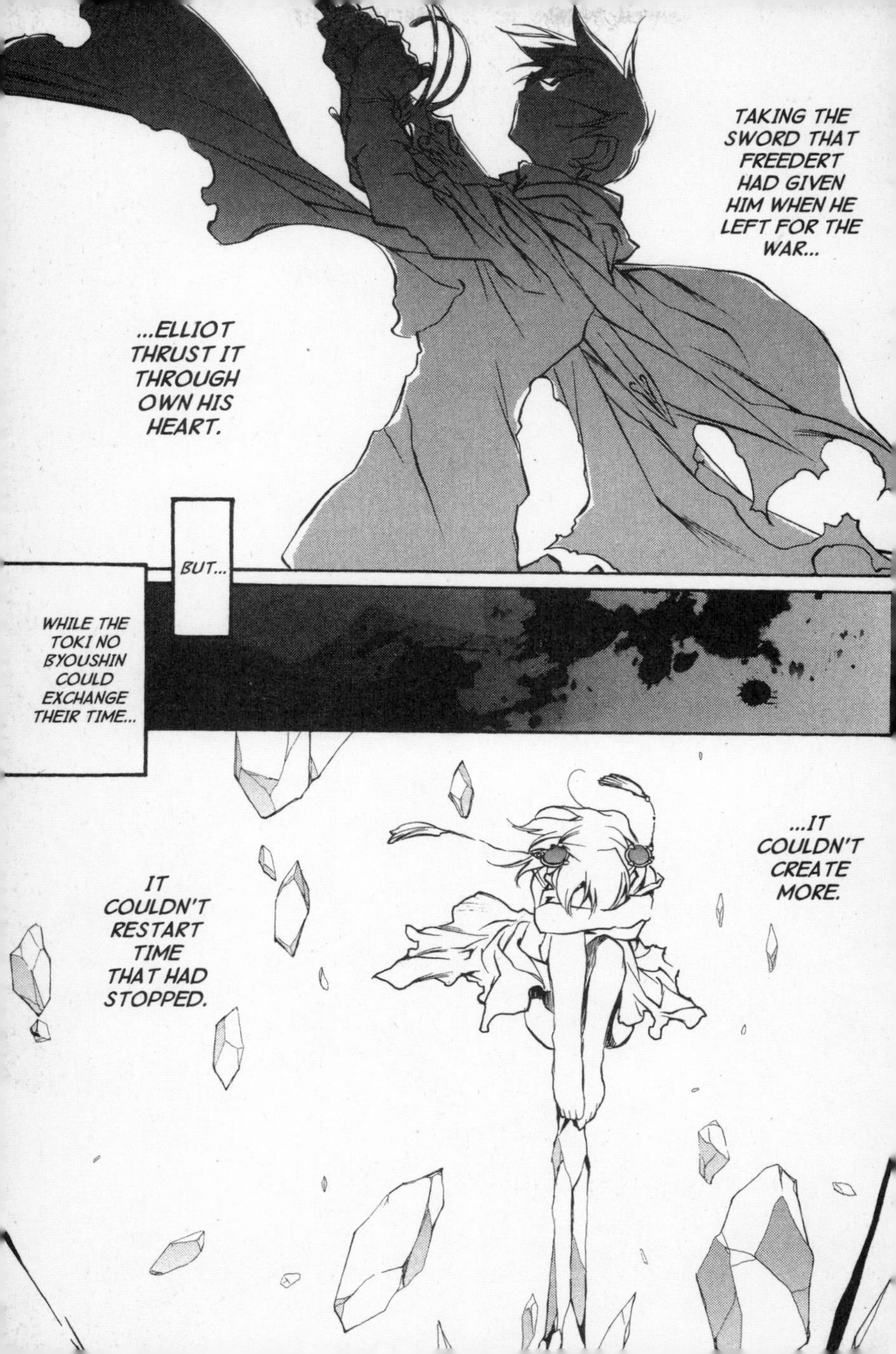

TAKING THE SWORD THAT FREEDERT HAD GIVEN HIM WHEN HE LEFT FOR THE WAR...
...ELLIOT THRUST IT THROUGH OWN HIS HEART.
BUT...
WHILE THE TOKI NO BYOUSHIN COULD EXCHANGE THEIR TIME...
...IT COULDN'T CREATE MORE.
IT COULDN'T RESTART TIME THAT HAD STOPPED.

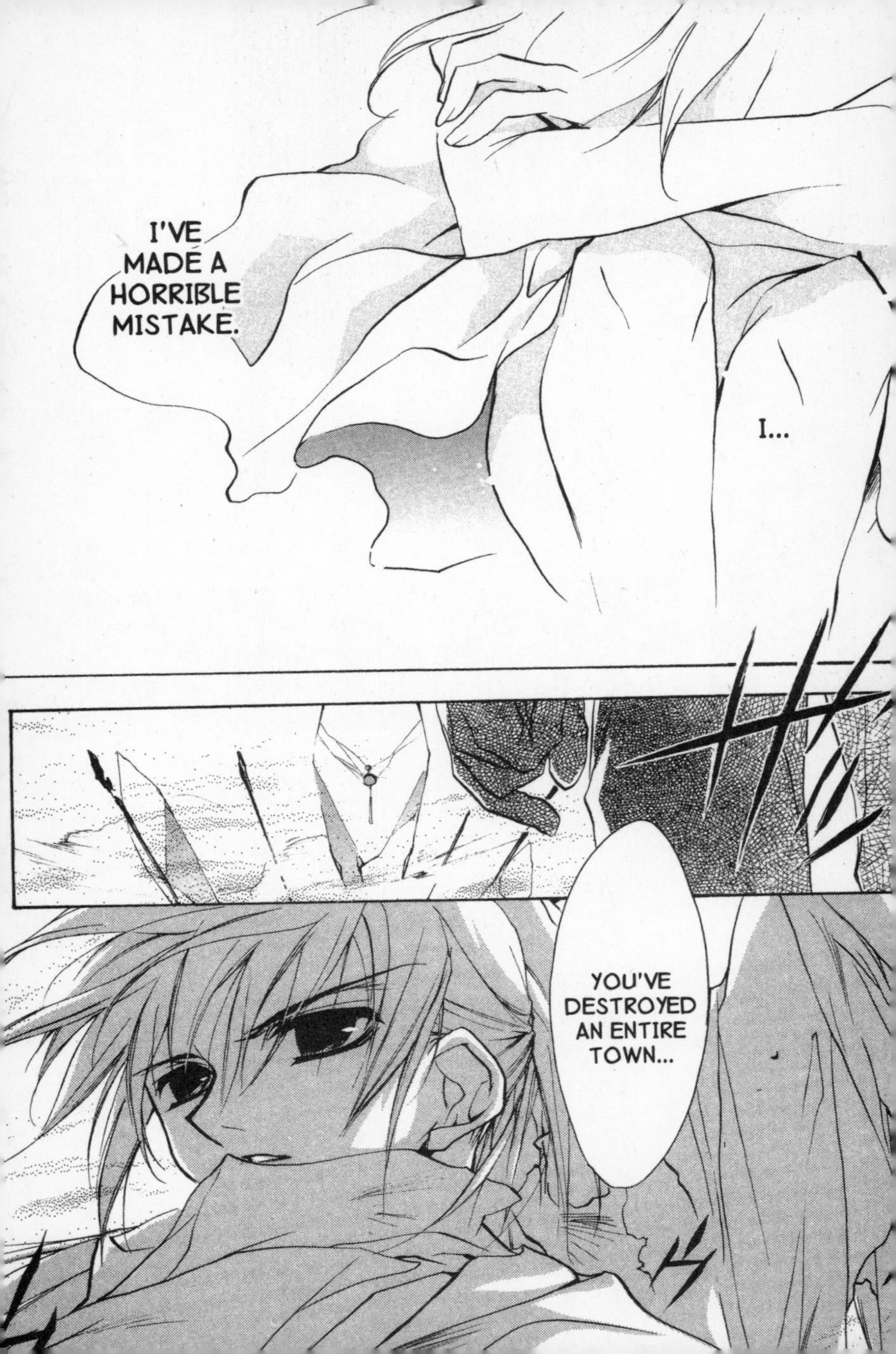
I...
I'VE MADE A HORRIBLE MISTAKE.
YOU'VE DESTROYED AN ENTIRE TOWN...

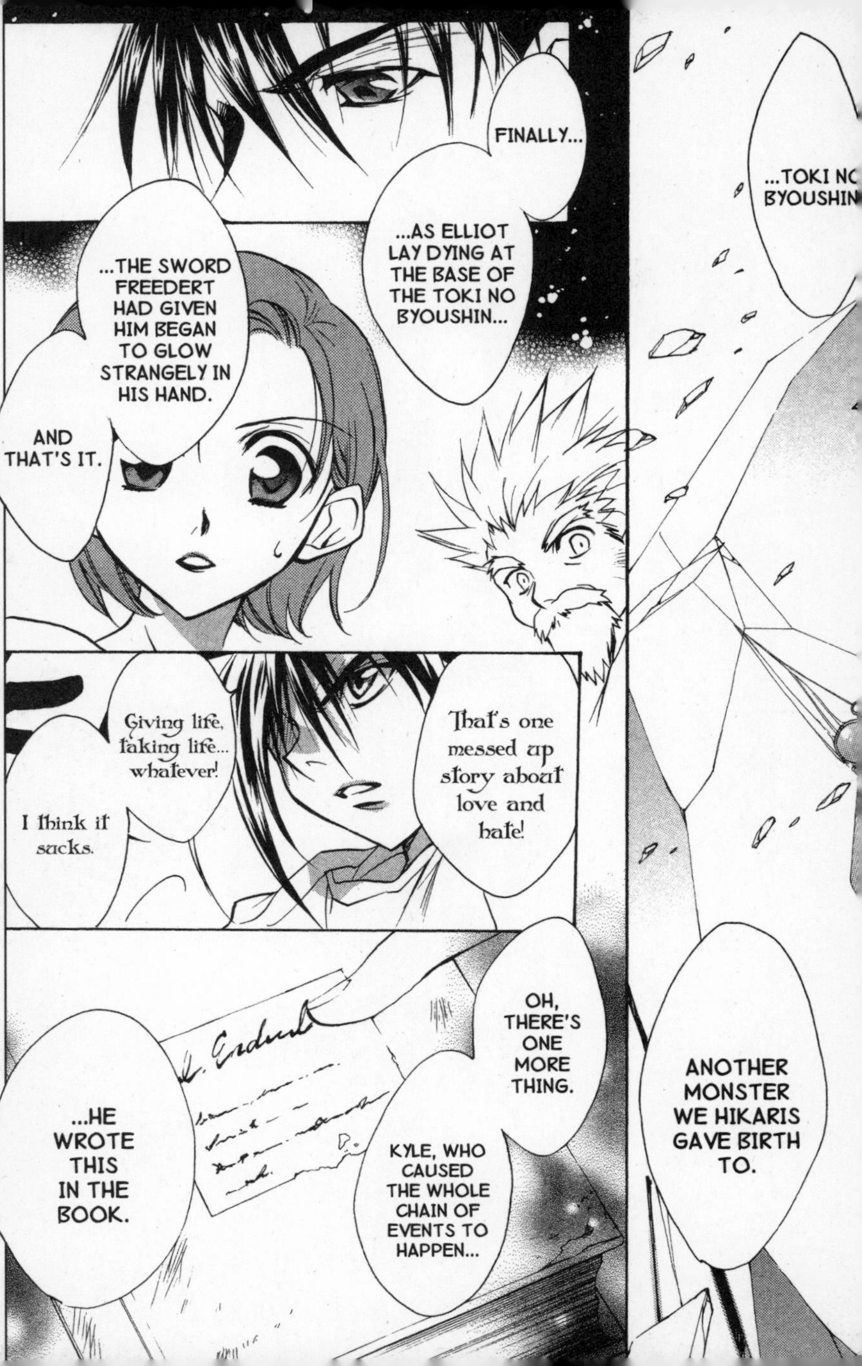

...TOKI NO BYOUSHIN
ANOTHER MONSTER WE HIKARIS GAVE BIRTH TO.
FINALLY...
...AS ELLIOT LAY DYING AT THE BASE OF THE TOKI NO BYOUSHIN...
...THE SWORD FREEDERT HAD GIVEN HIM BEGAN TO GLOW STRANGELY IN HIS HAND.
AND THAT'S IT.
That's one messed up story about love and hate!
Giving life, taking life... whatever!
I think it sucks.
OH, THERE'S ONE MORE THING.
KYLE, WHO CAUSED THE WHOLE CHAIN OF EVENTS TO HAPPEN...
...HE WROTE THIS IN THE BOOK.

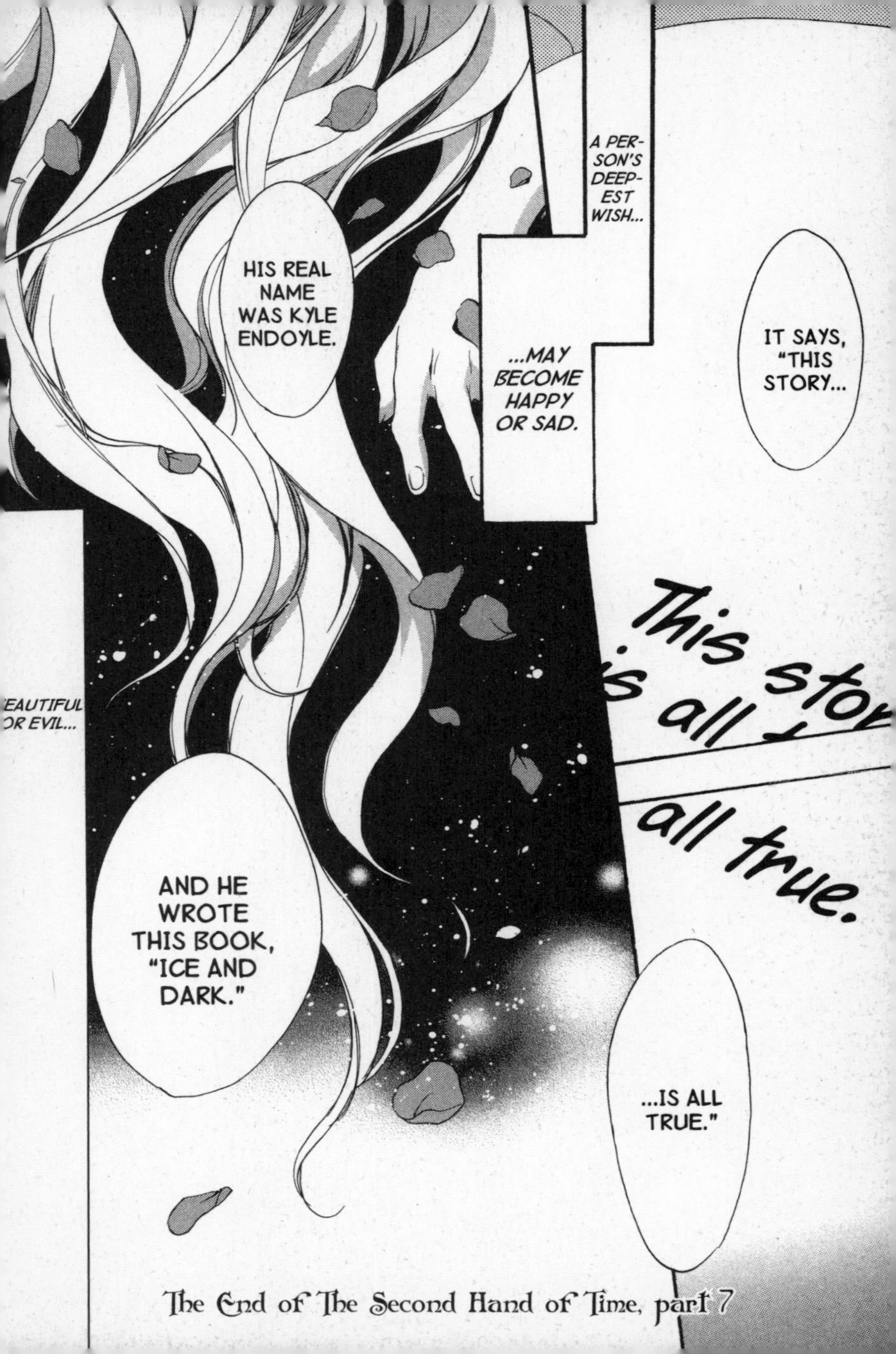
IT SAYS, "THIS STORY...
A PERSON'S DEEPEST WISH...
...MAY BECOME HAPPY OR SAD.
HIS REAL NAME WAS KYLE ENDOYLE.
EAUTIFUL OR EVIL...
This stor
is all
all true.
...IS ALL TRUE."
AND HE WROTE THIS BOOK, "ICE AND DARK."

The End of The Second Hand of Time, part 7

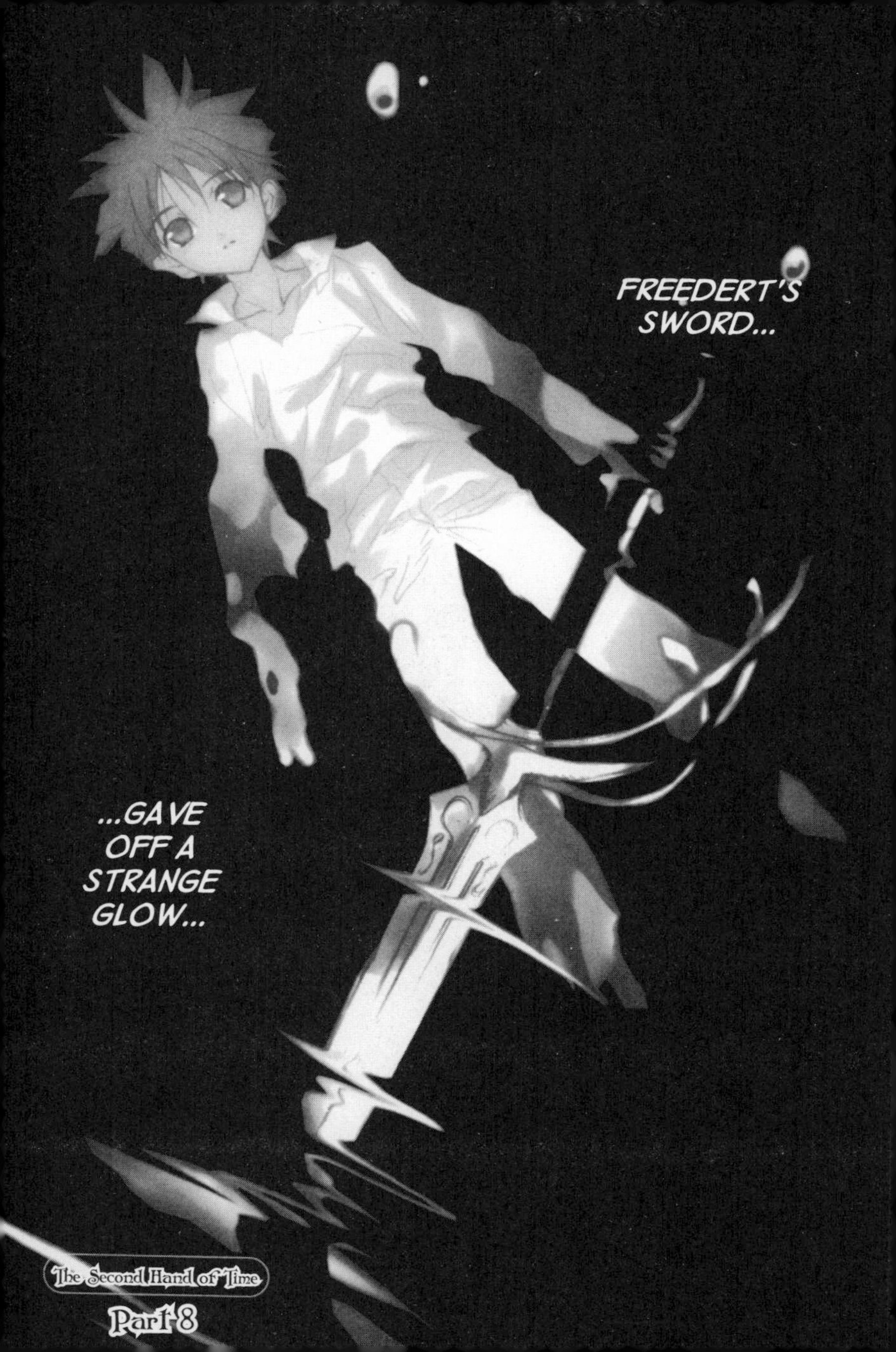
FREEDERT'S SWORD...
...GAVE OFF A STRANGE GLOW...
The Second Hand of Time
Part 8

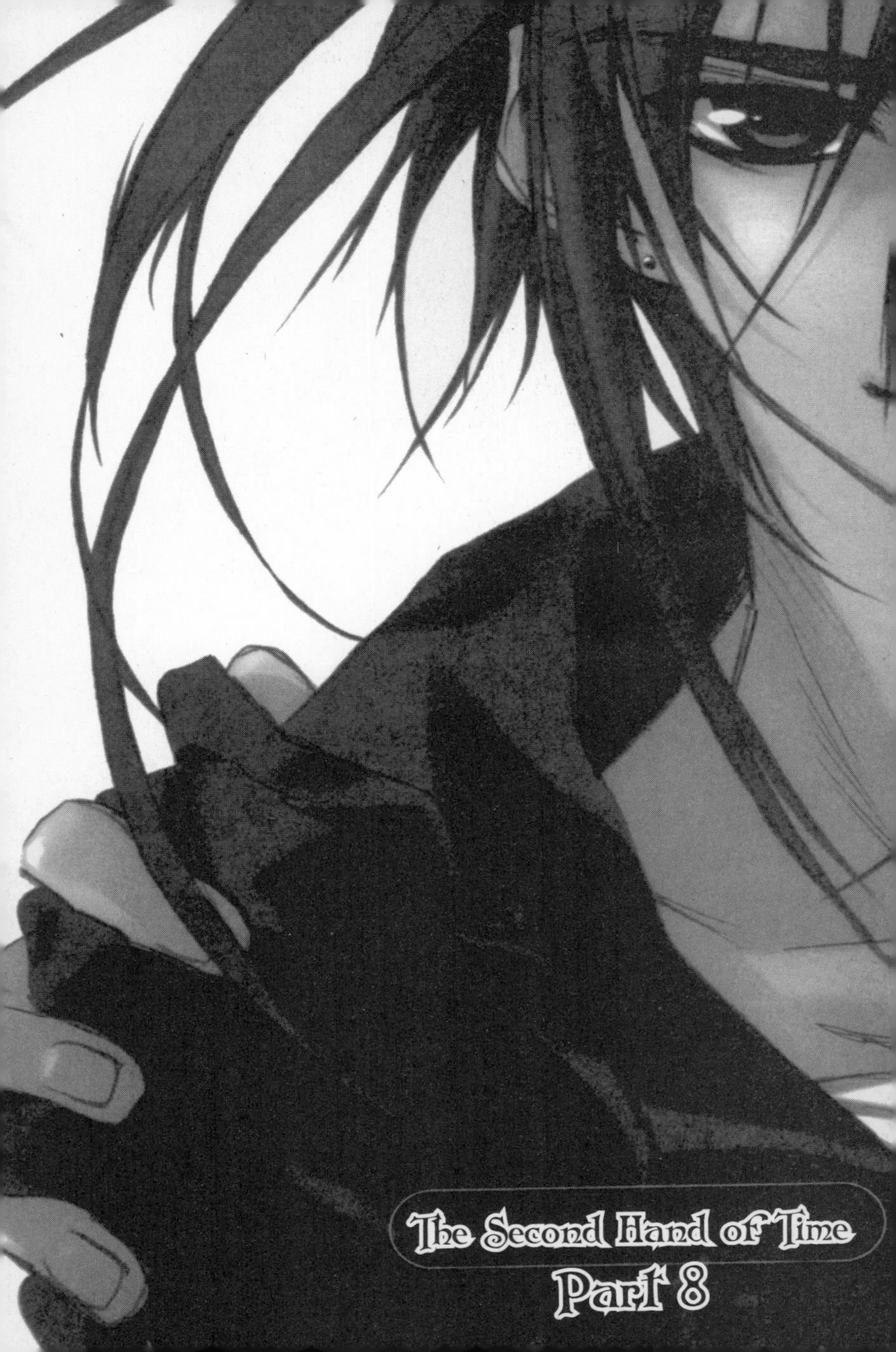
The Second Hand of Time
Part 8

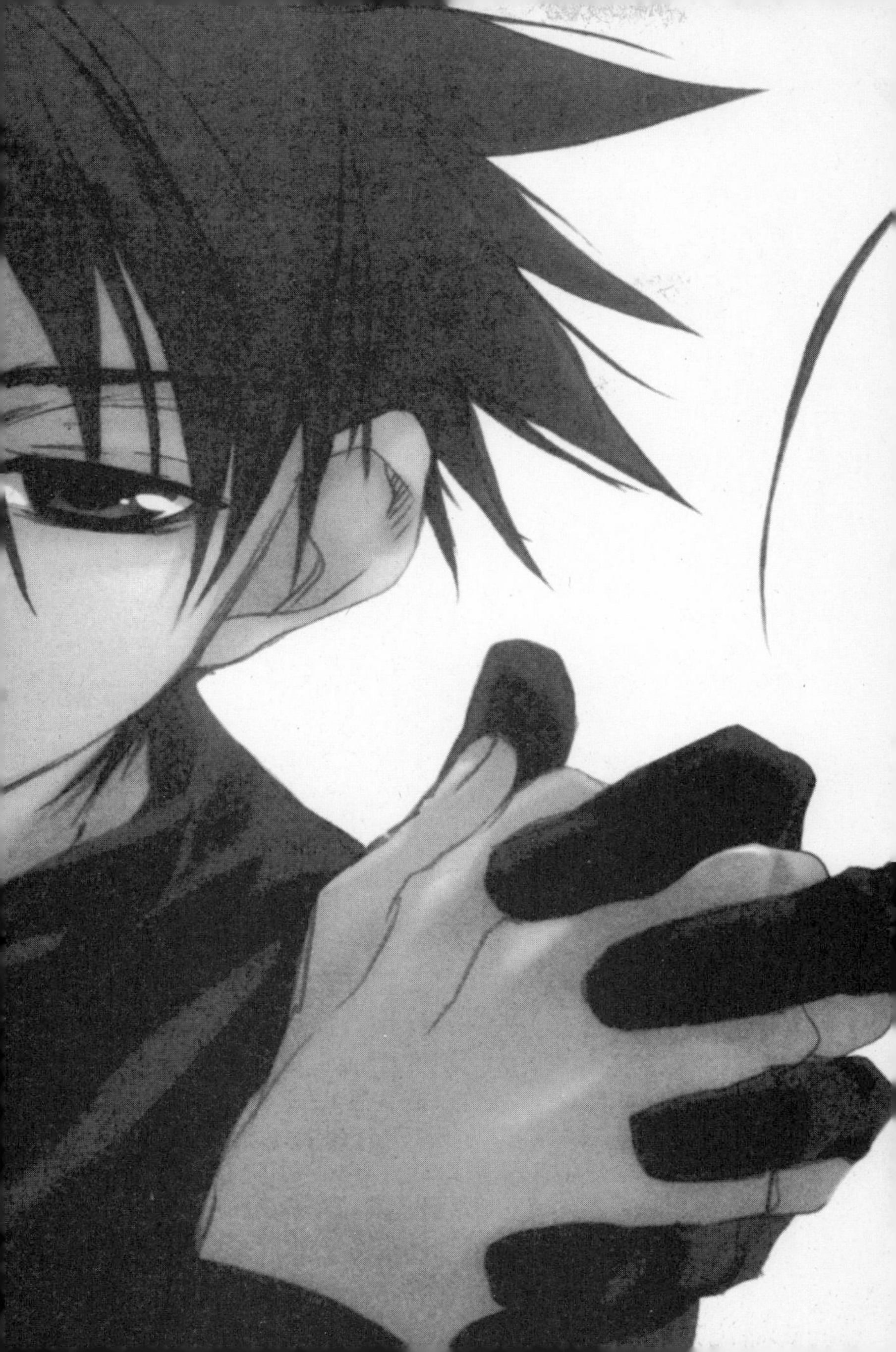

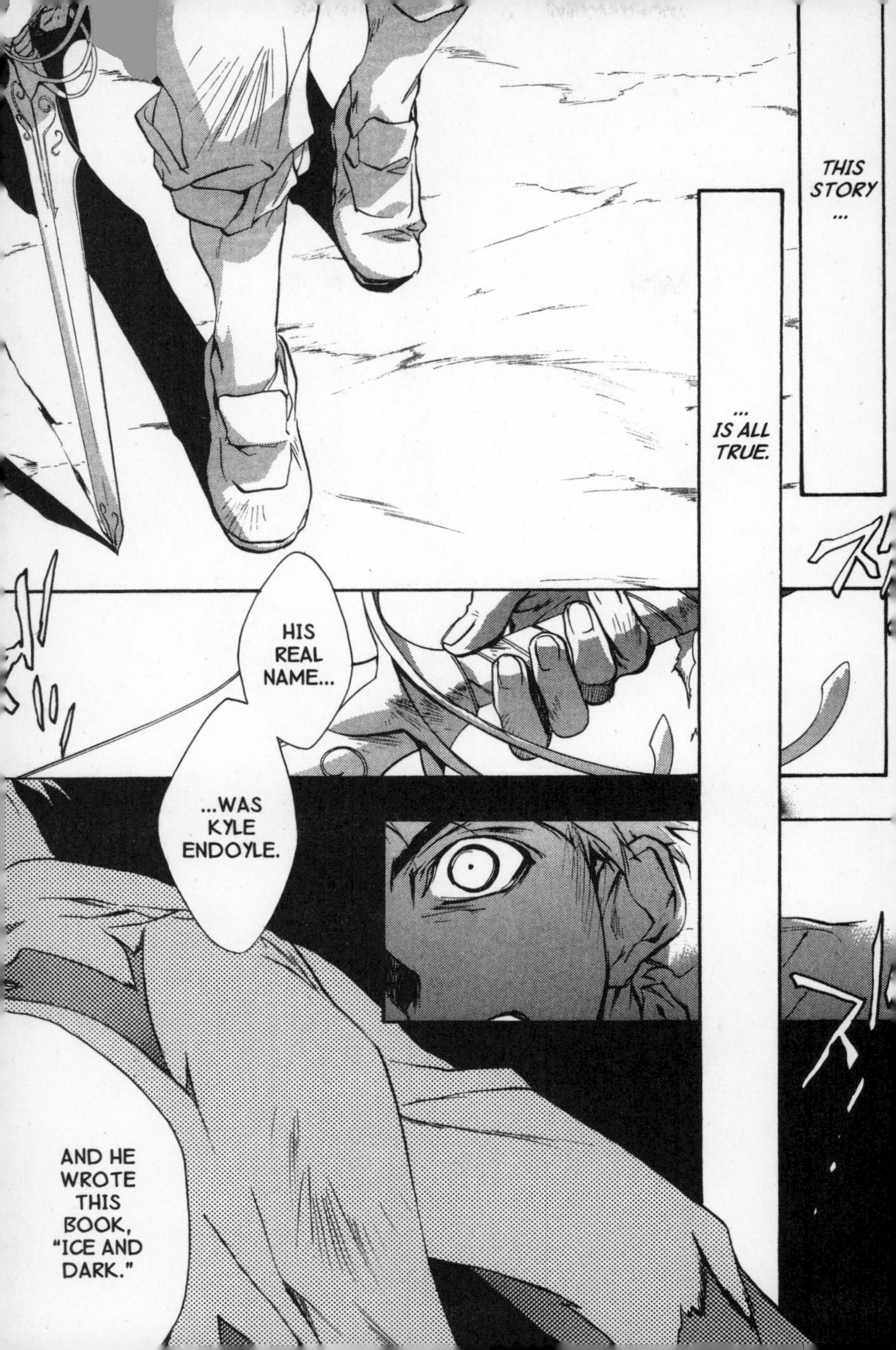
THIS STORY ...
... IS ALL TRUE.
HIS REAL NAME...
...WAS KYLE ENDOYLE.
AND HE WROTE THIS BOOK, "ICE AND DARK."

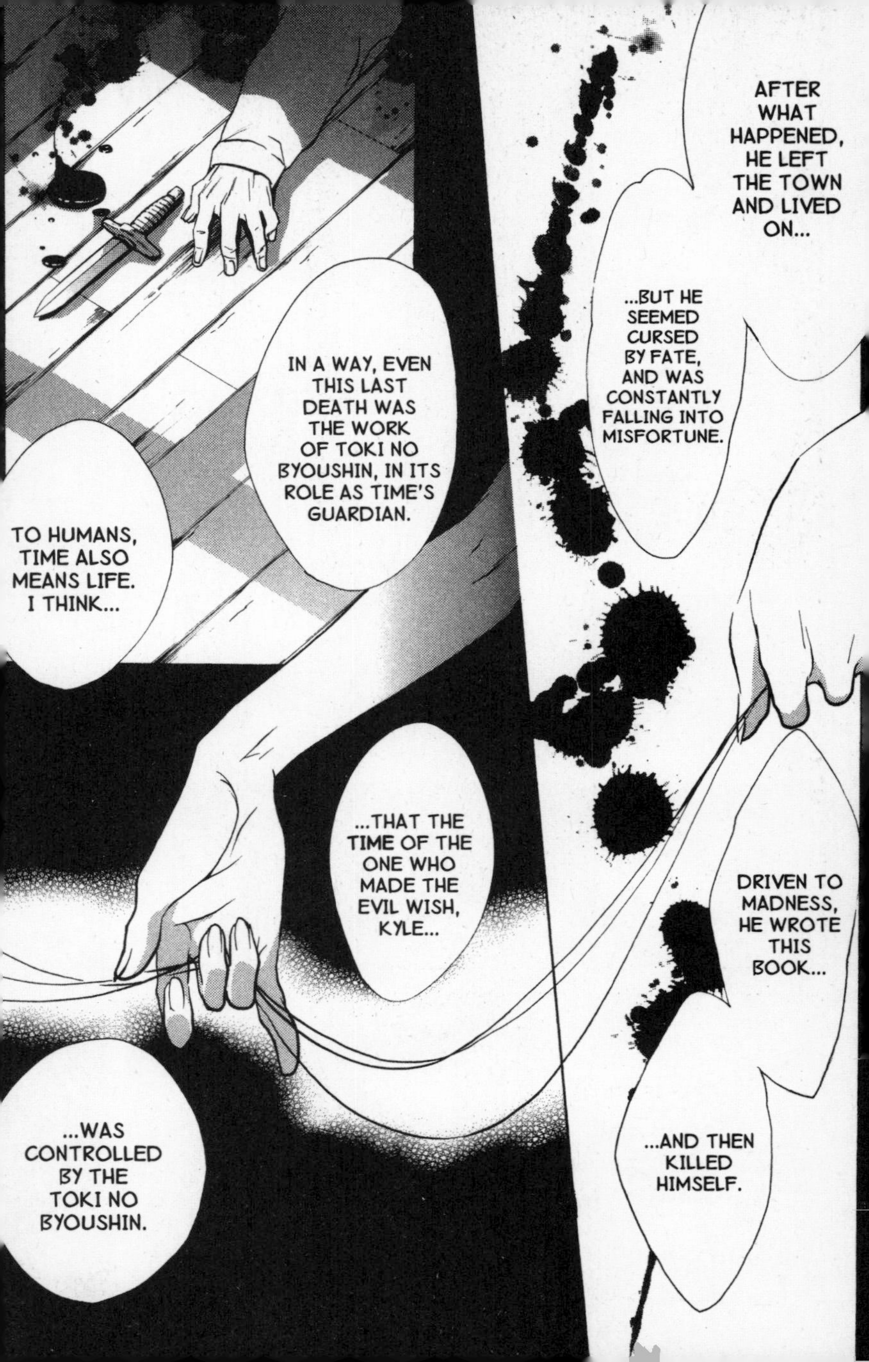
AFTER WHAT HAPPENED, HE LEFT THE TOWN AND LIVED ON...
...BUT HE SEEMED CURSED BY FATE, AND WAS CONSTANTLY FALLING INTO MISFORTUNE.
DRIVEN TO MADNESS, HE WROTE THIS BOOK...
...AND THEN KILLED HIMSELF.
IN A WAY, EVEN THIS LAST DEATH WAS THE WORK OF TOKI NO BYOUSHIN, IN ITS ROLE AS TIME'S GUARDIAN.
TO HUMANS, TIME ALSO MEANS LIFE. I THINK...
...THAT THE TIME OF THE ONE WHO MADE THE EVIL WISH, KYLE...
...WAS CONTROLLED BY THE TOKI NO BYOUSHIN.

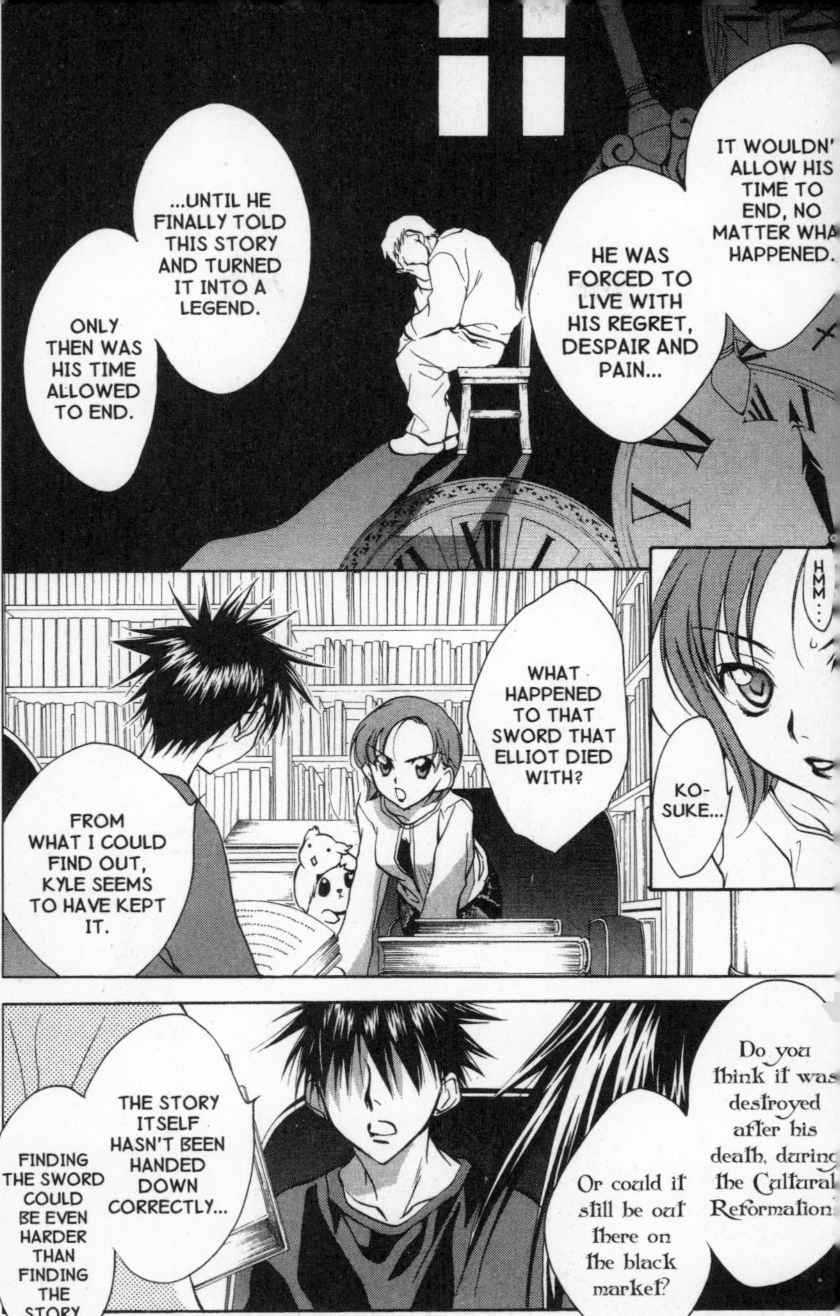
IT WOULDN' ALLOW HIS TIME TO END, NO MATTER WHA HAPPENED.
HE WAS FORCED TO LIVE WITH HIS REGRET, DESPAIR AND PAIN...
...UNTIL HE FINALLY TOLD THIS STORY AND TURNED IT INTO A LEGEND.
ONLY THEN WAS HIS TIME ALLOWED TO END.
HMM...
KO-SUKE...
WHAT HAPPENED TO THAT SWORD THAT ELLIOT DIED WITH?
FROM WHAT I COULD FIND OUT, KYLE SEEMS TO HAVE KEPT IT.
Do you think it was destroyed after his death, durin the Cultural Reformation
Or could it still be out there on the black market?
THE STORY ITSELF HASN'T BEEN HANDED DOWN CORRECTLY...
FINDING THE SWORD COULD BE EVEN HARDER THAN FINDING THE STORY.

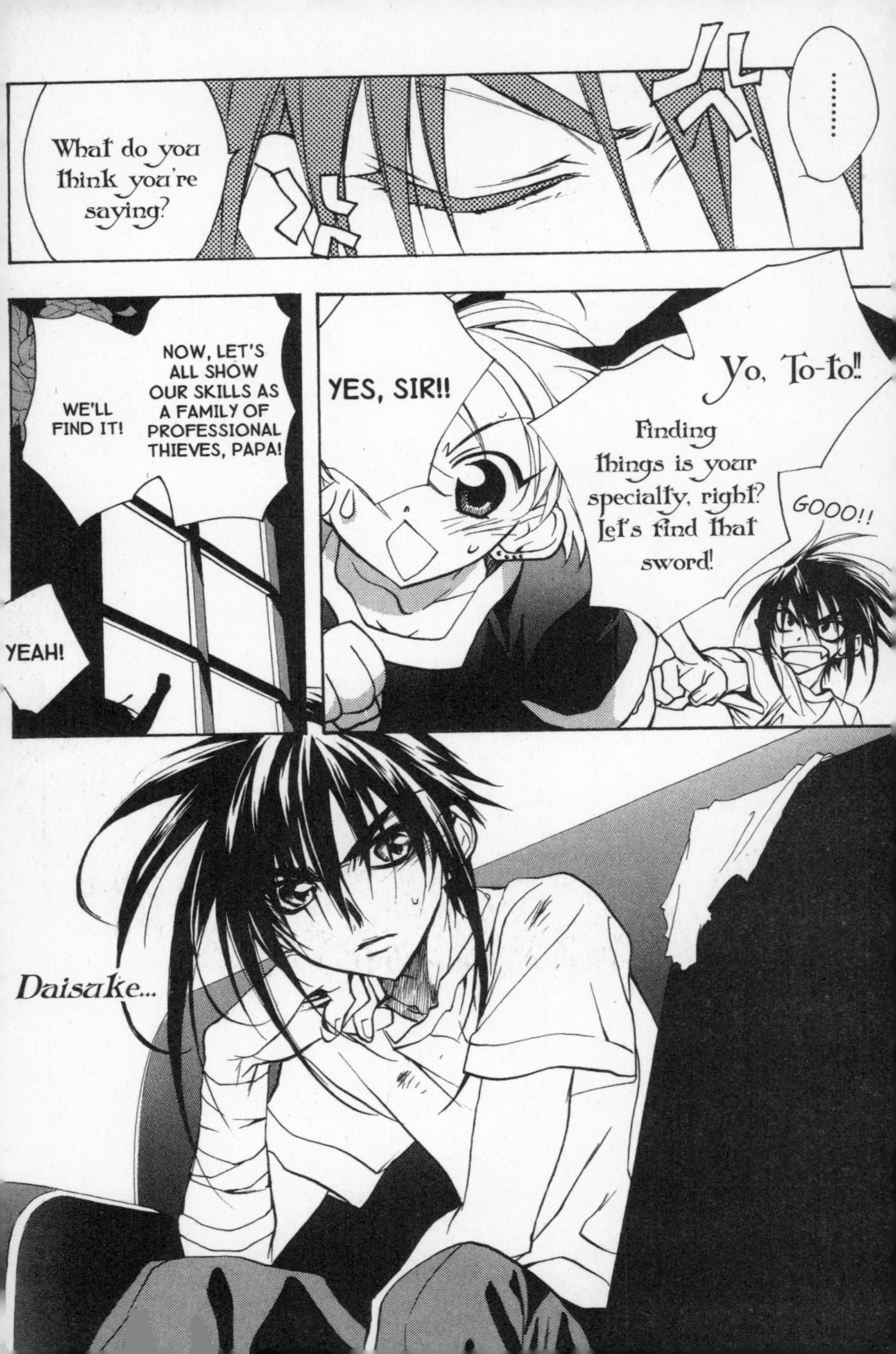
......
What do you think you're saying?
Yo, To-to!!
Finding things is your specialty, right? Let's find that sword!
GOOOO!!
YES, SIR!!
NOW, LET'S ALL SHOW OUR SKILLS AS A FAMILY OF PROFESSIONAL THIEVES, PAPA!
WE'LL FIND IT!
YEAH!
Daisuke...

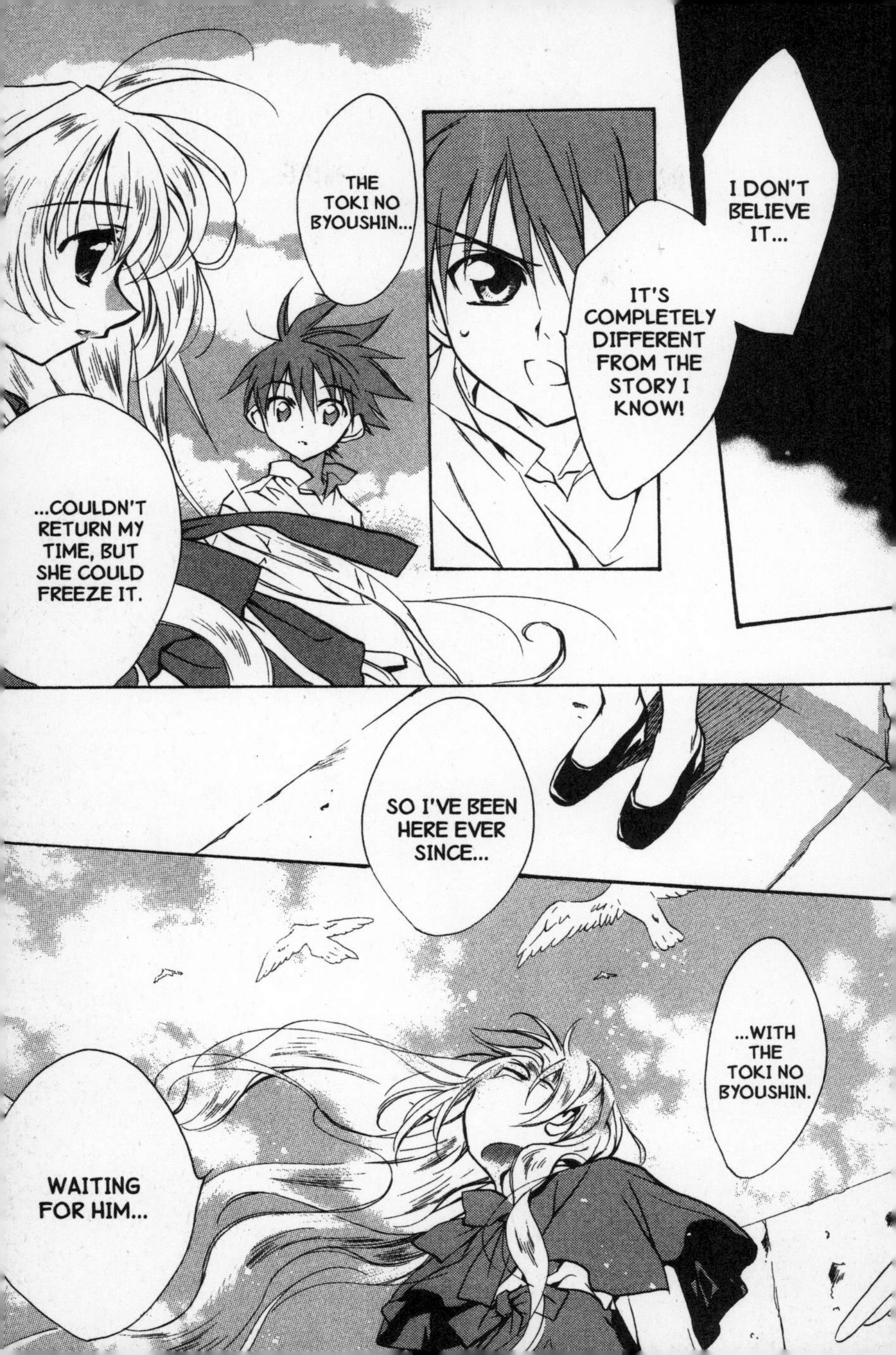
I DON'T BELIEVE IT...
IT'S COMPLETELY DIFFERENT FROM THE STORY I KNOW!
THE TOKI NO BYOUSHIN...
...COULDN'T RETURN MY TIME, BUT SHE COULD FREEZE IT.
SO I'VE BEEN HERE EVER SINCE...
...WITH THE TOKI NO BYOUSHIN.
WAITING FOR HIM...

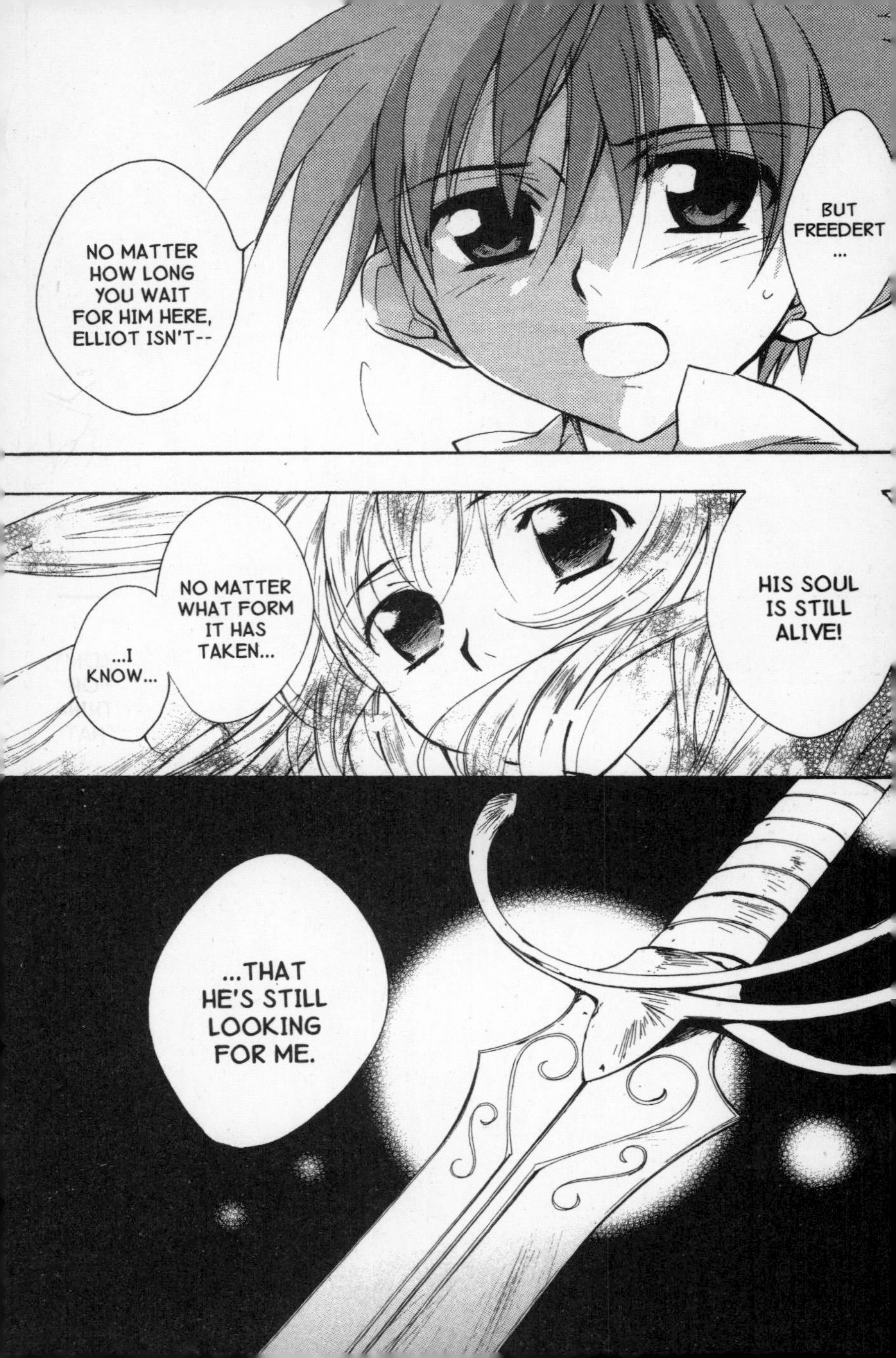
BUT FREEDERT ...
NO MATTER HOW LONG YOU WAIT FOR HIM HERE, ELLIOT ISN'T--
HIS SOUL IS STILL ALIVE!
NO MATTER WHAT FORM IT HAS TAKEN...
...I KNOW...
...THAT HE'S STILL LOOKING FOR ME.

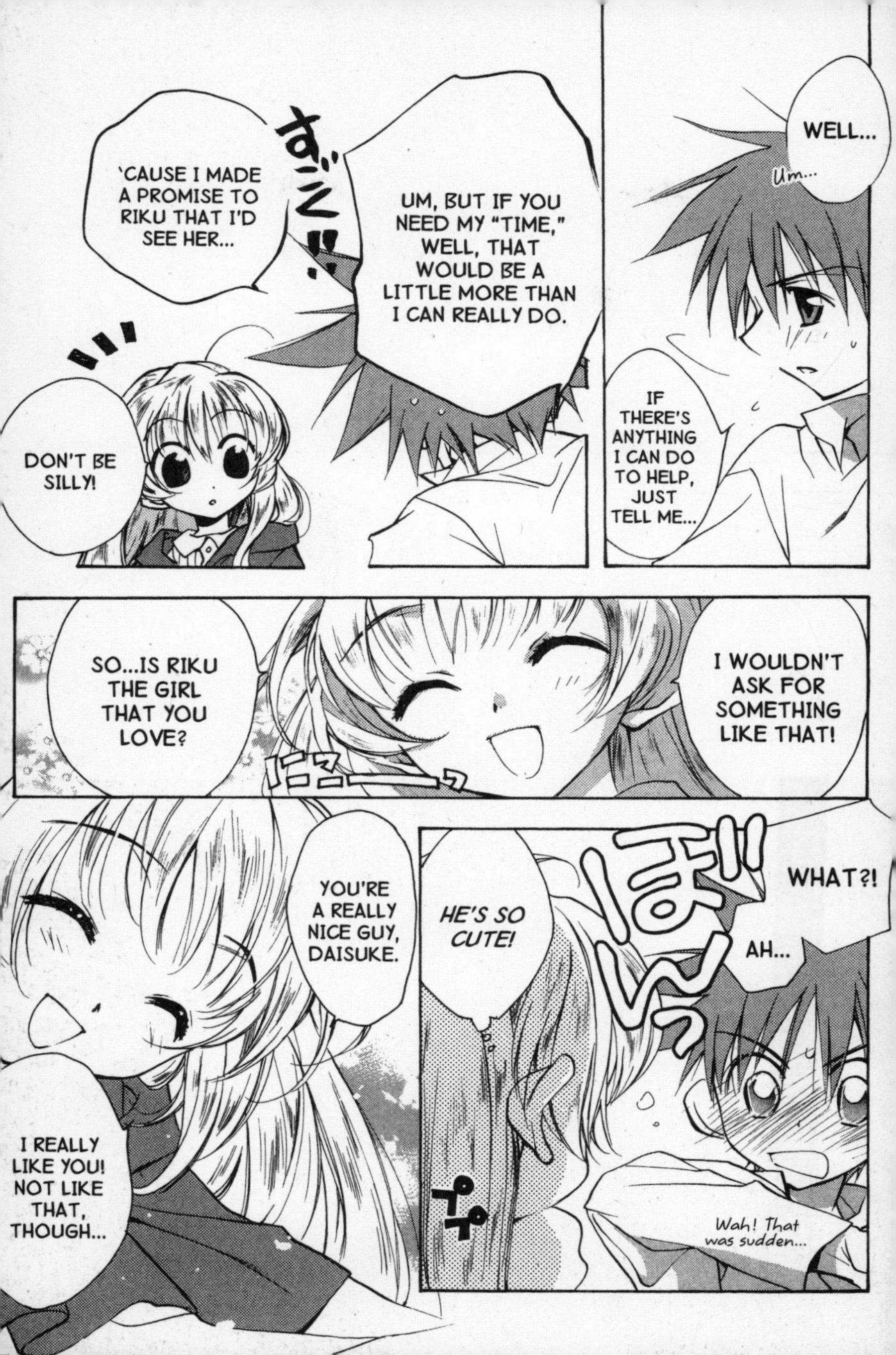
WELL...
Um...
IF THERE'S ANYTHING I CAN DO TO HELP, JUST TELL ME...
UM, BUT IF YOU NEED MY "TIME," WELL, THAT WOULD BE A LITTLE MORE THAN I CAN REALLY DO.
'CAUSE I MADE A PROMISE TO RIKU THAT I'D SEE HER...
DON'T BE SILLY!
I WOULDN'T ASK FOR SOMETHING LIKE THAT!
SO...IS RIKU THE GIRL THAT YOU LOVE?
WHAT?!
AH...
Wah! That was sudden...
HE'S SO CUTE!
YOU'RE A REALLY NICE GUY, DAISUKE.
I REALLY LIKE YOU! NOT LIKE THAT, THOUGH...

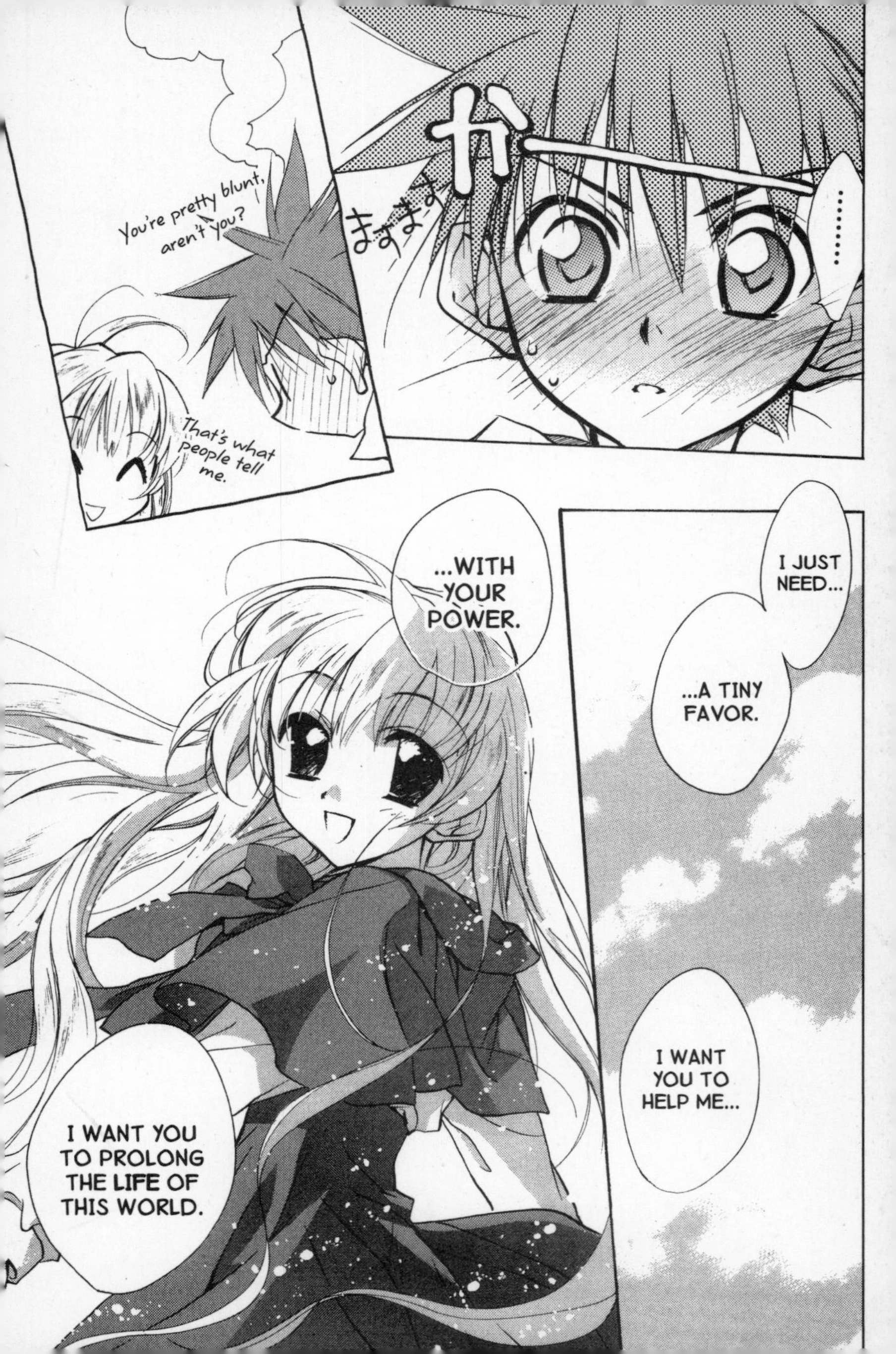
かー
ますます
......
You're pretty blunt, aren't you?
That's what people tell me.
I JUST NEED...
...A TINY FAVOR.
I WANT YOU TO HELP ME...
...WITH YOUR POWER.
I WANT YOU TO PROLONG THE LIFE OF THIS WORLD.

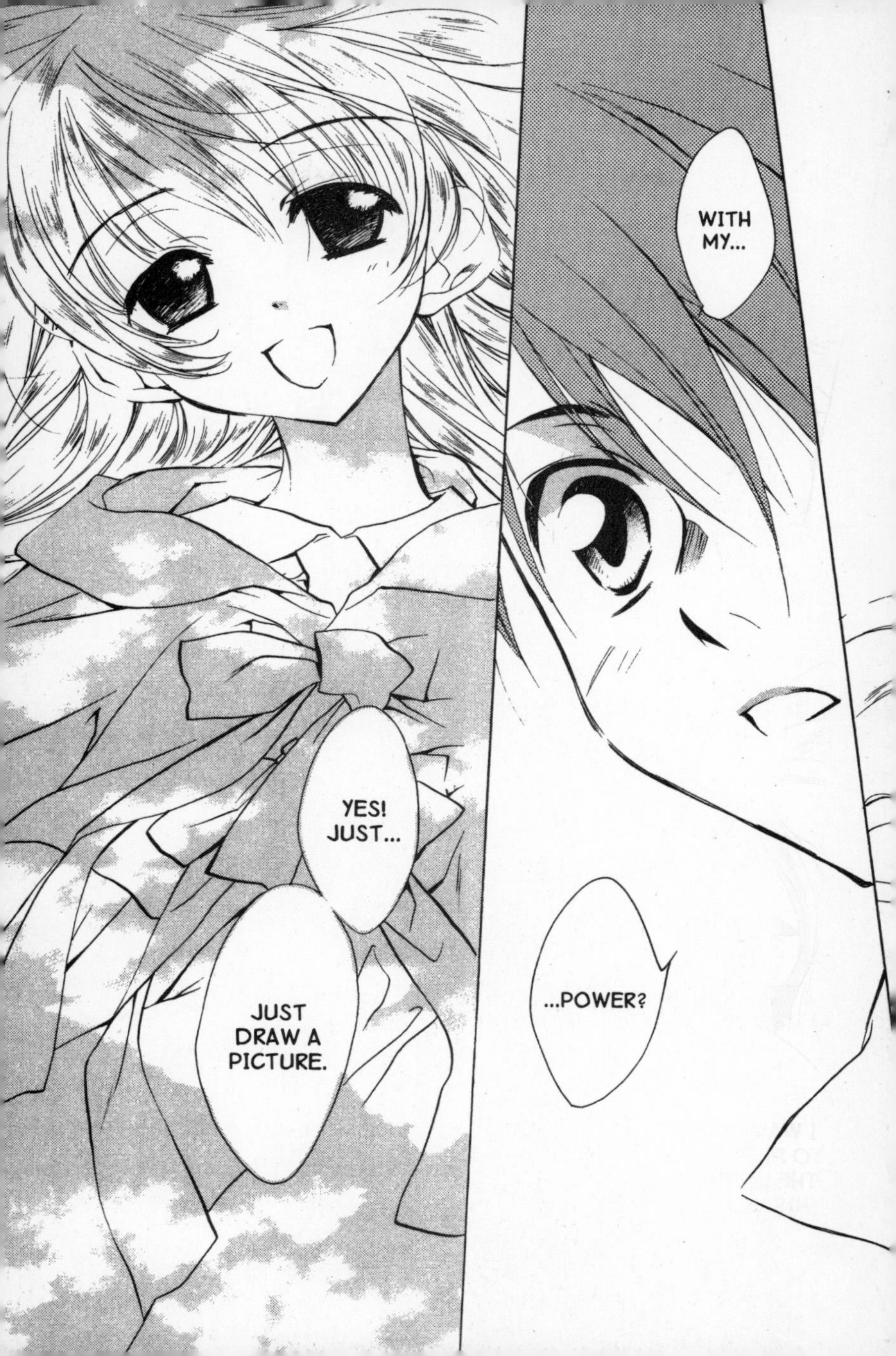
WITH MY...
...POWER?
YES! JUST...
JUST DRAW A PICTURE.

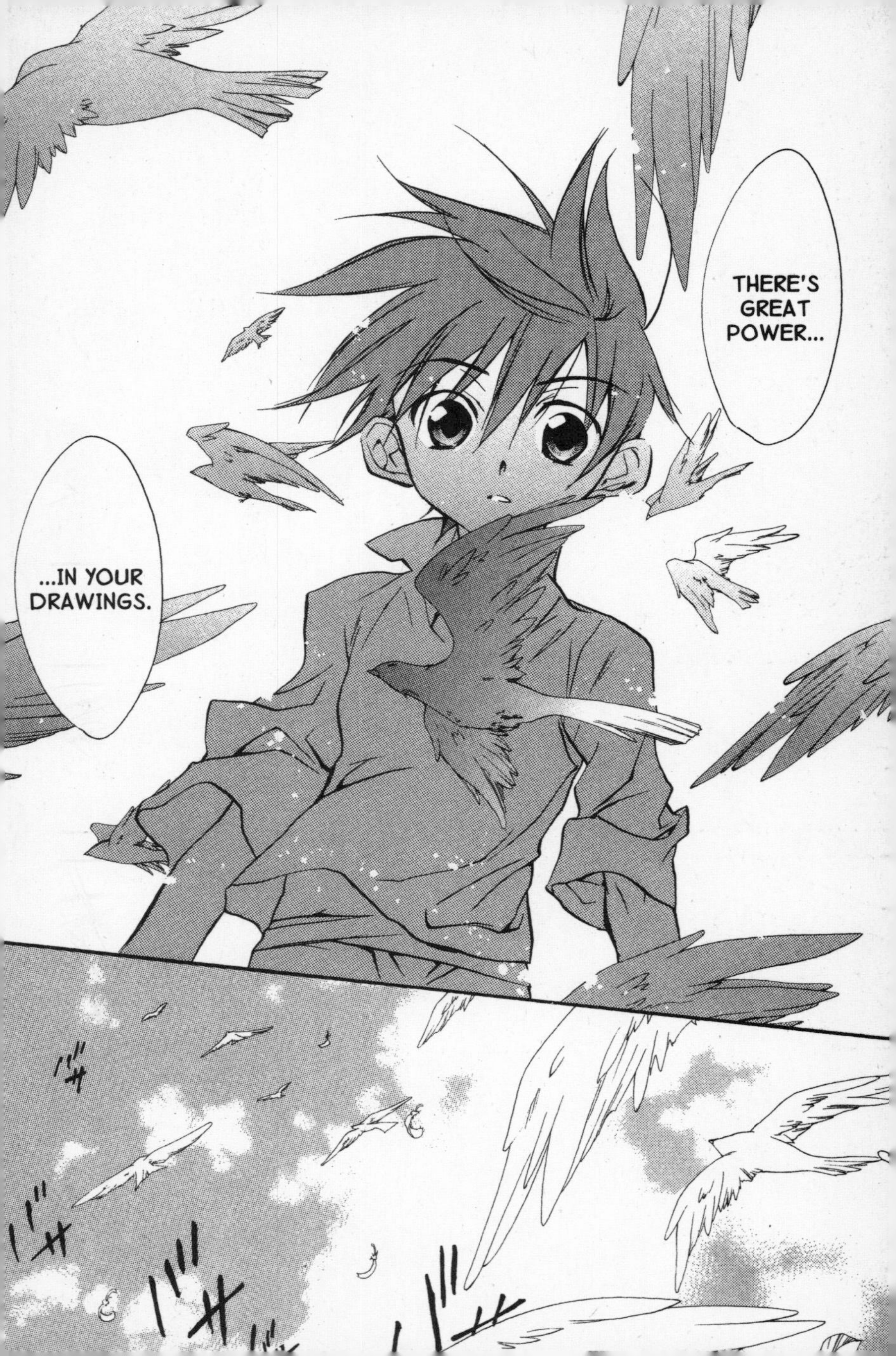
THERE'S GREAT POWER...
...IN YOUR DRAWINGS.

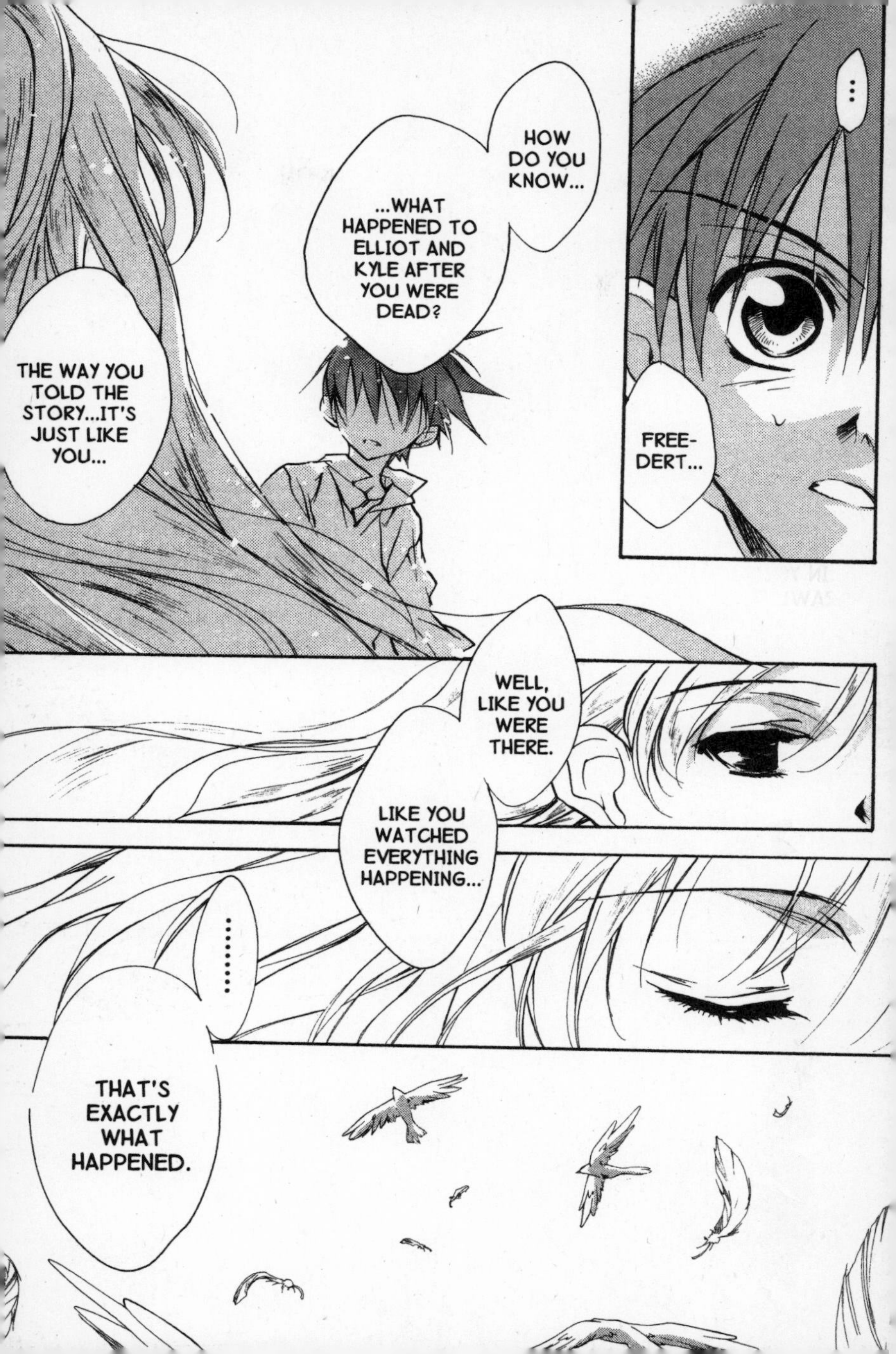
...
FREE-DERT...
HOW DO YOU KNOW...
...WHAT HAPPENED TO ELLIOT AND KYLE AFTER YOU WERE DEAD?
THE WAY YOU TOLD THE STORY...IT'S JUST LIKE YOU...
WELL, LIKE YOU WERE THERE.
LIKE YOU WATCHED EVERYTHING HAPPENING...
....
THAT'S EXACTLY WHAT HAPPENED.

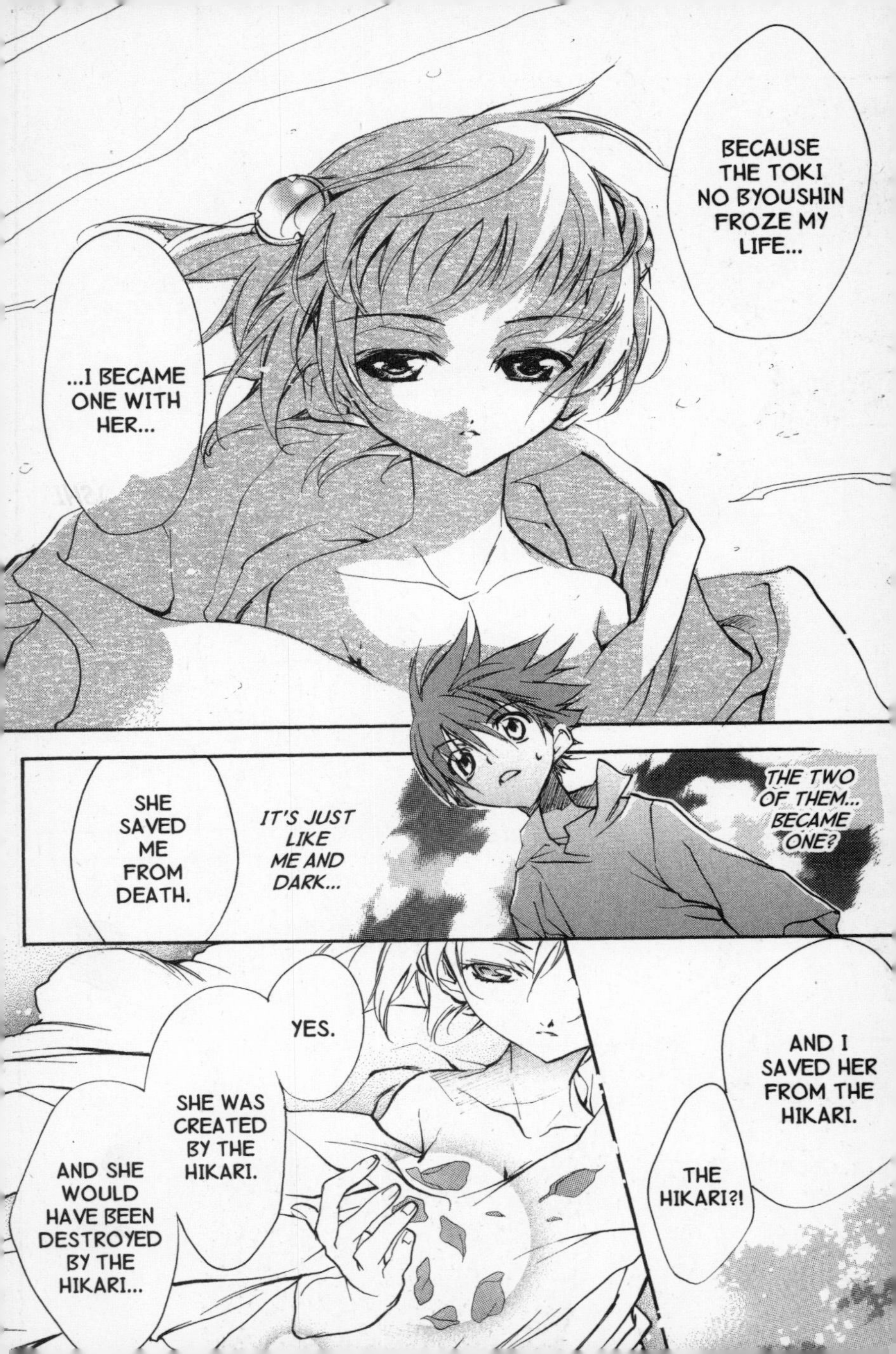
BECAUSE THE TOKI NO BYOUSHIN FROZE MY LIFE...
...I BECAME ONE WITH HER...
THE TWO OF THEM... BECAME ONE?
IT'S JUST LIKE ME AND DARK...
SHE SAVED ME FROM DEATH.
AND I SAVED HER FROM THE HIKARI.
THE HIKARI?!
YES.
SHE WAS CREATED BY THE HIKARI.
AND SHE WOULD HAVE BEEN DESTROYED BY THE HIKARI...

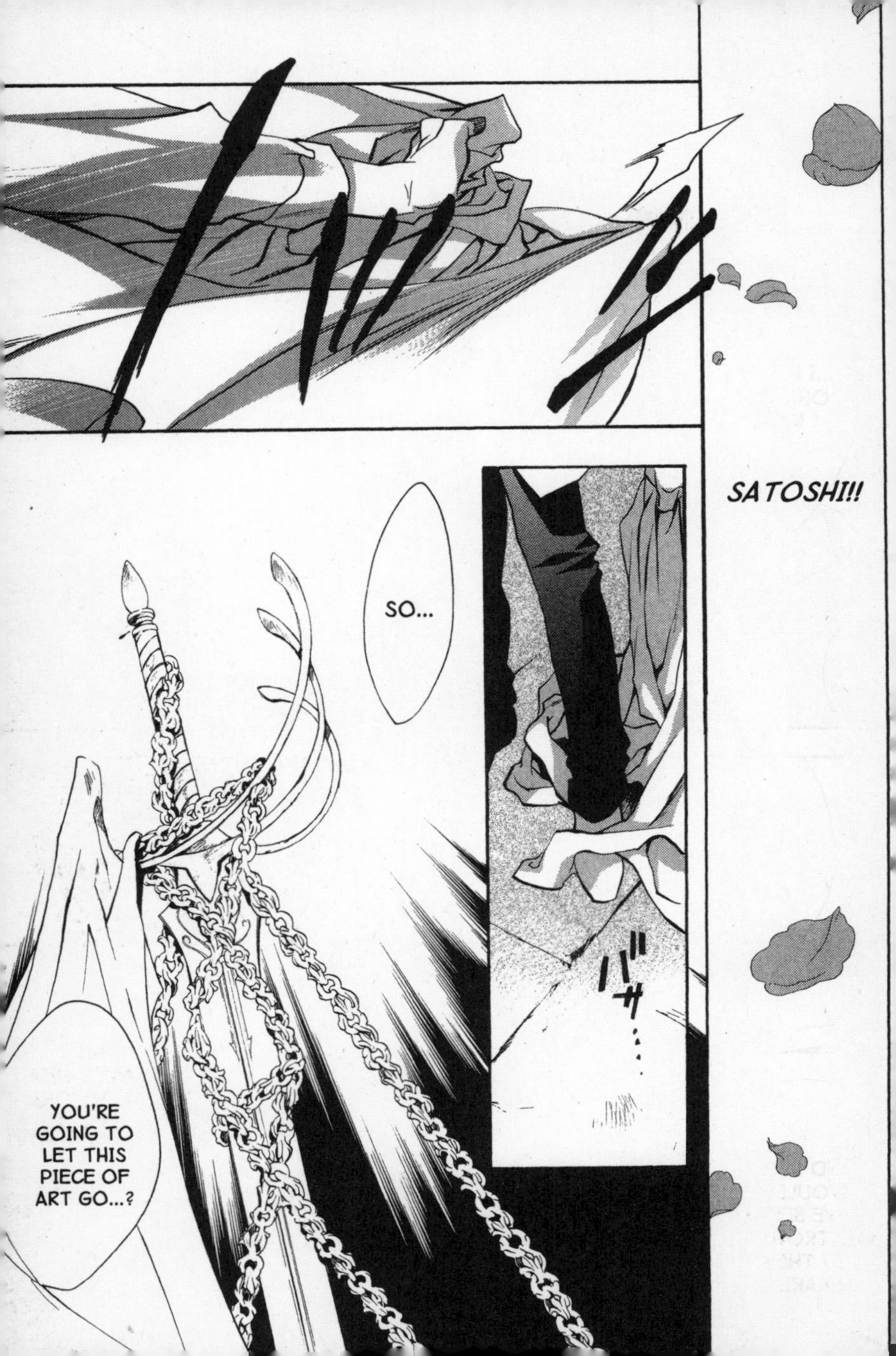
SATOSHI!!
SO...
YOU'RE GOING TO LET THIS PIECE OF ART GO...?

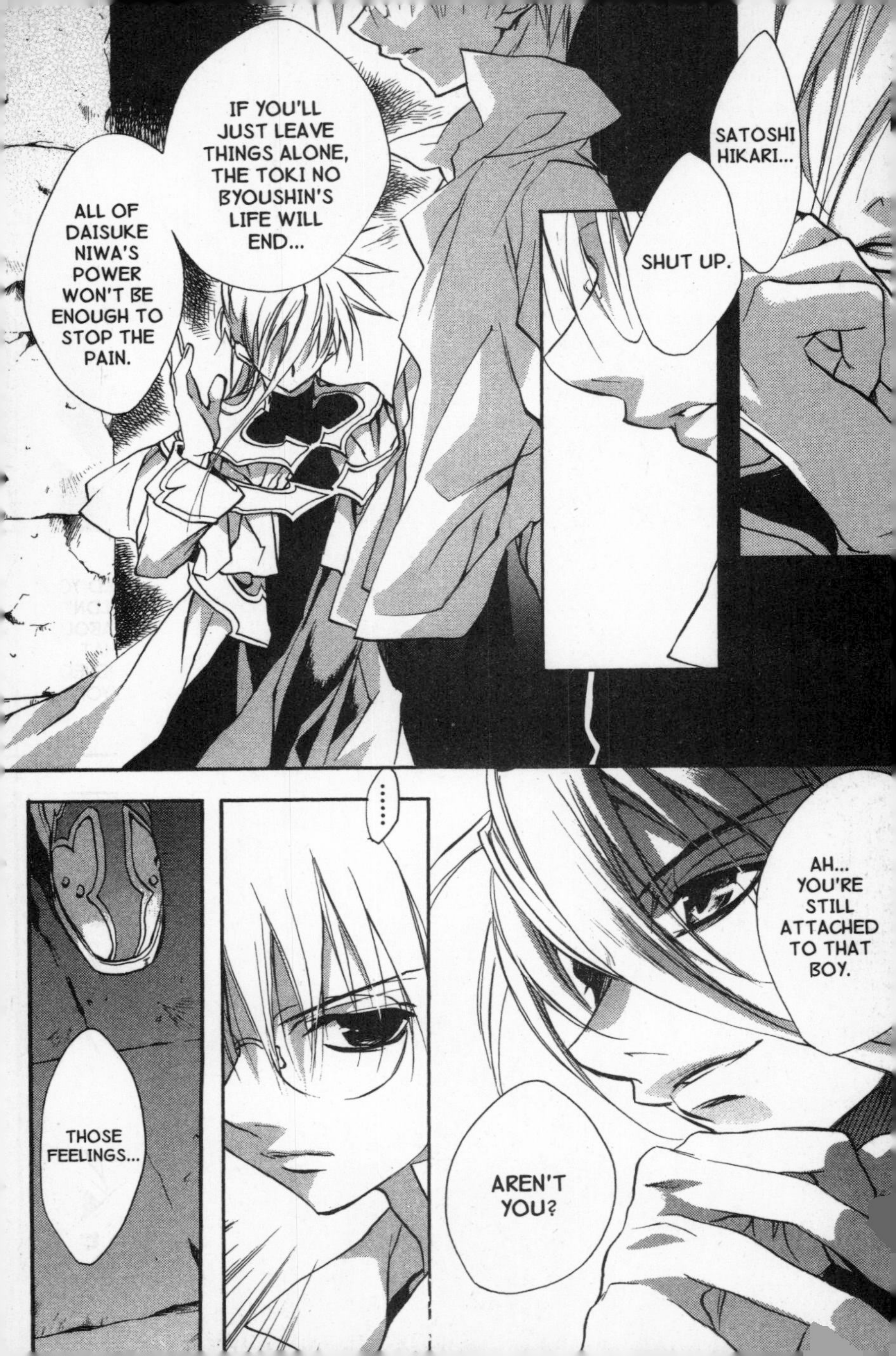
SATOSHI HIKARI...
SHUT UP.
IF YOU'LL JUST LEAVE THINGS ALONE, THE TOKI NO BYOUSHIN'S LIFE WILL END...
ALL OF DAISUKE NIWA'S POWER WON'T BE ENOUGH TO STOP THE PAIN.
AH... YOU'RE STILL ATTACHED TO THAT BOY.
AREN'T YOU?
......
THOSE FEELINGS...

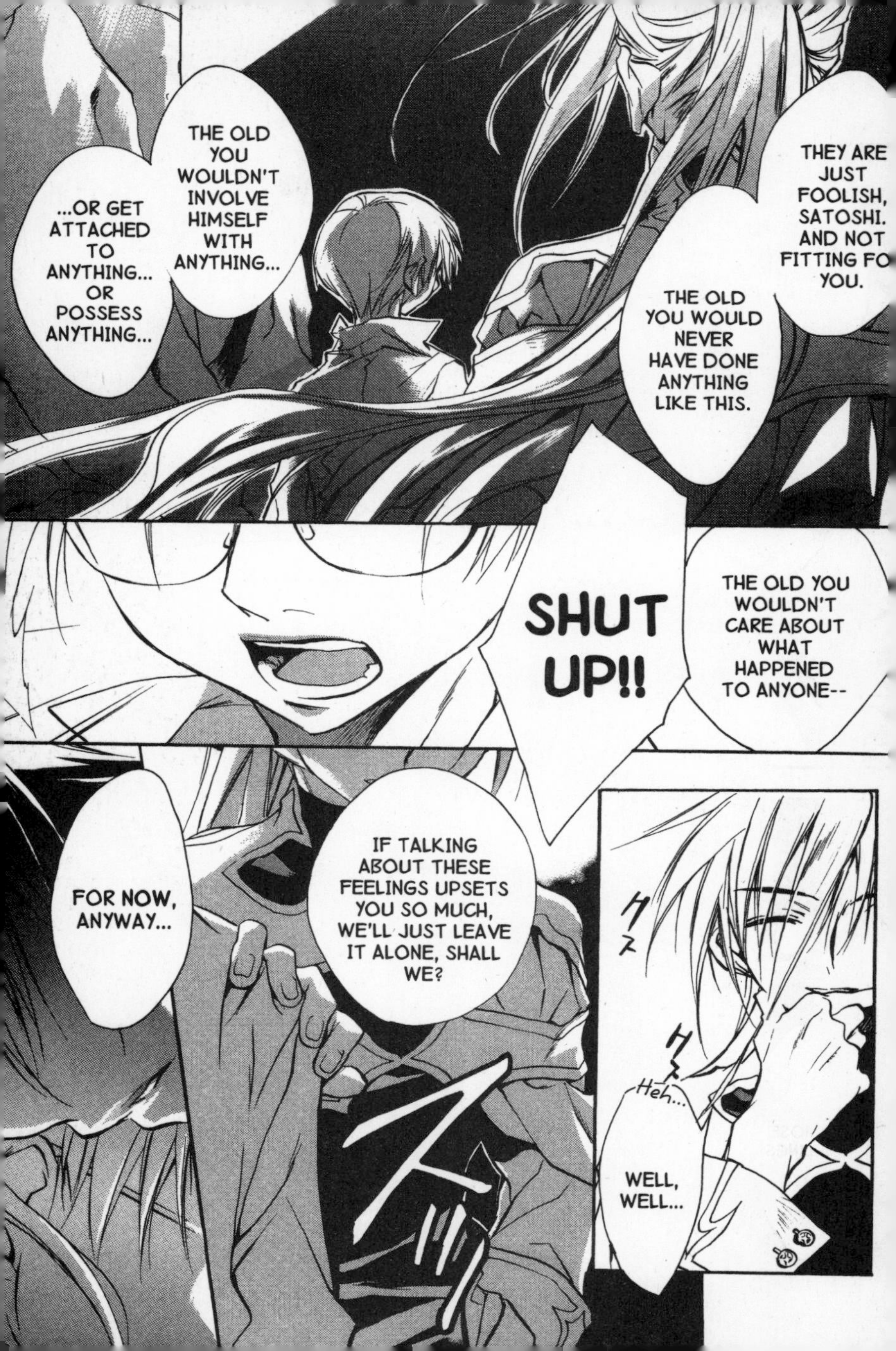
THEY ARE JUST FOOLISH, SATOSHI. AND NOT FITTING FO YOU.
THE OLD YOU WOULD NEVER HAVE DONE ANYTHING LIKE THIS.
THE OLD YOU WOULDN'T INVOLVE HIMSELF WITH ANYTHING...
...OR GET ATTACHED TO ANYTHING... OR POSSESS ANYTHING...
THE OLD YOU WOULDN'T CARE ABOUT WHAT HAPPENED TO ANYONE--
SHUT UP!!
クス
クス
Heh...
WELL, WELL...
IF TALKING ABOUT THESE FEELINGS UPSETS YOU SO MUCH, WE'LL JUST LEAVE IT ALONE, SHALL WE?
FOR NOW, ANYWAY...

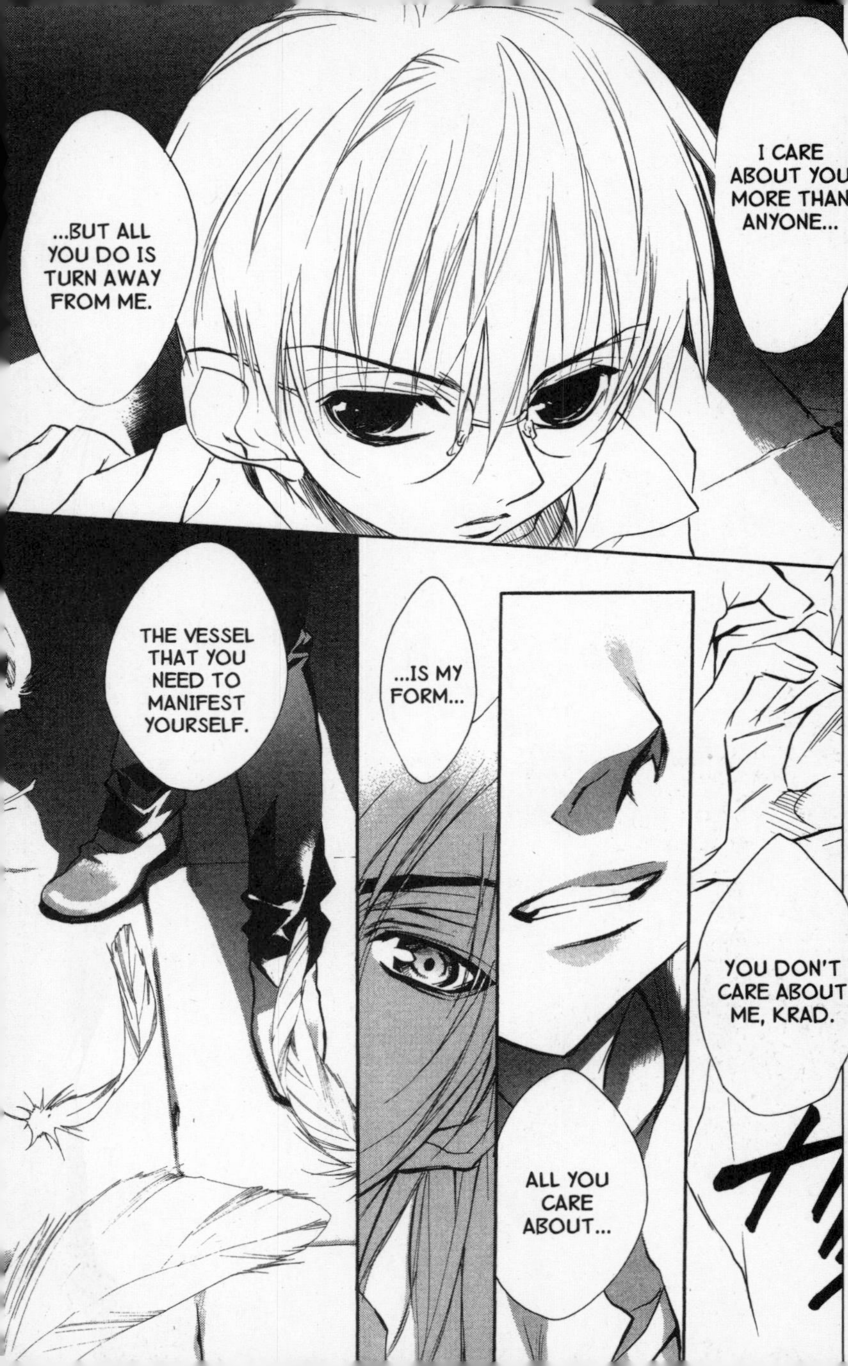
I CARE ABOUT YOU MORE THAN ANYONE...
...BUT ALL YOU DO IS TURN AWAY FROM ME.
YOU DON'T CARE ABOUT ME, KRAD.
ALL YOU CARE ABOUT...
...IS MY FORM...
THE VESSEL THAT YOU NEED TO MANIFEST YOURSELF.

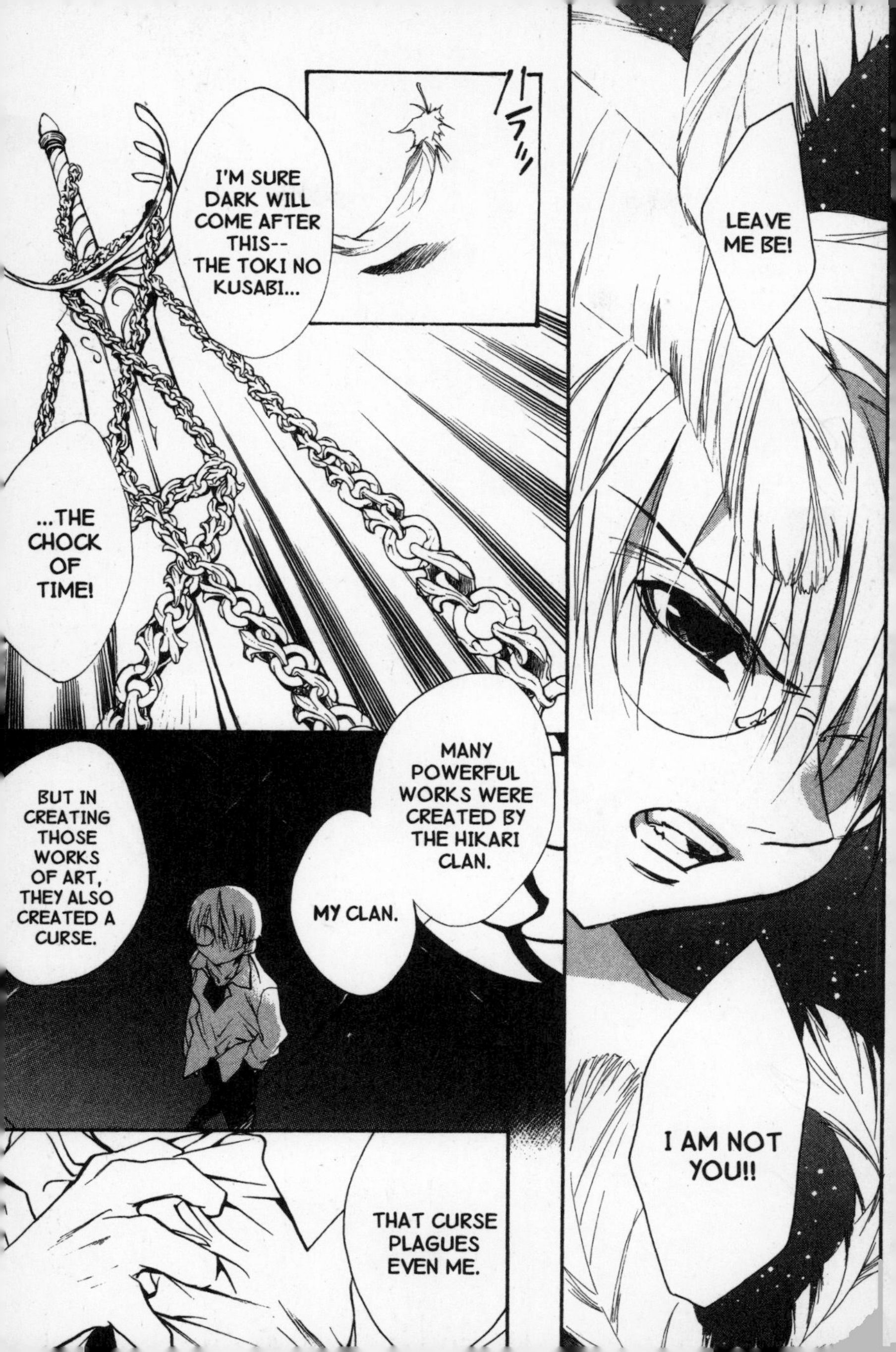
LEAVE ME BE!
I AM NOT YOU!!
ハラッ
I'M SURE DARK WILL COME AFTER THIS-- THE TOKI NO KUSABI...
...THE CHOCK OF TIME!
MANY POWERFUL WORKS WERE CREATED BY THE HIKARI CLAN.
MY CLAN.
BUT IN CREATING THOSE WORKS OF ART, THEY ALSO CREATED A CURSE.
THAT CURSE PLAGUES EVEN ME.

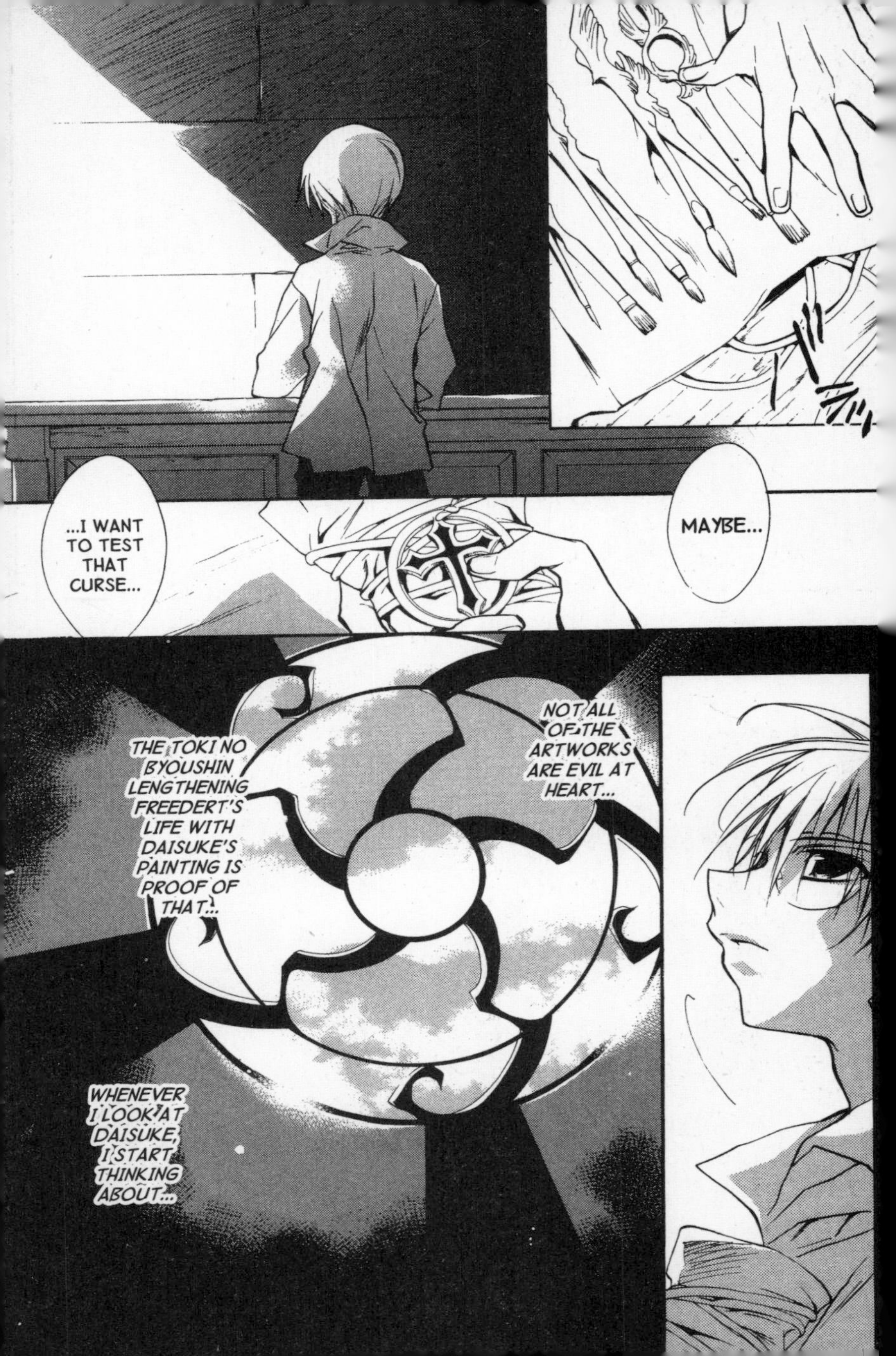
MAYBE...
...I WANT TO TEST THAT CURSE...
NOT ALL OF THE ARTWORKS ARE EVIL AT HEART...
THE TOKI NO BYOUSHIN LENGTHENING FREEDERT'S LIFE WITH DAISUKE'S PAINTING IS PROOF OF THAT...
WHENEVER I LOOK AT DAISUKE, I START THINKING ABOUT...

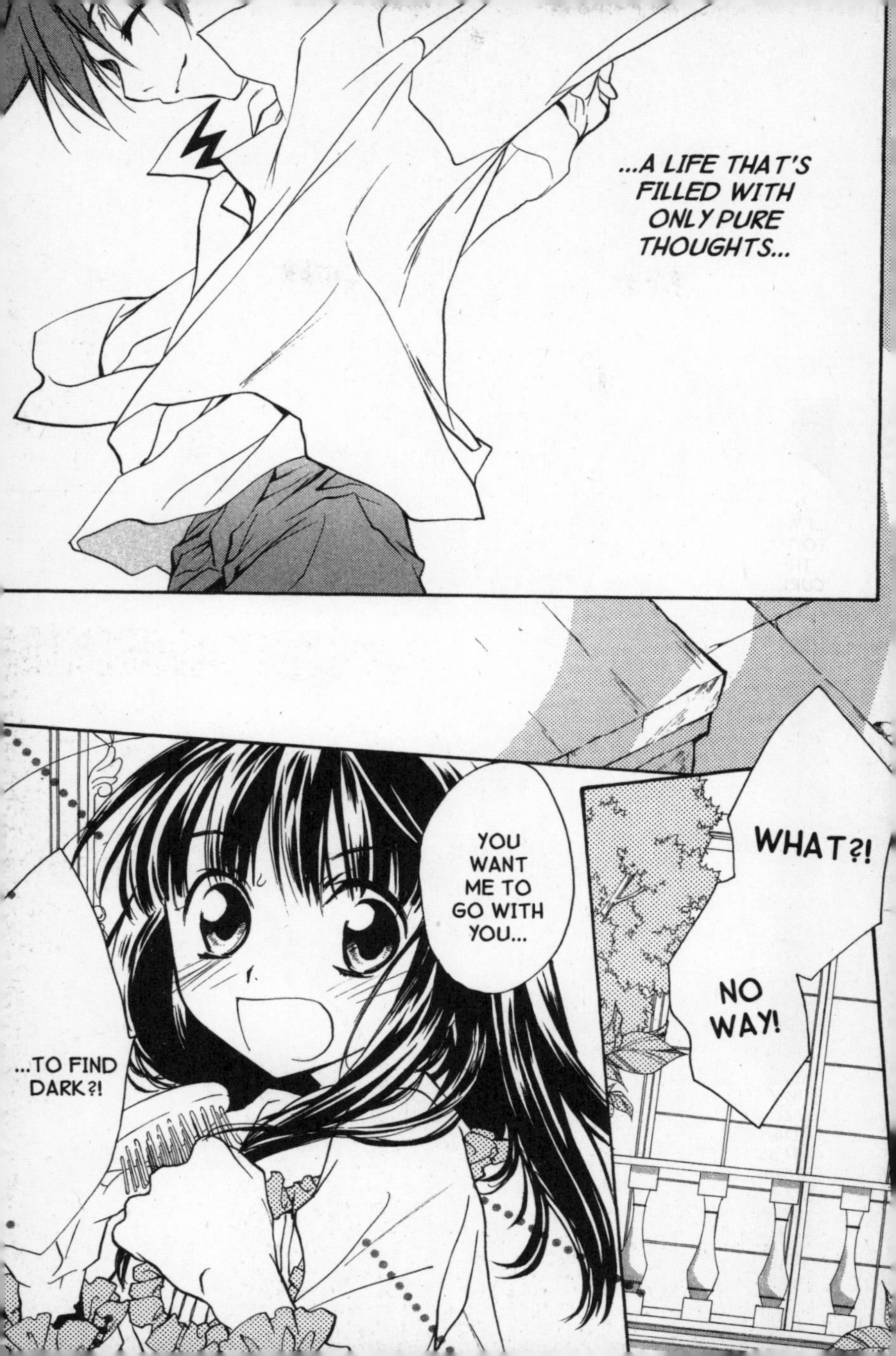
...A LIFE THAT'S FILLED WITH ONLY PURE THOUGHTS...
WHAT?!
NO WAY!
YOU WANT ME TO GO WITH YOU...
...TO FIND DARK?!

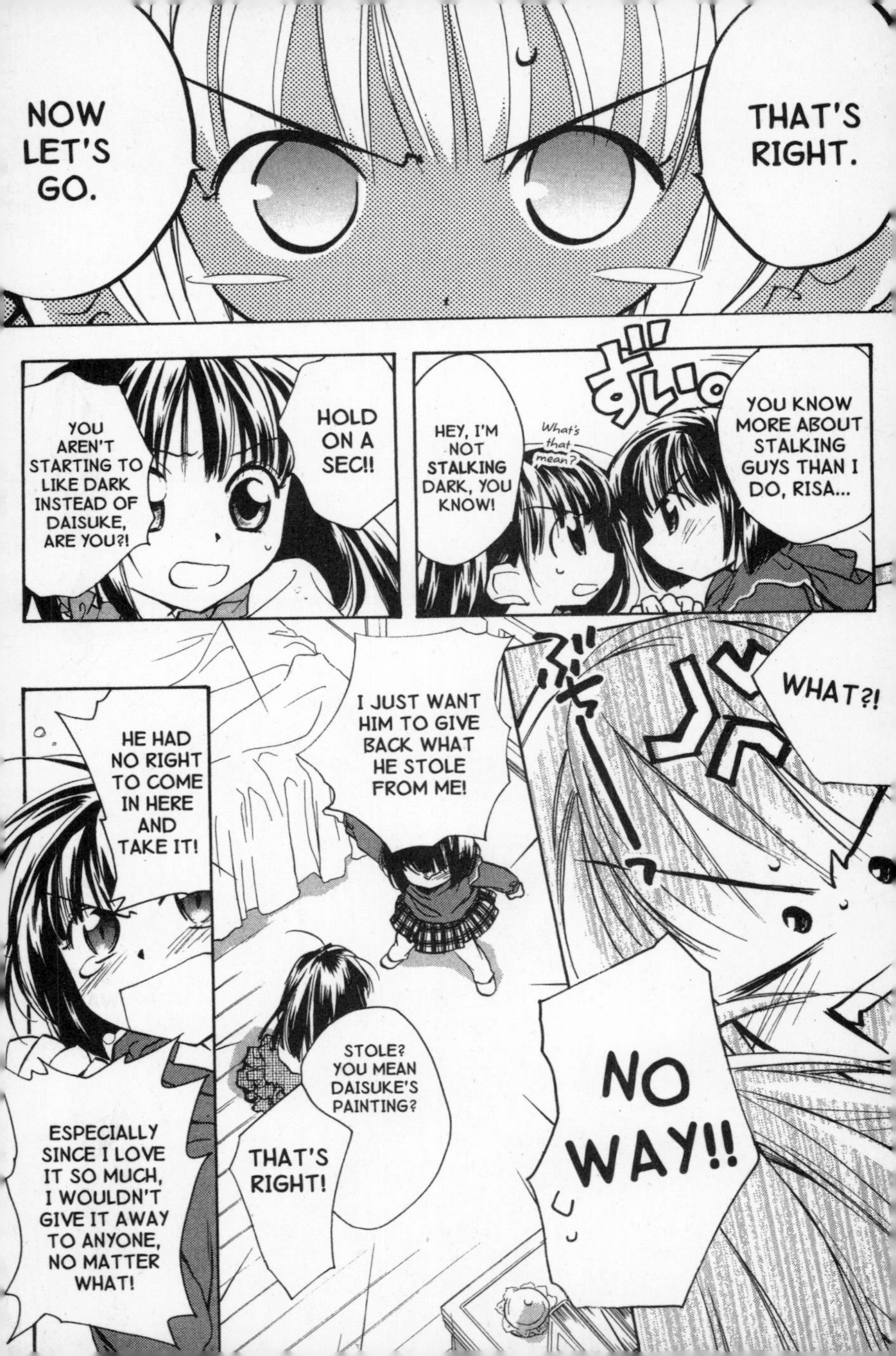
THAT'S RIGHT.
NOW LET'S GO.
YOU KNOW MORE ABOUT STALKING GUYS THAN I DO, RISA...
What's that mean?
HEY, I'M NOT STALKING DARK, YOU KNOW!
HOLD ON A SEC!!
YOU AREN'T STARTING TO LIKE DARK INSTEAD OF DAISUKE, ARE YOU?!
WHAT?!
NO WAY!!
I JUST WANT HIM TO GIVE BACK WHAT HE STOLE FROM ME!
STOLE? YOU MEAN DAISUKE'S PAINTING?
THAT'S RIGHT!
HE HAD NO RIGHT TO COME IN HERE AND TAKE IT!
ESPECIALLY SINCE I LOVE IT SO MUCH, I WOULDN'T GIVE IT AWAY TO ANYONE, NO MATTER WHAT!

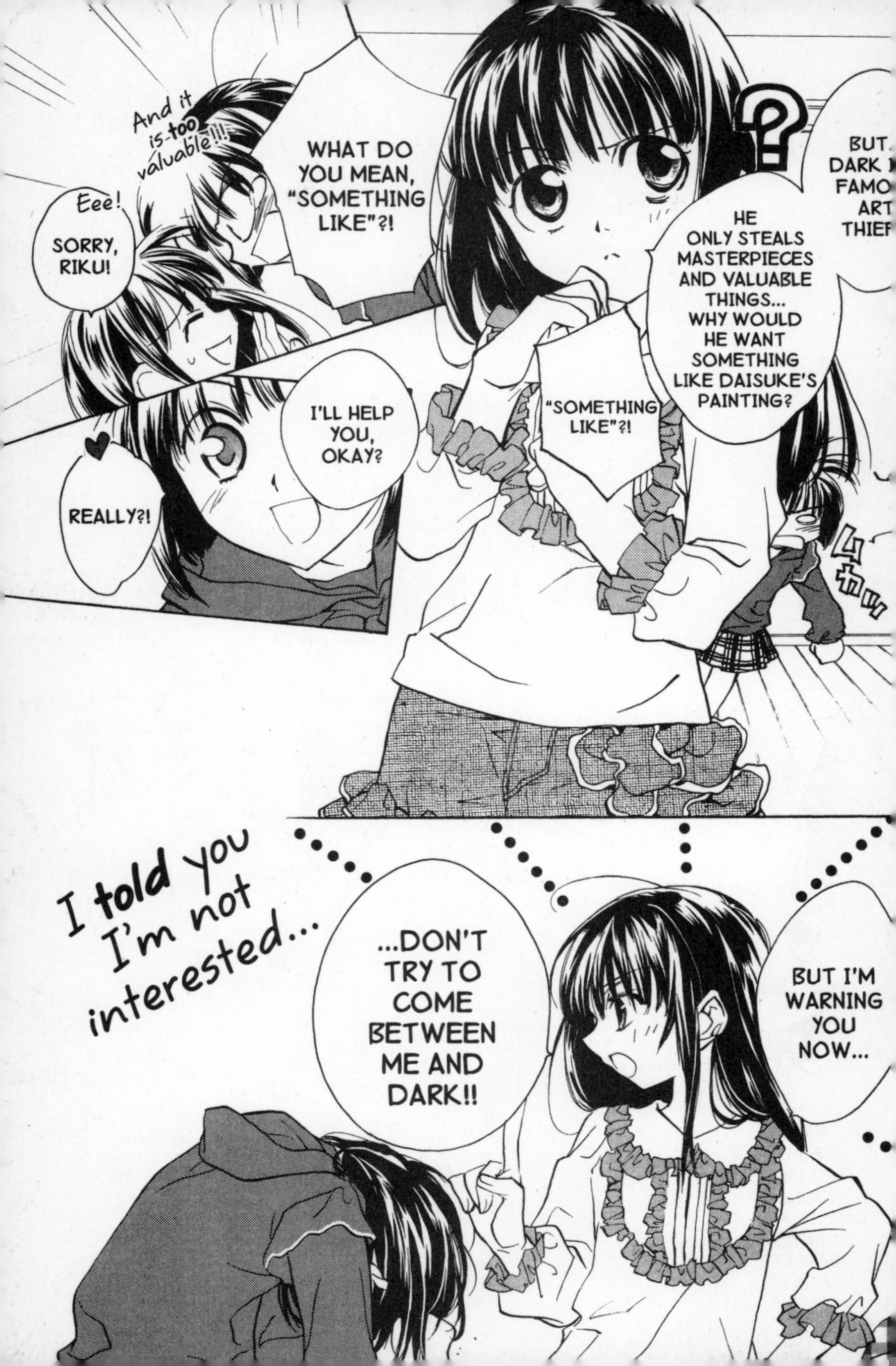
BUT. DARK I FAMO ART THIEF
HE ONLY STEALS MASTERPIECES AND VALUABLE THINGS... WHY WOULD HE WANT SOMETHING LIKE DAISUKE'S PAINTING?
"SOMETHING LIKE"?!
ムカッ
WHAT DO YOU MEAN, "SOMETHING LIKE"?!
And it is too valuable!!!
Eee!
SORRY, RIKU!
I'LL HELP YOU, OKAY?
REALLY?!
BUT I'M WARNING YOU NOW...
...DON'T TRY TO COME BETWEEN ME AND DARK!!
I told you I'm not interested...

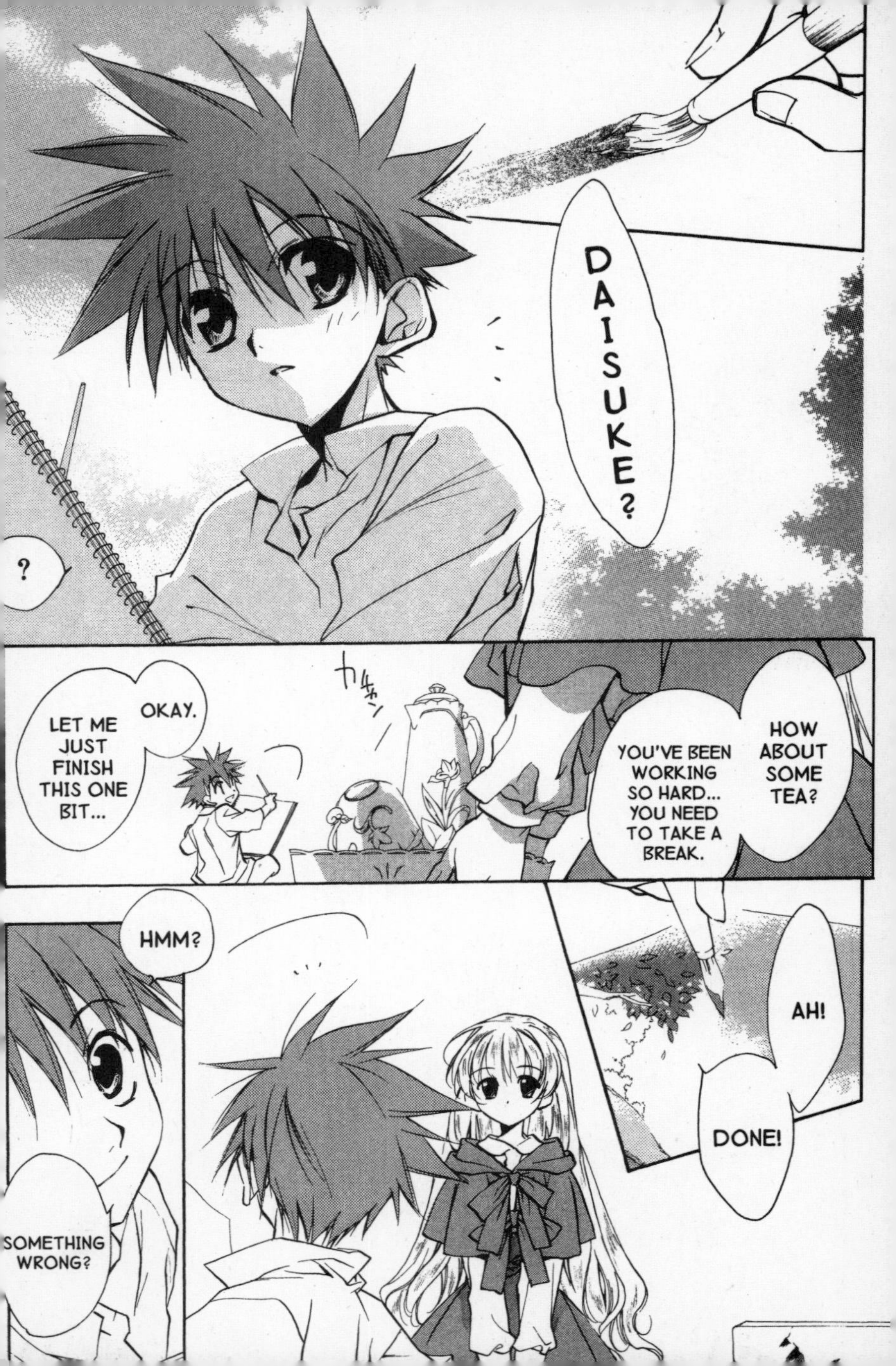
DAISUKE?
?
HOW ABOUT SOME TEA?
YOU'VE BEEN WORKING SO HARD... YOU NEED TO TAKE A BREAK.
OKAY.
LET ME JUST FINISH THIS ONE BIT...
AH!
DONE!
HMM?
...
SOMETHING WRONG?

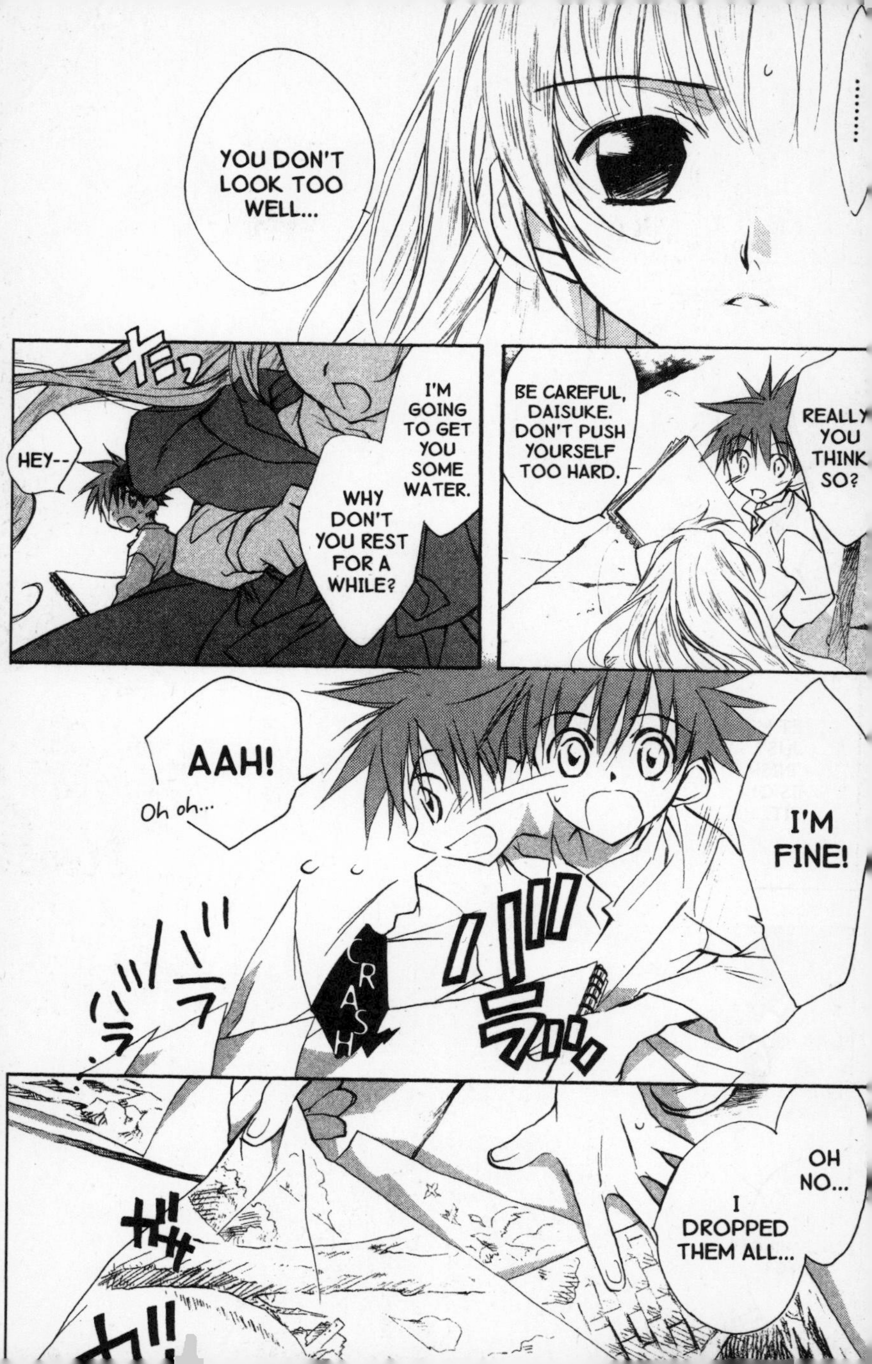
......
YOU DON'T LOOK TOO WELL...
REALLY YOU THINK SO?
BE CAREFUL, DAISUKE. DON'T PUSH YOURSELF TOO HARD.
I'M GOING TO GET YOU SOME WATER.
WHY DON'T YOU REST FOR A WHILE?
HEY--
I'M FINE!
AAH!
Oh oh...
CRASH
OH NO...
I DROPPED THEM ALL...

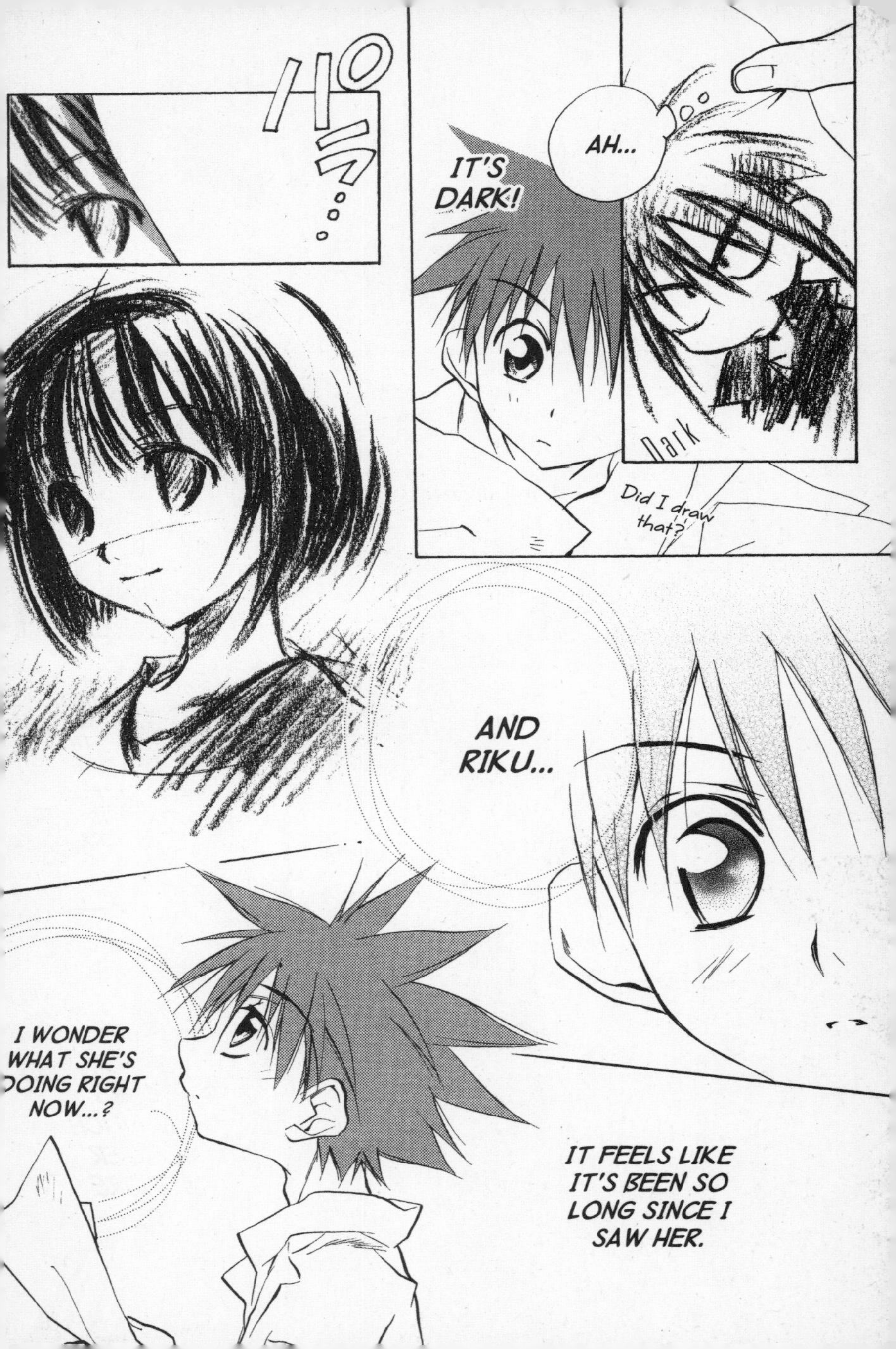

AH...
IT'S DARK!
Dark
Did I draw that?
パラ…
AND RIKU...
IT FEELS LIKE IT'S BEEN SO LONG SINCE I SAW HER.
I WONDER WHAT SHE'S DOING RIGHT NOW...?

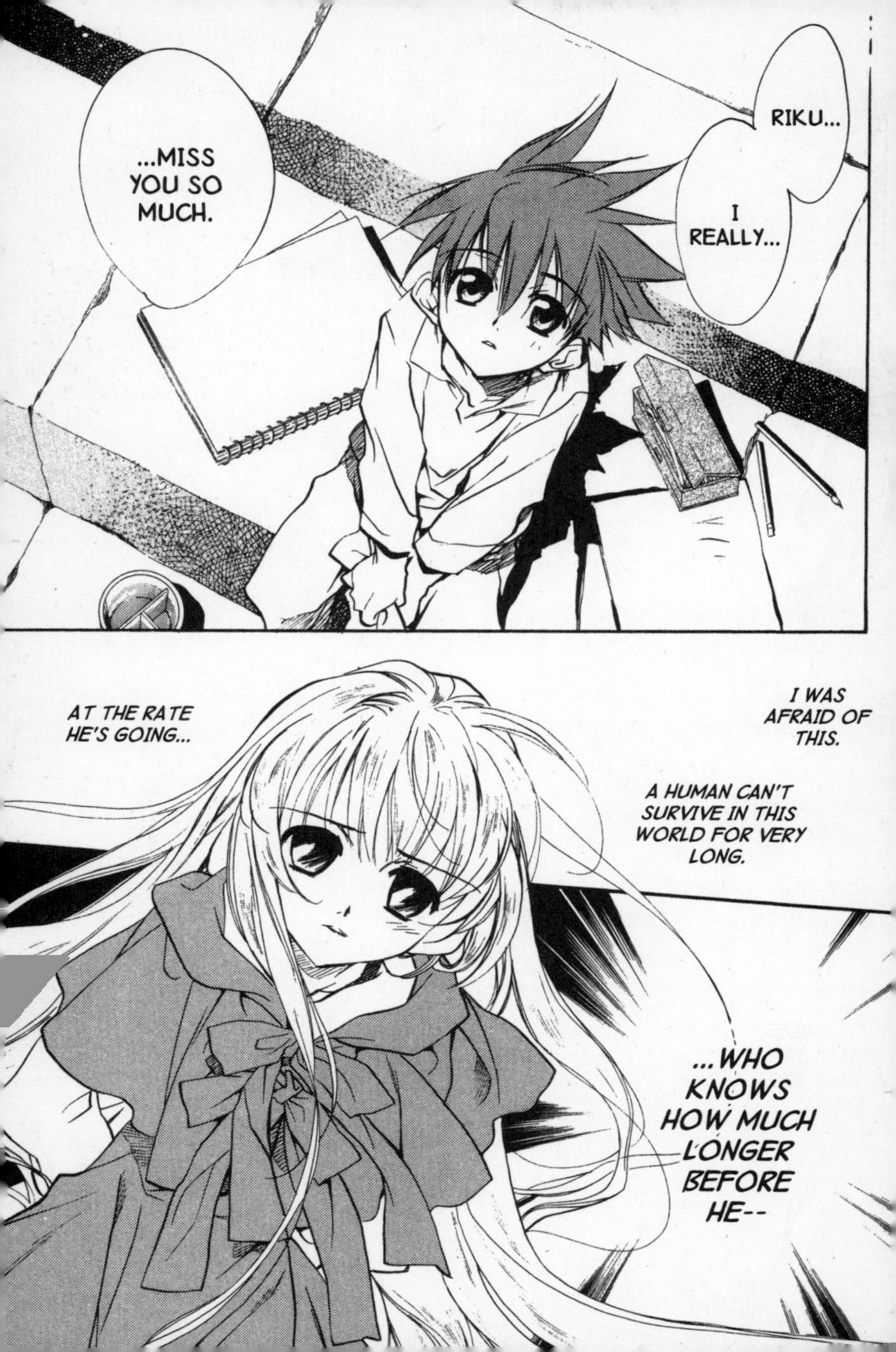
RIKU...
I REALLY...
...MISS YOU SO MUCH.
I WAS AFRAID OF THIS.
A HUMAN CAN'T SURVIVE IN THIS WORLD FOR VERY LONG.
AT THE RATE HE'S GOING...
...WHO KNOWS HOW MUCH LONGER BEFORE HE--

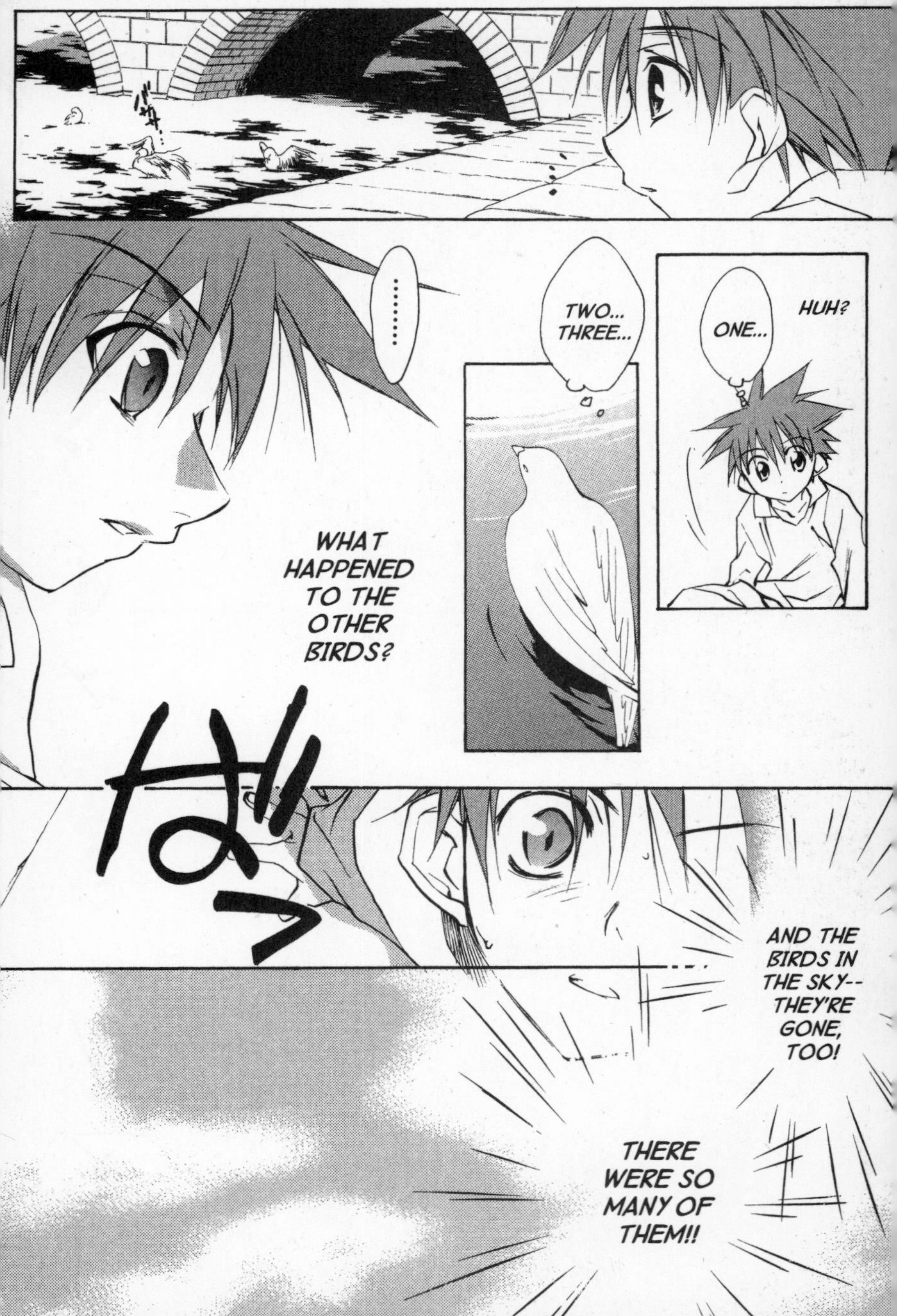
HUH?
ONE...
TWO... THREE...
......
WHAT HAPPENED TO THE OTHER BIRDS?
はっ
AND THE BIRDS IN THE SKY-- THEY'RE GONE, TOO!
THERE WERE SO MANY OF THEM!!

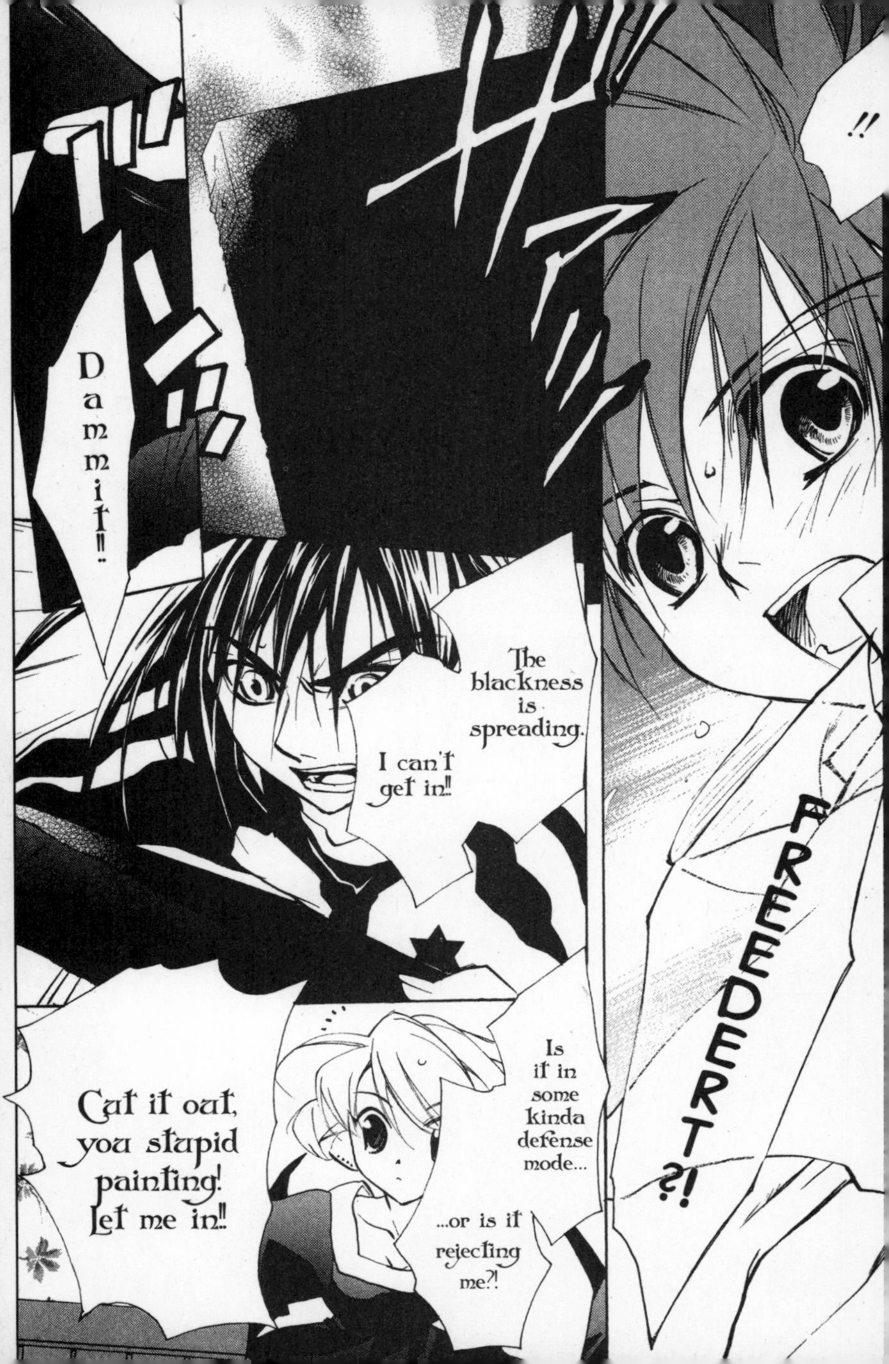
!!
FREEDERT?!
Dammit!!
The blackness is spreading.
I can't get in!!
Is it in some kinda defense mode...
...or is it rejecting me?!
Cut it out, you stupid painting! Let me in!!

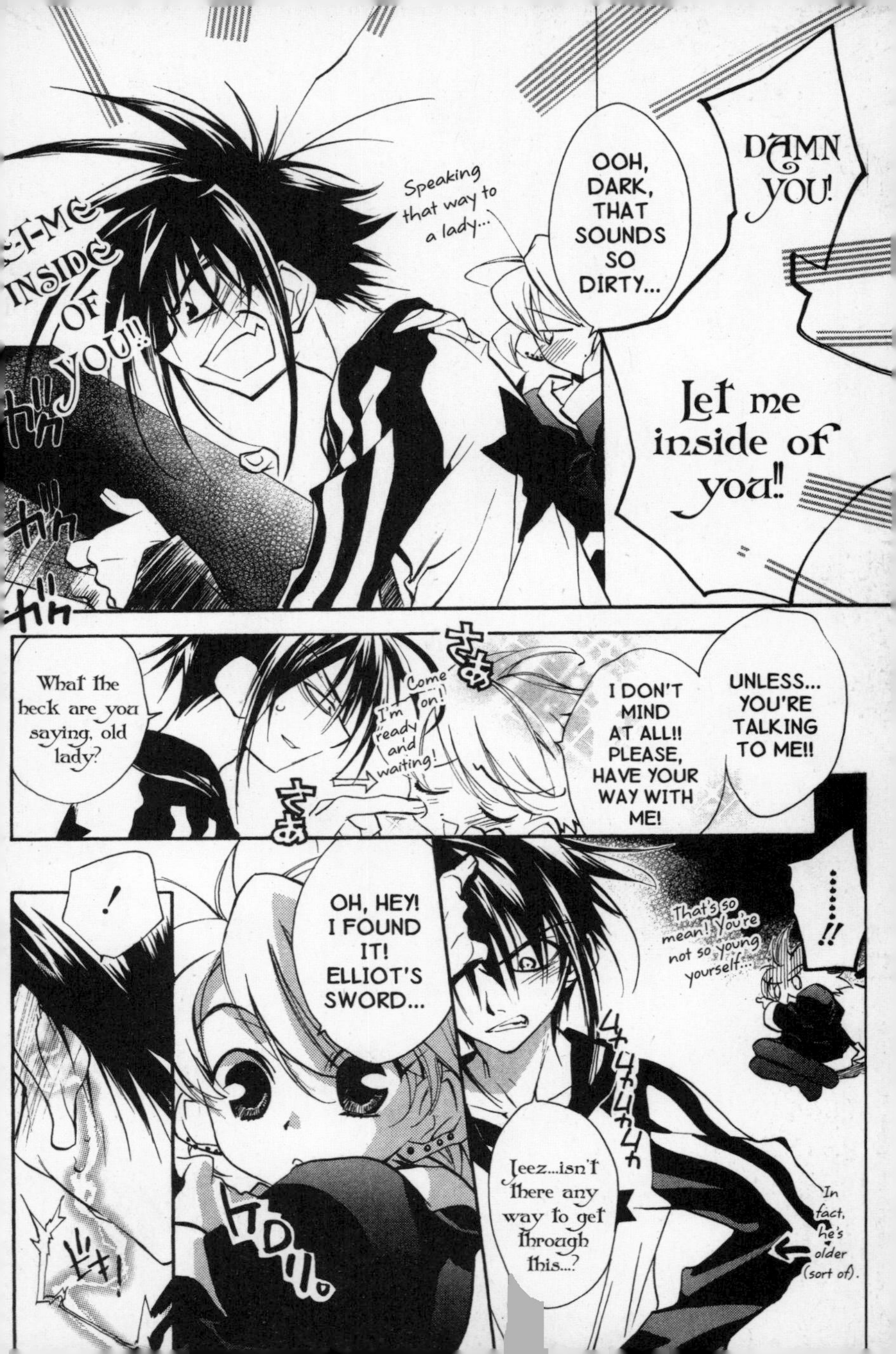
DAMN YOU!
Let me inside of you!!
OOH, DARK, THAT SOUNDS SO DIRTY...
Speaking that way to a lady...
T-ME INSIDE OF YOU!!
ガッ
ガッ
ガッ
UNLESS... YOU'RE TALKING TO ME!!
I DON'T MIND AT ALL!! PLEASE, HAVE YOUR WAY WITH ME!
さあ
Come on!
I'm ready and waiting!
さあ
What the heck are you saying, old lady?
......!!
That's so mean! You're not so young yourself...
In fact, he's older (sort of).
Jeez...isn't there any way to get through this...?
OH, HEY! I FOUND IT! ELLIOT'S SWORD...
!

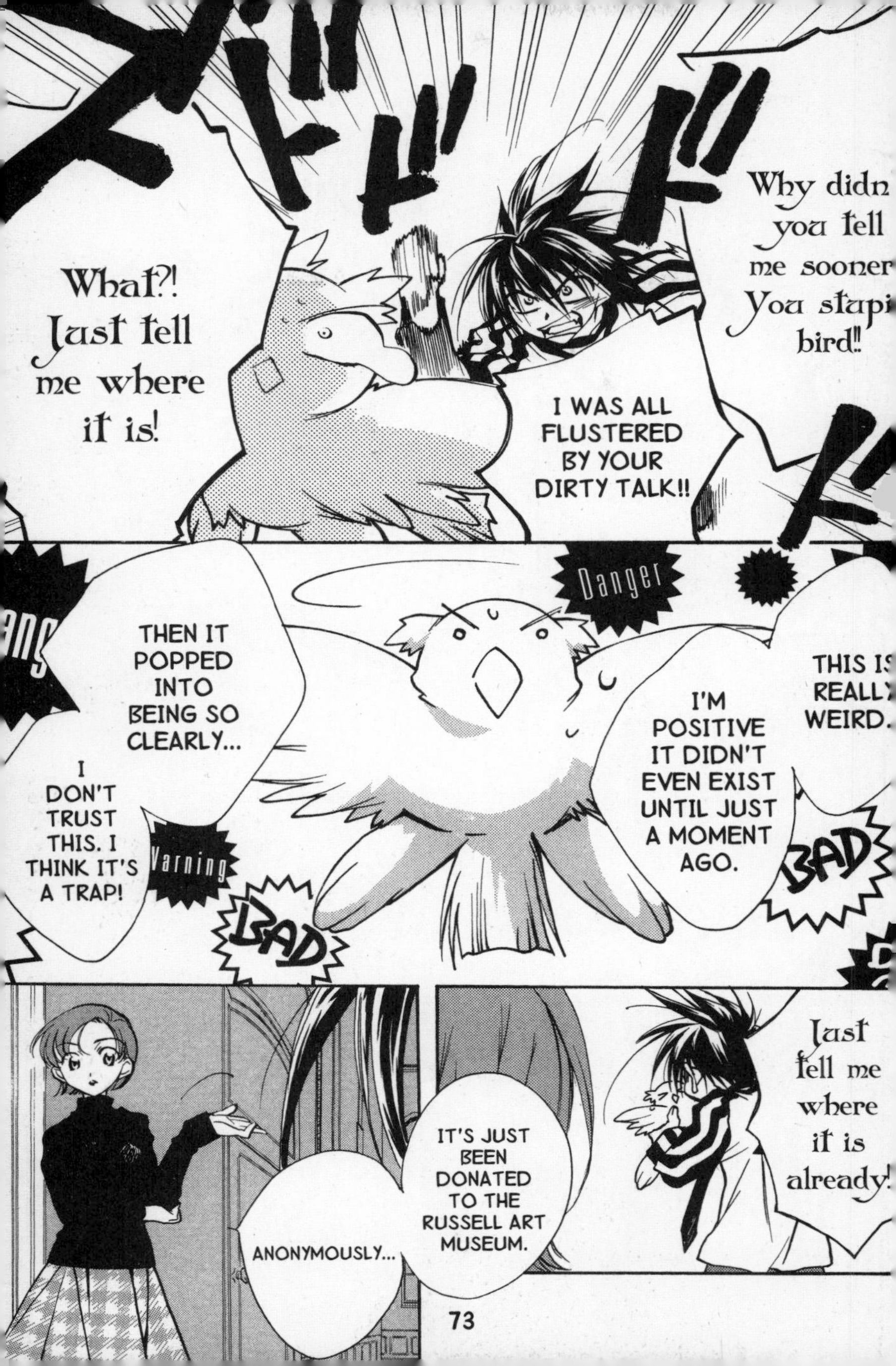
Why didn you tell me sooner You stupi bird!!
I WAS ALL FLUSTERED BY YOUR DIRTY TALK!!
What?! Just tell me where it is!
THIS IS REALLY WEIRD.
I'M POSITIVE IT DIDN'T EVEN EXIST UNTIL JUST A MOMENT AGO.
BAD
Danger
THEN IT POPPED INTO BEING SO CLEARLY...
I DON'T TRUST THIS. I THINK IT'S A TRAP!
Warning
BAD
Just tell me where it is already!
IT'S JUST BEEN DONATED TO THE RUSSELL ART MUSEUM.
ANONYMOUSLY...

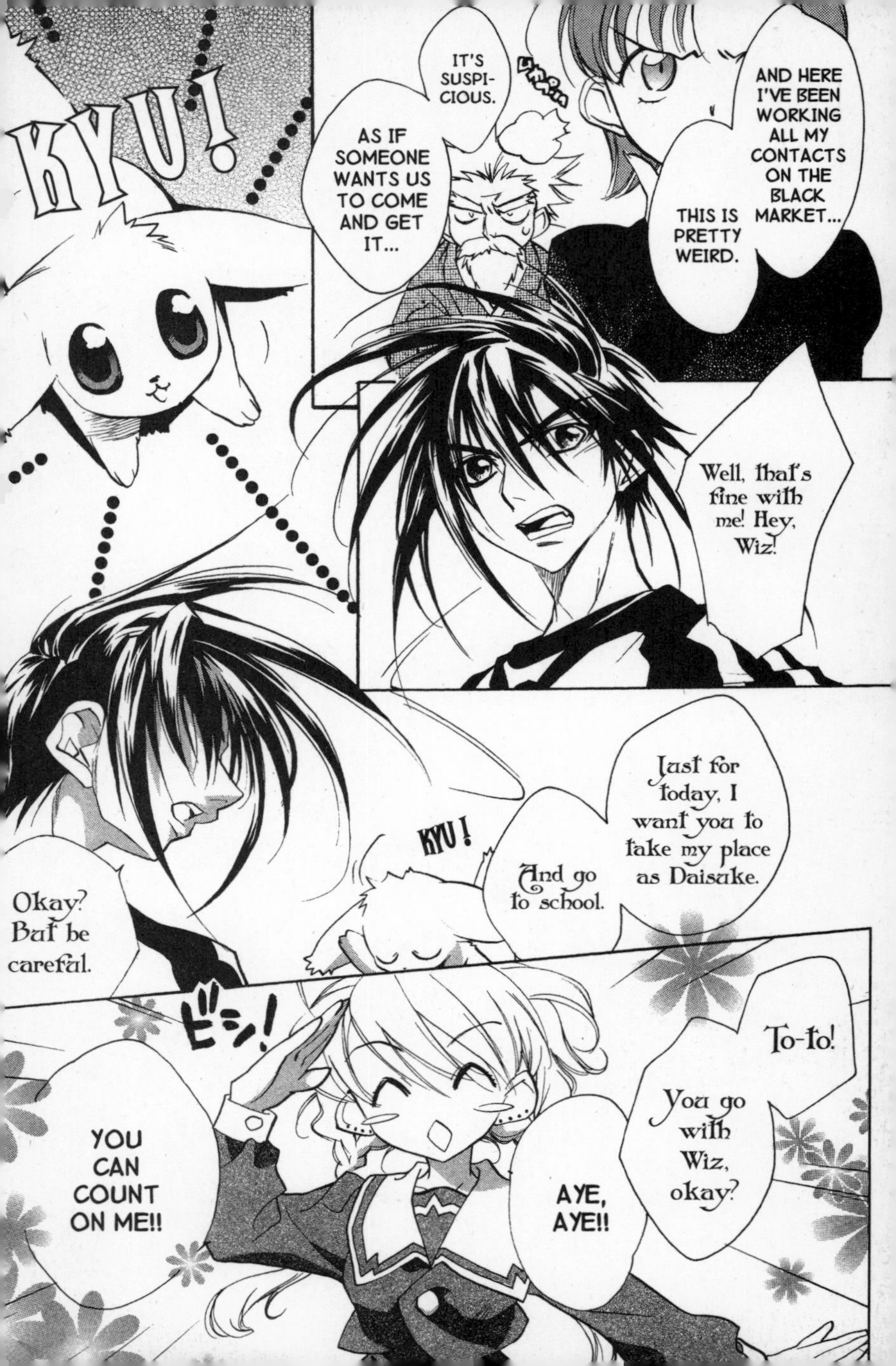
AND HERE I'VE BEEN WORKING ALL MY CONTACTS ON THE BLACK MARKET...
THIS IS PRETTY WEIRD.
IT'S SUSPICIOUS.
AS IF SOMEONE WANTS US TO COME AND GET IT...
KYU!
Well, that's fine with me! Hey, Wiz!
Just for today, I want you to take my place as Daisuke.
And go to school.
KYU!
Okay? But be careful.
To-to!
You go with Wiz, okay?
ビシッ!
AYE, AYE!!
YOU CAN COUNT ON ME!!

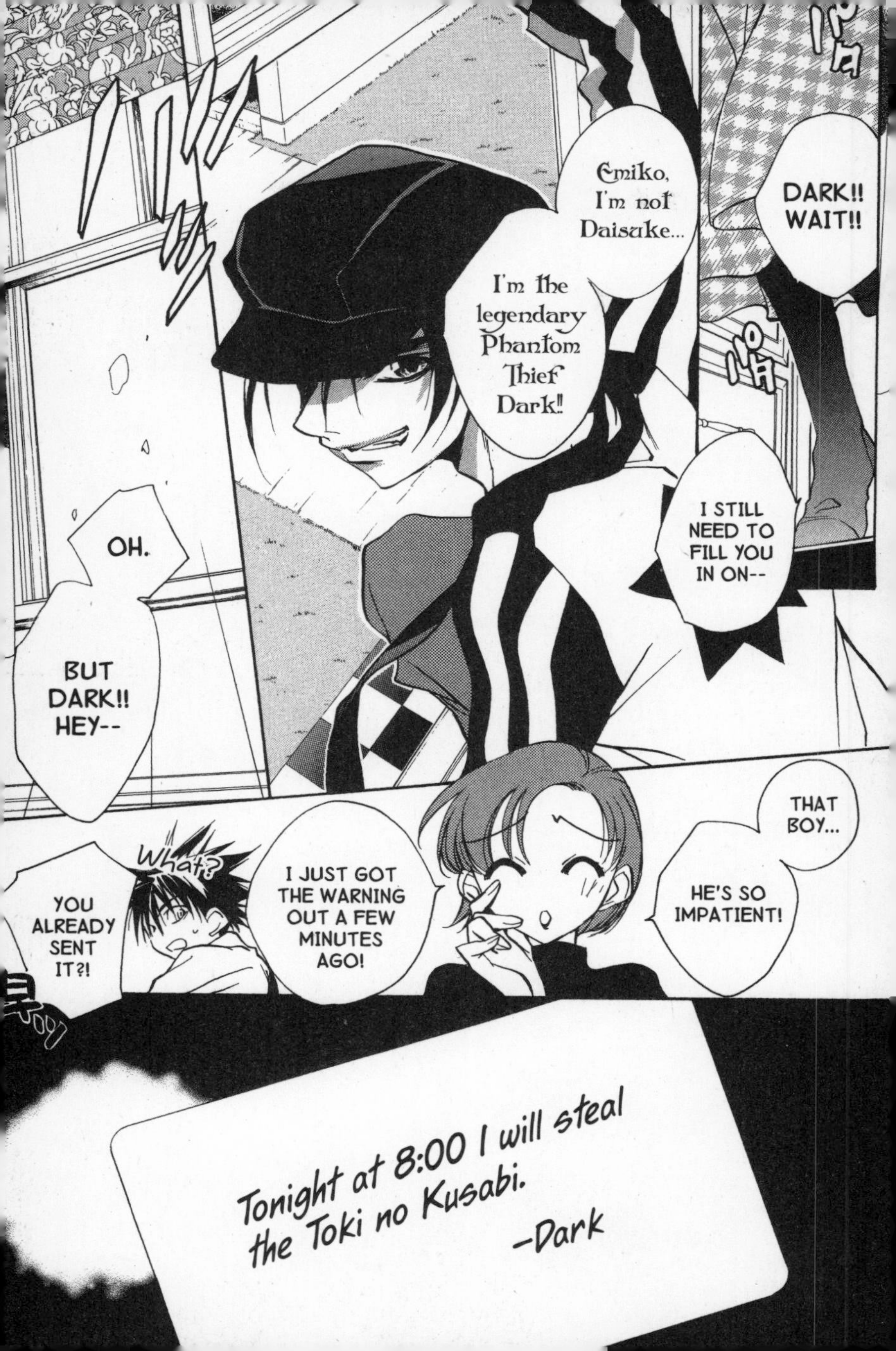
DARK!! WAIT!!
I STILL NEED TO FILL YOU IN ON--
Emiko, I'm not Daisuke...
I'm the legendary Phantom Thief Dark!!
OH.
BUT DARK!! HEY--
THAT BOY...
HE'S SO IMPATIENT!
I JUST GOT THE WARNING OUT A FEW MINUTES AGO!
What?
YOU ALREADY SENT IT?!
Tonight at 8:00 I will steal the Toki no Kusabi.
-Dark

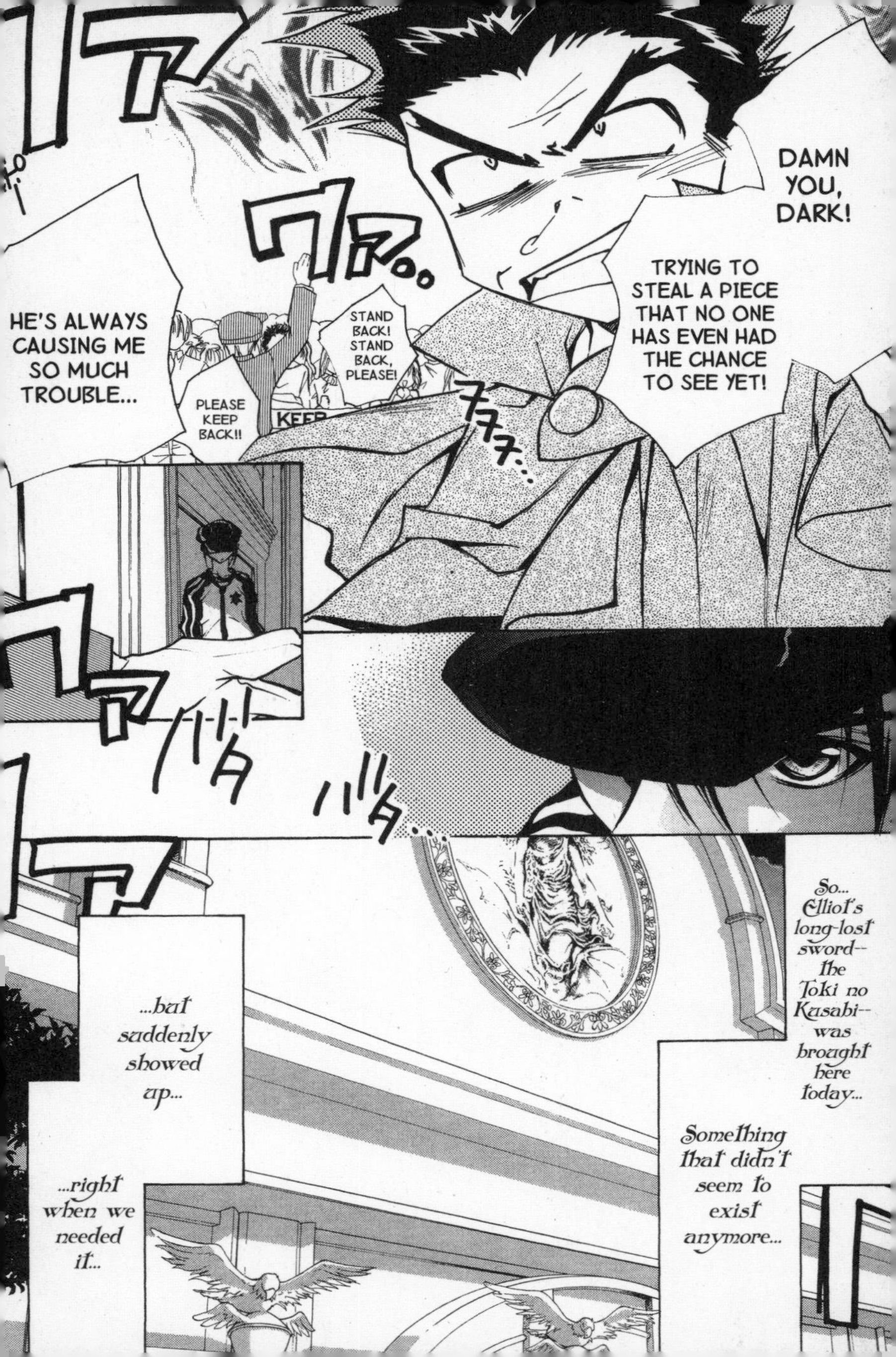
DAMN YOU, DARK!
TRYING TO STEAL A PIECE THAT NO ONE HAS EVEN HAD THE CHANCE TO SEE YET!
STAND BACK! STAND BACK, PLEASE!
PLEASE KEEP BACK!!
HE'S ALWAYS CAUSING ME SO MUCH TROUBLE...
So... Elliot's long-lost sword-- the Toki no Kusabi-- was brought here today...
Something that didn't seem to exist anymore...
...but suddenly showed up...
...right when we needed it...

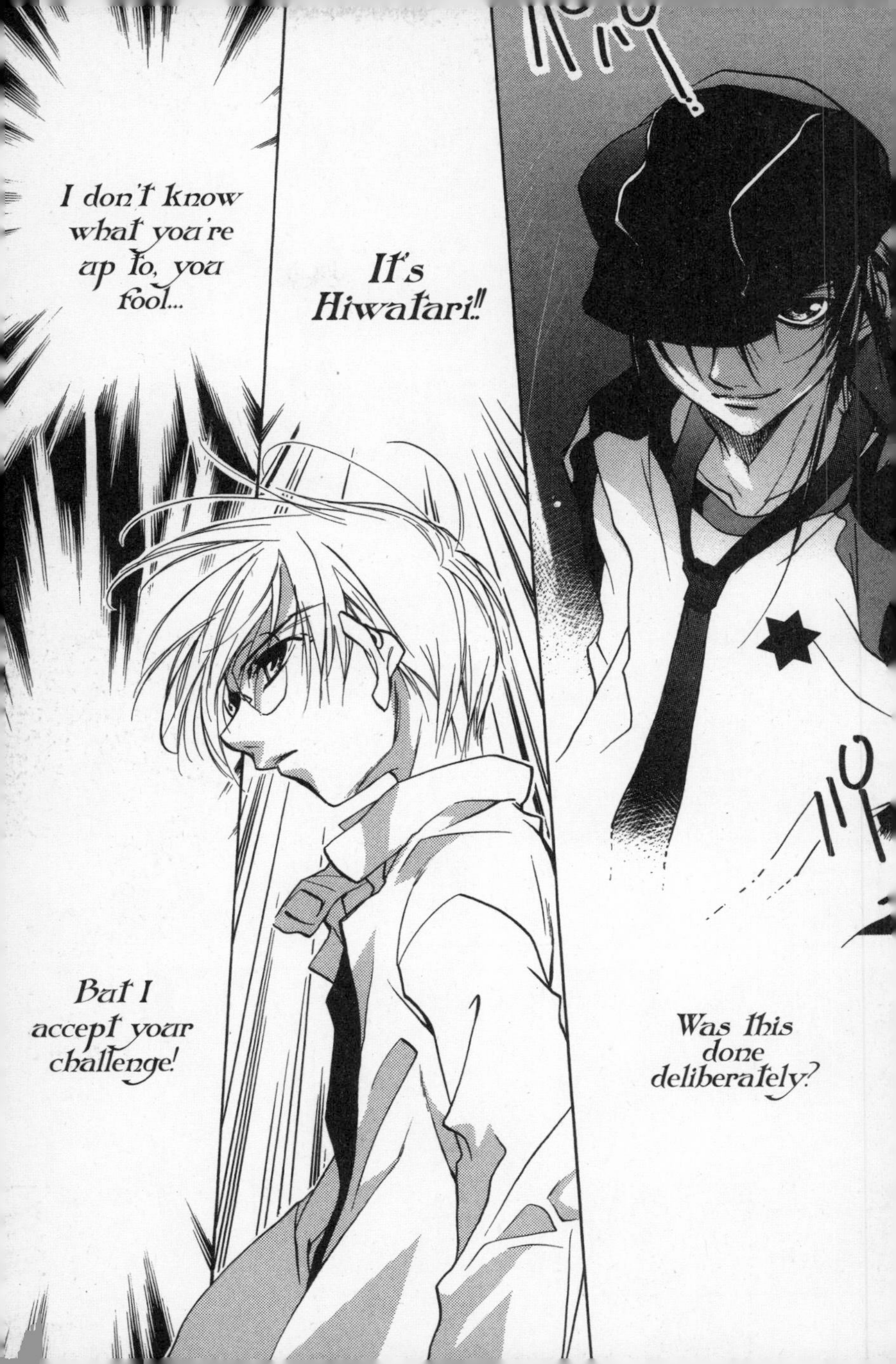
Was this done deliberately?
It's Hiwatari!!
I don't know what you're up to, you fool...
But I accept your challenge!

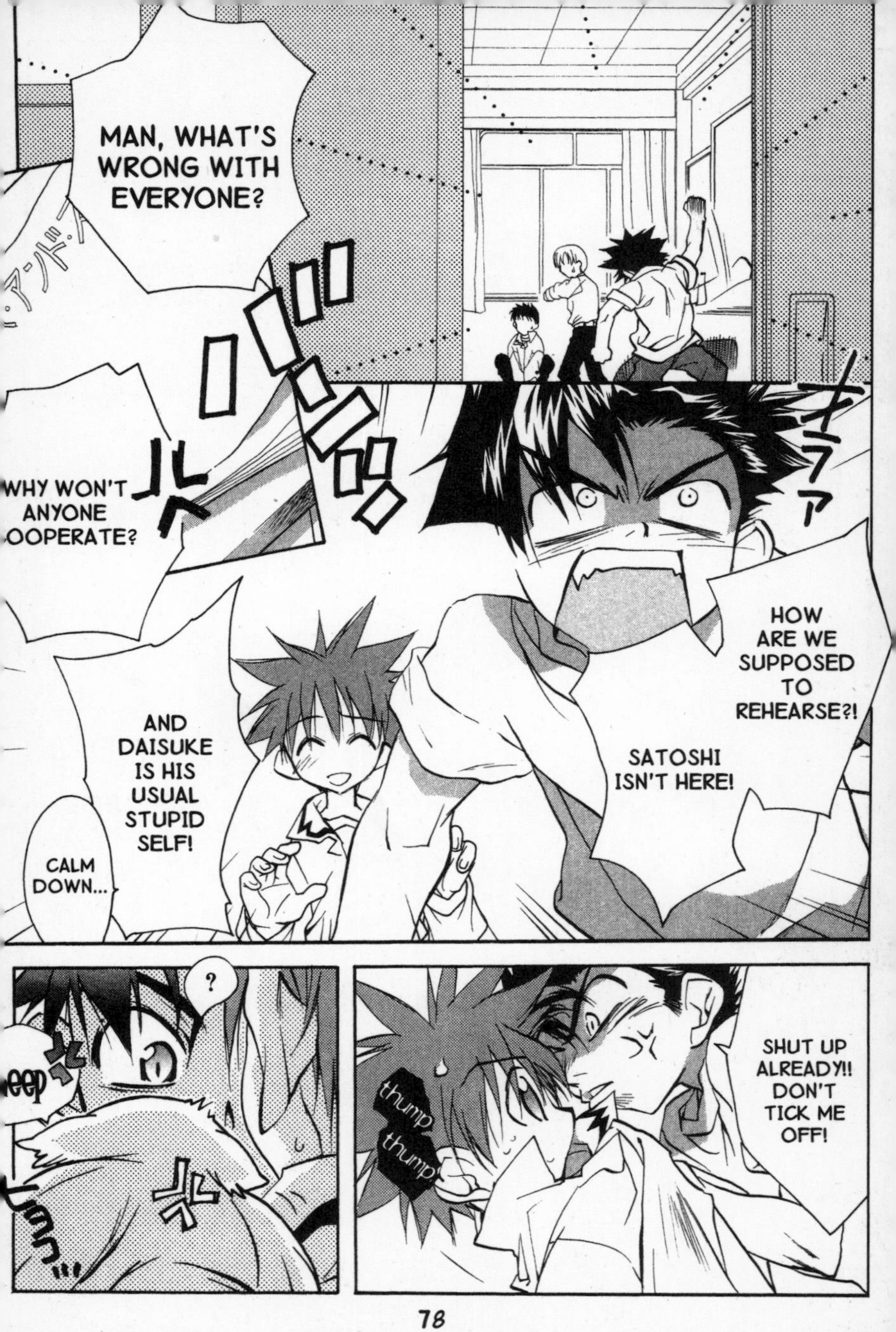
MAN, WHAT'S WRONG WITH EVERYONE?
オラァ
HOW ARE WE SUPPOSED TO REHEARSE?!
SATOSHI ISN'T HERE!
WHY WON'T ANYONE OOPERATE?
AND DAISUKE IS HIS USUAL STUPID SELF!
CALM DOWN...
SHUT UP ALREADY!! DON'T TICK ME OFF!
thump thump
?
eep

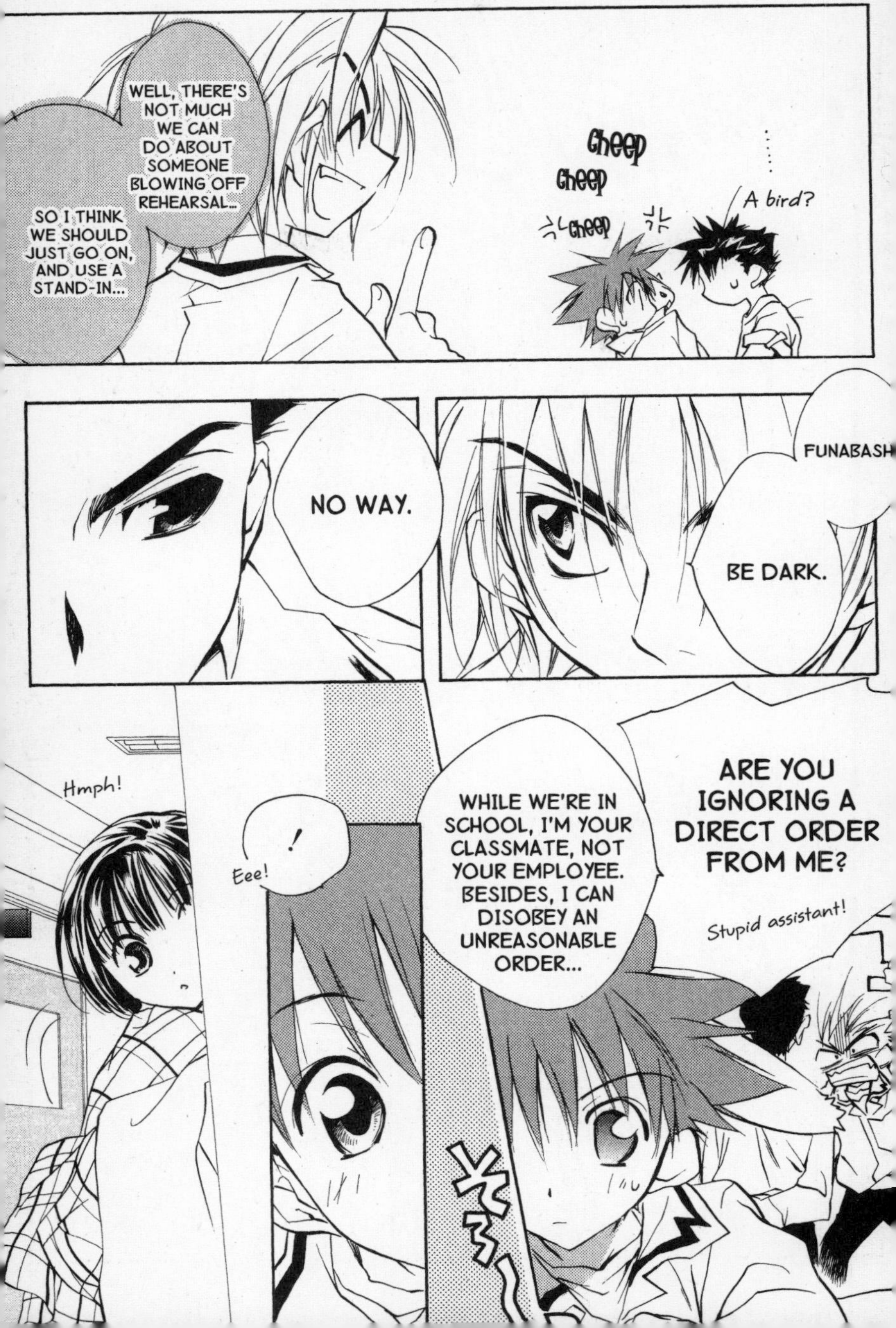
......
A bird?
Cheep
Cheep
Cheep
WELL, THERE'S NOT MUCH WE CAN DO ABOUT SOMEONE BLOWING OFF REHEARSAL...
SO I THINK WE SHOULD JUST GO ON, AND USE A STAND-IN...
FUNABASH
BE DARK.
NO WAY.
ARE YOU IGNORING A DIRECT ORDER FROM ME?
Stupid assistant!
WHILE WE'RE IN SCHOOL, I'M YOUR CLASSMATE, NOT YOUR EMPLOYEE. BESIDES, I CAN DISOBEY AN UNREASONABLE ORDER...
!
Eee!
Hmph!

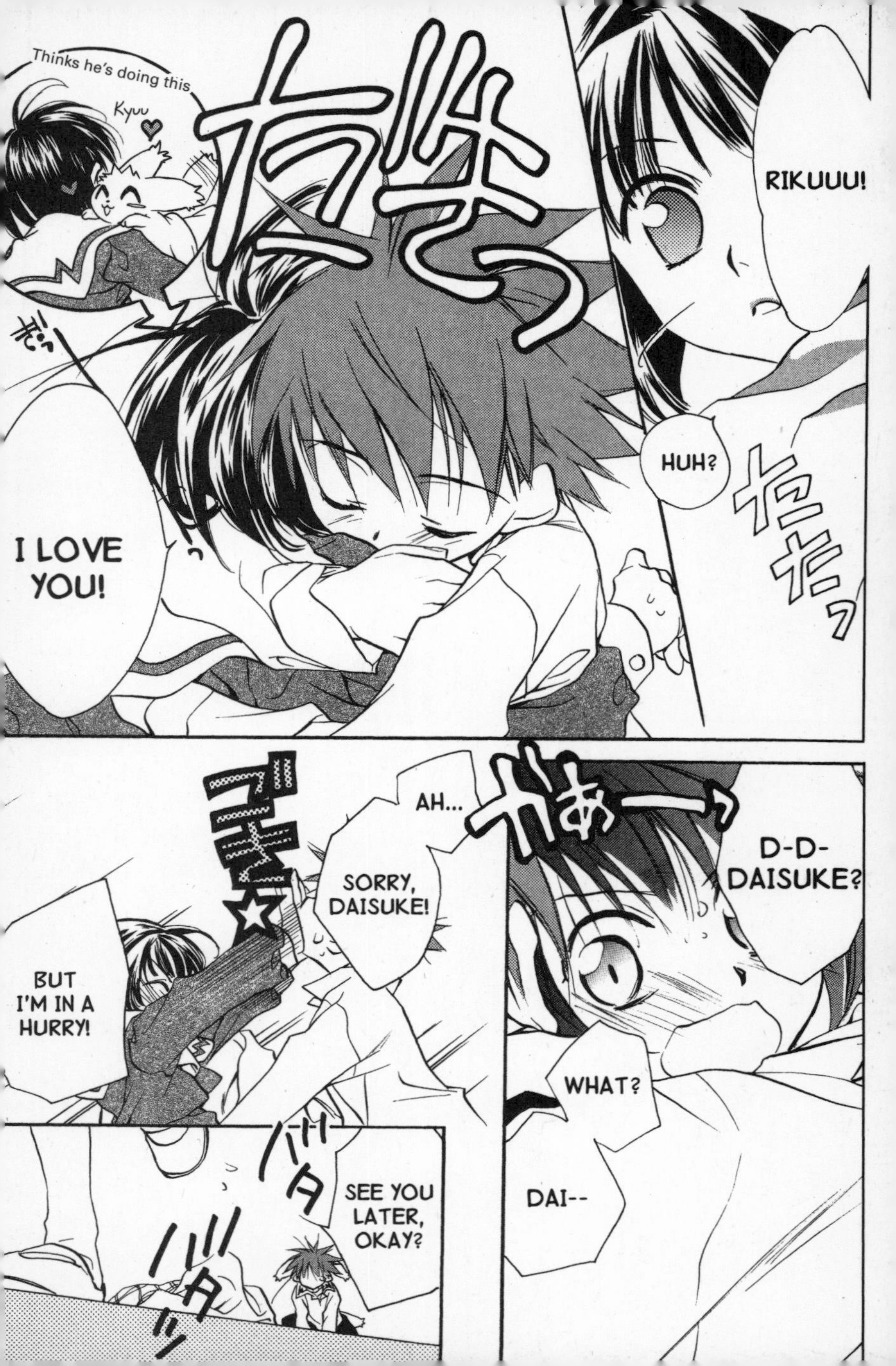
RIKUUU!
HUH?
Thinks he's doing this
Kyuu
I LOVE YOU!
D-D-DAISUKE?
WHAT?
DAI--
AH...
SORRY, DAISUKE!
BUT I'M IN A HURRY!
SEE YOU LATER, OKAY?

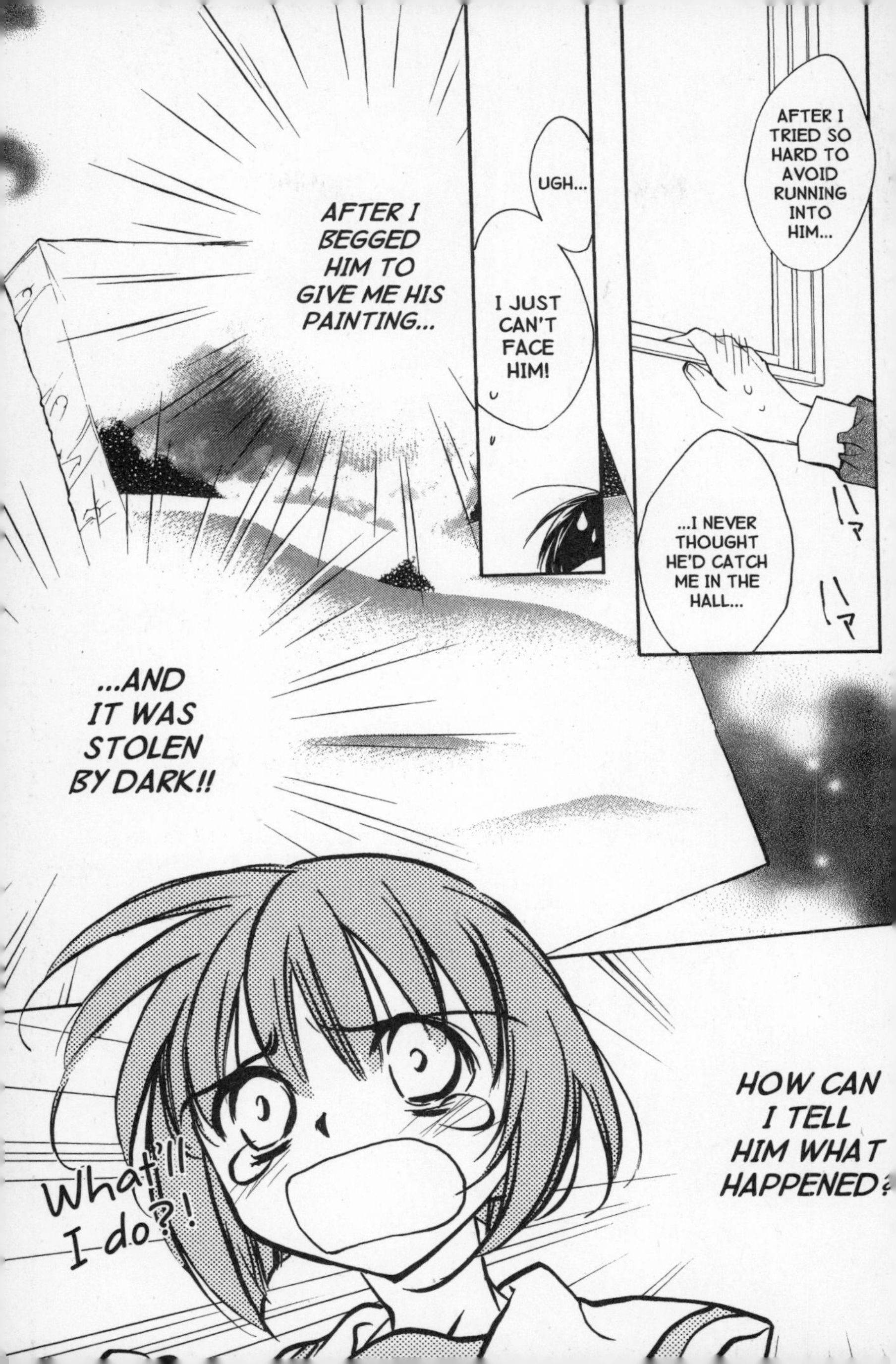

AFTER I TRIED SO HARD TO AVOID RUNNING INTO HIM...
...I NEVER THOUGHT HE'D CATCH ME IN THE HALL...
ハァ
ハァ
UGH...
I JUST CAN'T FACE HIM!
AFTER I BEGGED HIM TO GIVE ME HIS PAINTING...
...AND IT WAS STOLEN BY DARK!!
HOW CAN I TELL HIM WHAT HAPPENED?
What'll I do?!

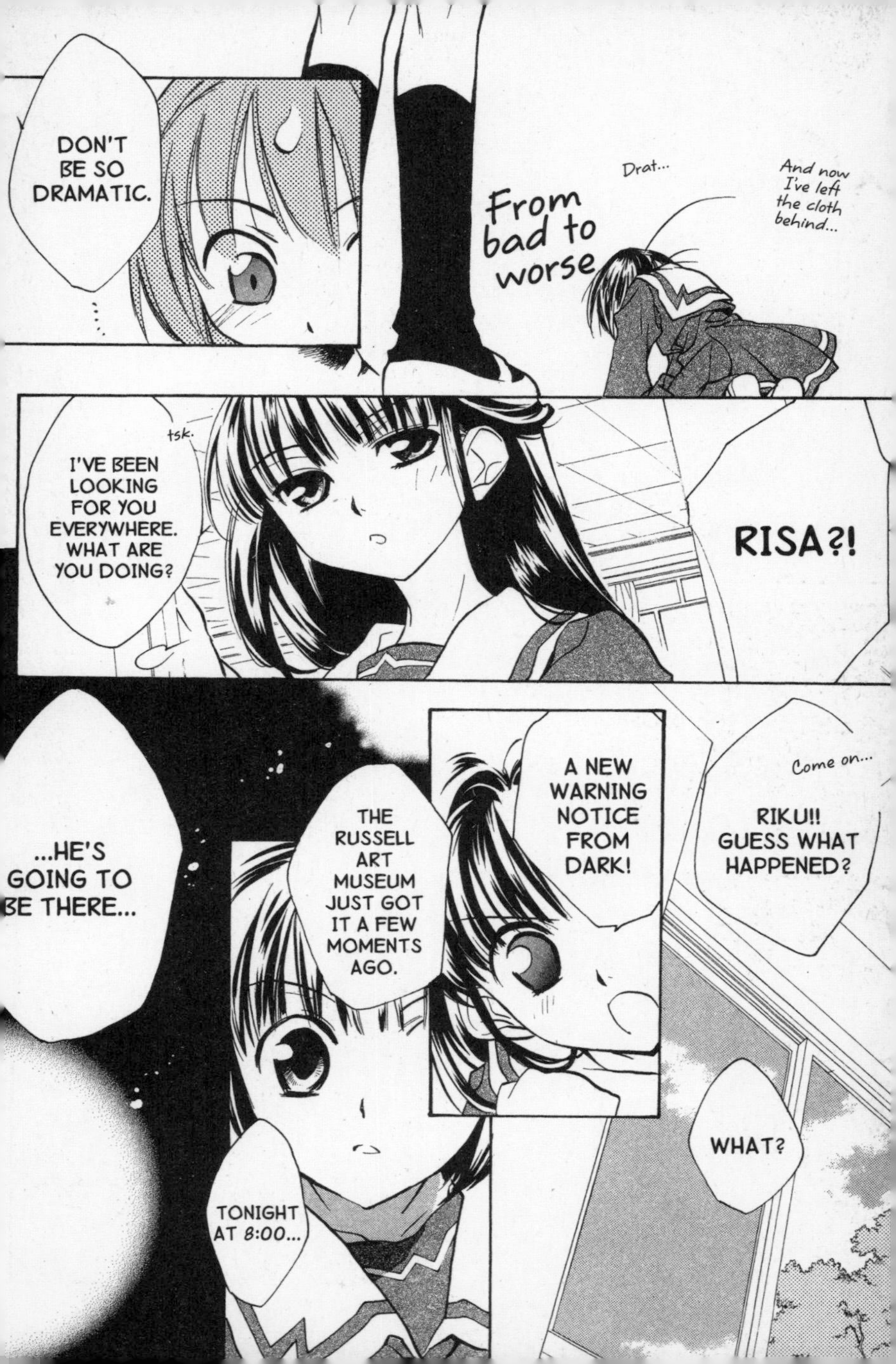
Drat...
And now I've left the cloth behind...
From bad to worse
DON'T BE SO DRAMATIC.
...
RISA?!
tsk.
I'VE BEEN LOOKING FOR YOU EVERYWHERE. WHAT ARE YOU DOING?
Come on...
RIKU!! GUESS WHAT HAPPENED?
WHAT?
A NEW WARNING NOTICE FROM DARK!
THE RUSSELL ART MUSEUM JUST GOT IT A FEW MOMENTS AGO.
TONIGHT AT 8:00...
...HE'S GOING TO BE THERE...

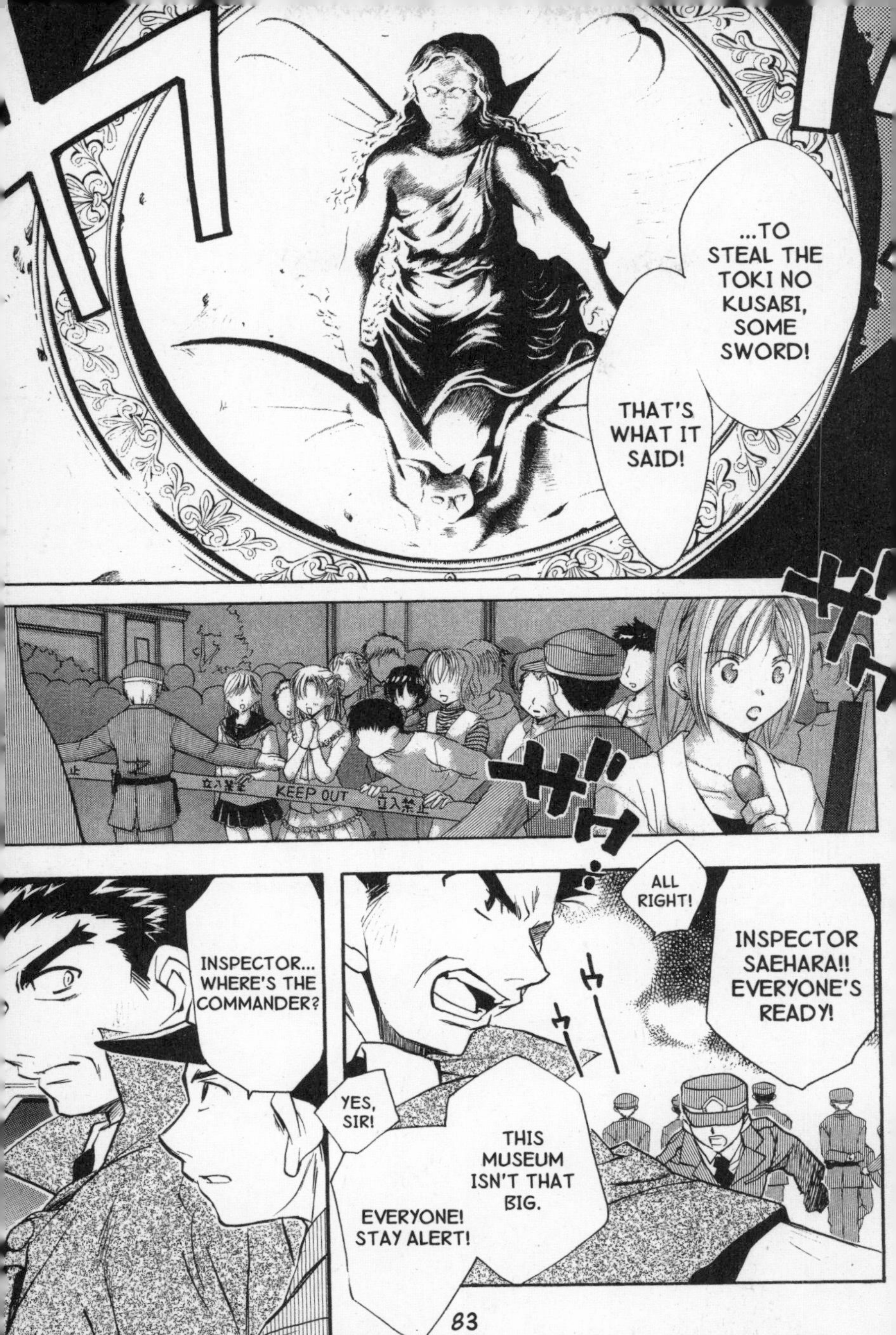
...TO STEAL THE TOKI NO KUSABI, SOME SWORD!
THAT'S WHAT IT SAID!
KEEP OUT
立入禁止
INSPECTOR SAEHARA!! EVERYONE'S READY!
ALL RIGHT!
THIS MUSEUM ISN'T THAT BIG.
EVERYONE! STAY ALERT!
YES, SIR!
INSPECTOR... WHERE'S THE COMMANDER?

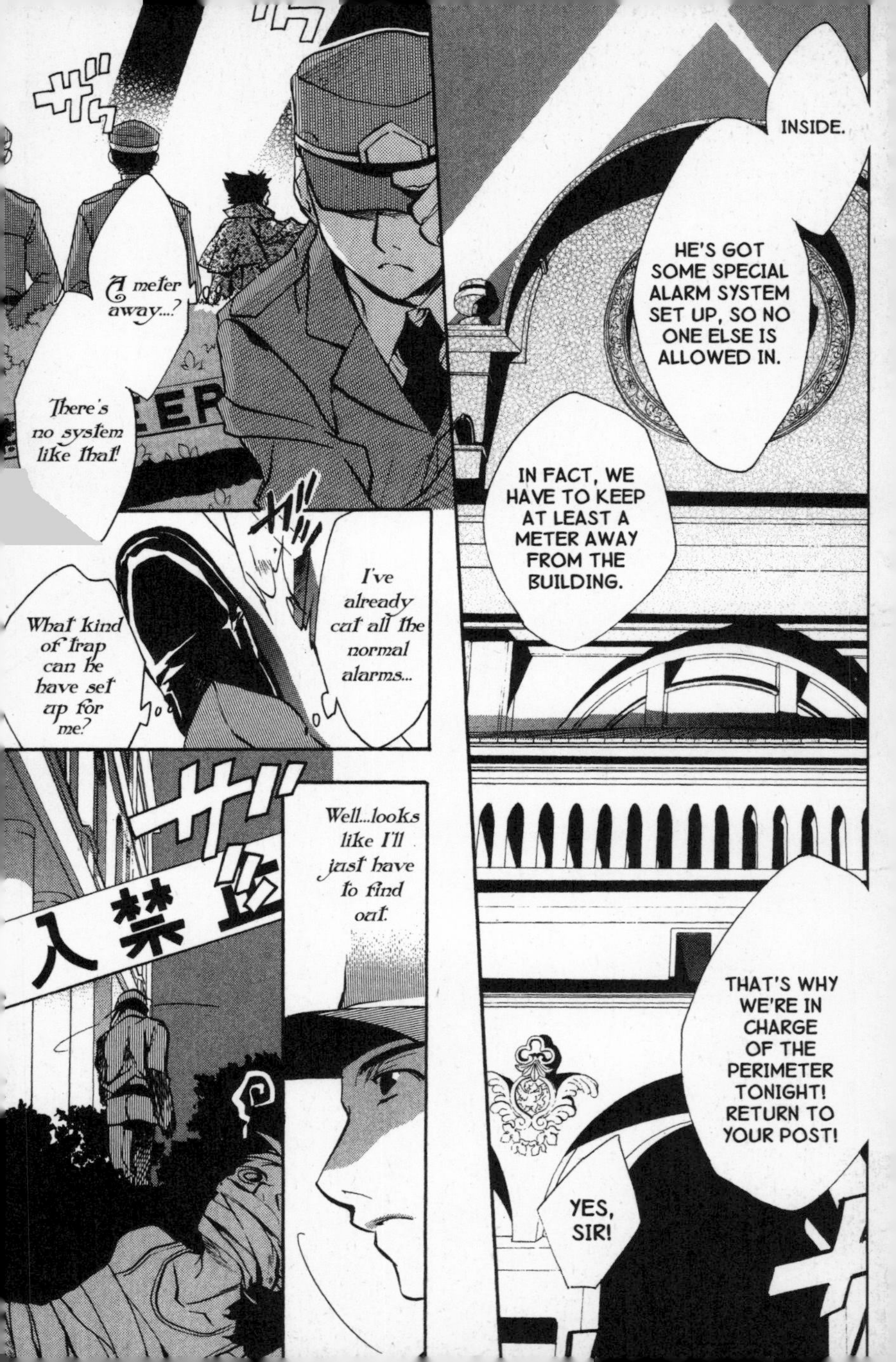

INSIDE.
HE'S GOT SOME SPECIAL ALARM SYSTEM SET UP, SO NO ONE ELSE IS ALLOWED IN.
IN FACT, WE HAVE TO KEEP AT LEAST A METER AWAY FROM THE BUILDING.
THAT'S WHY WE'RE IN CHARGE OF THE PERIMETER TONIGHT! RETURN TO YOUR POST!
YES, SIR!
A meter away...?
There's no system like that!
I've already cut all the normal alarms...
What kind of trap can he have set up for me?
Well...looks like I'll just have to find out.
入禁

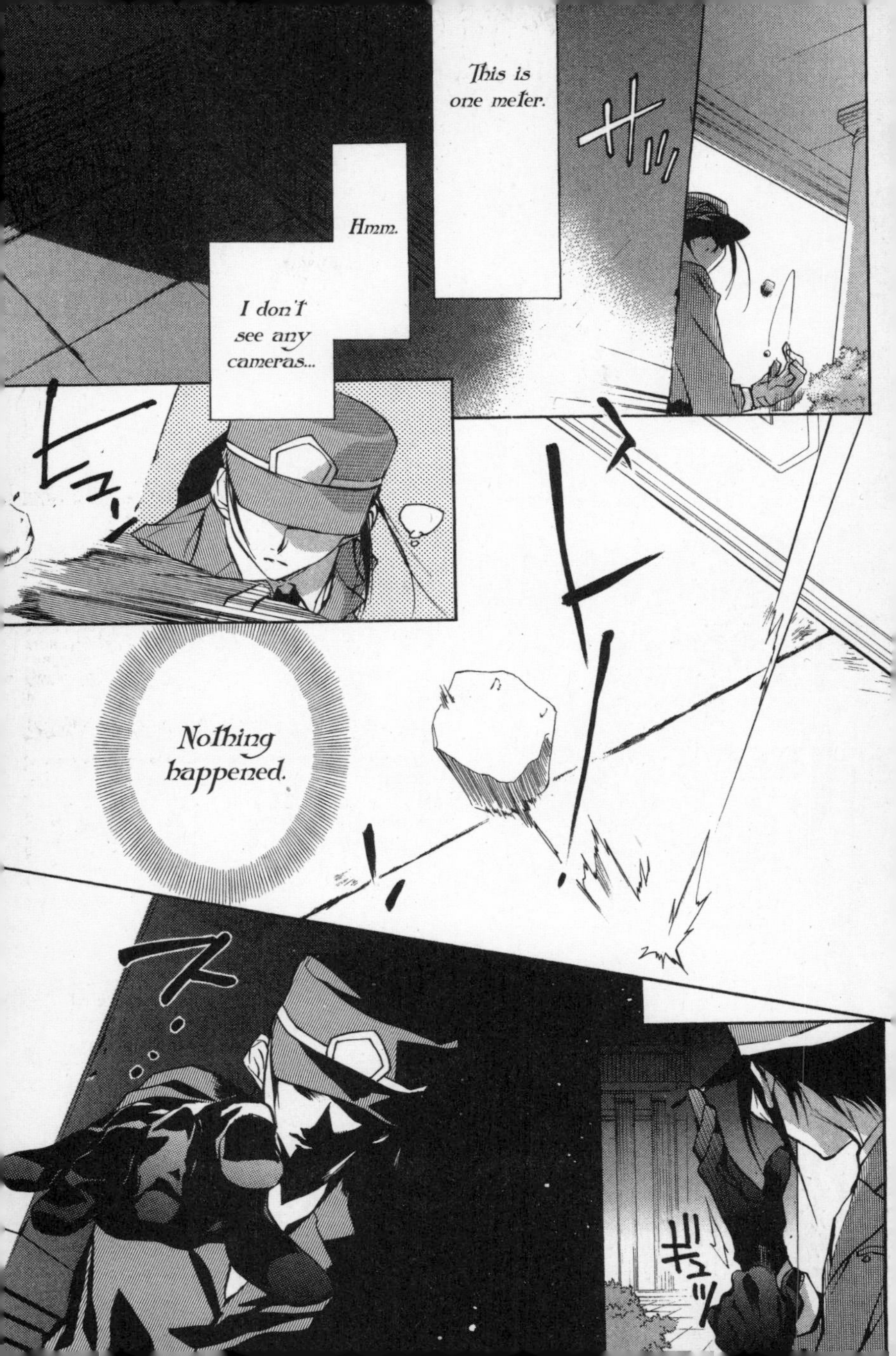
This is one meter.
Hmm.
I don't see any cameras...
Nothing happened.

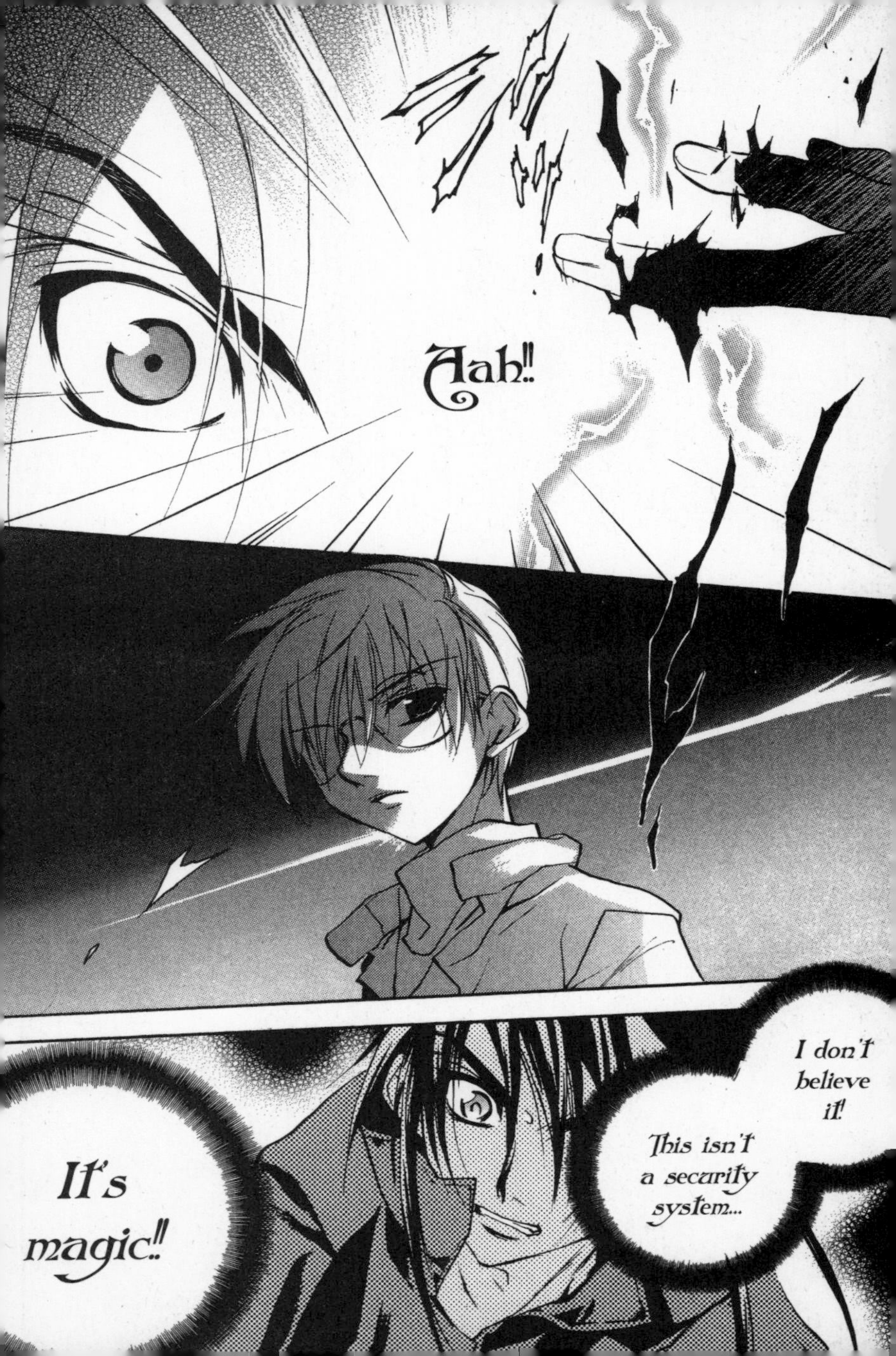
Aah!!
I don't believe it!
This isn't a security system...
It's magic!!

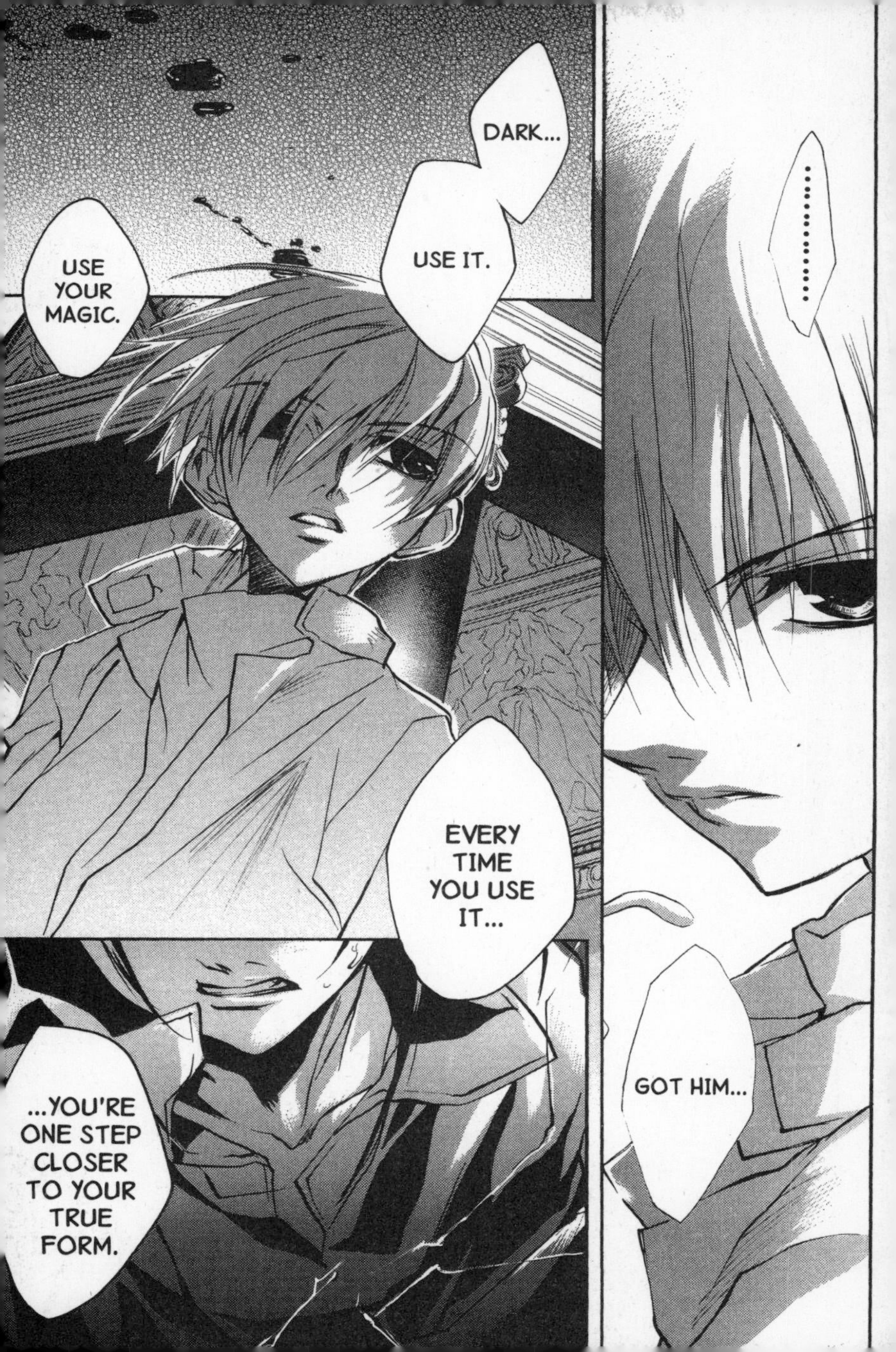
……………
GOT HIM...
DARK...
USE IT.
USE YOUR MAGIC.
EVERY TIME YOU USE IT...
...YOU'RE ONE STEP CLOSER TO YOUR TRUE FORM.

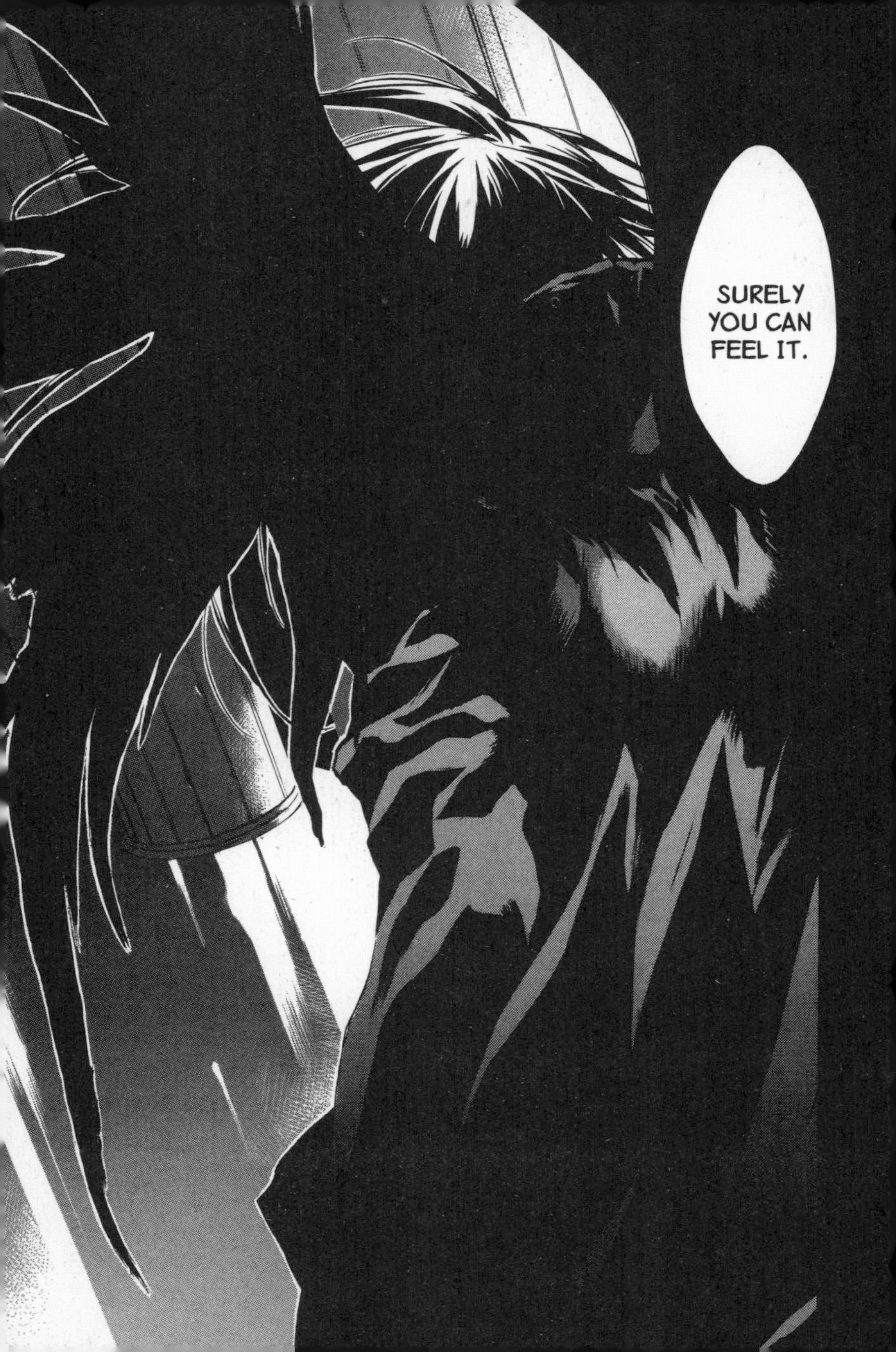
SURELY YOU CAN FEEL IT.

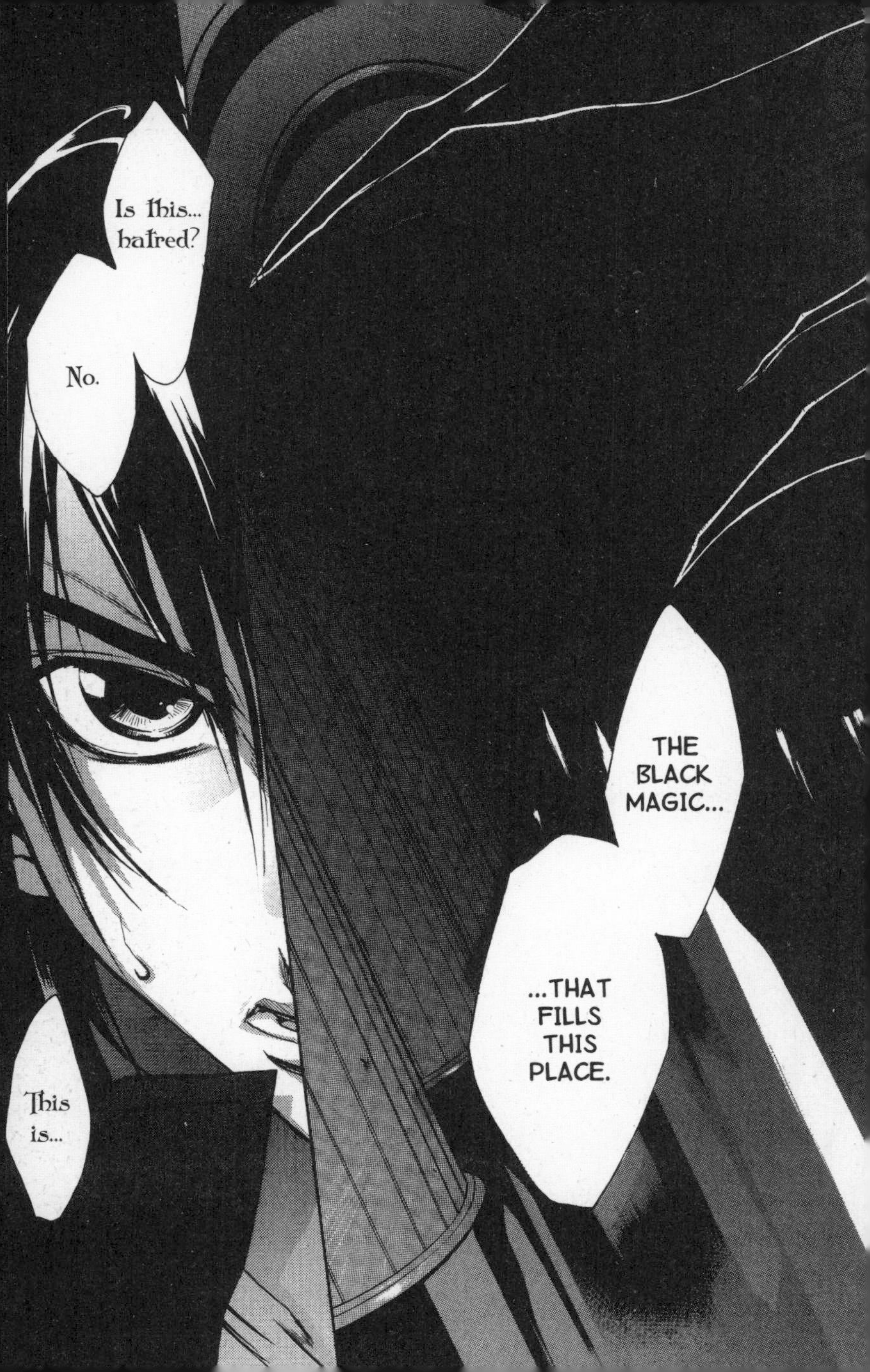
Is this... hatred?
No.
This is...
THE BLACK MAGIC...
...THAT FILLS THIS PLACE.

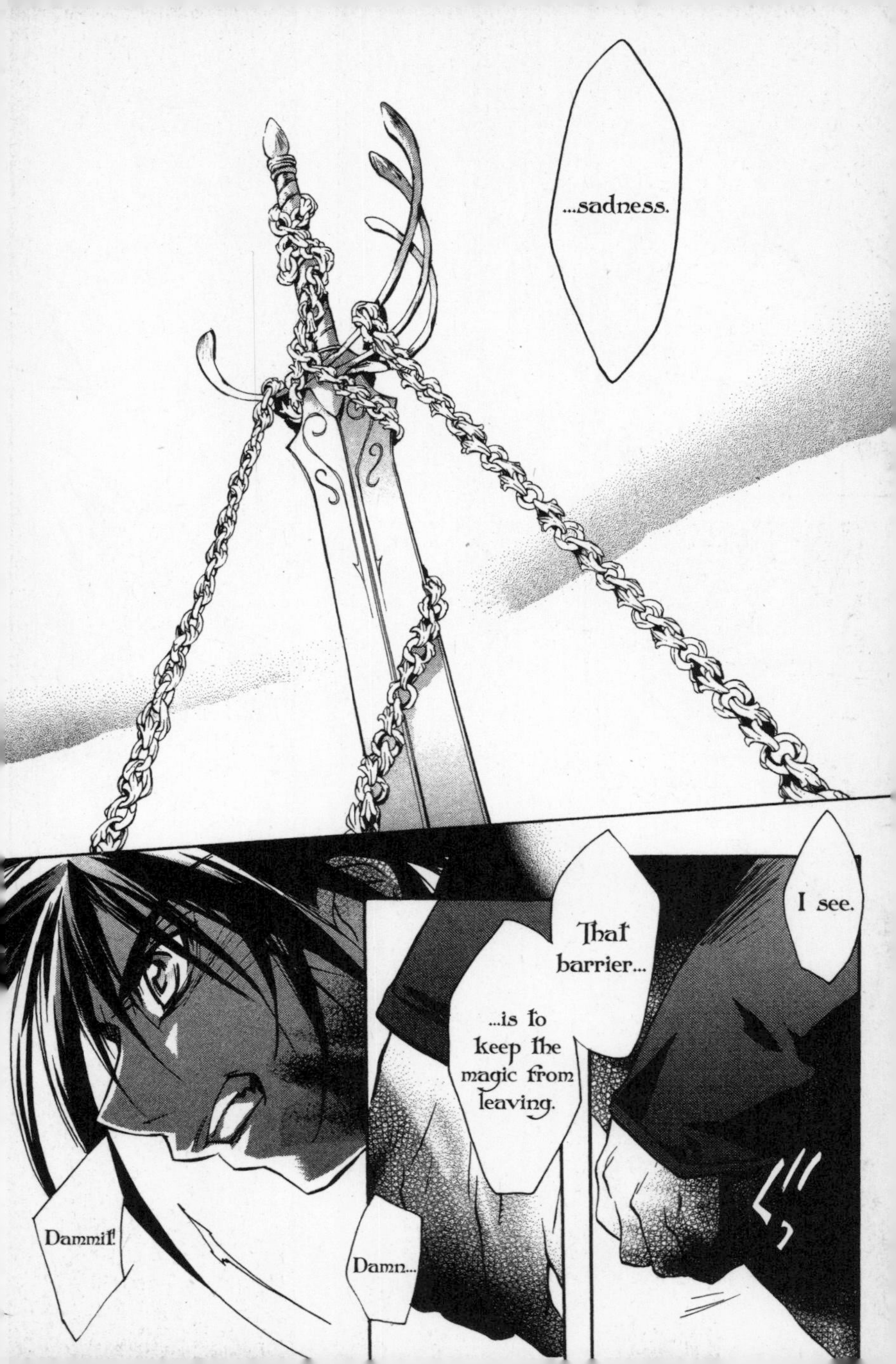
...sadness.
I see.
That barrier...
...is to keep the magic from leaving.
Damn...
Dammit!

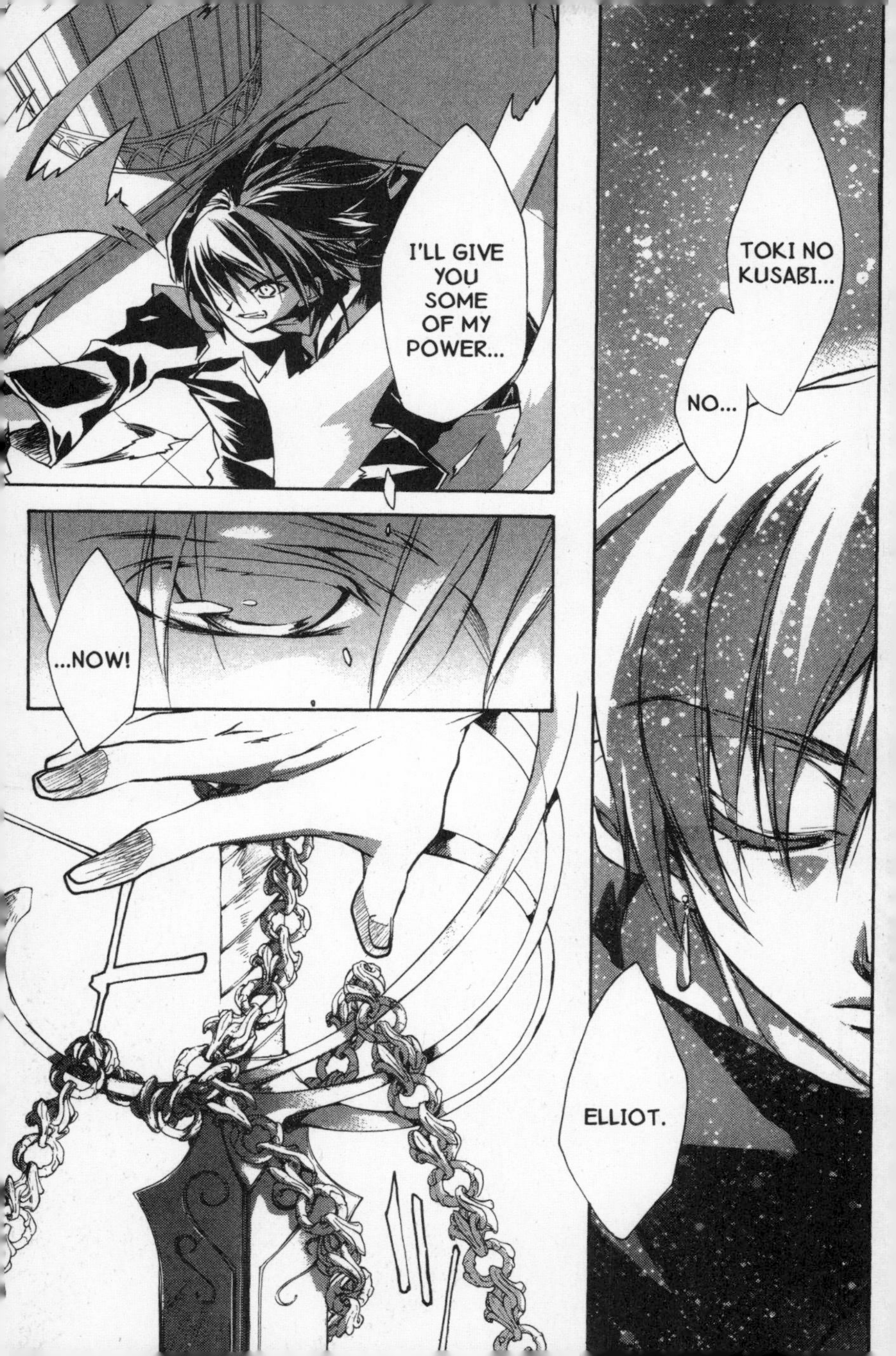
TOKI NO KUSABI...
NO...
ELLIOT.
I'LL GIVE YOU SOME OF MY POWER...
...NOW!

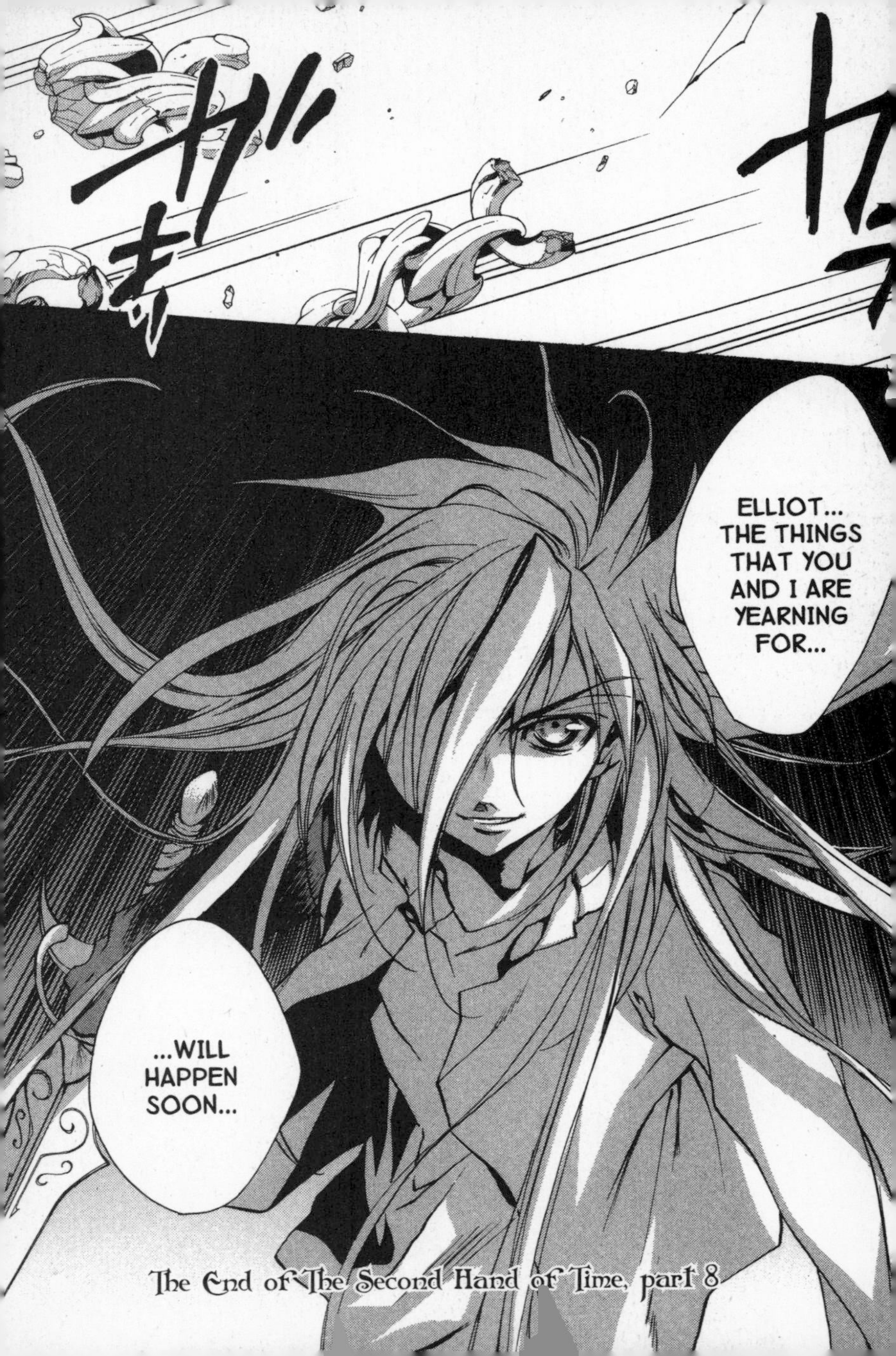
ELLIOT... THE THINGS THAT YOU AND I ARE YEARNING FOR...
...WILL HAPPEN SOON...
The End of The Second Hand of Time, part 8

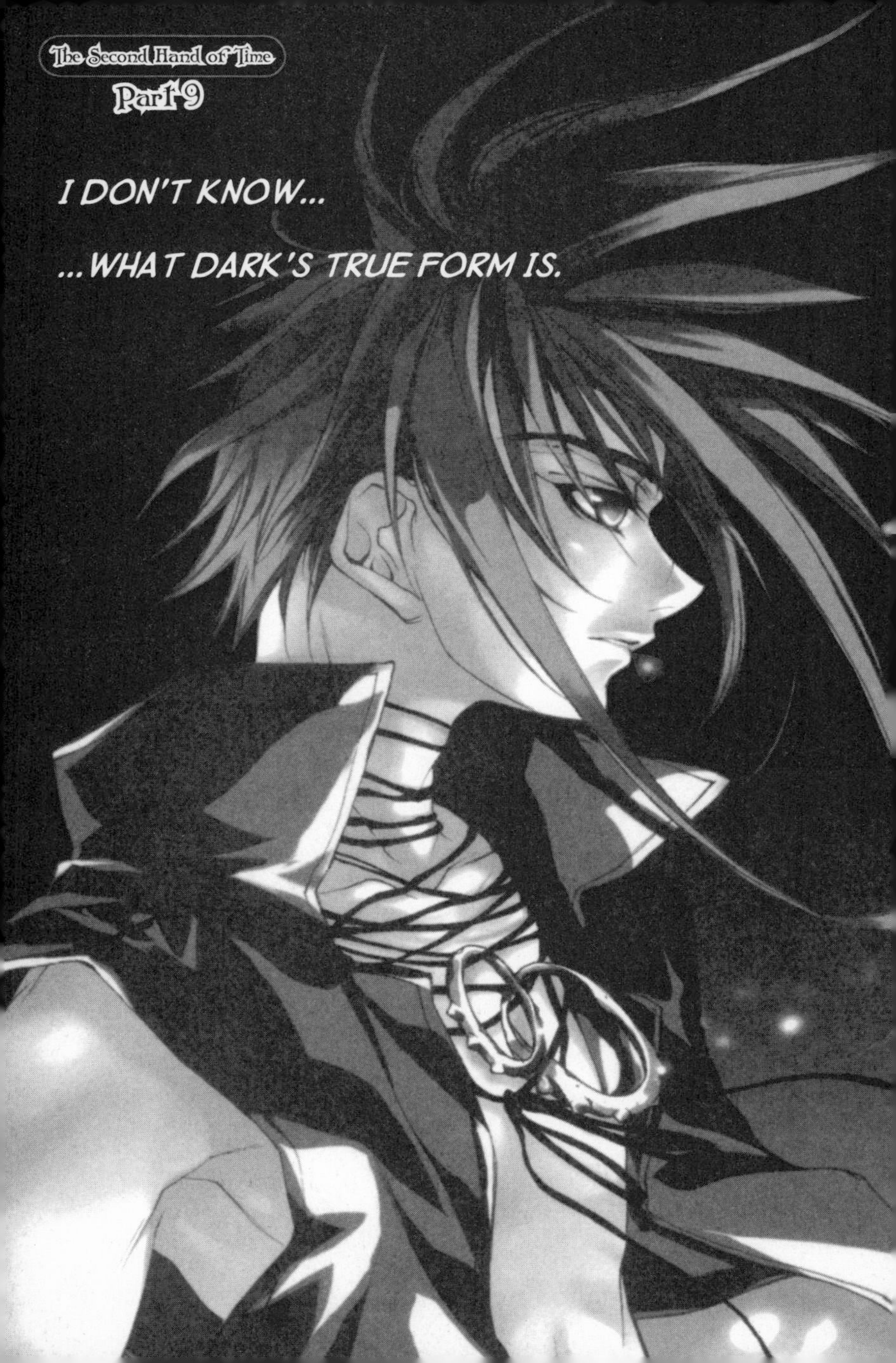
The Second Hand of Time
Part 9
I DON'T KNOW...
...WHAT DARK'S TRUE FORM IS.

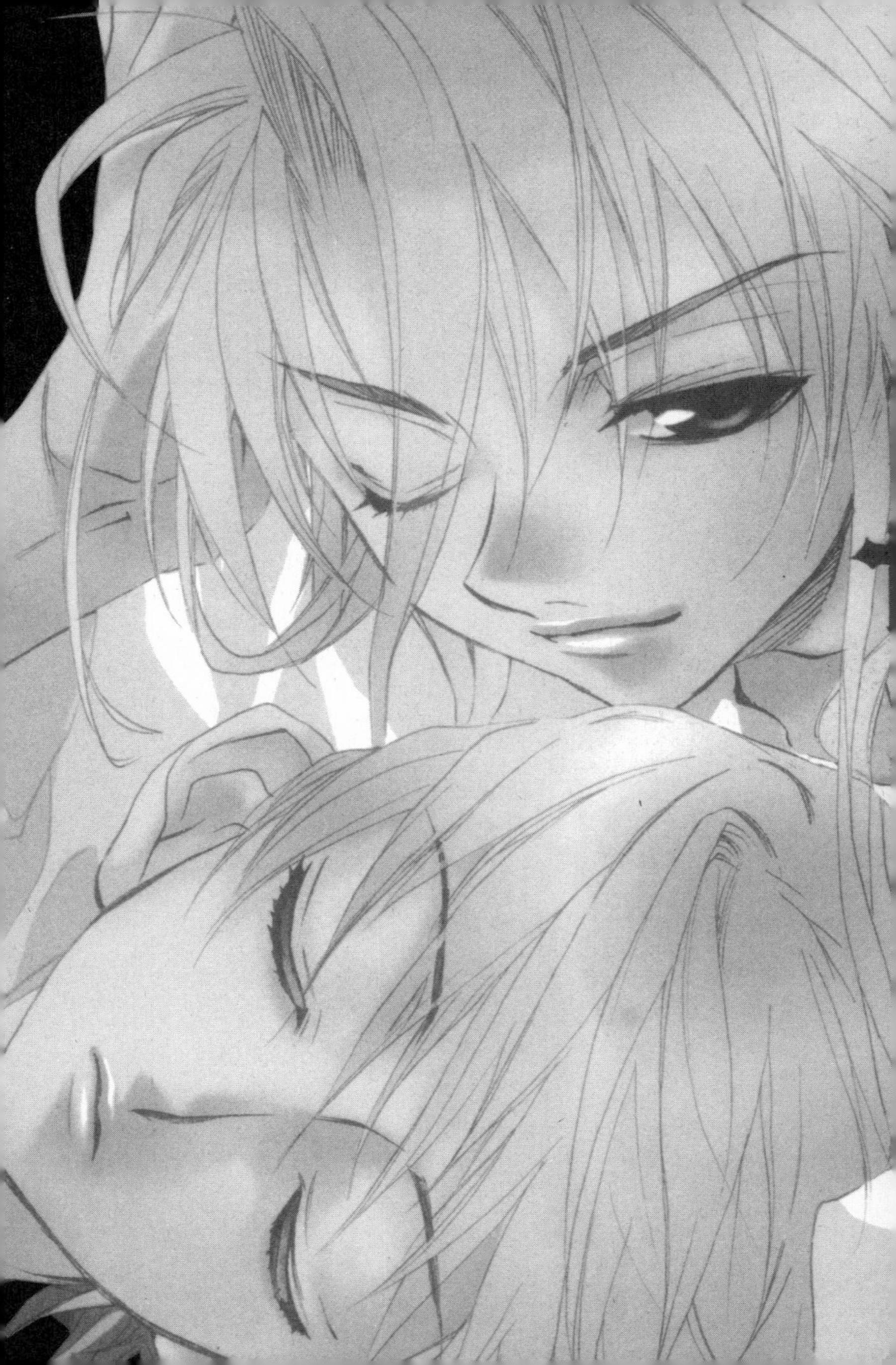

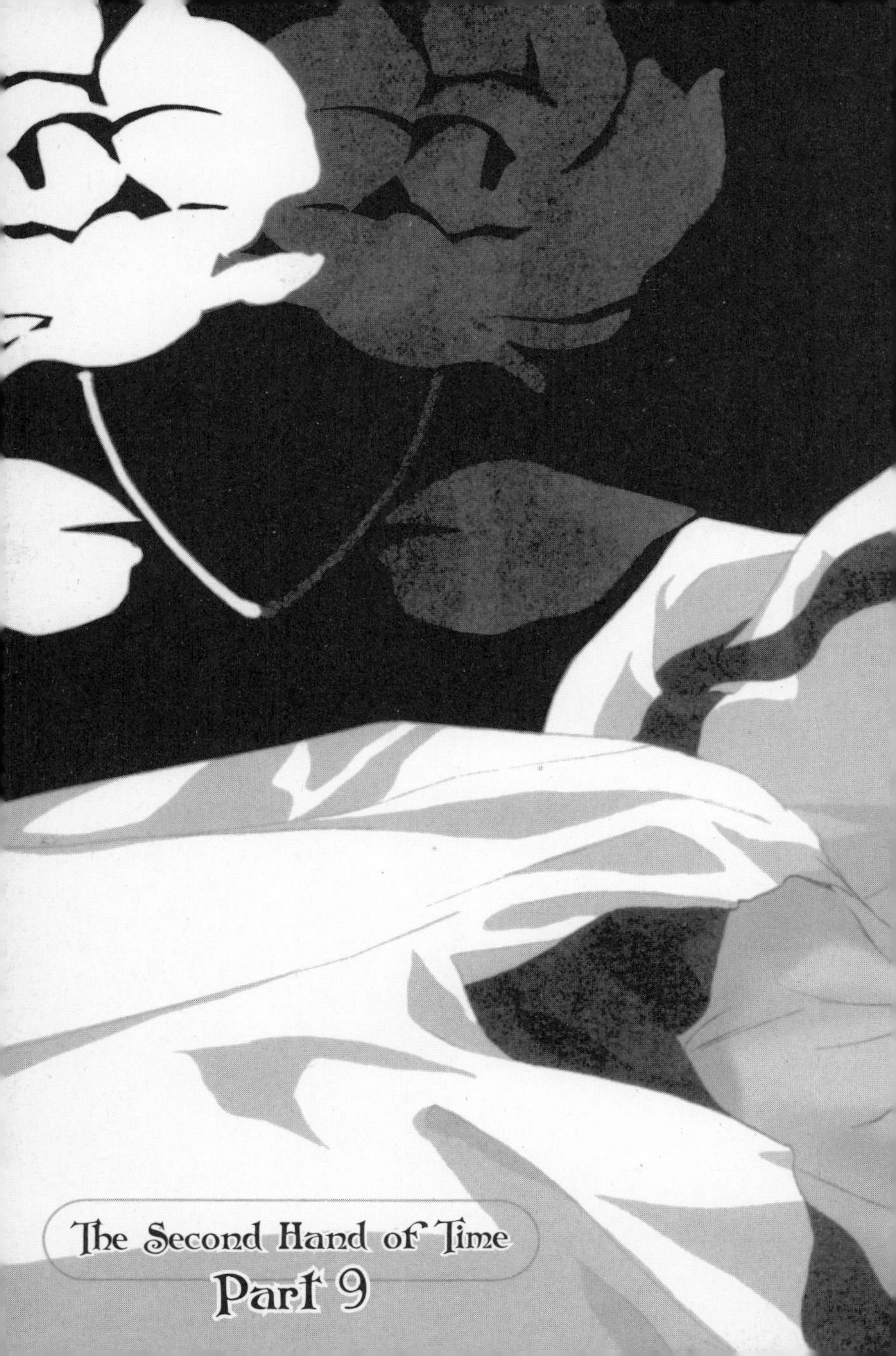
The Second Hand of Time
Part 9

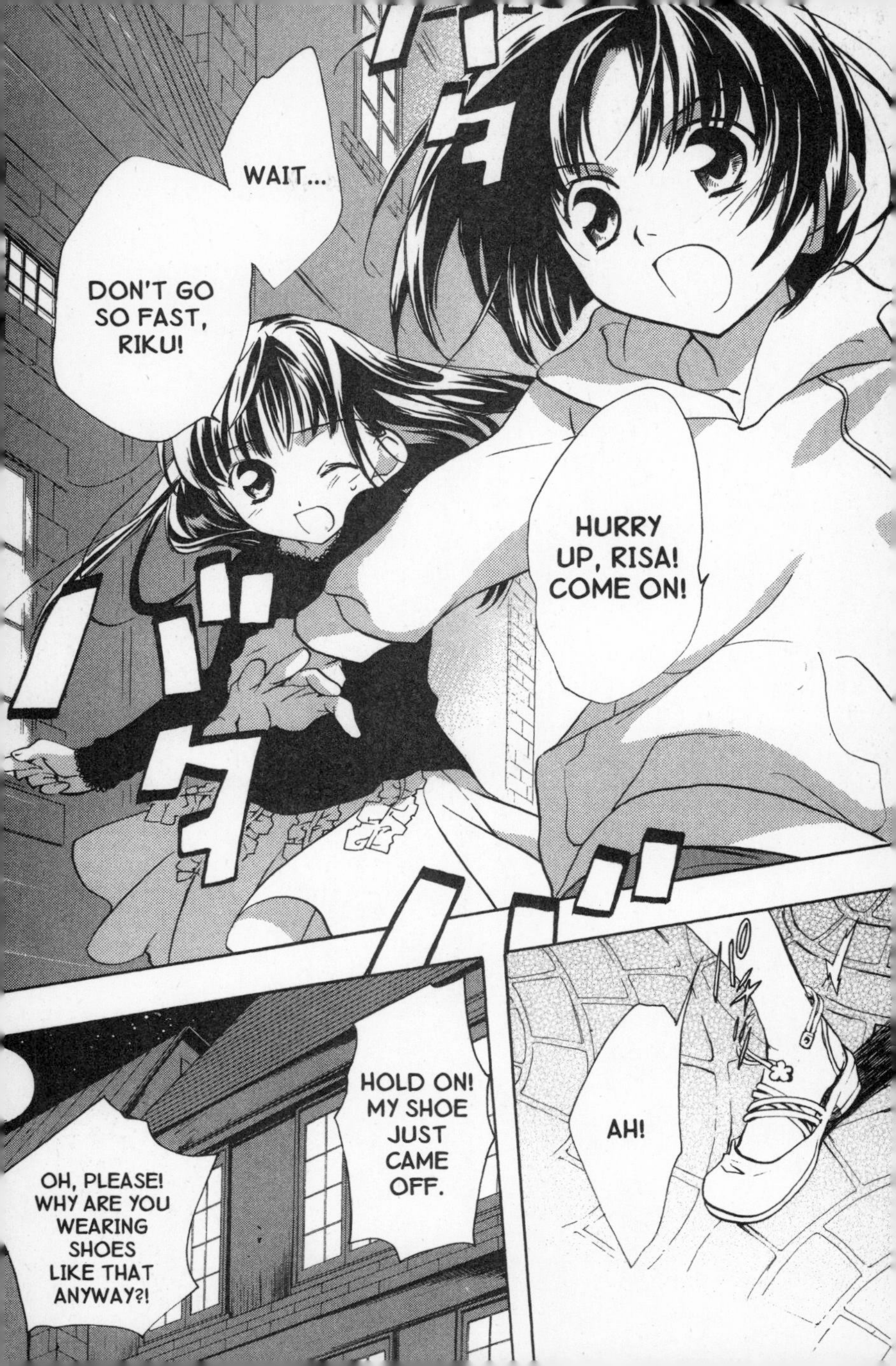
HURRY UP, RISA! COME ON!
WAIT...
DON'T GO SO FAST, RIKU!
AH!
HOLD ON! MY SHOE JUST CAME OFF.
OH, PLEASE! WHY ARE YOU WEARING SHOES LIKE THAT ANYWAY?!

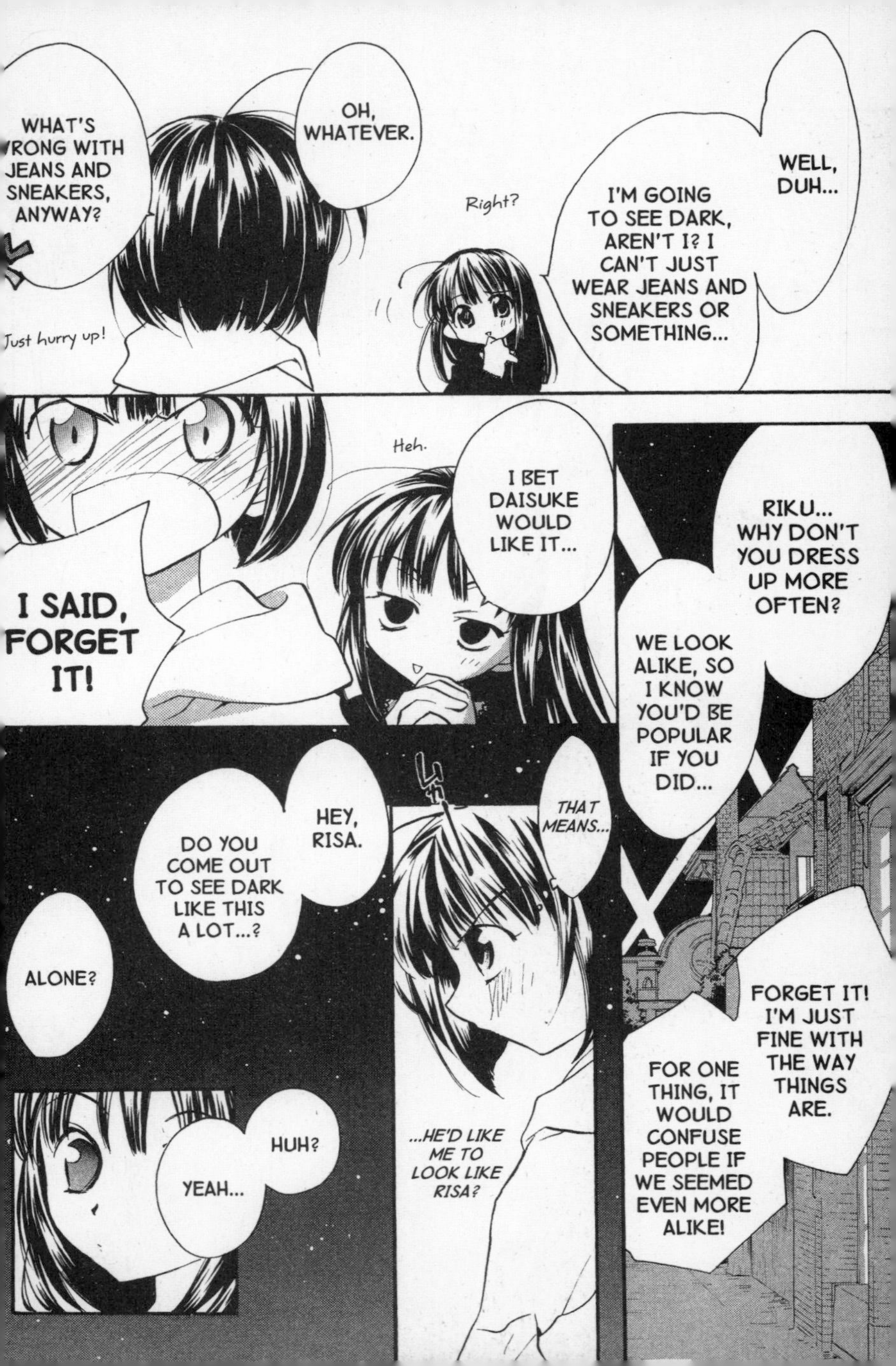

WELL, DUH...
I'M GOING TO SEE DARK, AREN'T I? I CAN'T JUST WEAR JEANS AND SNEAKERS OR SOMETHING...
Right?
OH, WHATEVER.
WHAT'S RONG WITH JEANS AND SNEAKERS, ANYWAY?
Just hurry up!
RIKU... WHY DON'T YOU DRESS UP MORE OFTEN?
WE LOOK ALIKE, SO I KNOW YOU'D BE POPULAR IF YOU DID...
FORGET IT! I'M JUST FINE WITH THE WAY THINGS ARE.
FOR ONE THING, IT WOULD CONFUSE PEOPLE IF WE SEEMED EVEN MORE ALIKE!
Heh.
I BET DAISUKE WOULD LIKE IT...
I SAID, FORGET IT!
THAT MEANS...
...HE'D LIKE ME TO LOOK LIKE RISA?
HEY, RISA.
DO YOU COME OUT TO SEE DARK LIKE THIS A LOT...?
ALONE?
HUH?
YEAH...

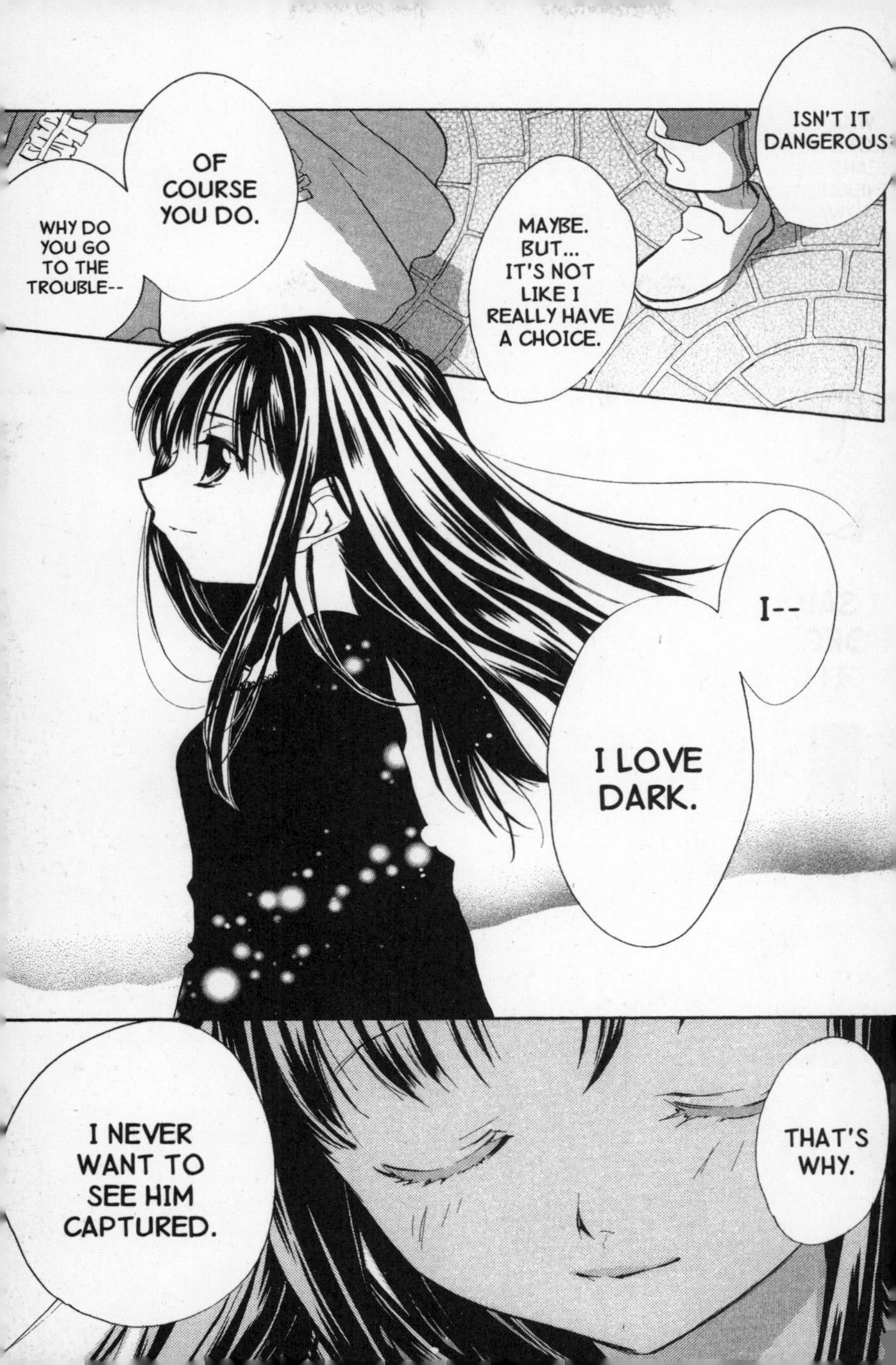

ISN'T IT DANGEROUS
MAYBE. BUT... IT'S NOT LIKE I REALLY HAVE A CHOICE.
OF COURSE YOU DO.
WHY DO YOU GO TO THE TROUBLE--
I--
I LOVE DARK.
THAT'S WHY.
I NEVER WANT TO SEE HIM CAPTURED.

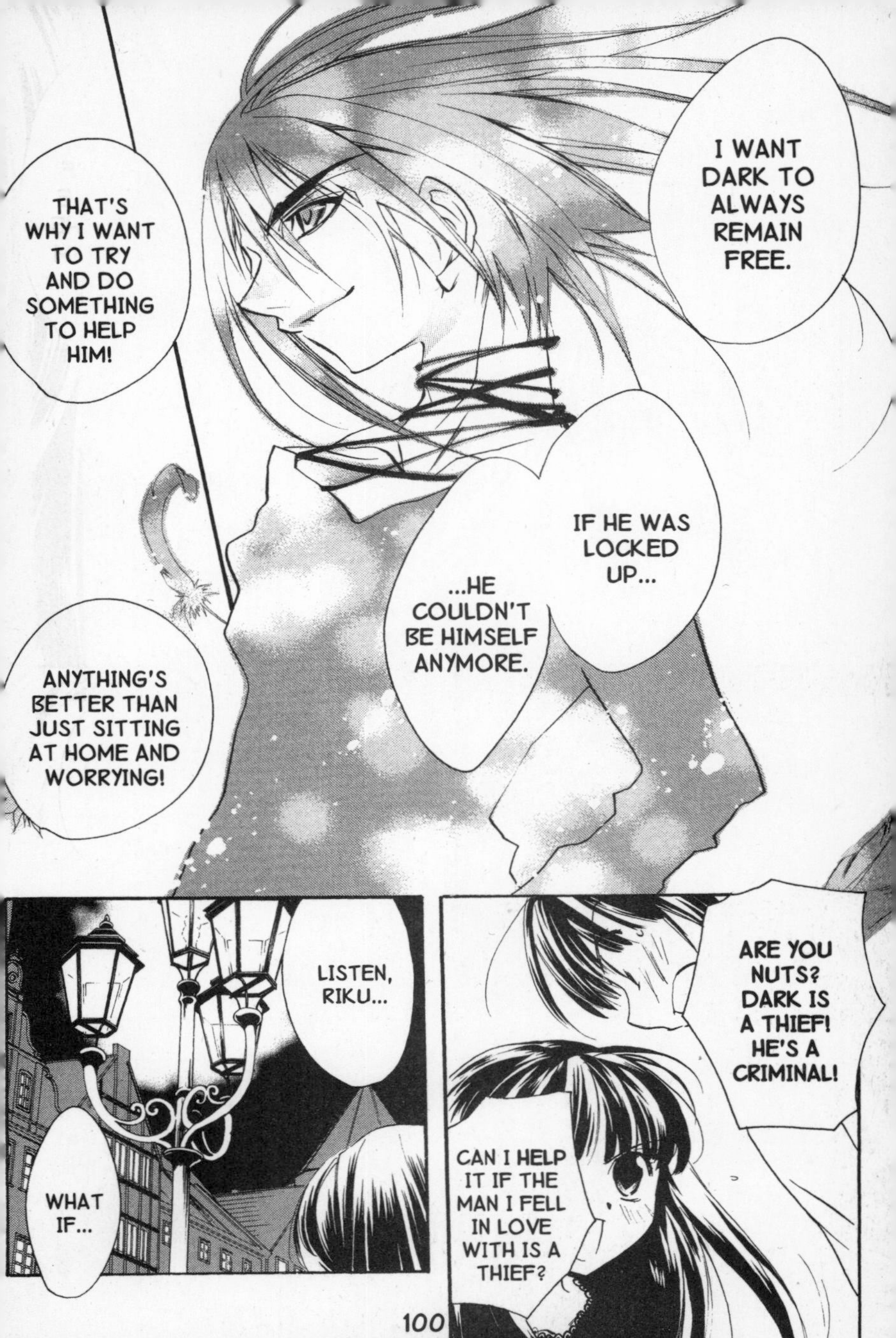
I WANT DARK TO ALWAYS REMAIN FREE.
IF HE WAS LOCKED UP...
...HE COULDN'T BE HIMSELF ANYMORE.
THAT'S WHY I WANT TO TRY AND DO SOMETHING TO HELP HIM!
ANYTHING'S BETTER THAN JUST SITTING AT HOME AND WORRYING!
ARE YOU NUTS? DARK IS A THIEF! HE'S A CRIMINAL!
CAN I HELP IT IF THE MAN I FELL IN LOVE WITH IS A THIEF?
LISTEN, RIKU...
WHAT IF...

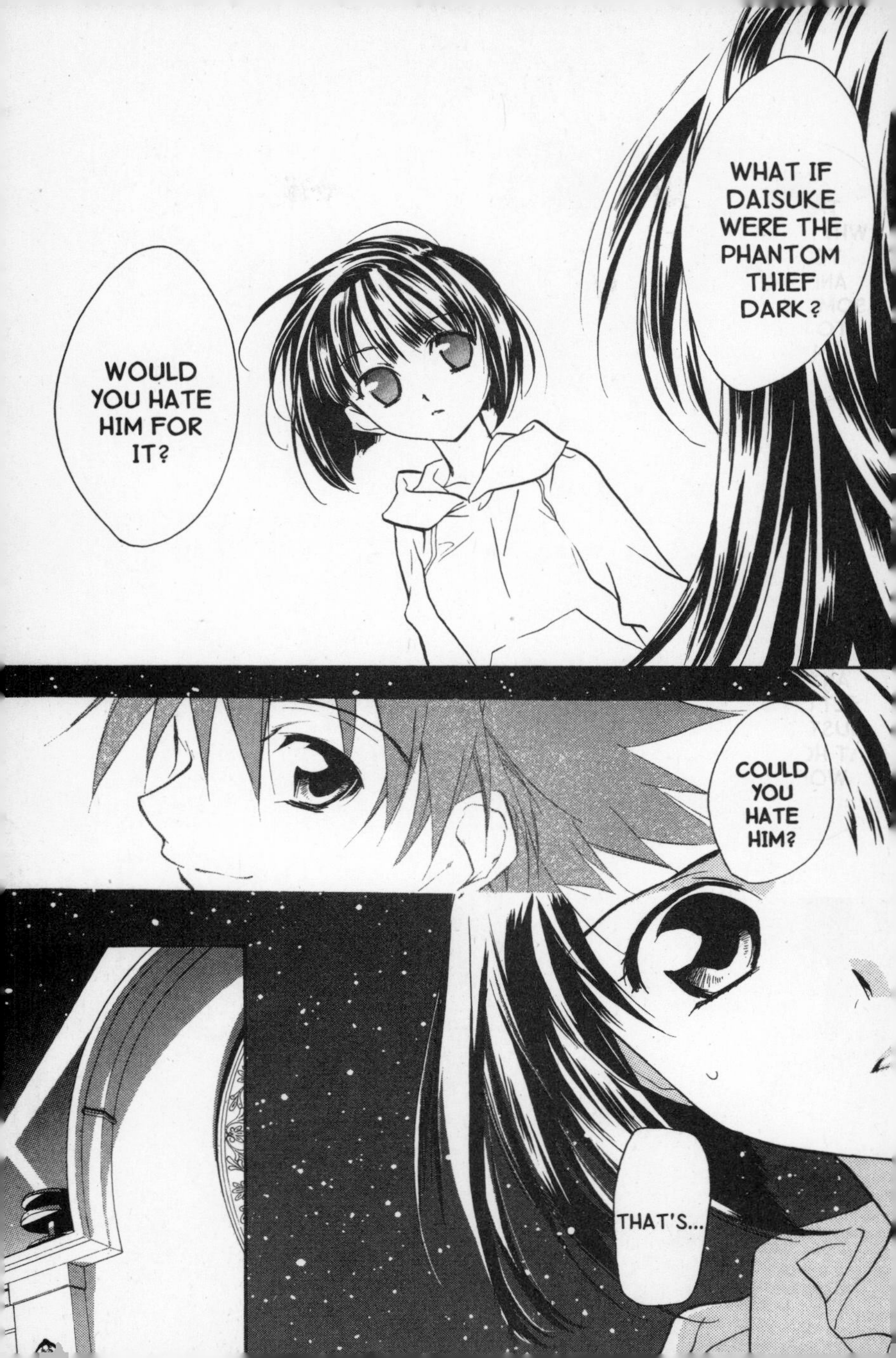
WHAT IF DAISUKE WERE THE PHANTOM THIEF DARK?
WOULD YOU HATE HIM FOR IT?
COULD YOU HATE HIM?
THAT'S...

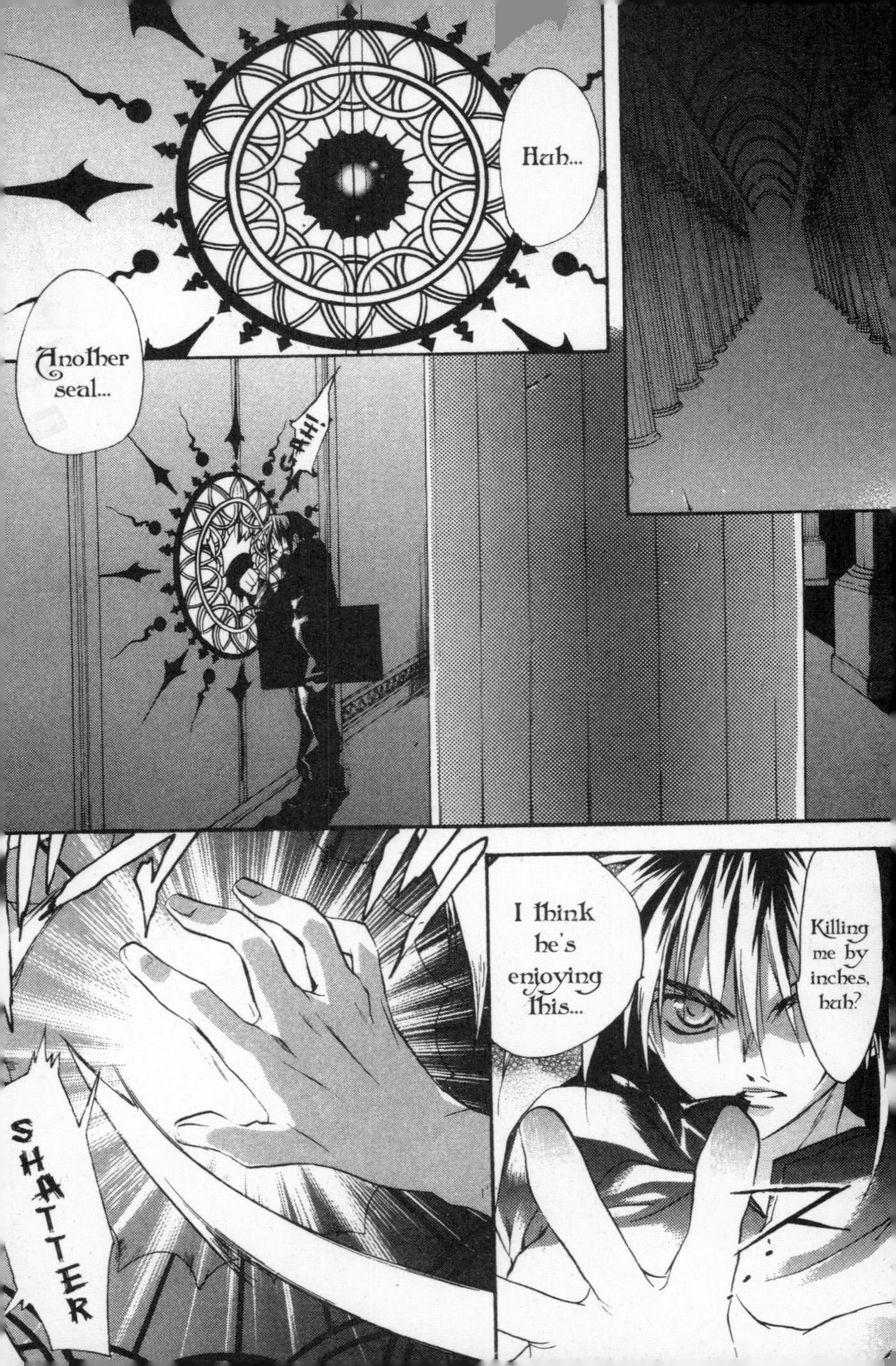
Huh...
Another seal...
GAH!
Killing me by inches, huh?
I think he's enjoying this...
SHATTER

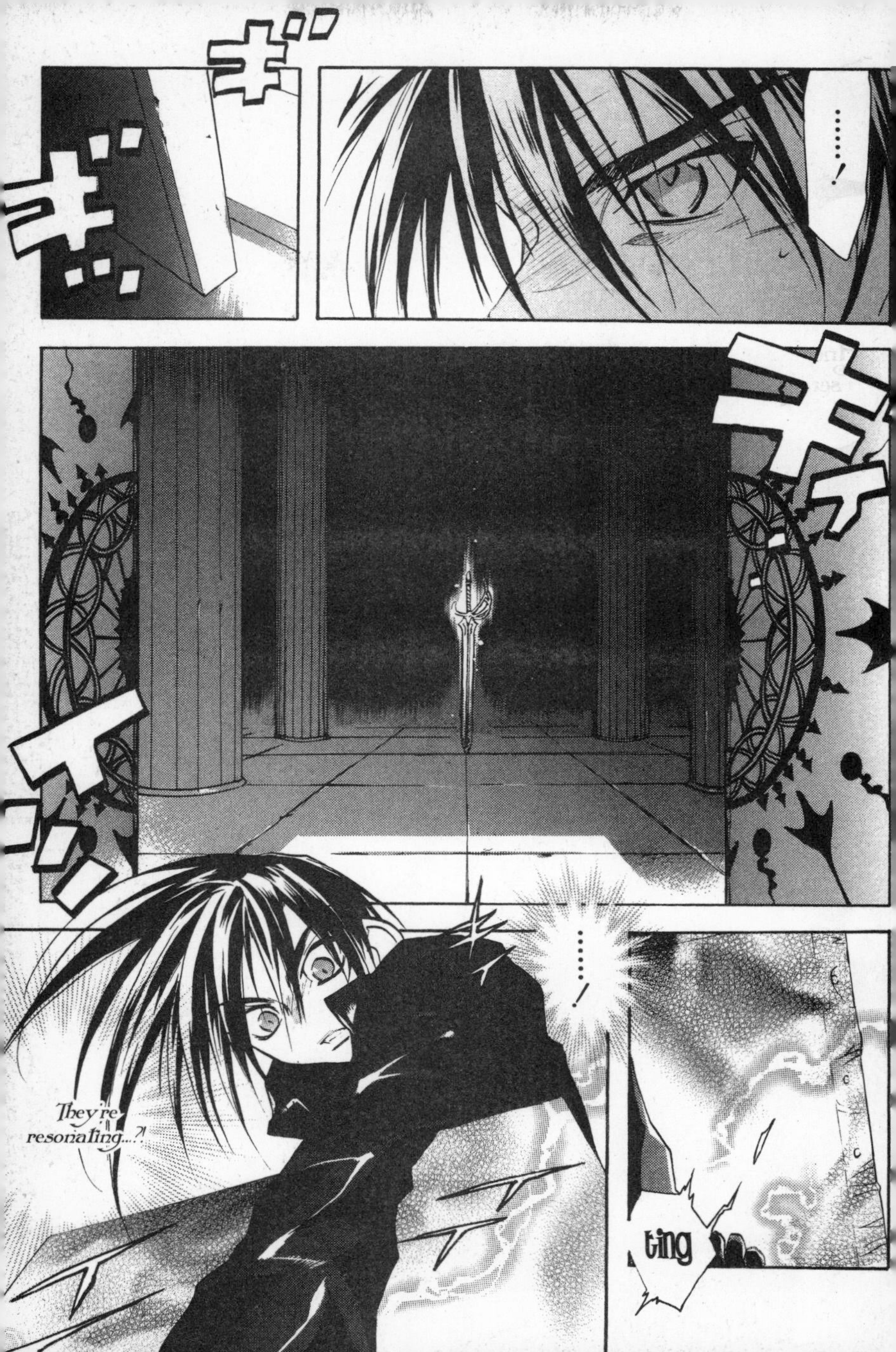
......!
ting
......!
They're resonating...?!

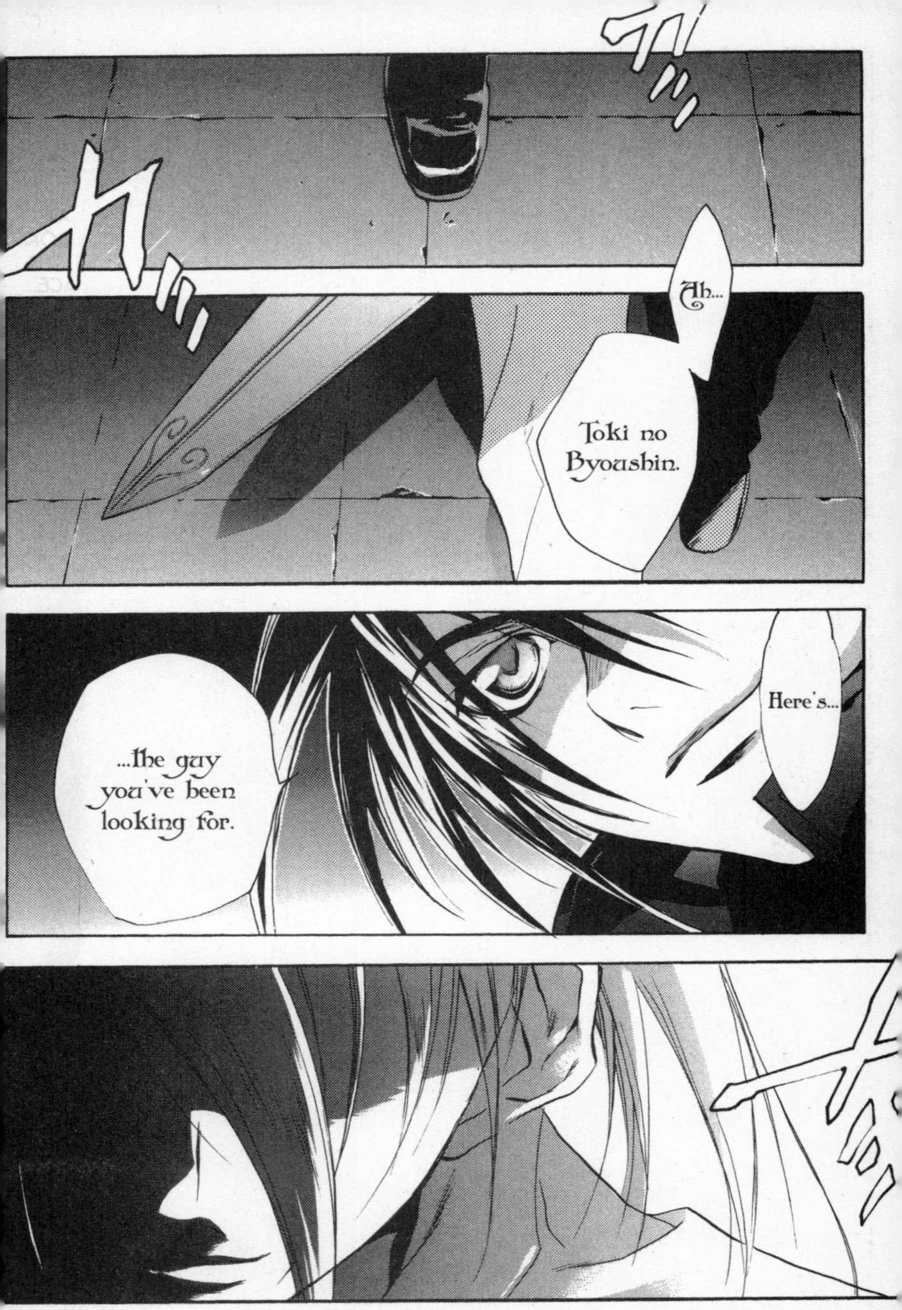
Ah...
Toki no Byoushin.
Here's...
...The guy you've been looking for.

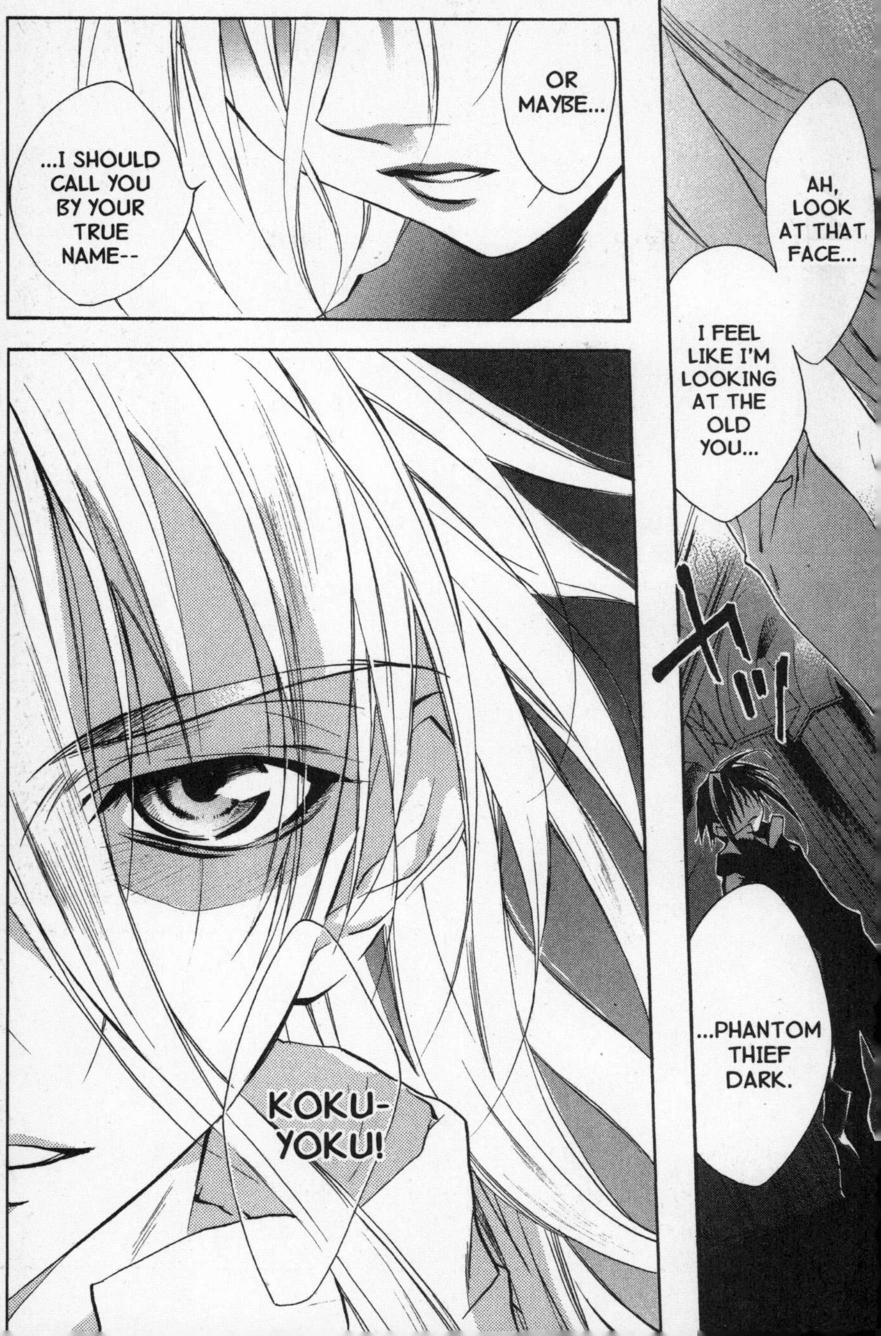
AH, LOOK AT THAT FACE...
I FEEL LIKE I'M LOOKING AT THE OLD YOU...
...PHANTOM THIEF DARK.
OR MAYBE...
...I SHOULD CALL YOU BY YOUR TRUE NAME--
KOKU-YOKU!

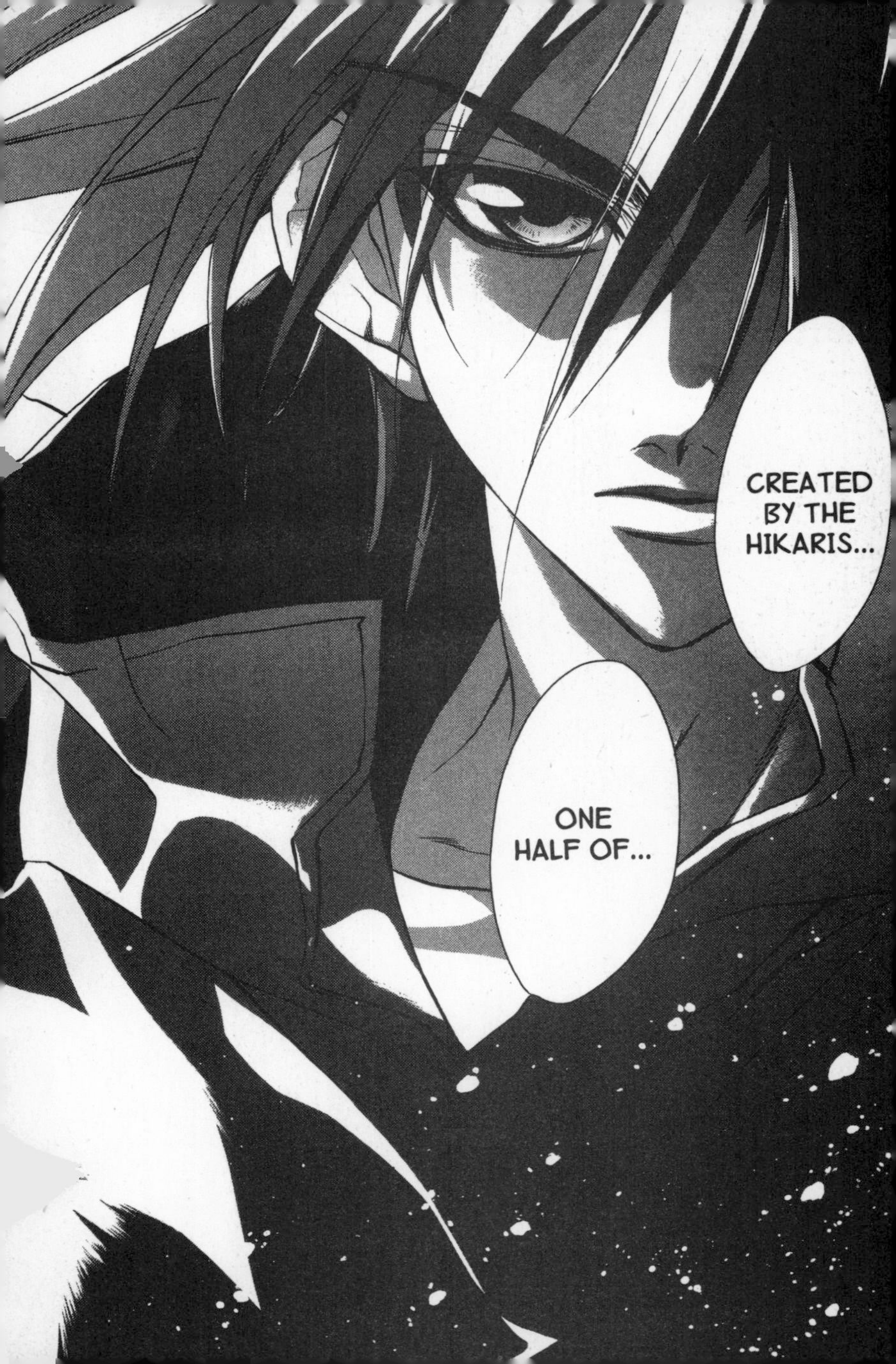
CREATED BY THE HIKARIS...
ONE HALF OF...

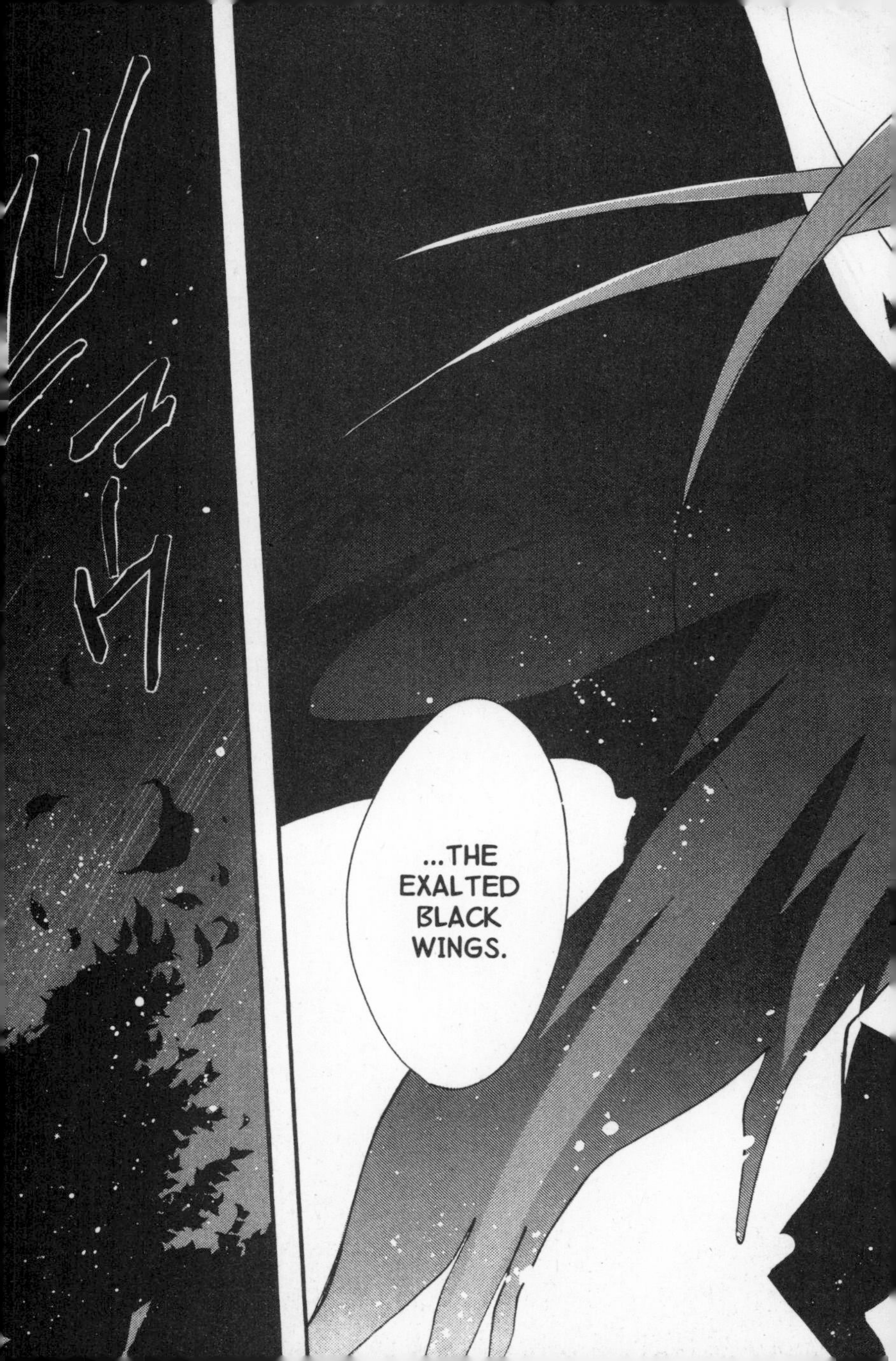
...THE EXALTED BLACK WINGS.

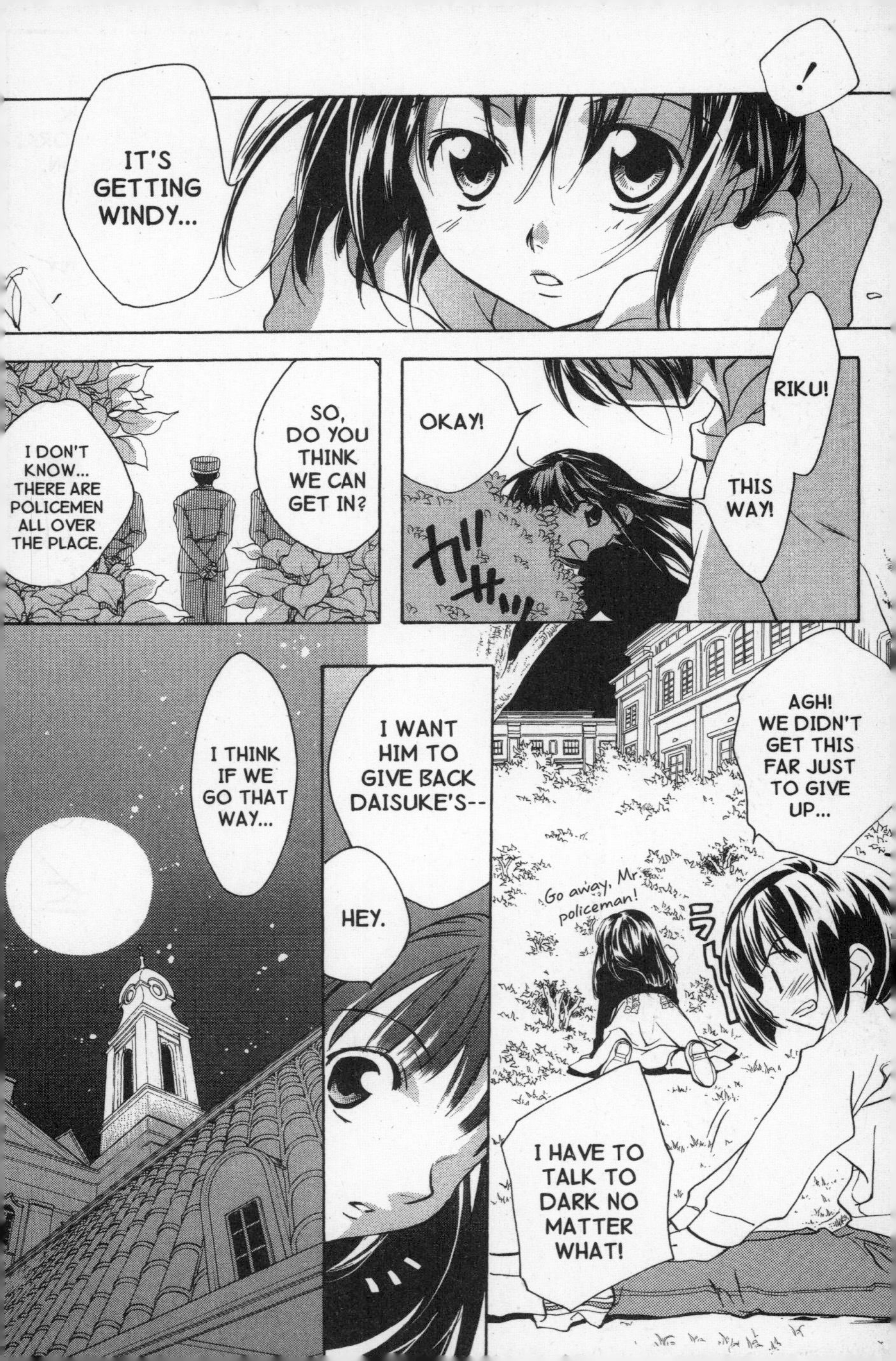
!
IT'S GETTING WINDY...
RIKU!
THIS WAY!
OKAY!
SO, DO YOU THINK WE CAN GET IN?
I DON'T KNOW... THERE ARE POLICEMEN ALL OVER THE PLACE.
AGH! WE DIDN'T GET THIS FAR JUST TO GIVE UP...
Go away, Mr. policeman!
I HAVE TO TALK TO DARK NO MATTER WHAT!
I WANT HIM TO GIVE BACK DAISUKE'S--
HEY.
I THINK IF WE GO THAT WAY...

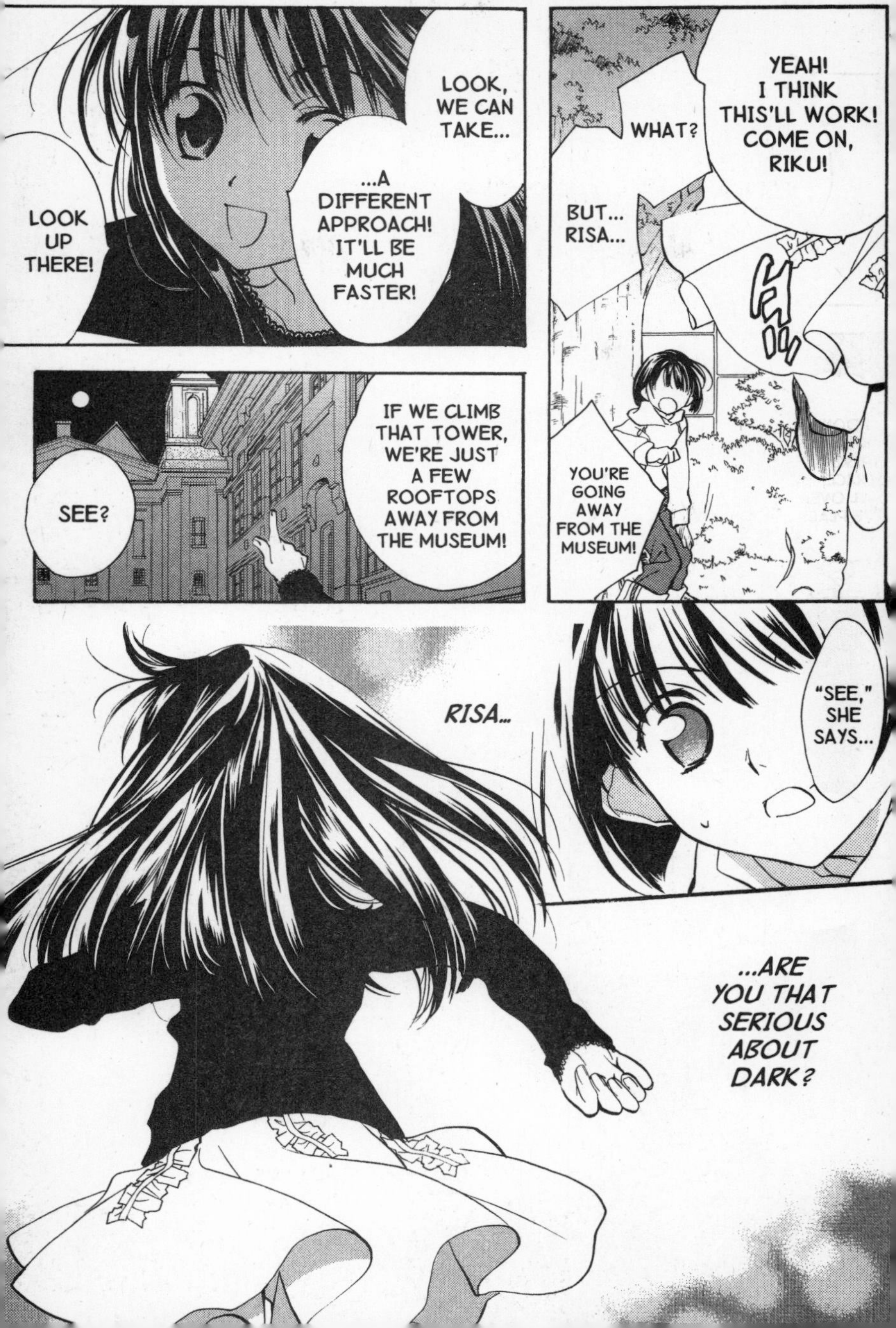
YEAH! I THINK THIS'LL WORK! COME ON, RIKU!
WHAT?
BUT... RISA...
YOU'RE GOING AWAY FROM THE MUSEUM!
LOOK, WE CAN TAKE...
...A DIFFERENT APPROACH! IT'LL BE MUCH FASTER!
LOOK UP THERE!
IF WE CLIMB THAT TOWER, WE'RE JUST A FEW ROOFTOPS AWAY FROM THE MUSEUM!
SEE?
"SEE," SHE SAYS...
RISA...
...ARE YOU THAT SERIOUS ABOUT DARK?

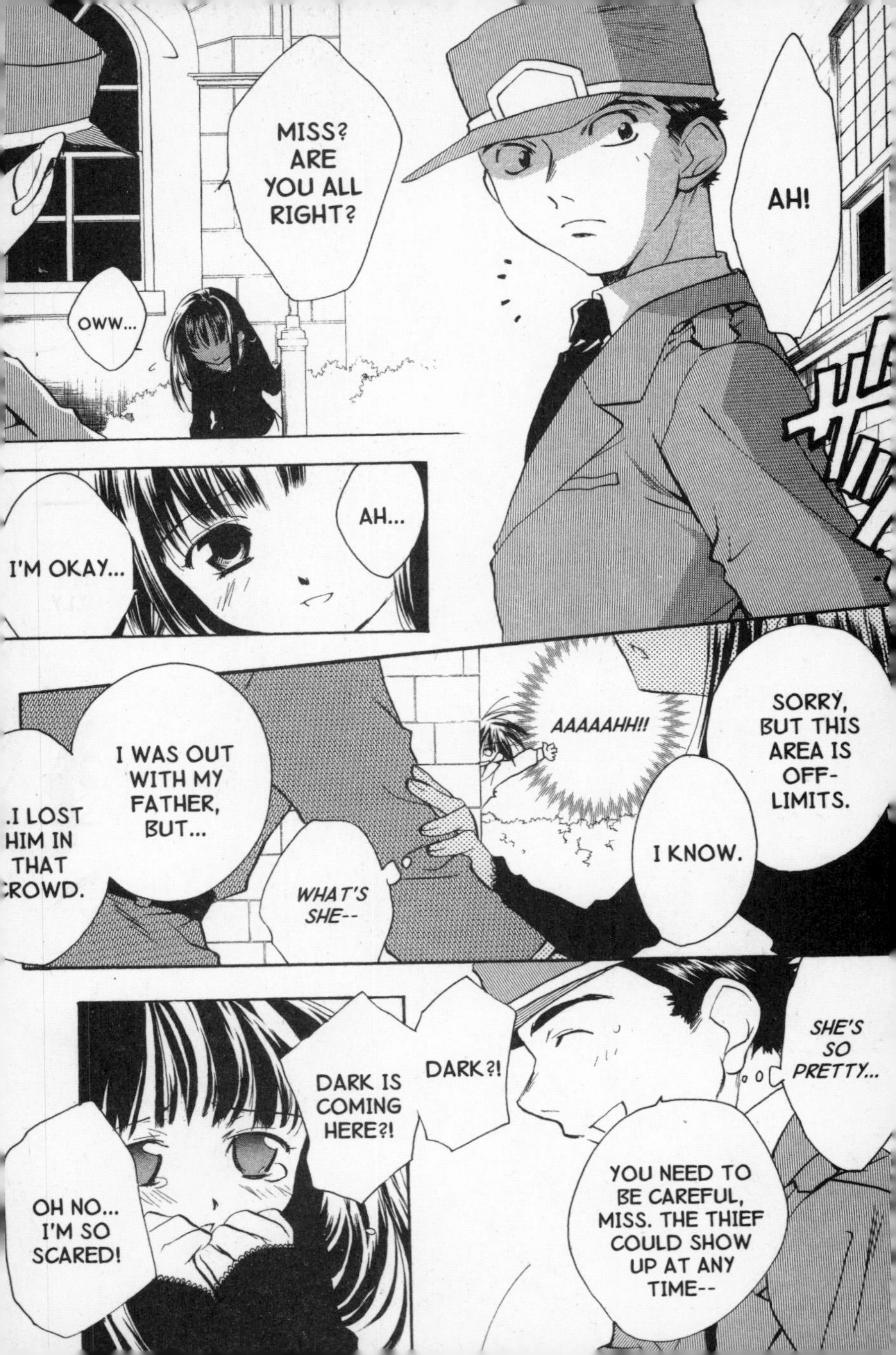

AH!
MISS? ARE YOU ALL RIGHT?
OWW...
AH...
I'M OKAY...
SORRY, BUT THIS AREA IS OFF-LIMITS.
I KNOW.
AAAAAHH!!
WHAT'S SHE--
I WAS OUT WITH MY FATHER, BUT...
.I LOST HIM IN THAT CROWD.
SHE'S SO PRETTY...
YOU NEED TO BE CAREFUL, MISS. THE THIEF COULD SHOW UP AT ANY TIME--
DARK?!
DARK IS COMING HERE?!
OH NO... I'M SO SCARED!

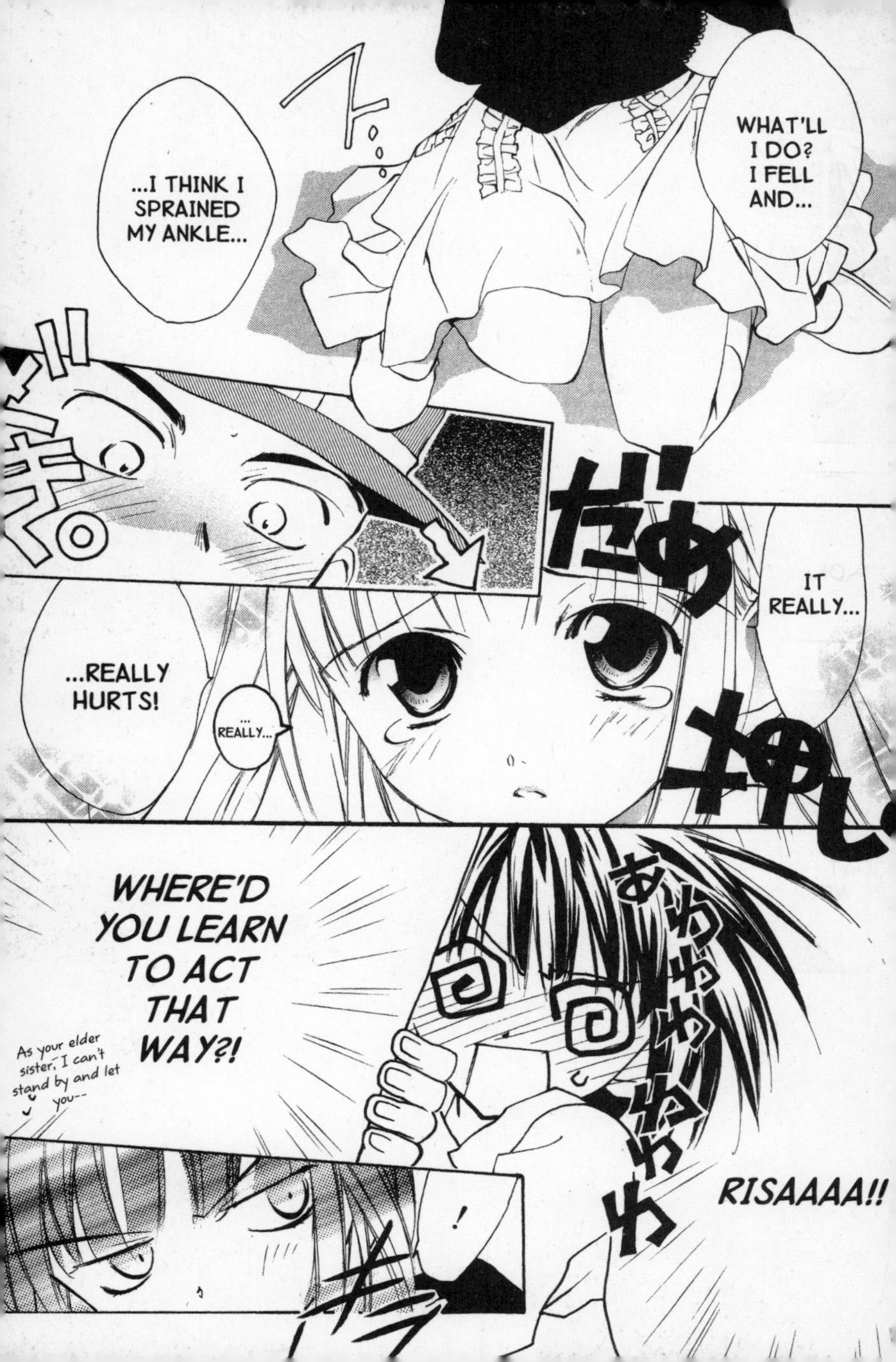
WHAT'LL I DO? I FELL AND...
...I THINK I SPRAINED MY ANKLE...
IT REALLY...
だめ押し
...REALLY...
...REALLY HURTS!
WHERE'D YOU LEARN TO ACT THAT WAY?!
As your elder sister, I can't stand by and let you--
RISAAAA!!
!

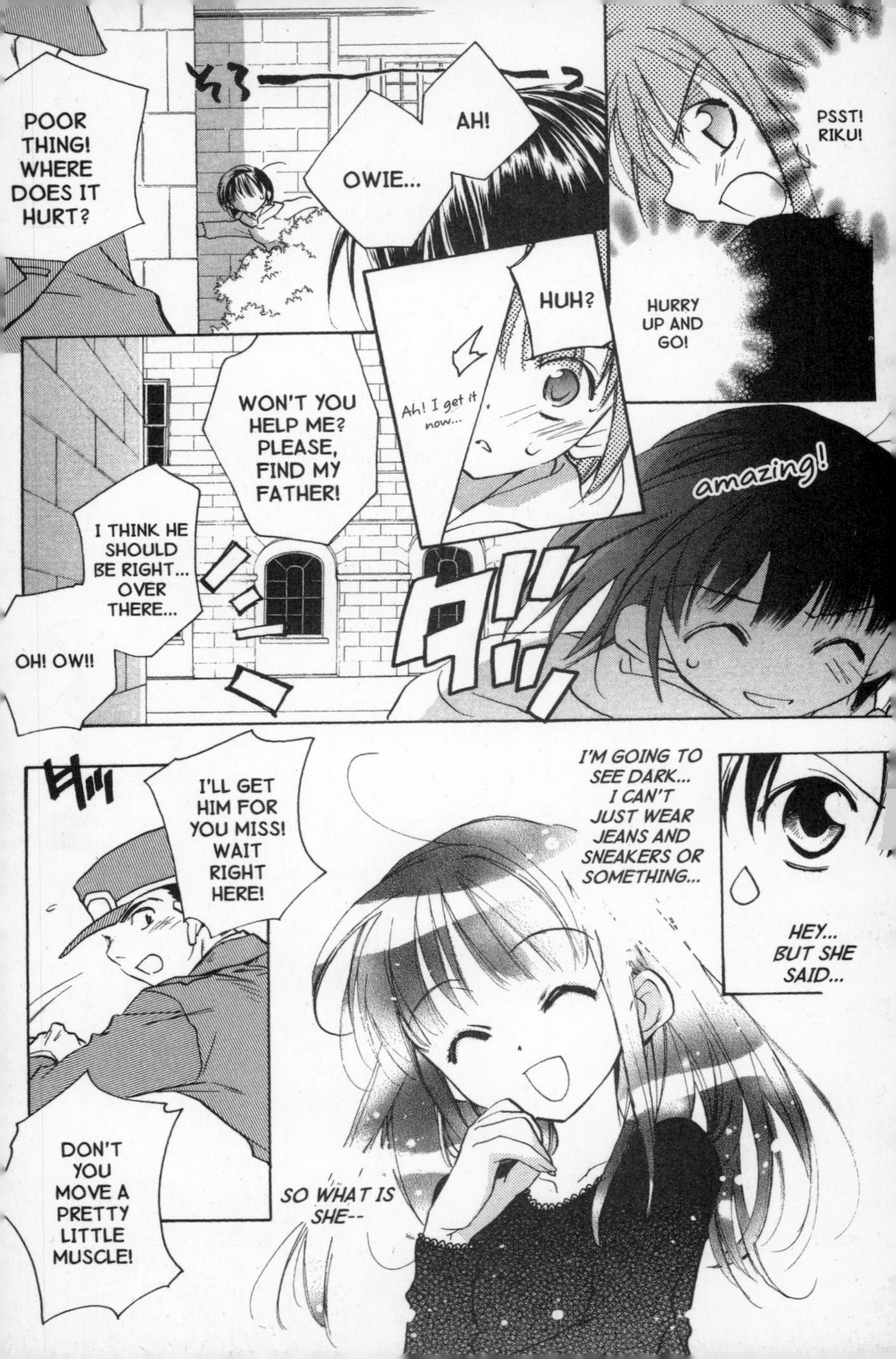
PSST! RIKU!
HURRY UP AND GO!
AH!
OWIE...
POOR THING! WHERE DOES IT HURT?
HUH?
Ah! I get it now...
amazing!
WON'T YOU HELP ME? PLEASE, FIND MY FATHER!
I THINK HE SHOULD BE RIGHT... OVER THERE...
OH! OW!!
HEY... BUT SHE SAID...
I'M GOING TO SEE DARK... I CAN'T JUST WEAR JEANS AND SNEAKERS OR SOMETHING...
SO WHAT IS SHE--
I'LL GET HIM FOR YOU MISS! WAIT RIGHT HERE!
DON'T YOU MOVE A PRETTY LITTLE MUSCLE!

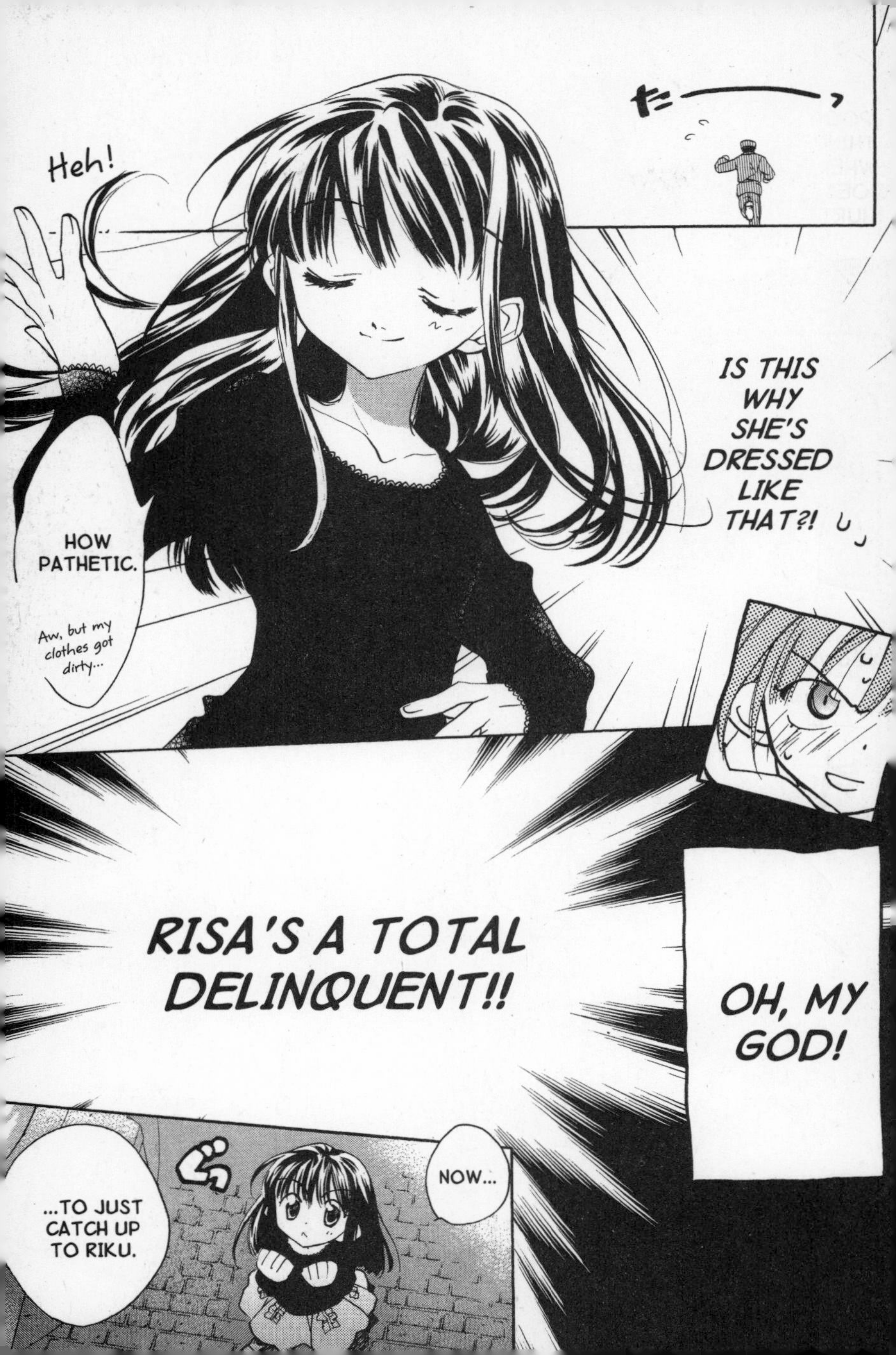

た——っ
Heh!
HOW PATHETIC.
Aw, but my clothes got dirty...
IS THIS WHY SHE'S DRESSED LIKE THAT?!
OH, MY GOD!
RISA'S A TOTAL DELINQUENT!!
NOW...
...TO JUST CATCH UP TO RIKU.

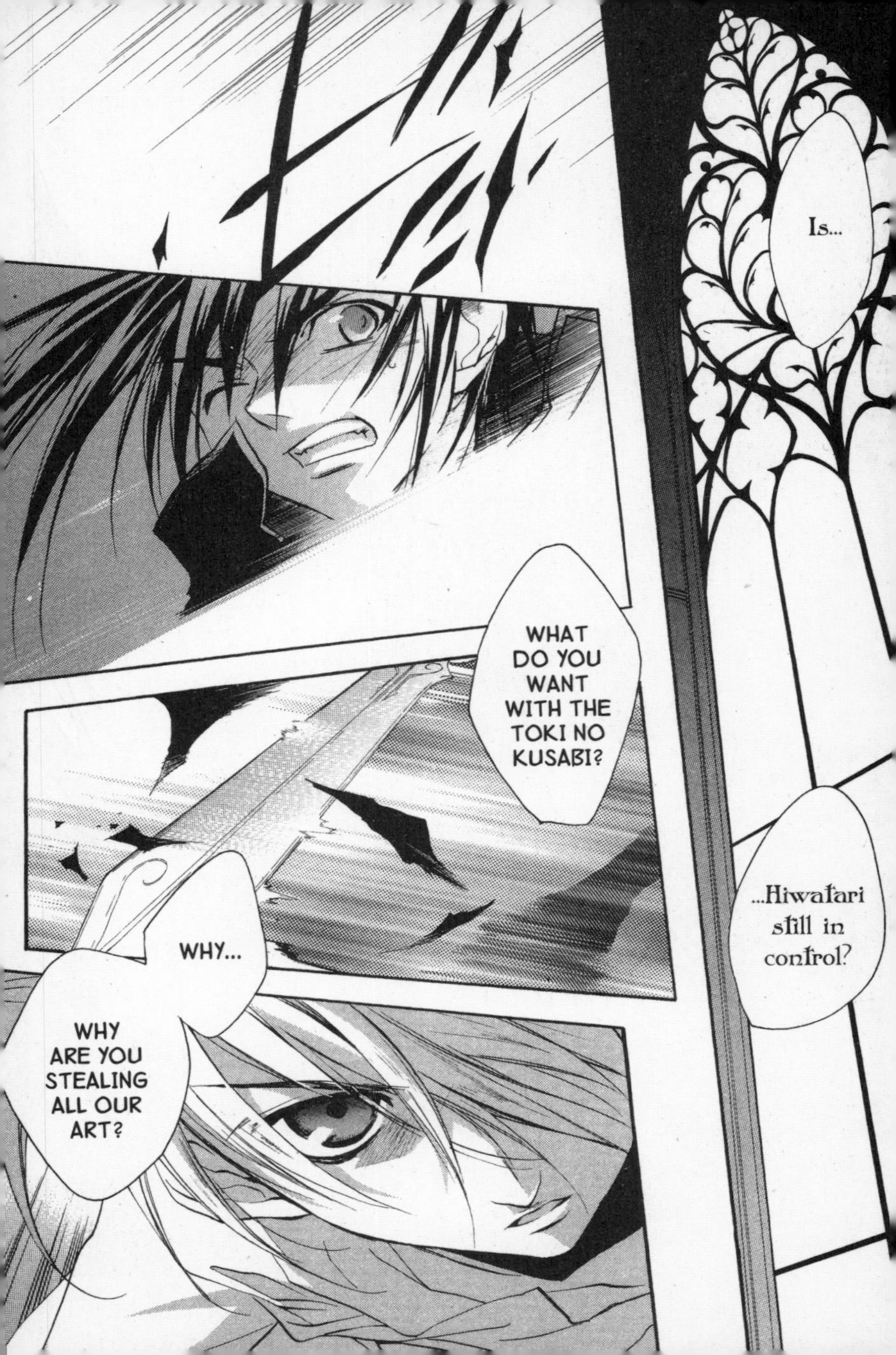
Is...
...Hiwatari still in control?
WHAT DO YOU WANT WITH THE TOKI NO KUSABI?
WHY...
WHY ARE YOU STEALING ALL OUR ART?

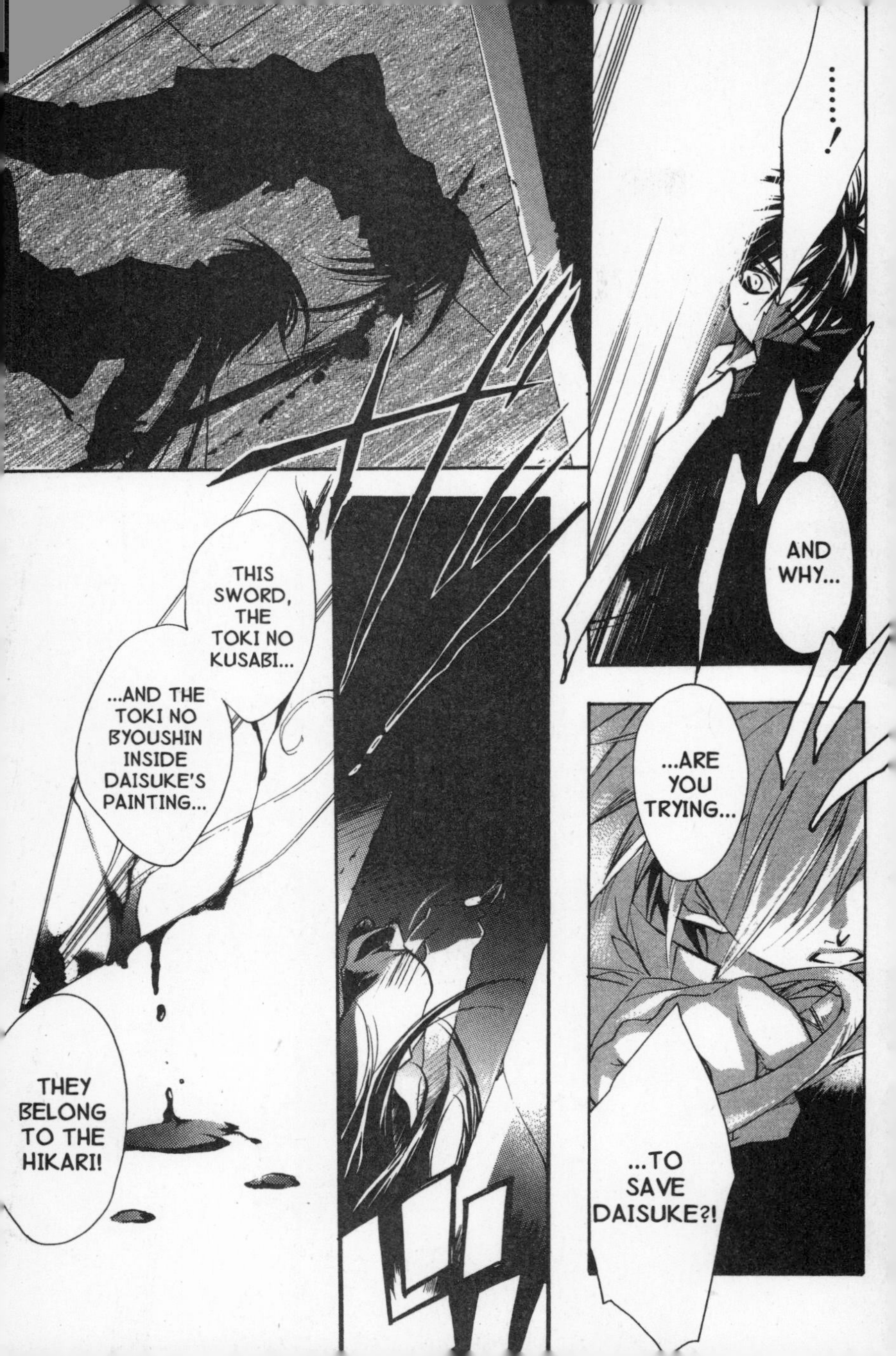
......!
AND WHY...
...ARE YOU TRYING...
...TO SAVE DAISUKE?!
THIS SWORD, THE TOKI NO KUSABI...
...AND THE TOKI NO BYOUSHIN INSIDE DAISUKE'S PAINTING...
THEY BELONG TO THE HIKARI!

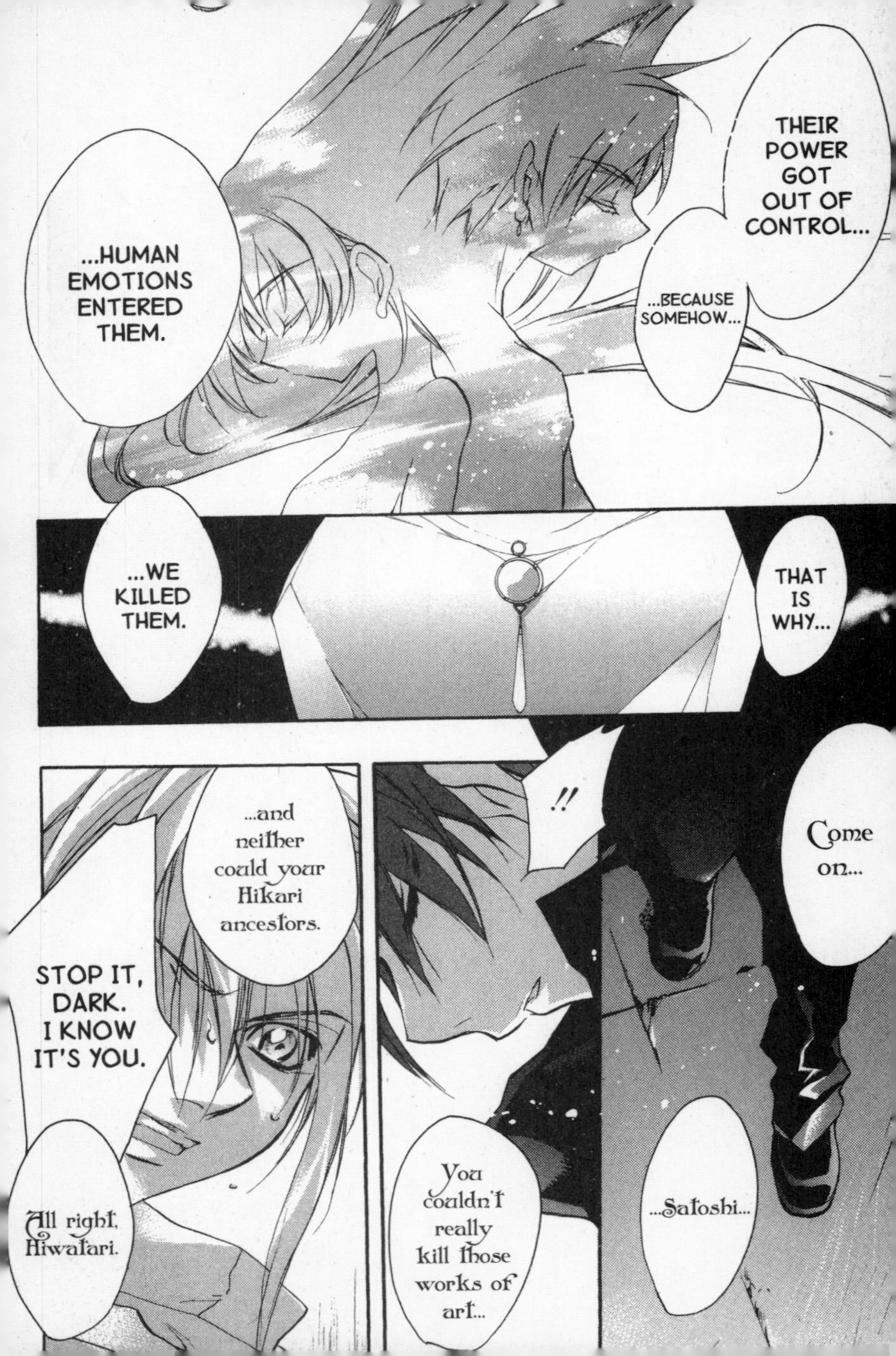
THEIR POWER GOT OUT OF CONTROL...
...BECAUSE SOMEHOW...
...HUMAN EMOTIONS ENTERED THEM.
THAT IS WHY...
...WE KILLED THEM.
Come on...
!!
...Satoshi...
You couldn't really kill those works of art...
...and neither could your Hikari ancestors.
STOP IT, DARK. I KNOW IT'S YOU.
All right, Hiwatari.

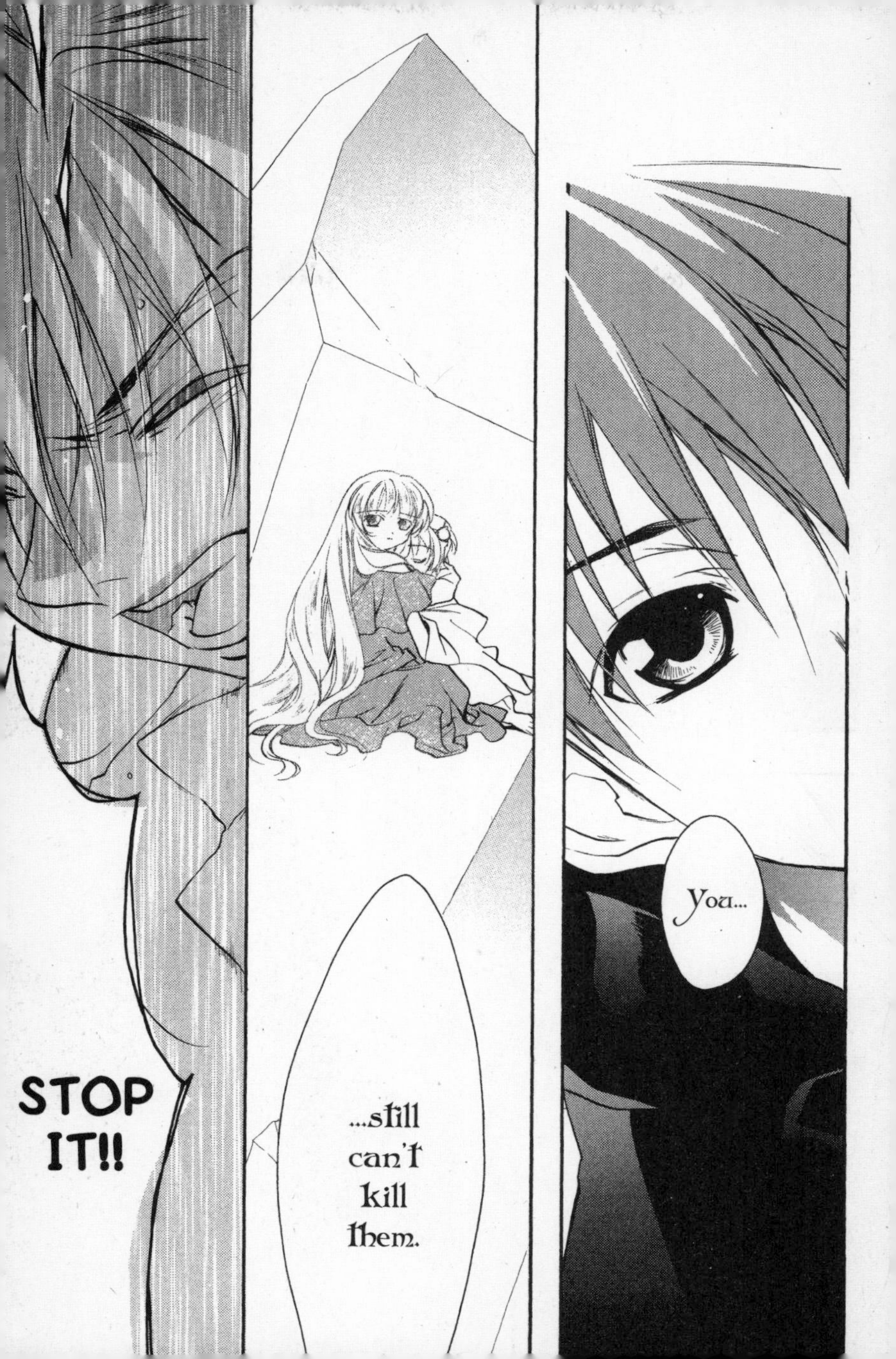
you...
...still can't kill them.
STOP IT!!

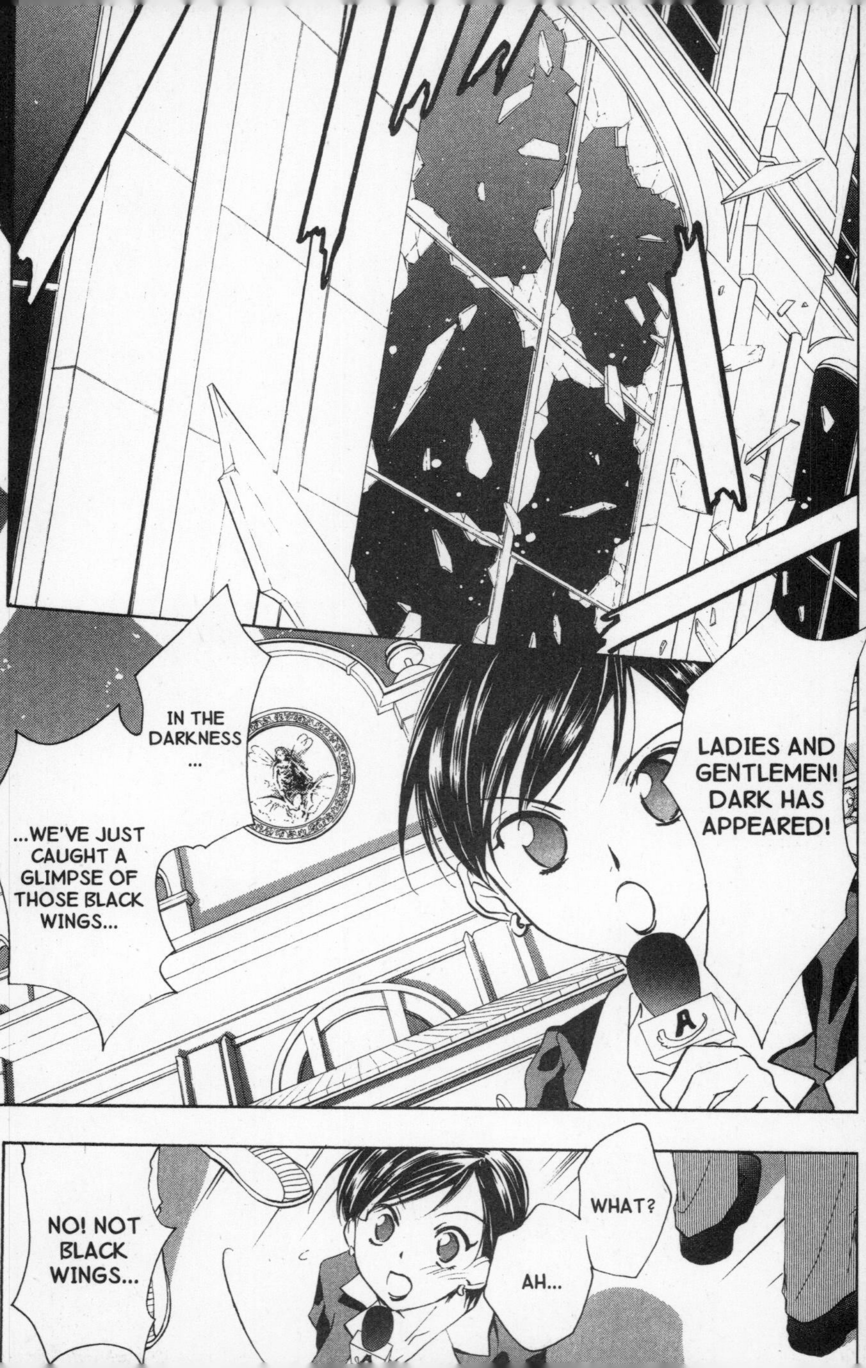
LADIES AND GENTLEMEN! DARK HAS APPEARED!
IN THE DARKNESS ...
...WE'VE JUST CAUGHT A GLIMPSE OF THOSE BLACK WINGS...
WHAT?
NO! NOT BLACK WINGS...
AH...

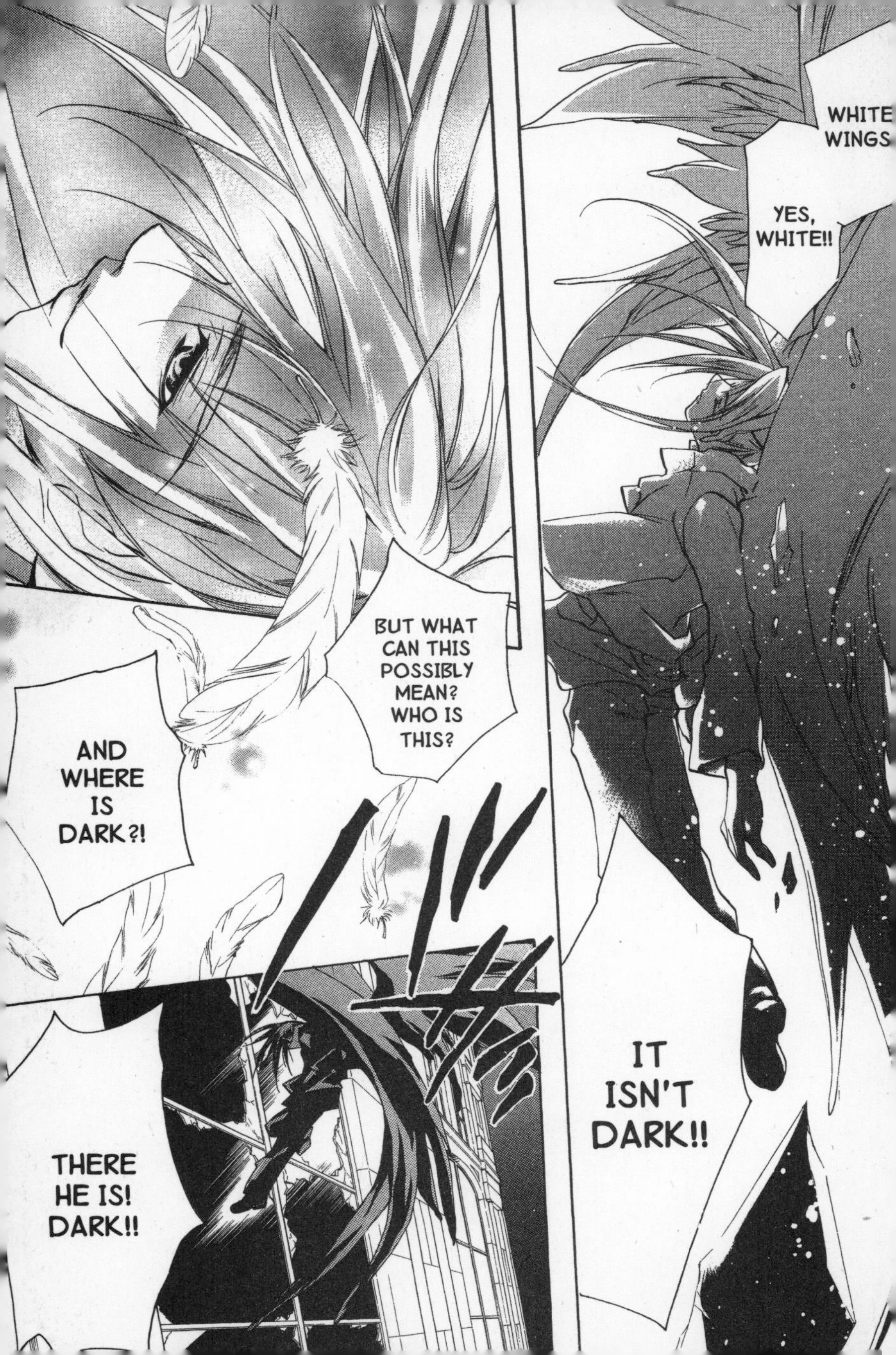
WHITE WINGS
YES, WHITE!!
IT ISN'T DARK!!
BUT WHAT CAN THIS POSSIBLY MEAN? WHO IS THIS?
AND WHERE IS DARK?!
THERE HE IS! DARK!!

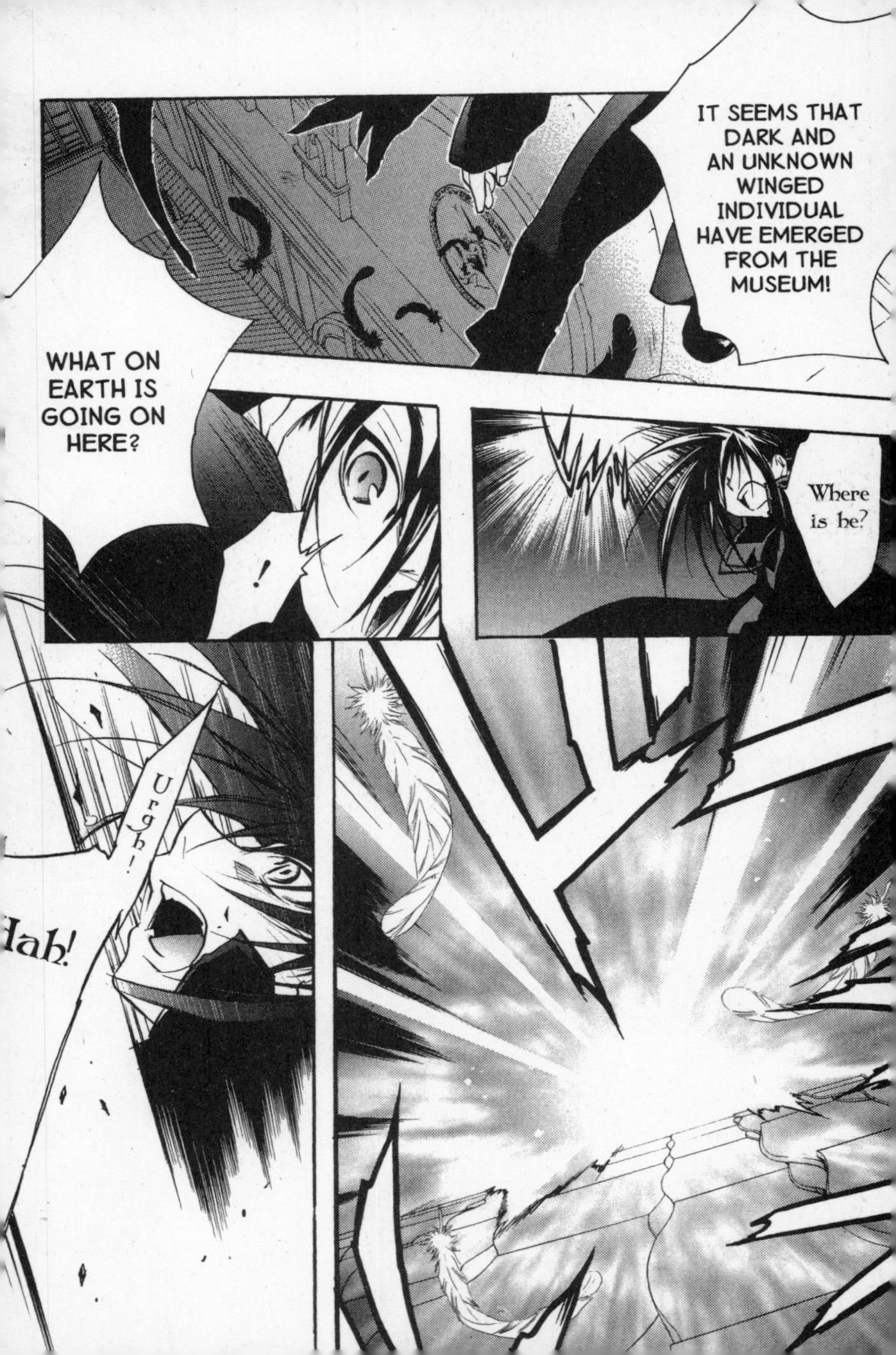
IT SEEMS THAT DARK AND AN UNKNOWN WINGED INDIVIDUAL HAVE EMERGED FROM THE MUSEUM!
Where is he?
WHAT ON EARTH IS GOING ON HERE?
!
Urgh!

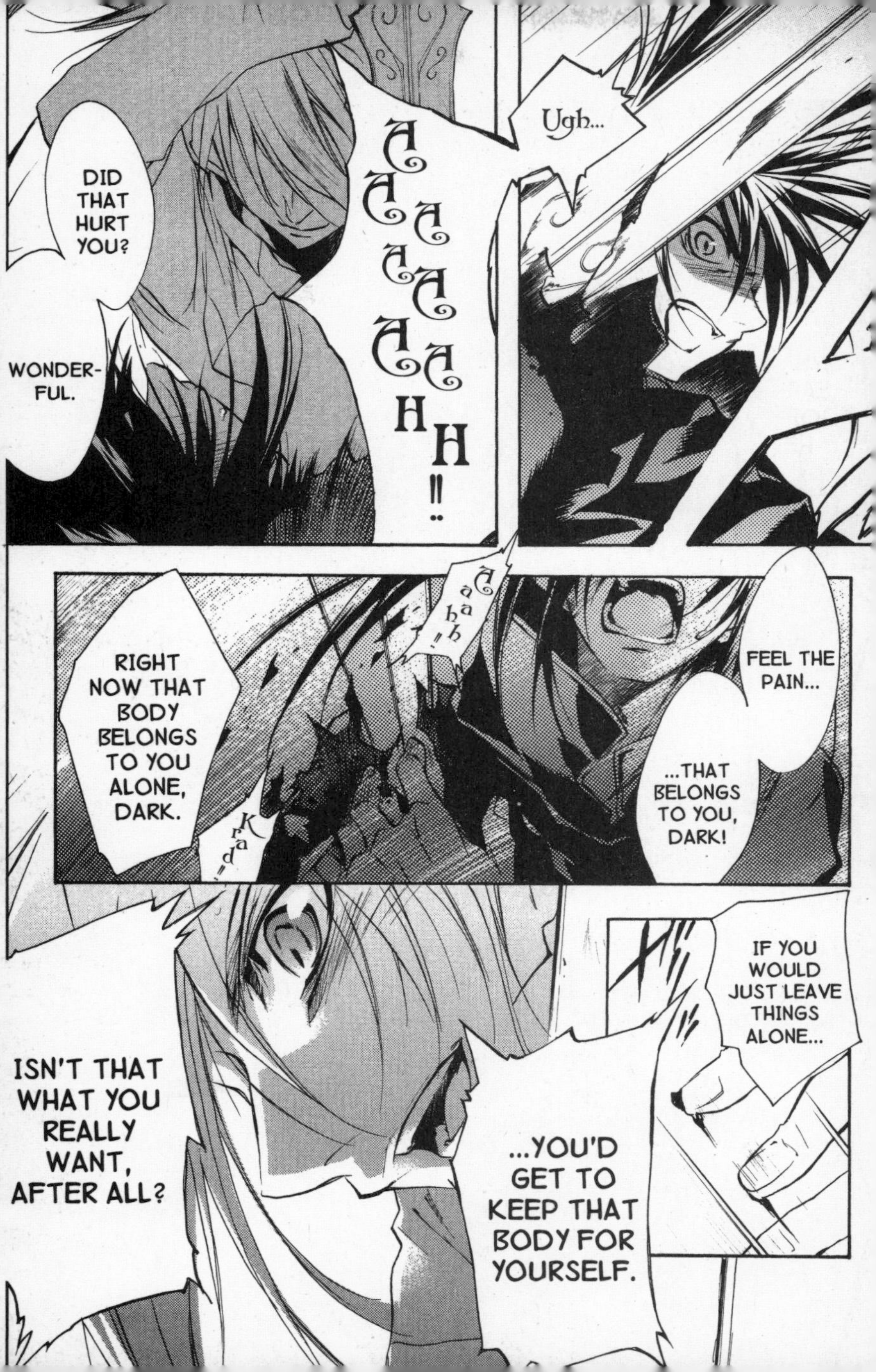
Ugh...
AAAAAAAH!!
DID THAT HURT YOU?
WONDERFUL.
FEEL THE PAIN...
...THAT BELONGS TO YOU, DARK!
Aaahh!!
Krad!!
RIGHT NOW THAT BODY BELONGS TO YOU ALONE, DARK.
IF YOU WOULD JUST LEAVE THINGS ALONE...
...YOU'D GET TO KEEP THAT BODY FOR YOURSELF.
ISN'T THAT WHAT YOU REALLY WANT, AFTER ALL?

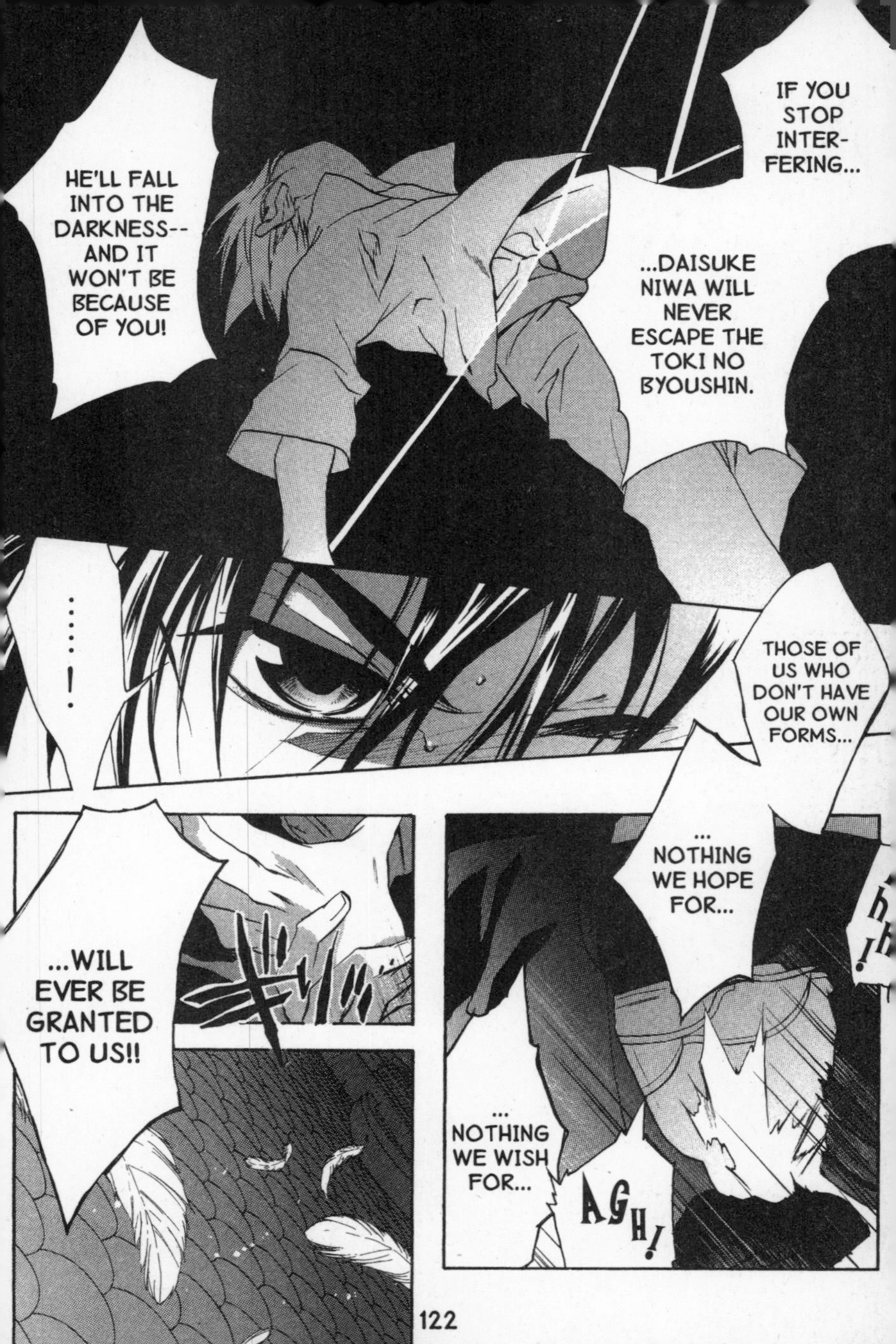
IF YOU STOP INTER-FERING...
...DAISUKE NIWA WILL NEVER ESCAPE THE TOKI NO BYOUSHIN.
HE'LL FALL INTO THE DARKNESS-- AND IT WON'T BE BECAUSE OF YOU!
THOSE OF US WHO DON'T HAVE OUR OWN FORMS...
......!
... NOTHING WE HOPE FOR...
... NOTHING WE WISH FOR...
AGH!
...WILL EVER BE GRANTED TO US!!

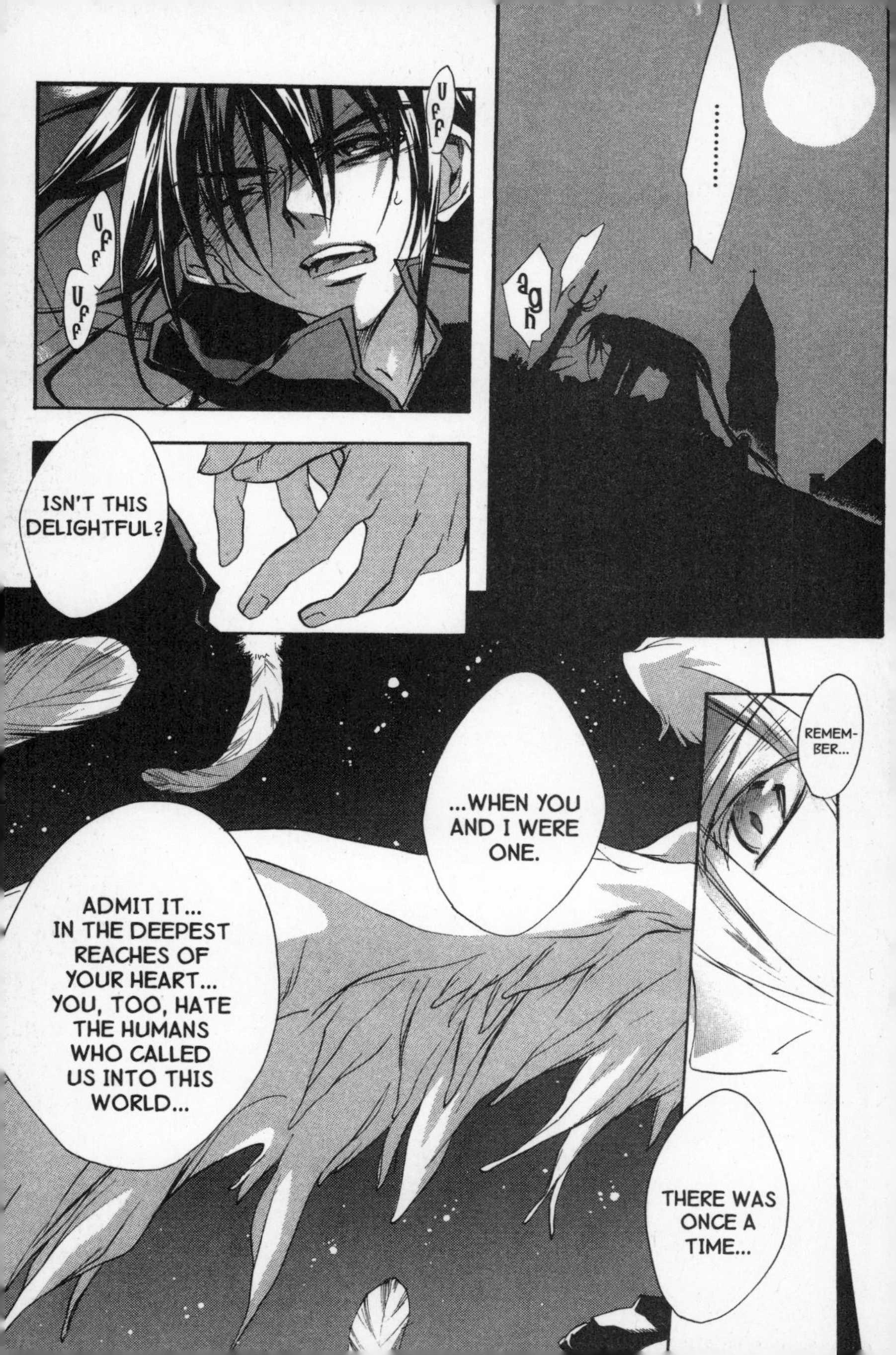
......
agh
Uff
Uff
Uff
ISN'T THIS DELIGHTFUL?
REMEMBER...
THERE WAS ONCE A TIME...
...WHEN YOU AND I WERE ONE.
ADMIT IT... IN THE DEEPEST REACHES OF YOUR HEART... YOU, TOO, HATE THE HUMANS WHO CALLED US INTO THIS WORLD...

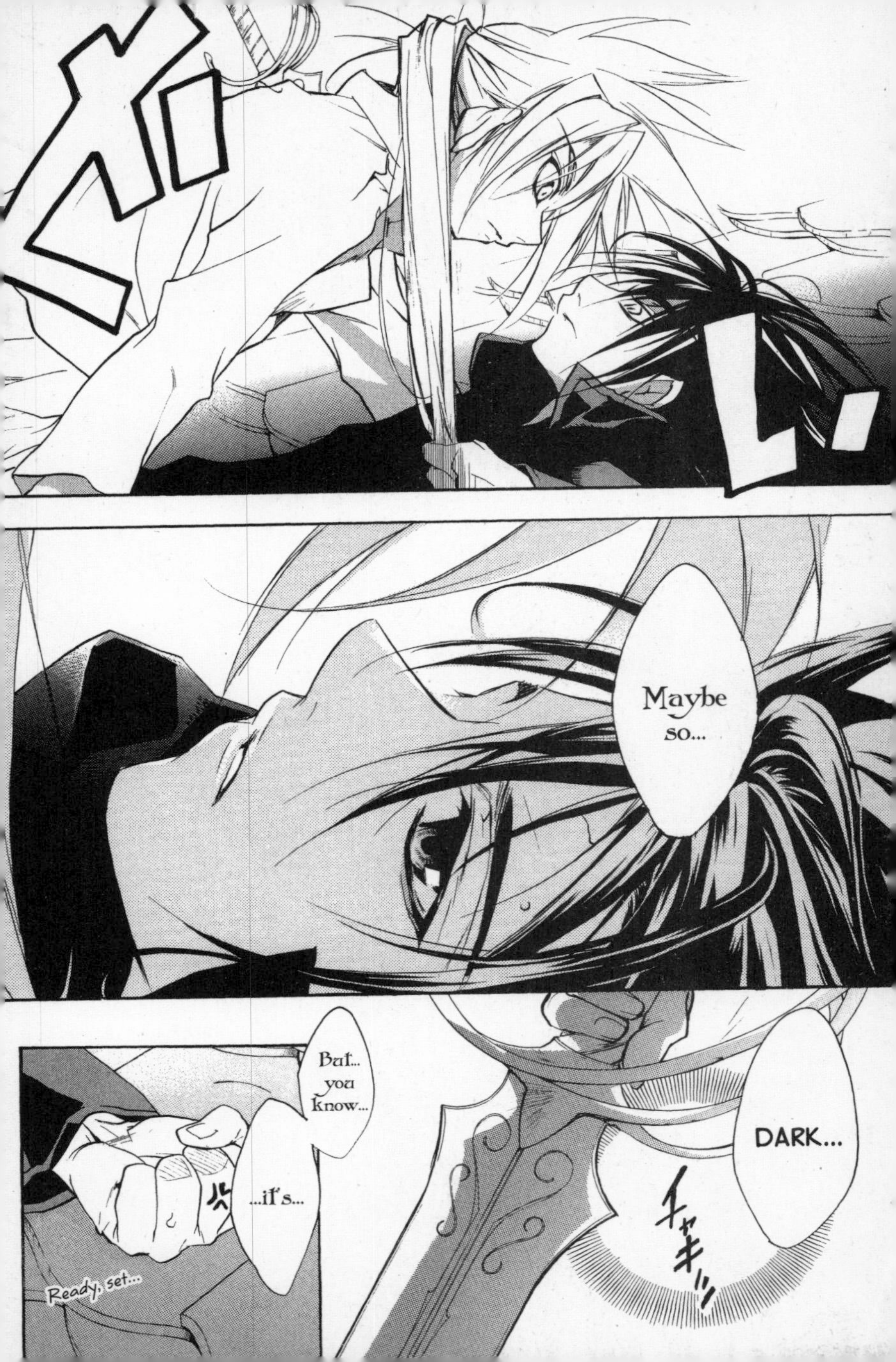
Maybe so...
DARK...
But... you know...
...it's...
Ready, set...

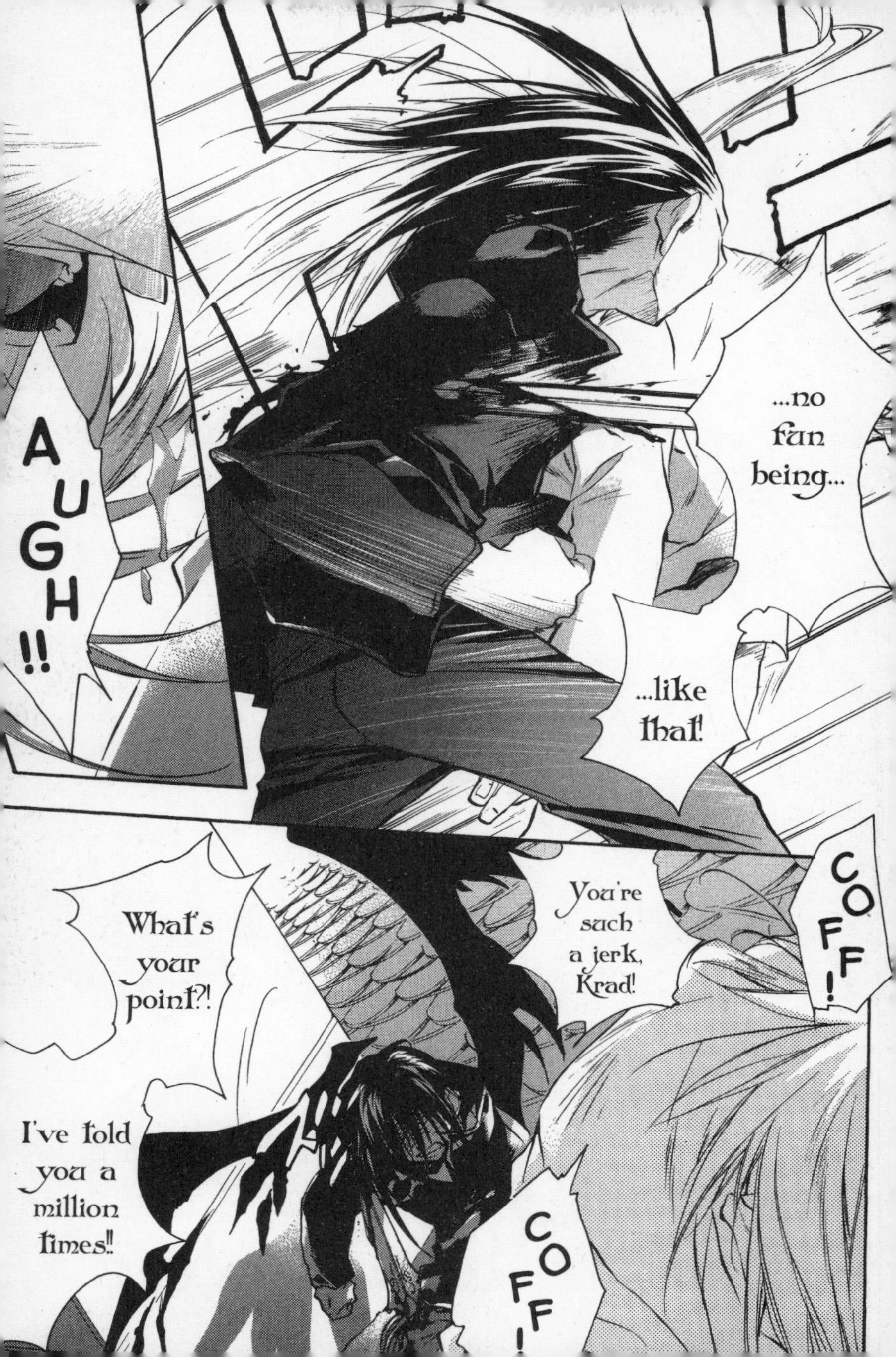
...no fun being...
...like that!
AUGH!!
COFF!
You're such a jerk, Krad!
What's your point?!
I've told you a million times!!
COFF!

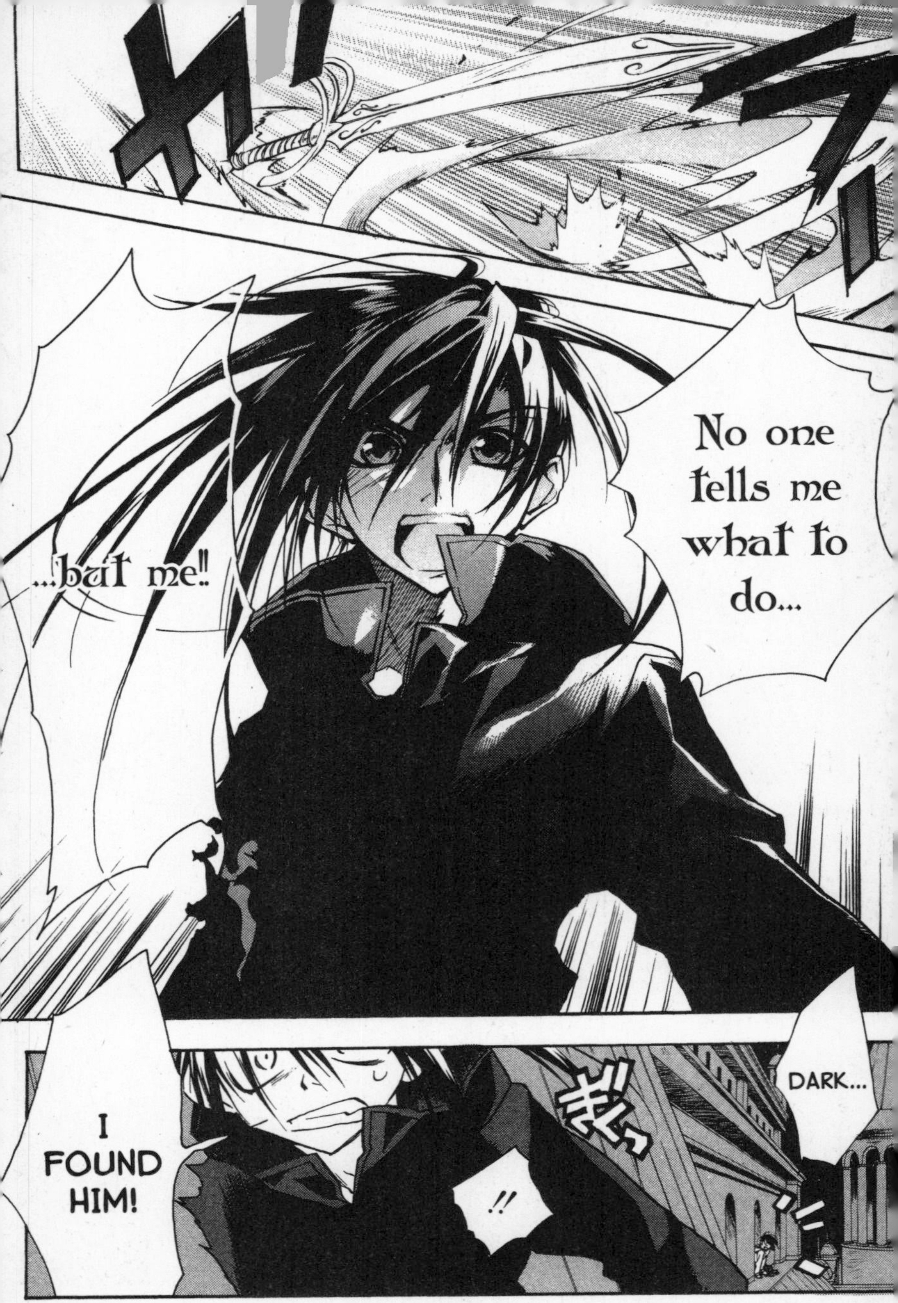
No one tells me what to do...
...but me!!
DARK...
I FOUND HIM!
!!

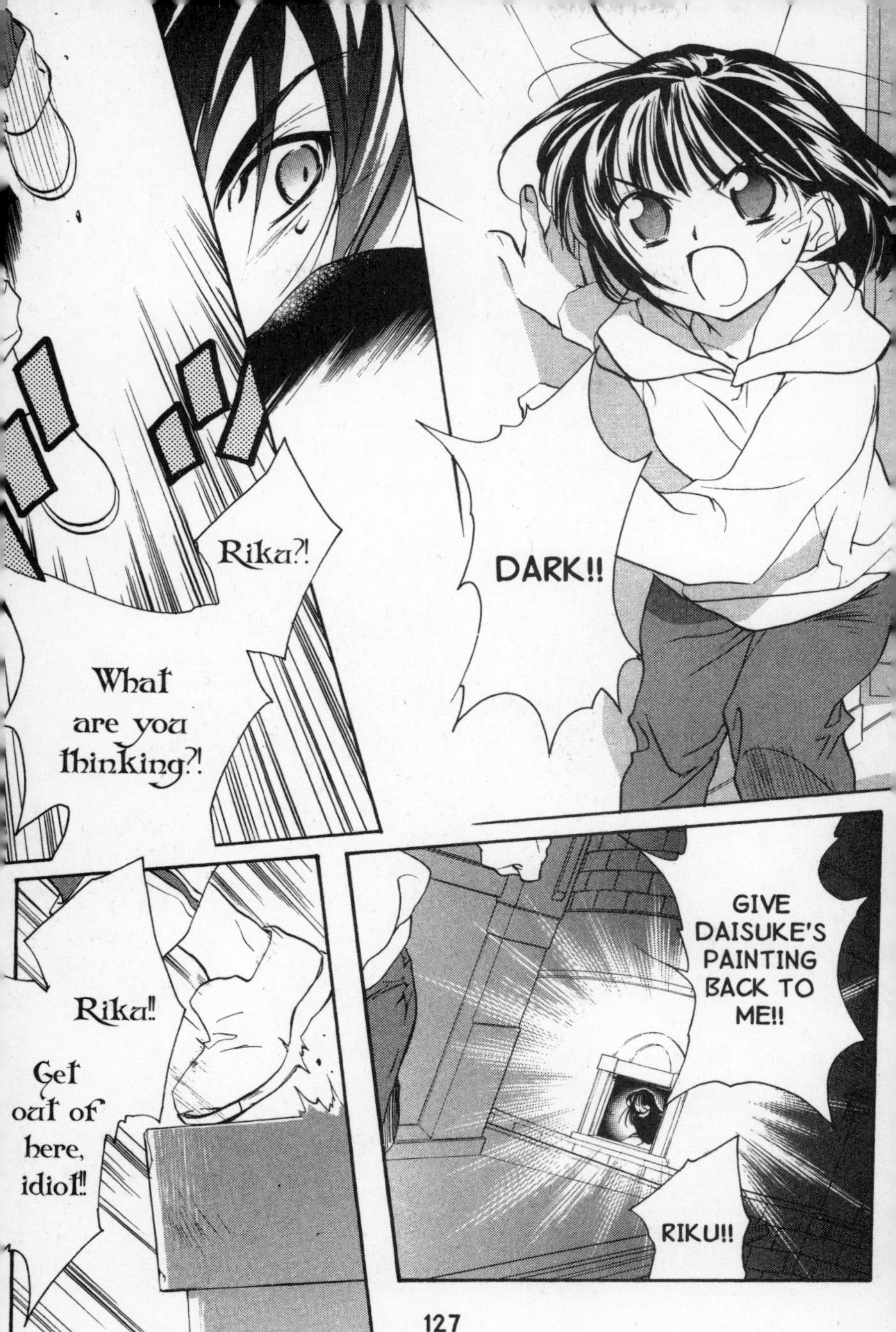
DARK!!
Riku?!
What are you thinking?!
GIVE DAISUKE'S PAINTING BACK TO ME!!
RIKU!!
Riku!!
Get out of here, idiot!!

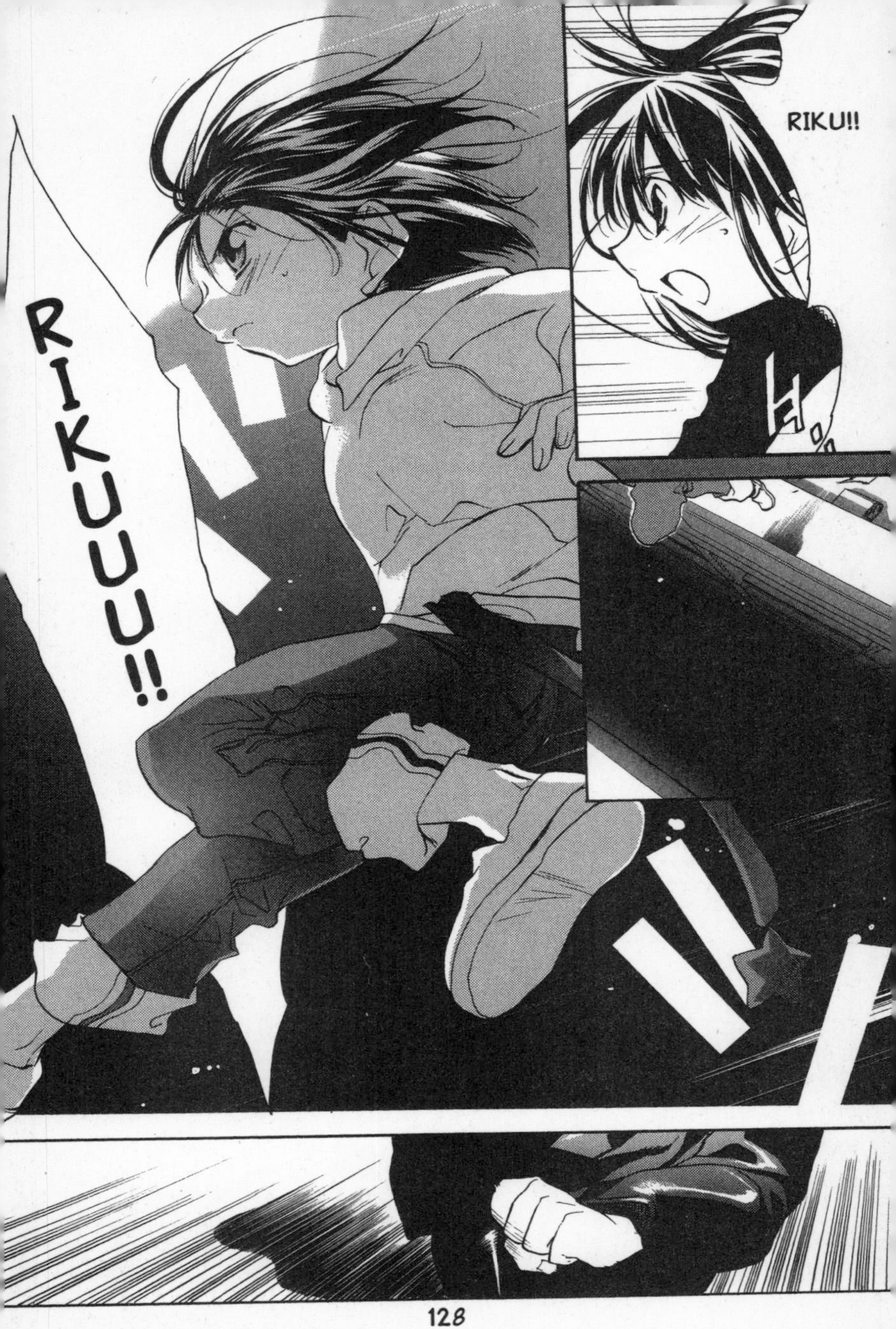
RIKU!!
RIKUUU!!

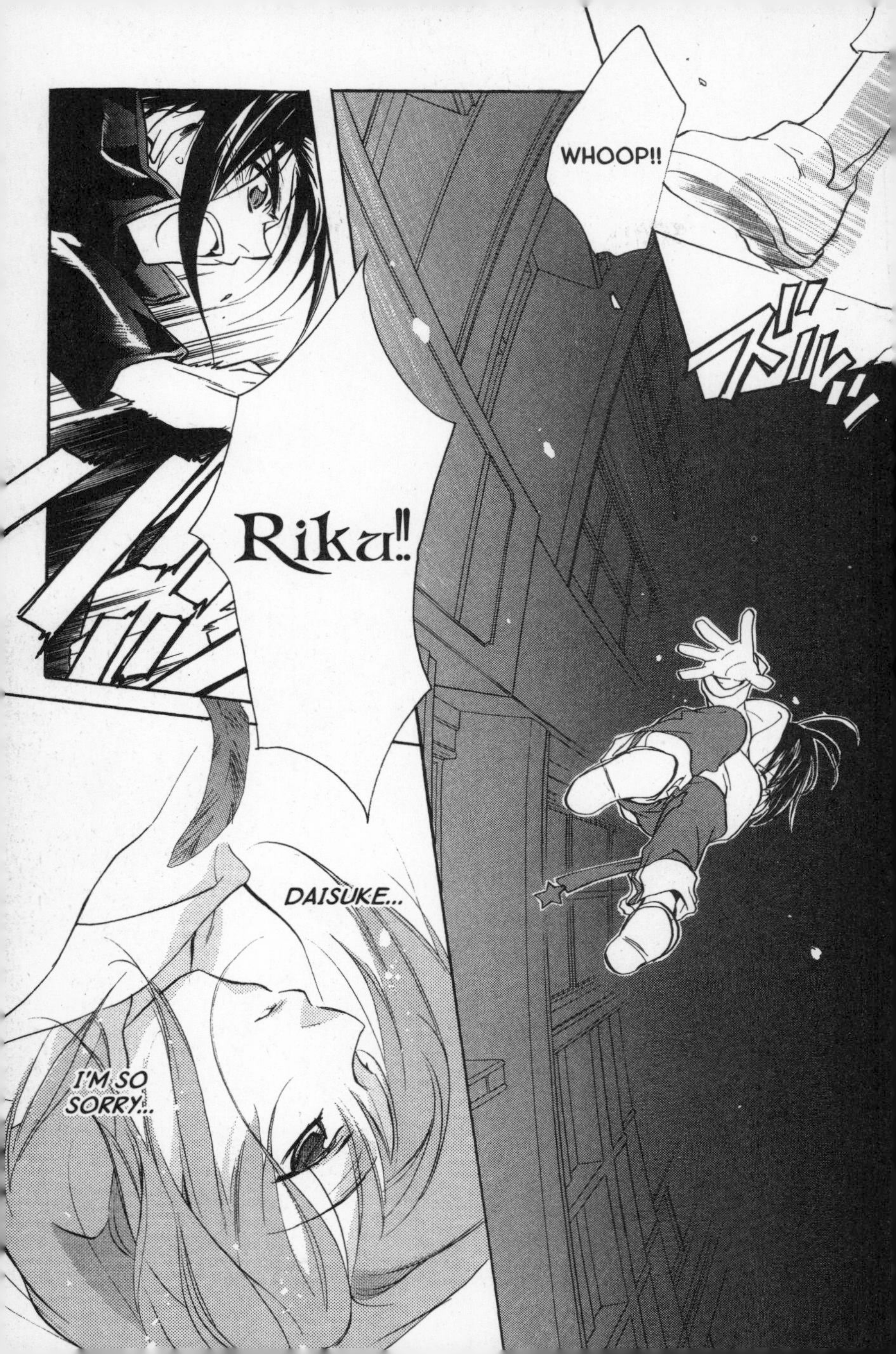
WHOOP!!
Riku!!
DAISUKE...
I'M SO SORRY...

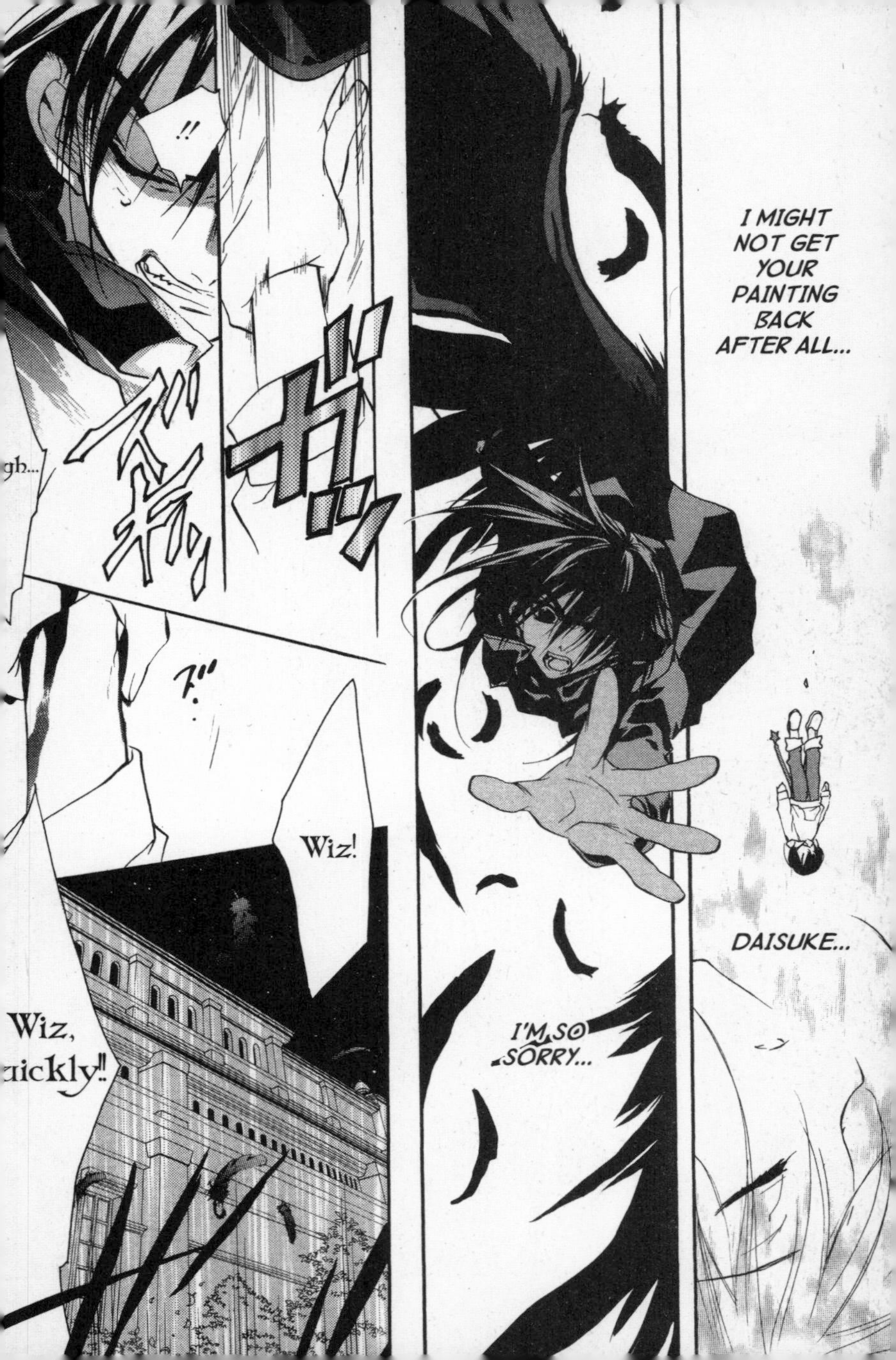
I MIGHT NOT GET YOUR PAINTING BACK AFTER ALL...
DAISUKE...
I'M SO SORRY...
!!
gh...
Wiz!
Wiz, uickly!!

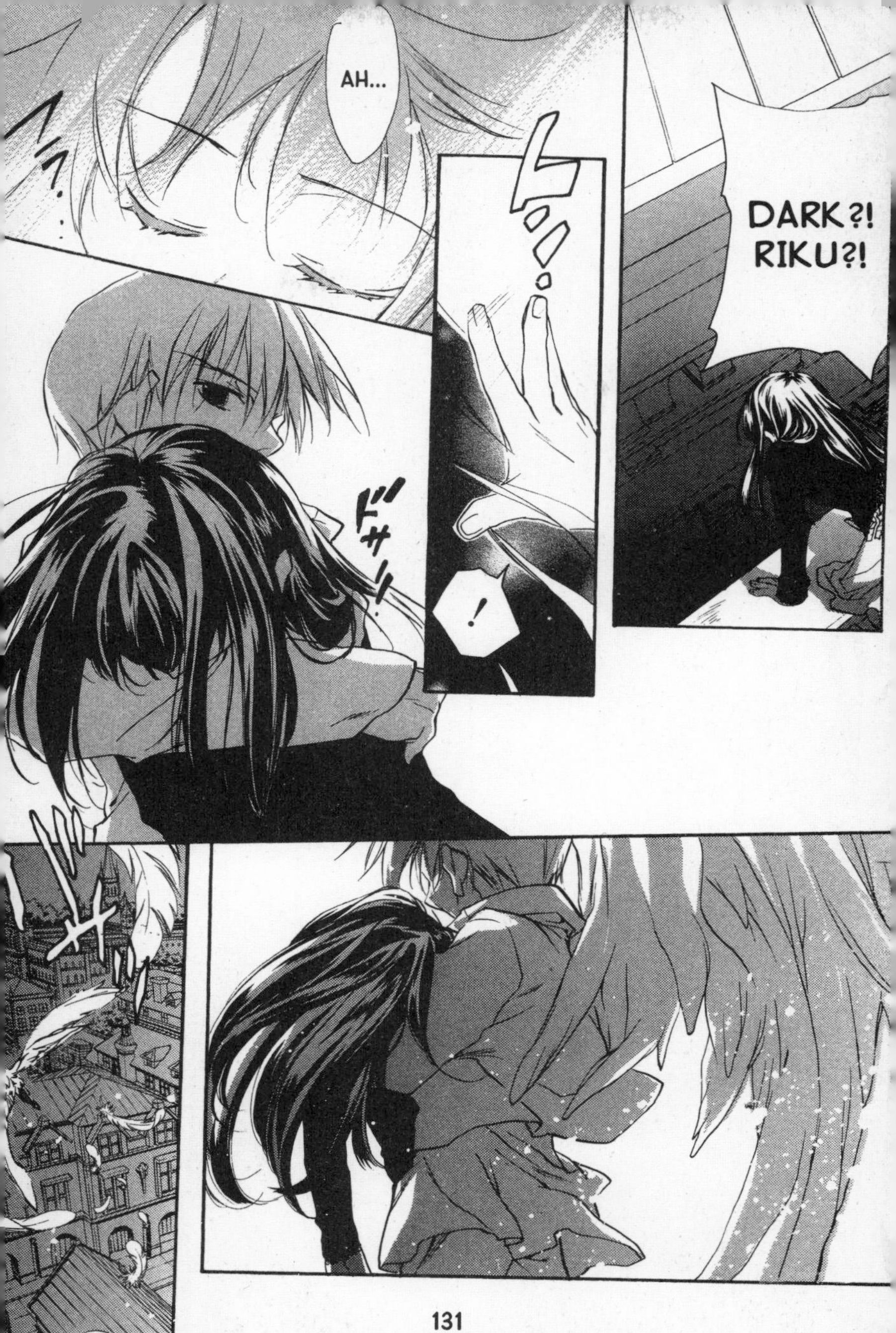
DARK?!
RIKU?!
AH...
!

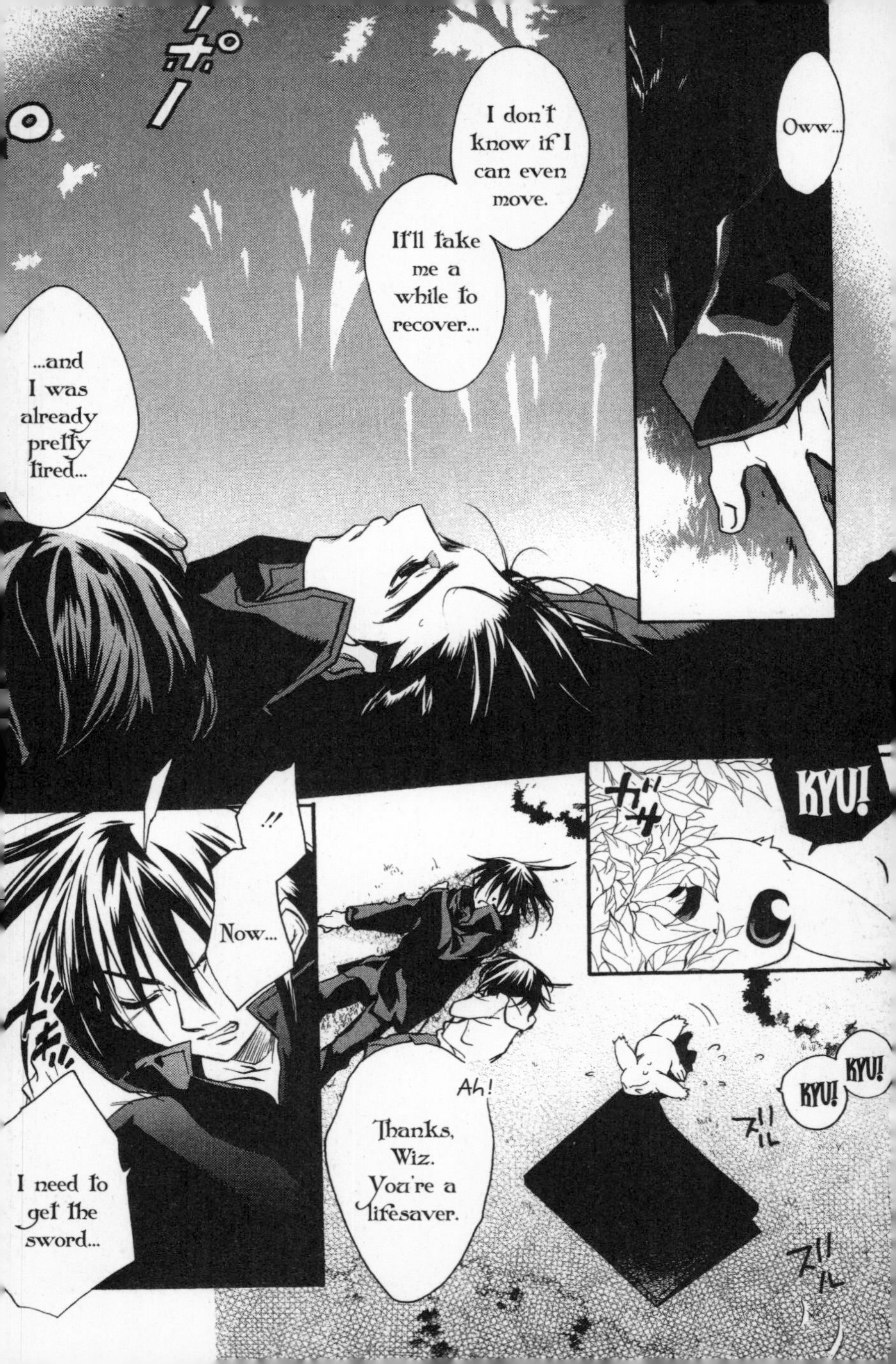
Oww...
I don't know if I can even move.
It'll take me a while to recover...
...and I was already pretty tired...
Now...
I need to get the sword...
!!
KYU!
KYU!
KYU!
Ah!
Thanks, Wiz. You're a lifesaver.

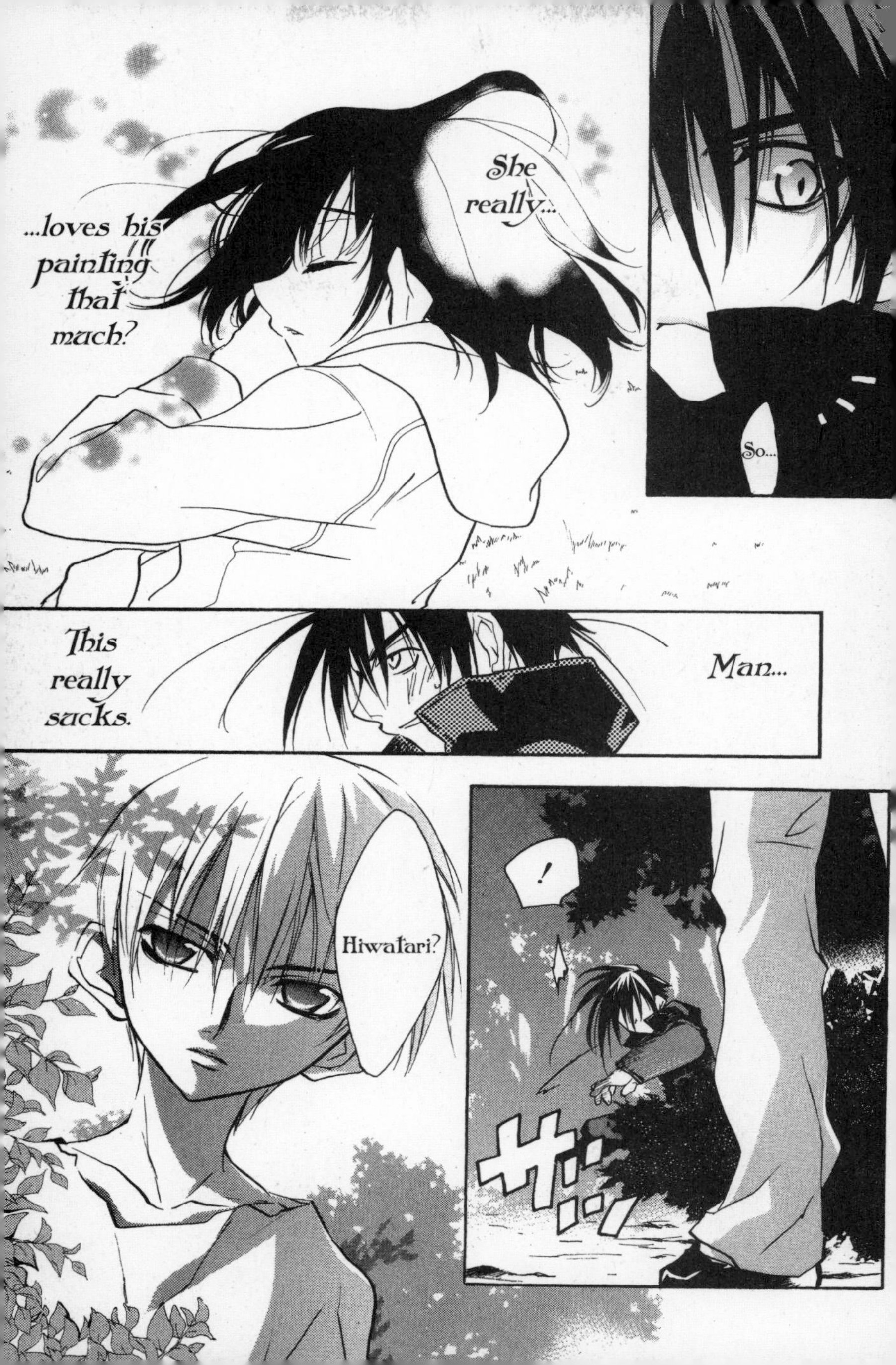
So...
She really...
...loves his painting that much?
Man...
This really sucks.
!
Hiwatari?

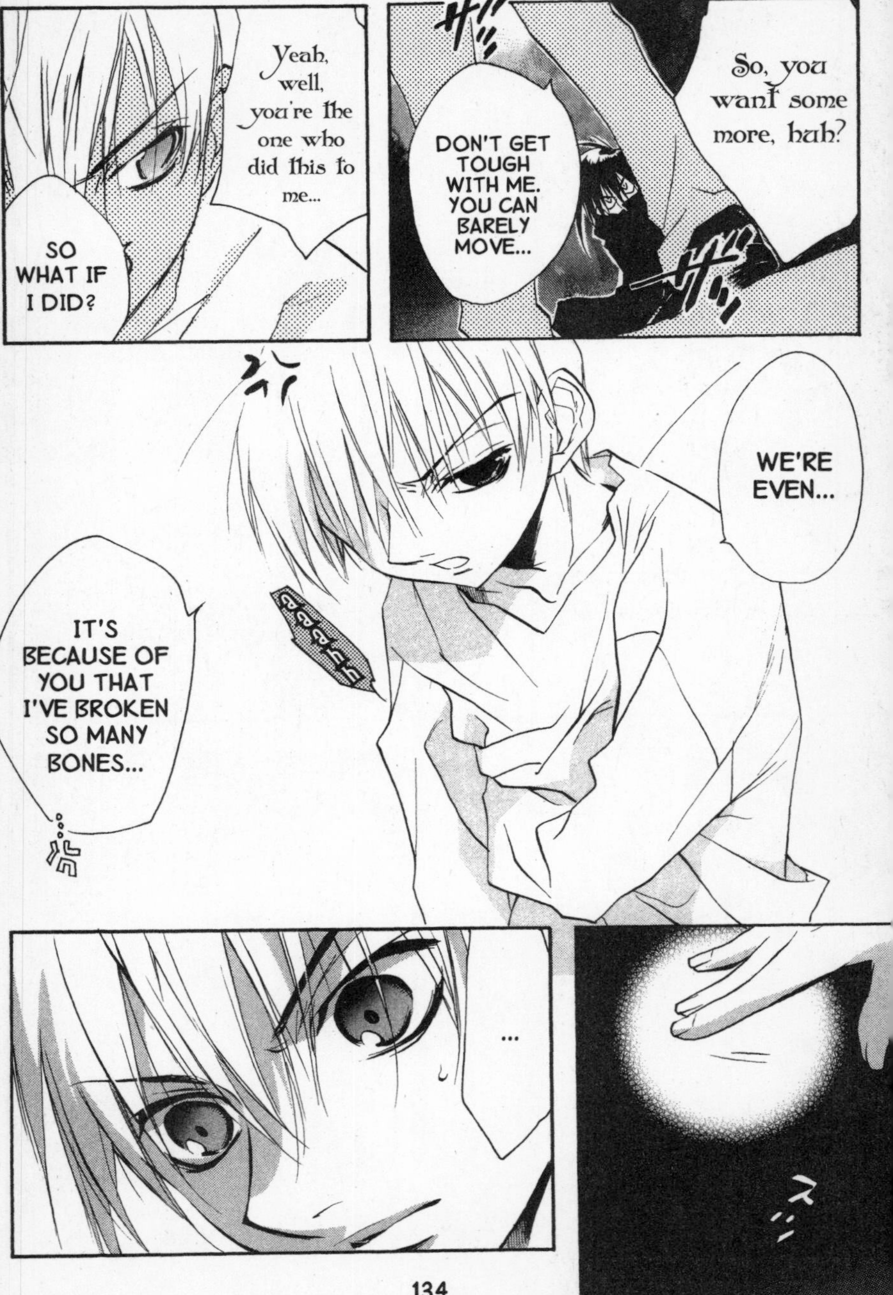
So, you want some more, huh?
DON'T GET TOUGH WITH ME. YOU CAN BARELY MOVE...
Yeah, well, you're the one who did this to me...
SO WHAT IF I DID?
WE'RE EVEN...
IT'S BECAUSE OF YOU THAT I'VE BROKEN SO MANY BONES...
...

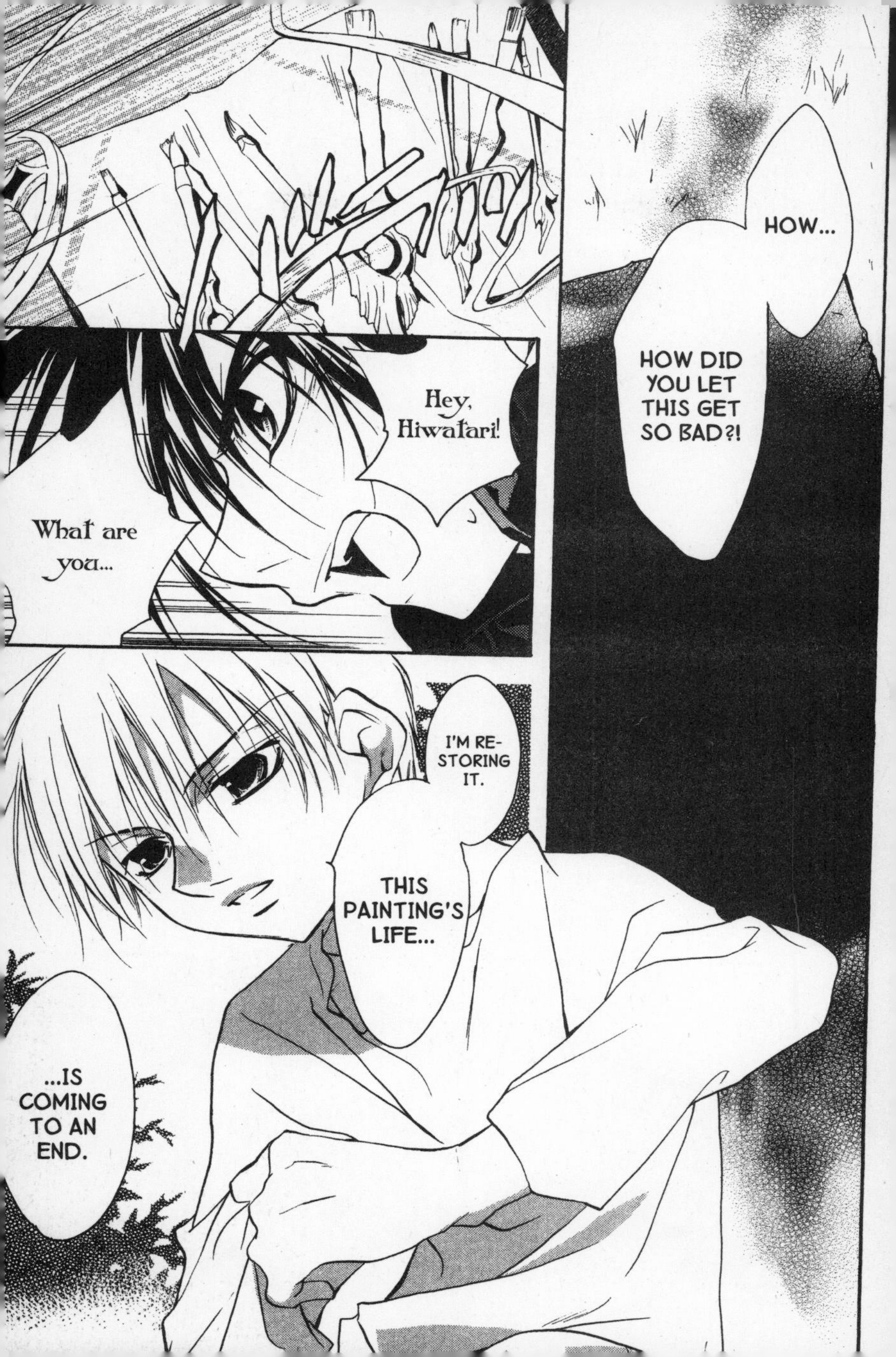
HOW...
HOW DID YOU LET THIS GET SO BAD?!
Hey, Hiwatari!
What are you...
I'M RE-STORING IT.
THIS PAINTING'S LIFE...
...IS COMING TO AN END.

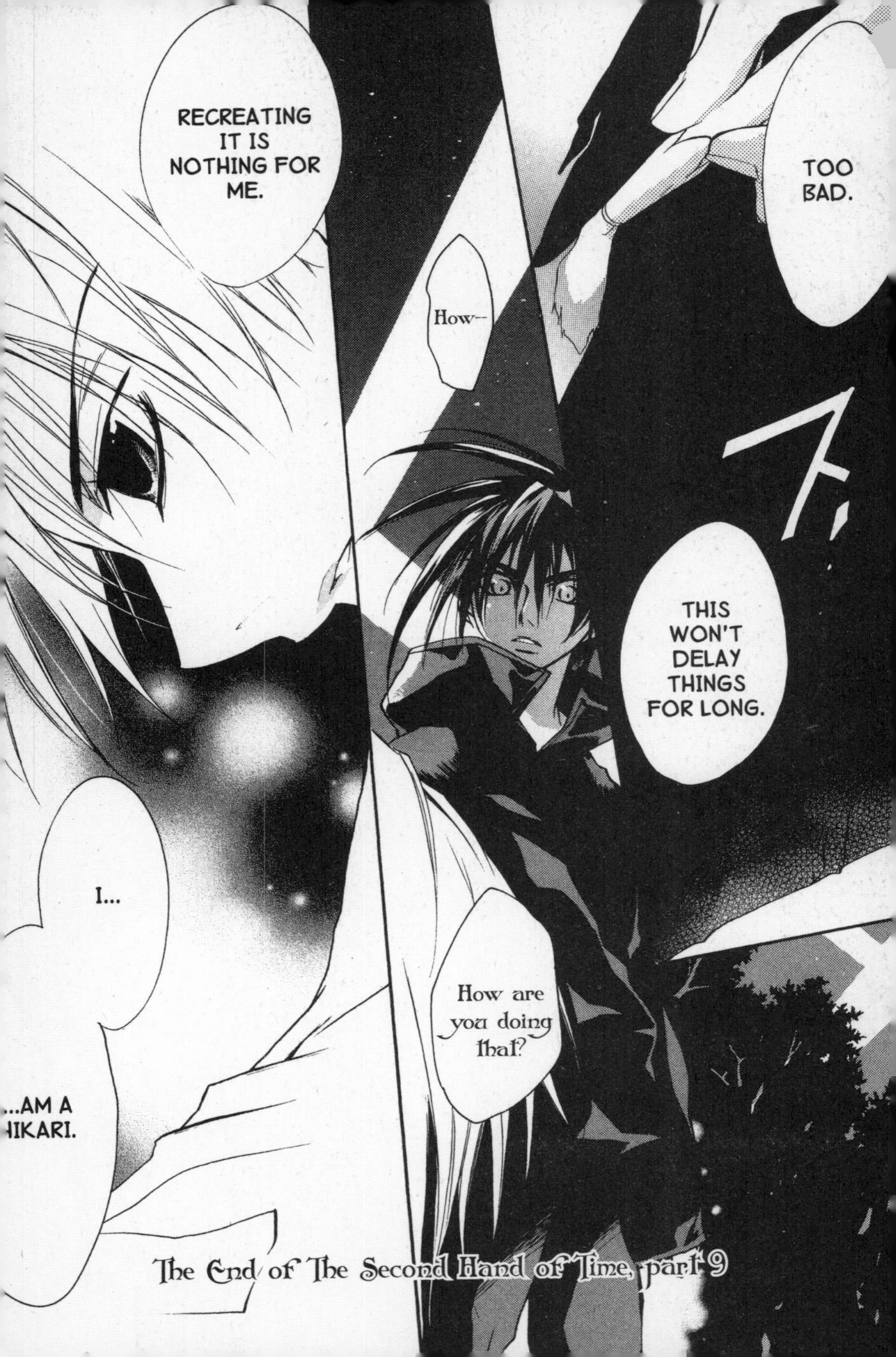
TOO BAD.
How--
THIS WON'T DELAY THINGS FOR LONG.
How are you doing that?
RECREATING IT IS NOTHING FOR ME.
I...
...AM A
IKARI.
The End of The Second Hand of Time, part 9

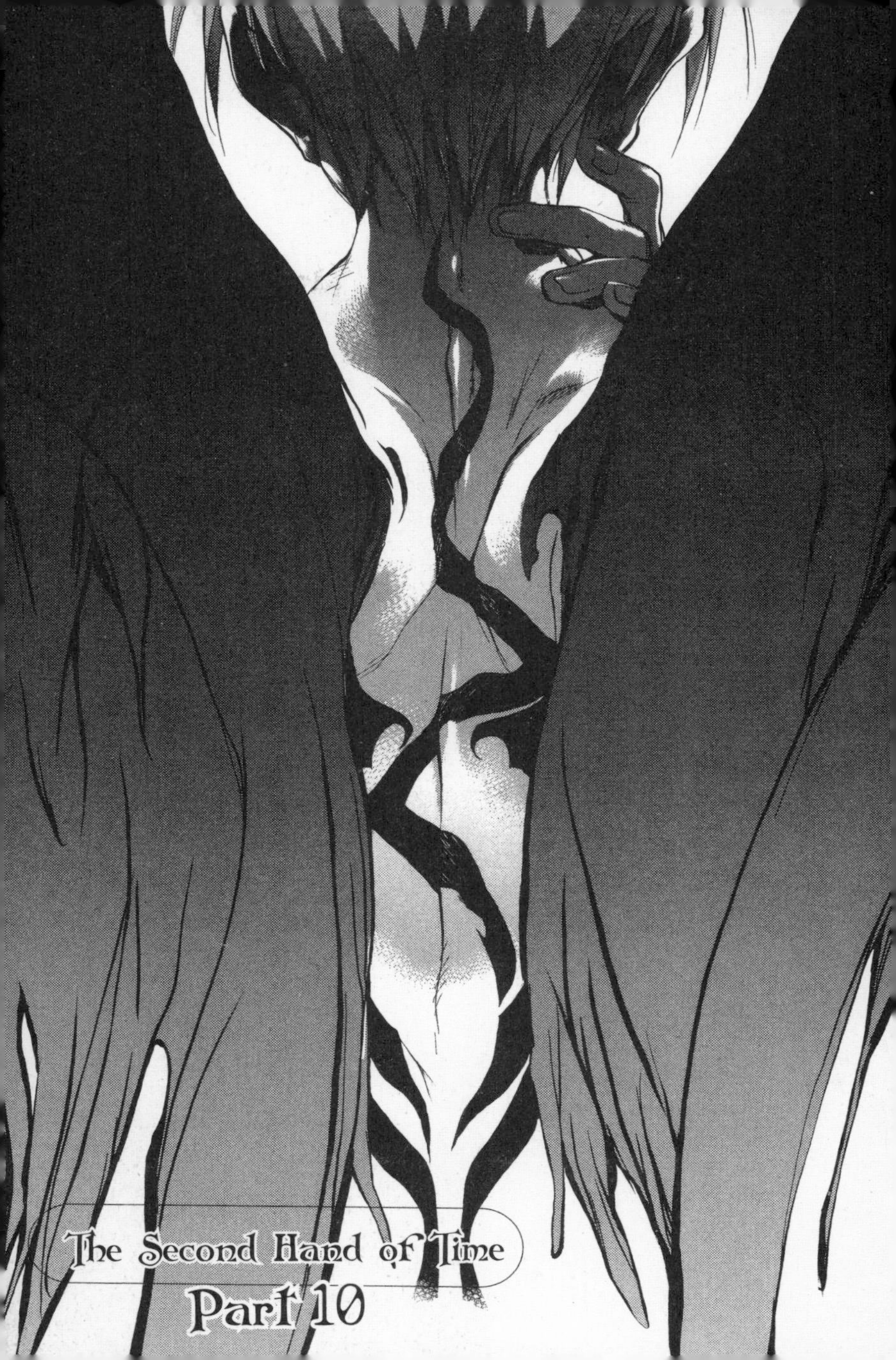
The Second Hand of Time
Part 10

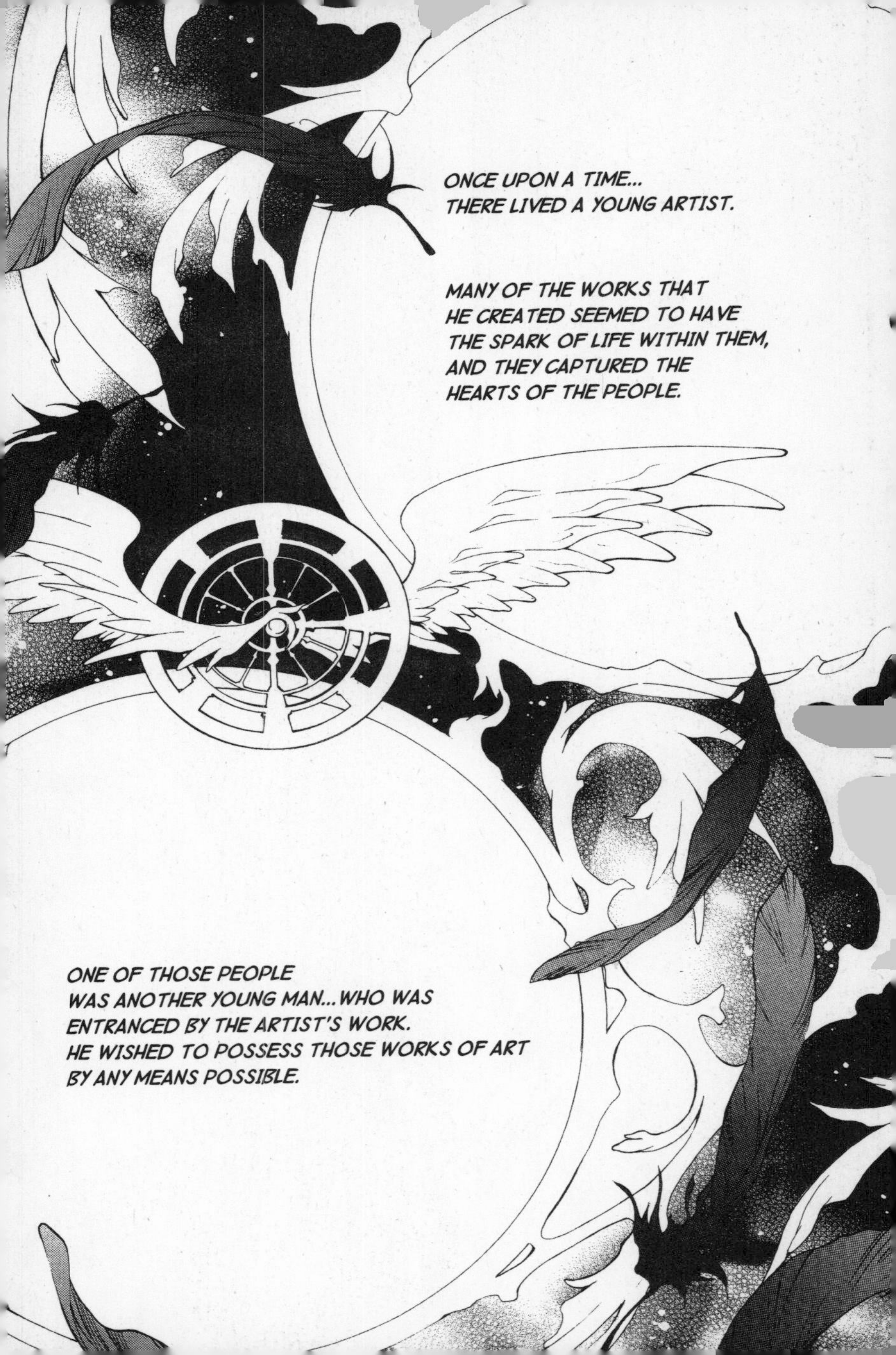
ONCE UPON A TIME...
THERE LIVED A YOUNG ARTIST.
MANY OF THE WORKS THAT HE CREATED SEEMED TO HAVE THE SPARK OF LIFE WITHIN THEM, AND THEY CAPTURED THE HEARTS OF THE PEOPLE.
ONE OF THOSE PEOPLE WAS ANOTHER YOUNG MAN...WHO WAS ENTRANCED BY THE ARTIST'S WORK. HE WISHED TO POSSESS THOSE WORKS OF ART BY ANY MEANS POSSIBLE.

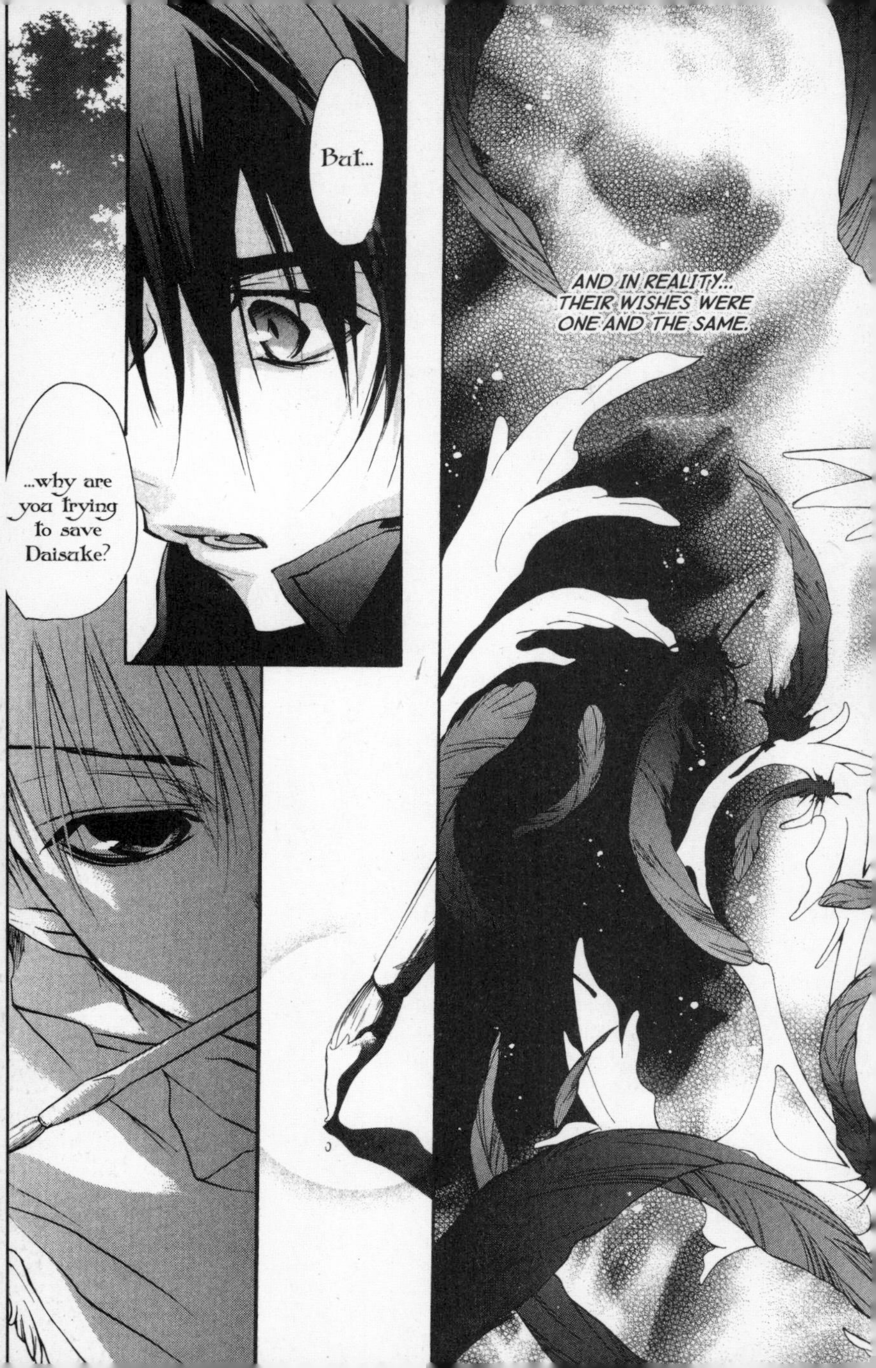
AND IN REALITY... THEIR WISHES WERE ONE AND THE SAME.
But...
...why are you trying to save Daisuke?

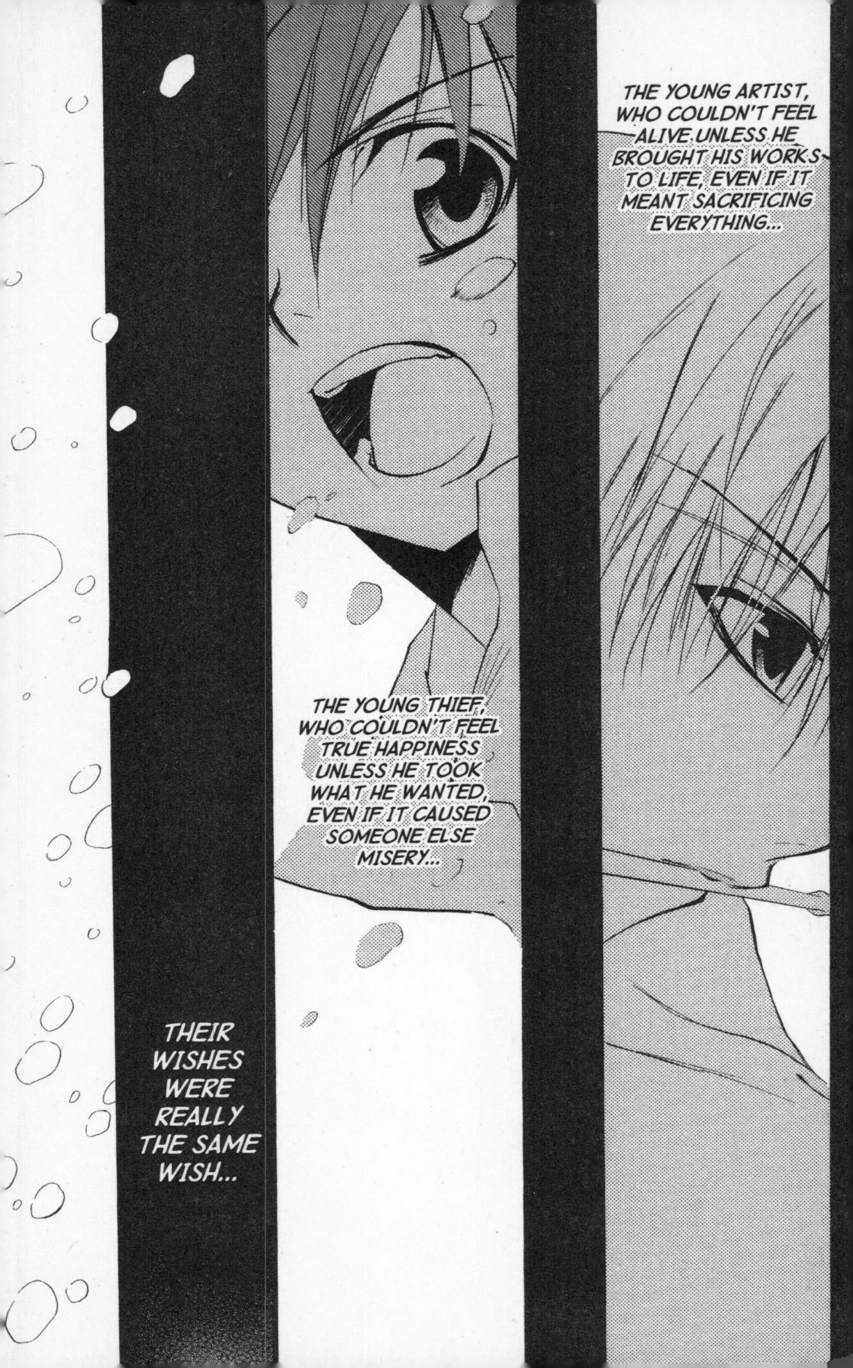
THE YOUNG ARTIST, WHO COULDN'T FEEL ALIVE UNLESS HE BROUGHT HIS WORKS TO LIFE, EVEN IF IT MEANT SACRIFICING EVERYTHING...
THE YOUNG THIEF, WHO COULDN'T FEEL TRUE HAPPINESS UNLESS HE TOOK WHAT HE WANTED, EVEN IF IT CAUSED SOMEONE ELSE MISERY...
THEIR WISHES WERE REALLY THE SAME WISH...

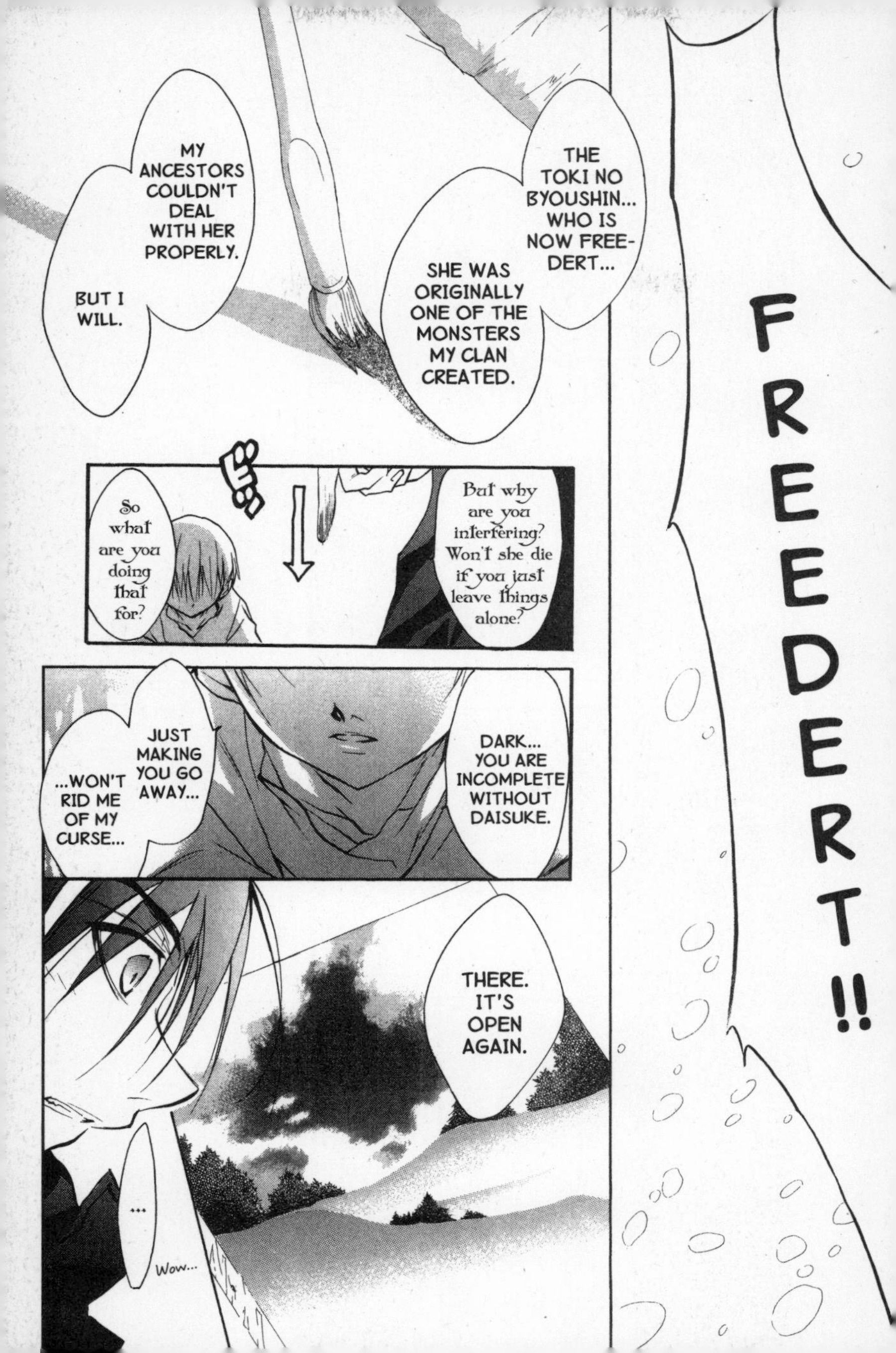

FREDERT!!
THE TOKI NO BYOUSHIN... WHO IS NOW FREE-DERT...
SHE WAS ORIGINALLY ONE OF THE MONSTERS MY CLAN CREATED.
MY ANCESTORS COULDN'T DEAL WITH HER PROPERLY.
BUT I WILL.
But why are you interfering? Won't she die if you just leave things alone?
So what are you doing that for?
DARK... YOU ARE INCOMPLETE WITHOUT DAISUKE.
JUST MAKING YOU GO AWAY...
...WON'T RID ME OF MY CURSE...
THERE. IT'S OPEN AGAIN.
...
Wow...

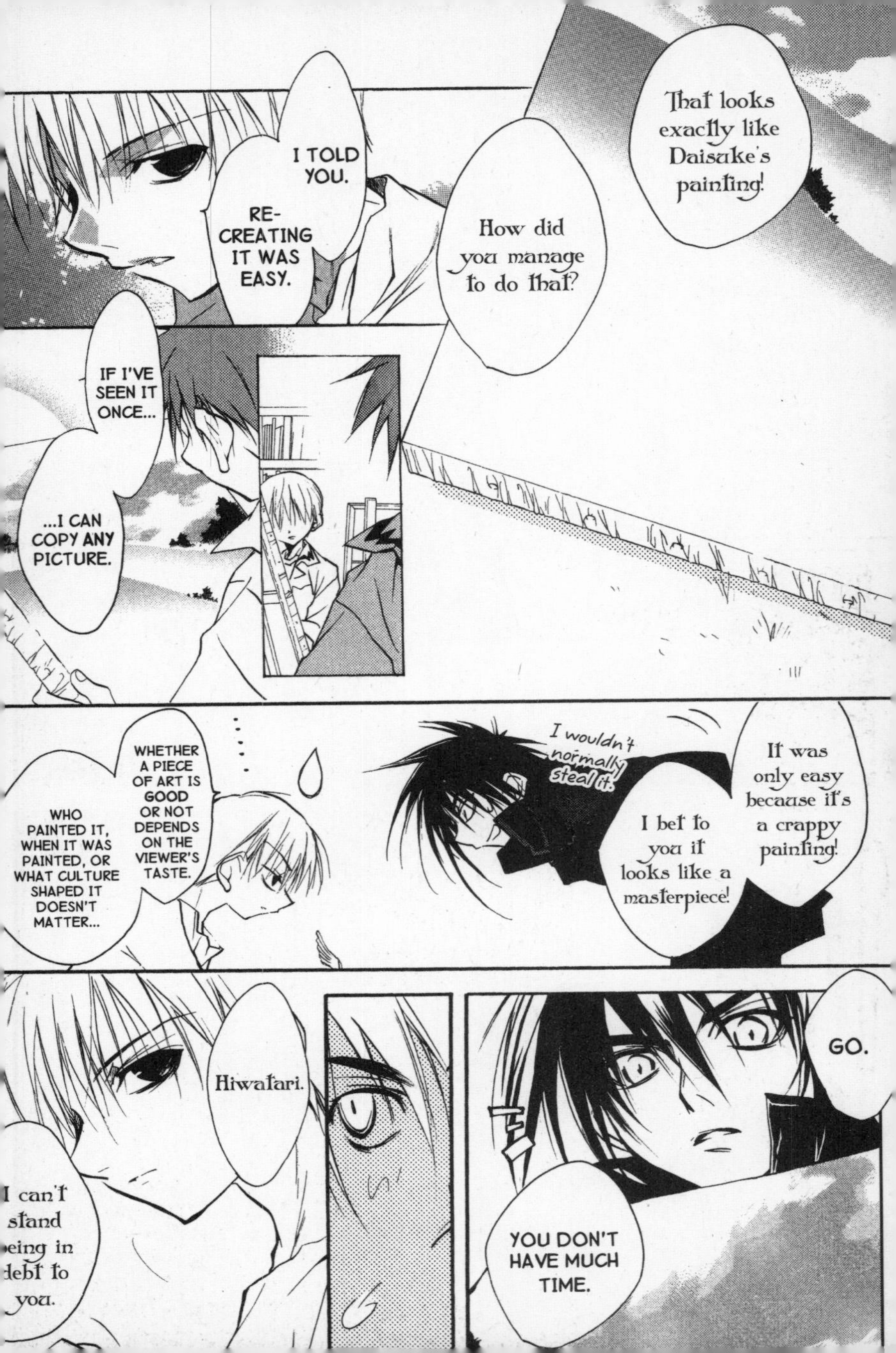
That looks exactly like Daisuke's painting!
How did you manage to do that?
I TOLD YOU.
RE-CREATING IT WAS EASY.
IF I'VE SEEN IT ONCE...
...I CAN COPY ANY PICTURE.
It was only easy because it's a crappy painting!
I bet to you it looks like a masterpiece!
I wouldn't normally steal it.
WHETHER A PIECE OF ART IS GOOD OR NOT DEPENDS ON THE VIEWER'S TASTE.
WHO PAINTED IT, WHEN IT WAS PAINTED, OR WHAT CULTURE SHAPED IT DOESN'T MATTER...
GO.
YOU DON'T HAVE MUCH TIME.
Hiwatari.
I can't stand eing in debt to you.

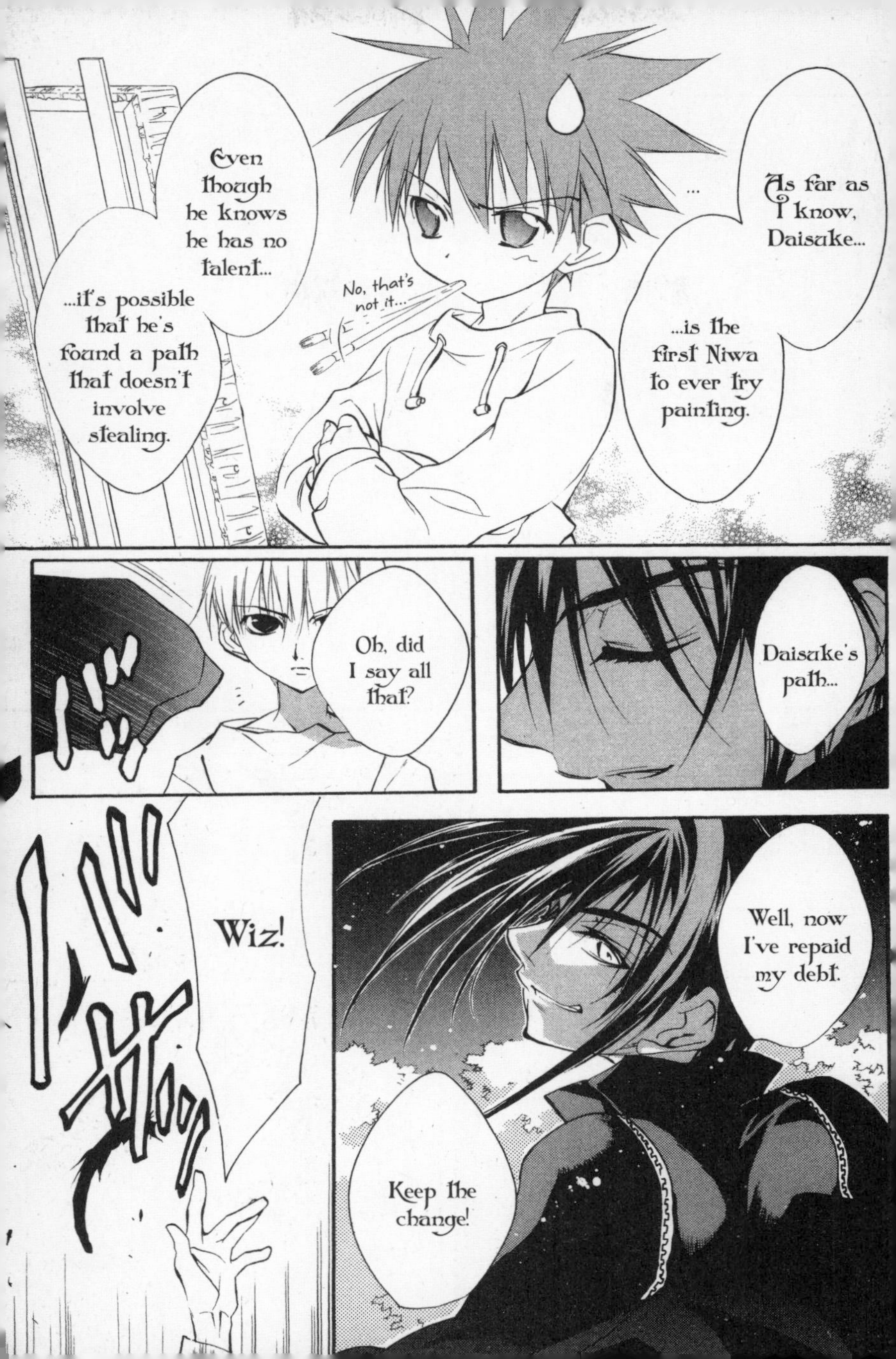
As far as I know, Daisuke...
...is the first Niwa to ever try painting.
...
No, that's not it...
Even though he knows he has no talent...
...it's possible that he's found a path that doesn't involve stealing.
Daisuke's path...
Oh, did I say all that?
Well, now I've repaid my debt.
Keep the change!
Wiz!

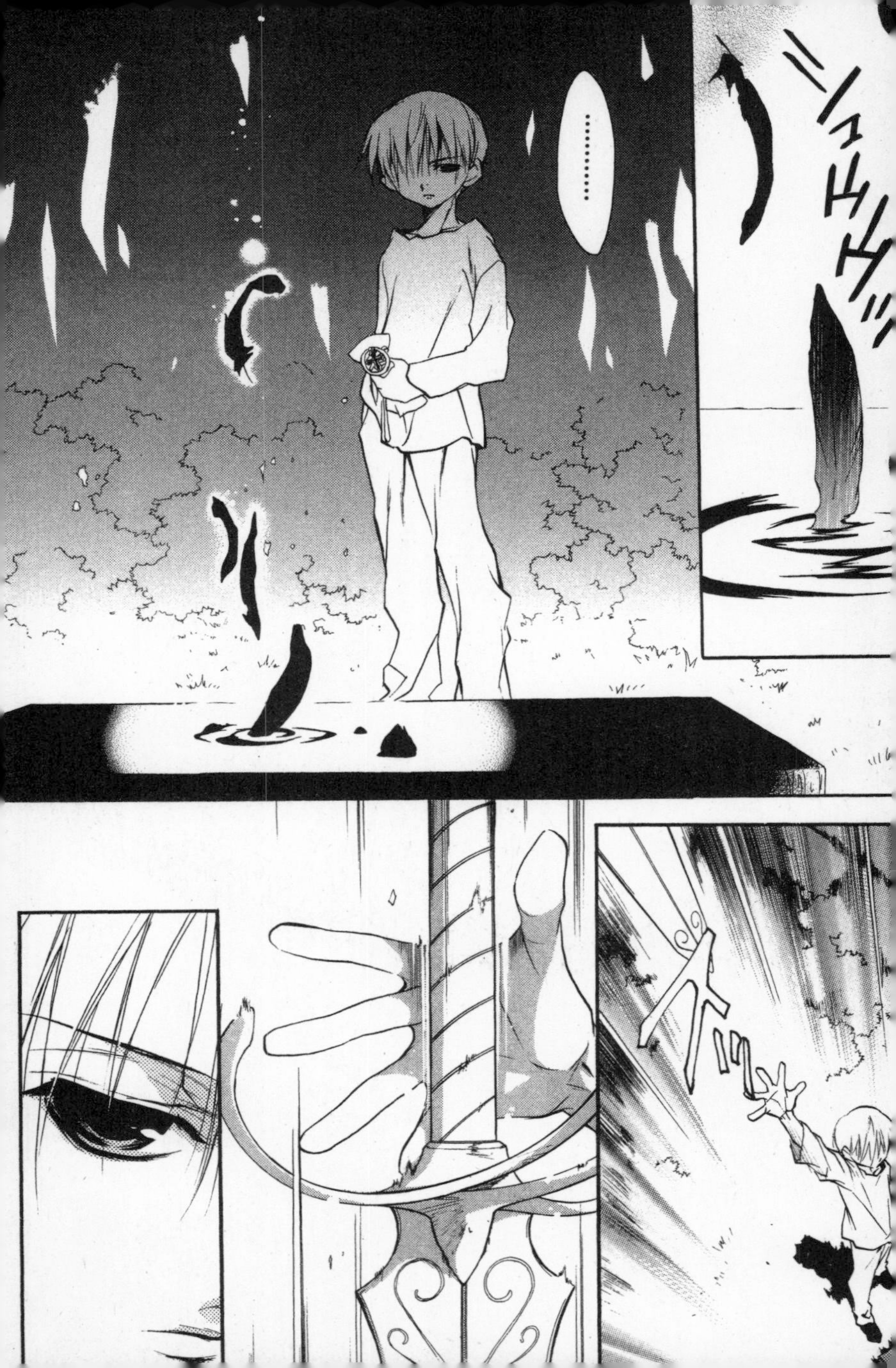
シュムムッ
……
ズッ

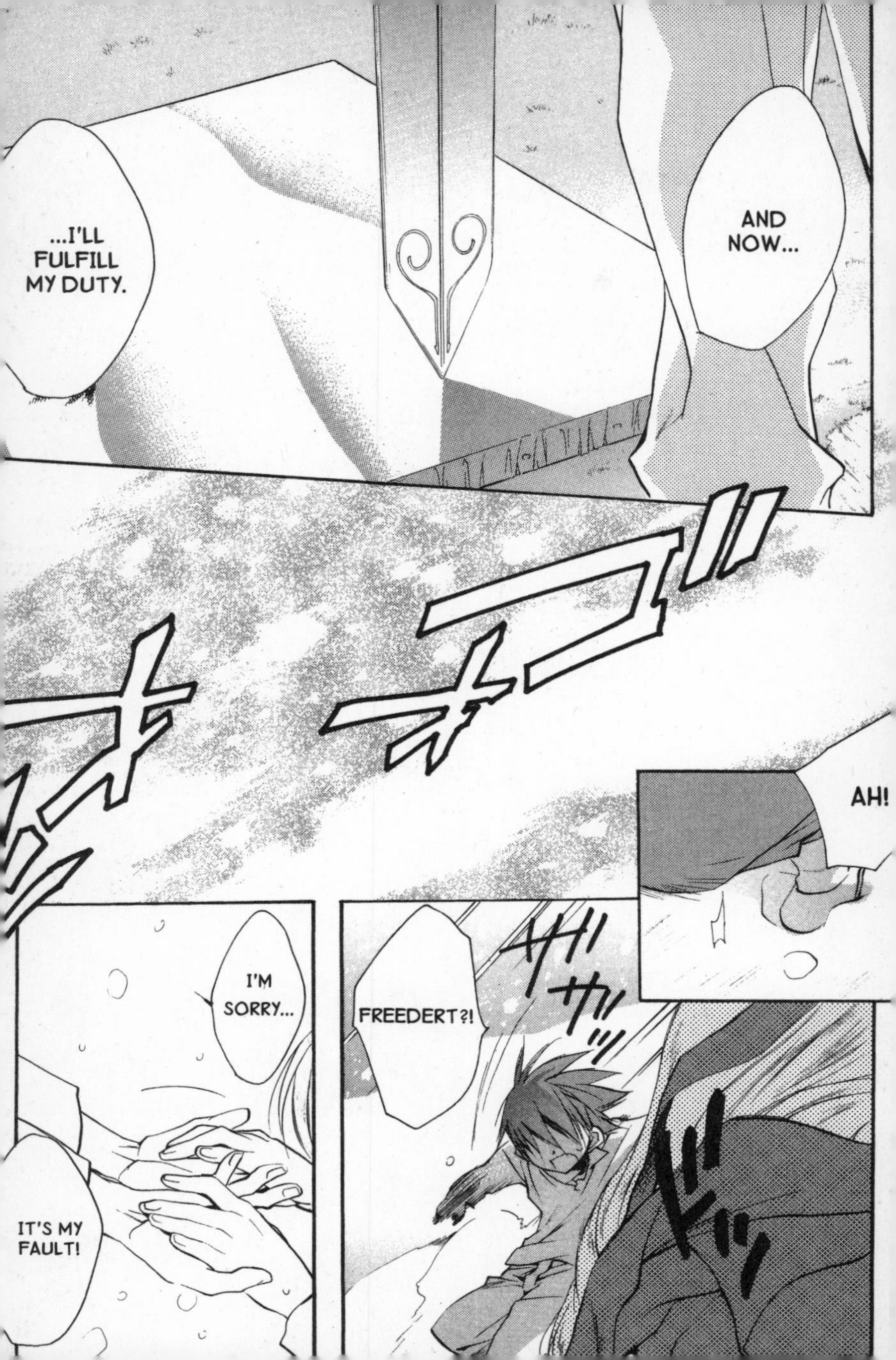
AND NOW...
...I'LL FULFILL MY DUTY.
AH!
FREEDERT?!
I'M SORRY...
IT'S MY FAULT!

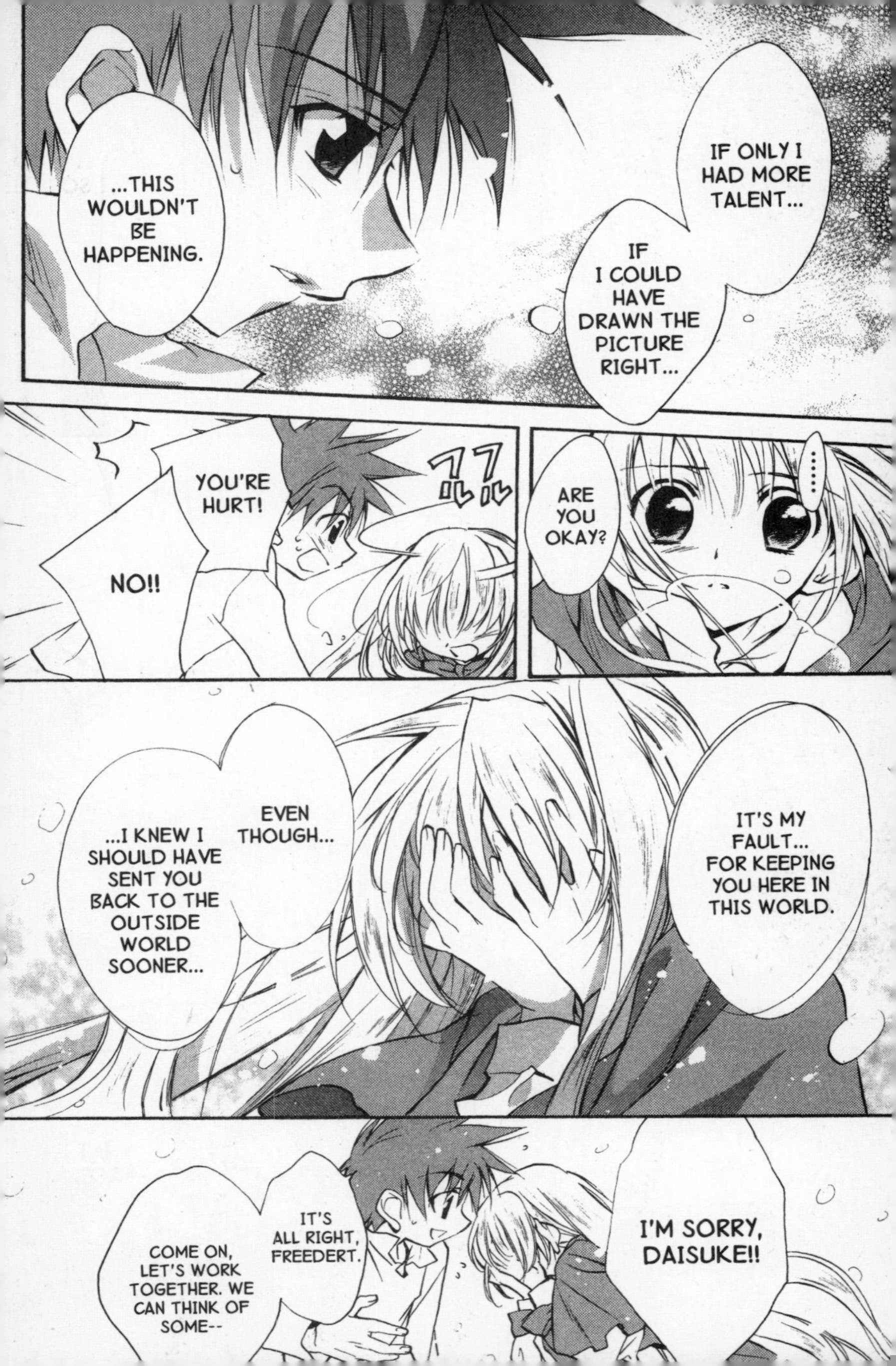
IF ONLY I HAD MORE TALENT...
IF I COULD HAVE DRAWN THE PICTURE RIGHT...
...THIS WOULDN'T BE HAPPENING.
......
ARE YOU OKAY?
YOU'RE HURT!
NO!!
IT'S MY FAULT... FOR KEEPING YOU HERE IN THIS WORLD.
EVEN THOUGH...
...I KNEW I SHOULD HAVE SENT YOU BACK TO THE OUTSIDE WORLD SOONER...
I'M SORRY, DAISUKE!!
IT'S ALL RIGHT, FREEDERT.
COME ON, LET'S WORK TOGETHER. WE CAN THINK OF SOME--

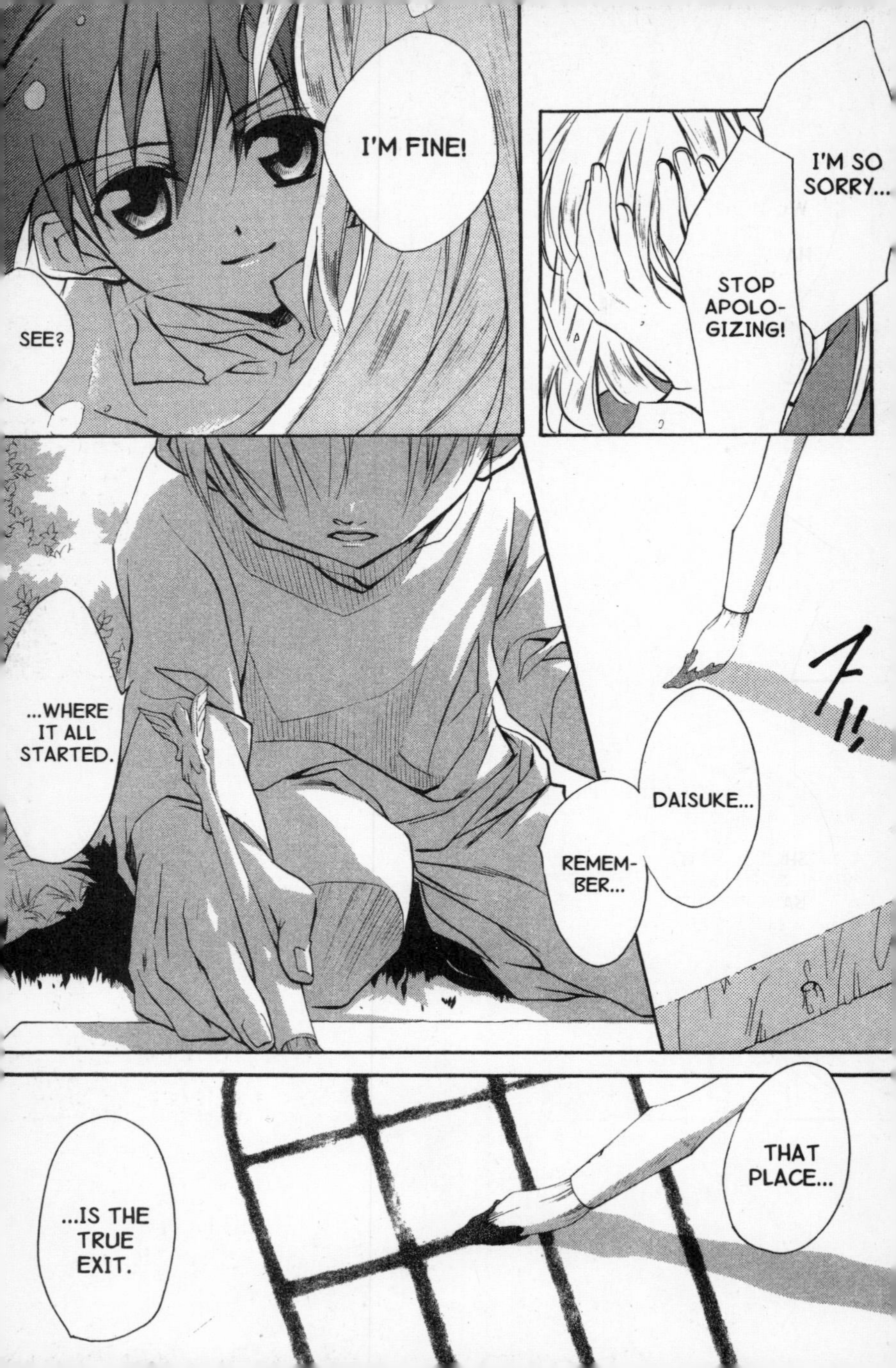
I'M SO SORRY...
STOP APOLOGIZING!
I'M FINE!
SEE?
DAISUKE...
REMEMBER...
...WHERE IT ALL STARTED.
THAT PLACE...
...IS THE TRUE EXIT.

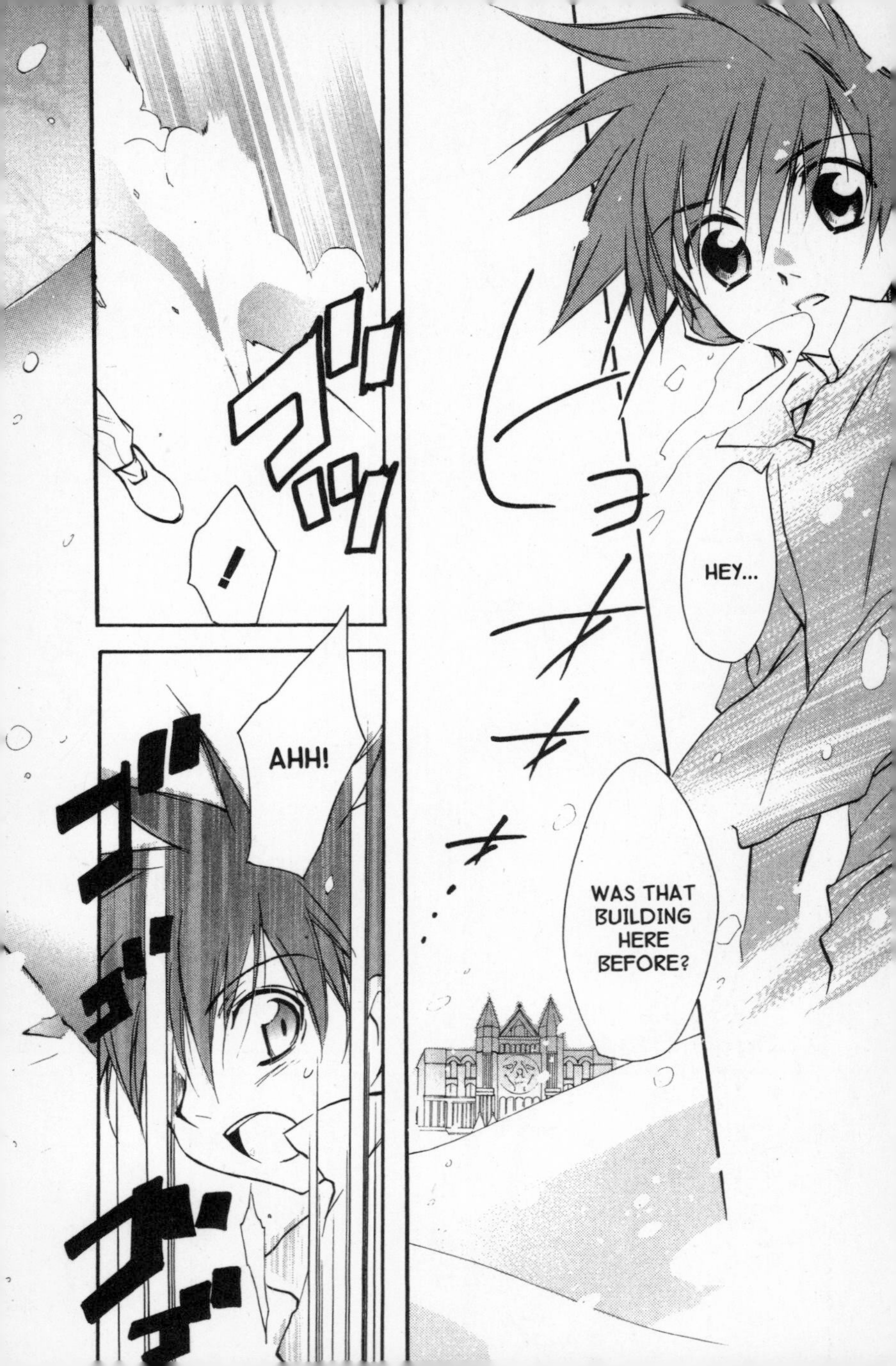
HEY...
WAS THAT BUILDING HERE BEFORE?
!
AHH!

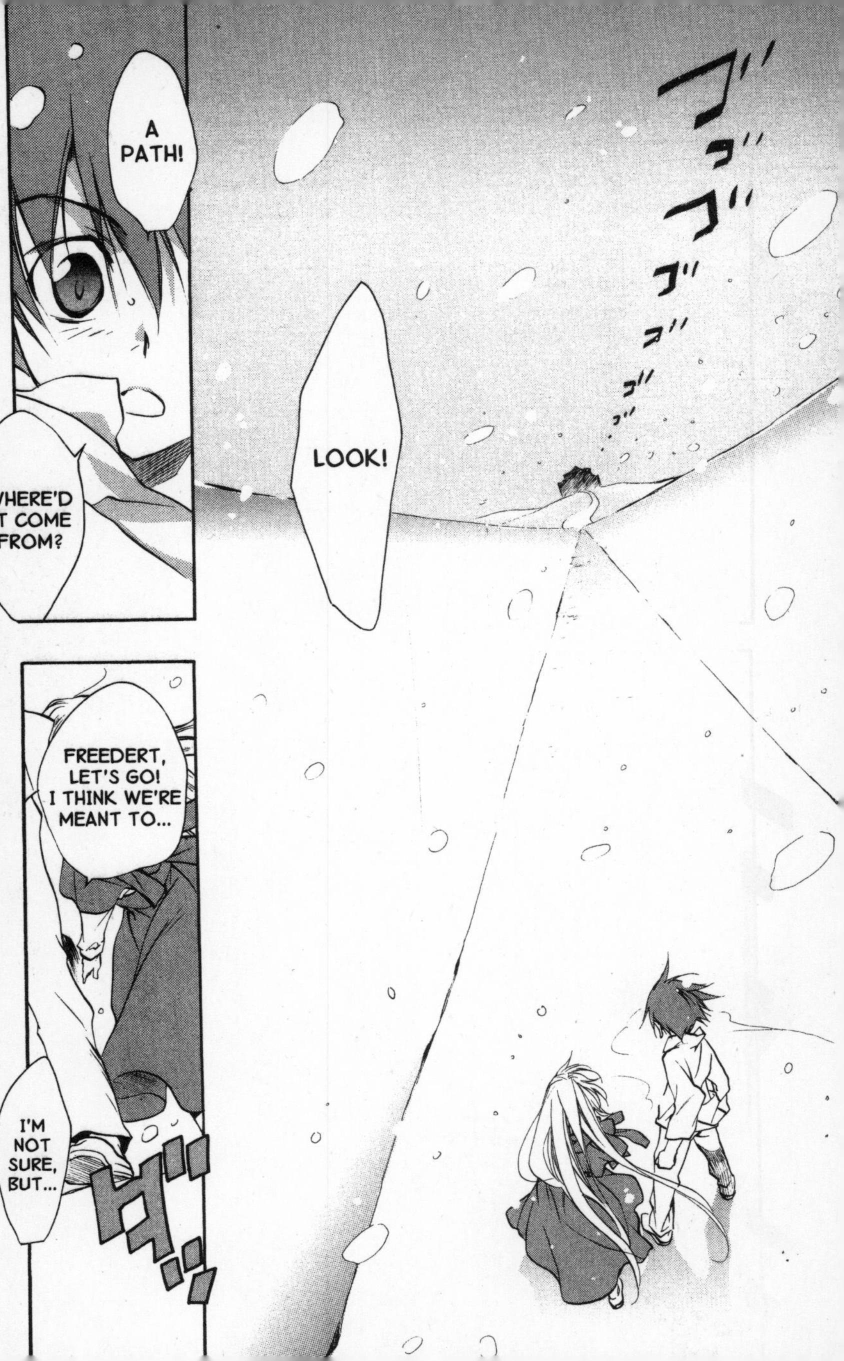
LOOK!
A PATH!
WHERE'D IT COME FROM?
FREEDERT, LET'S GO! I THINK WE'RE MEANT TO...
I'M NOT SURE, BUT...

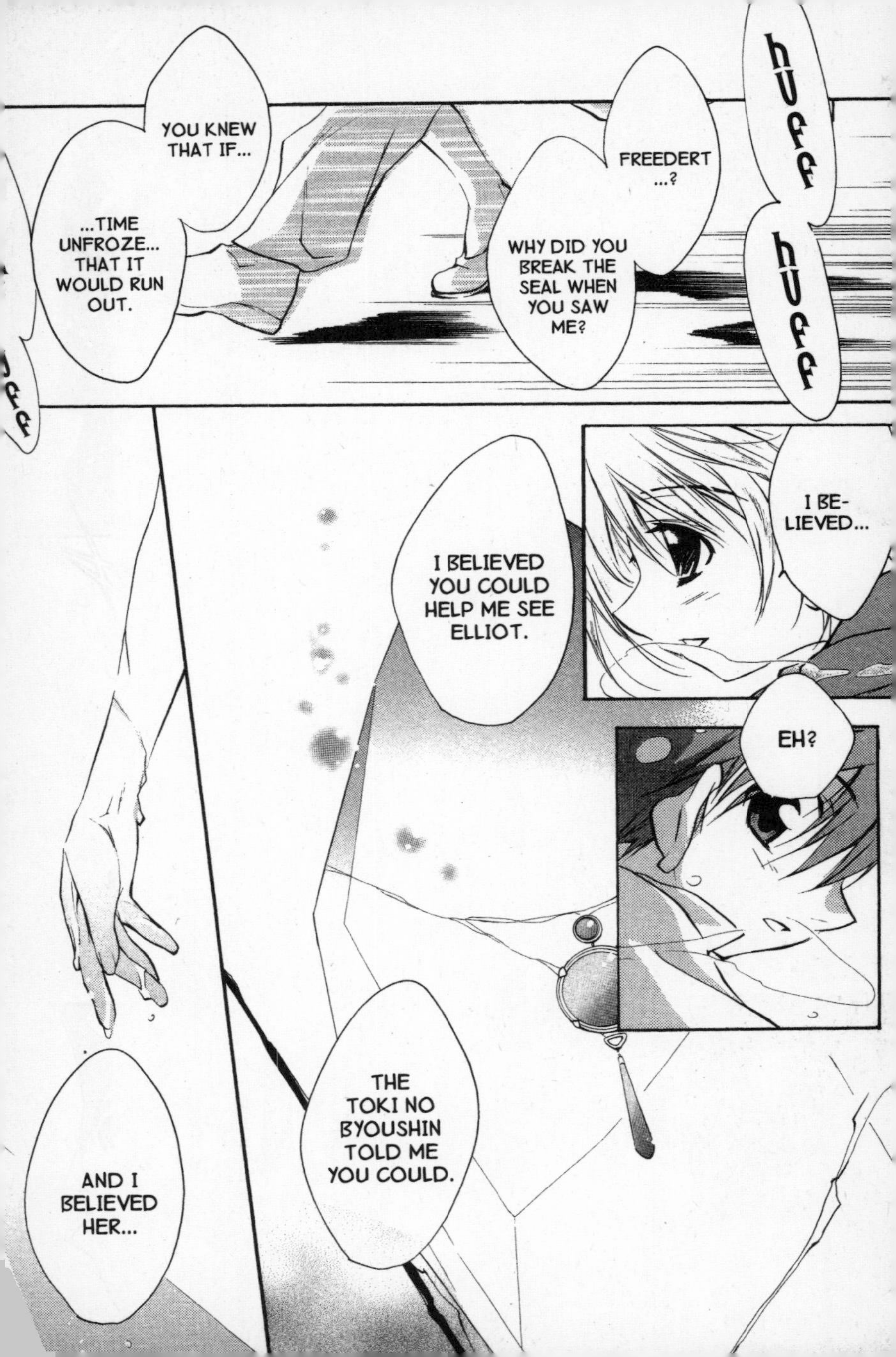
HUFF
HUFF
FREEDERT ...?
WHY DID YOU BREAK THE SEAL WHEN YOU SAW ME?
YOU KNEW THAT IF...
...TIME UNFROZE... THAT IT WOULD RUN OUT.
I BE-LIEVED...
EH?
I BELIEVED YOU COULD HELP ME SEE ELLIOT.
THE TOKI NO BYOUSHIN TOLD ME YOU COULD.
AND I BELIEVED HER...

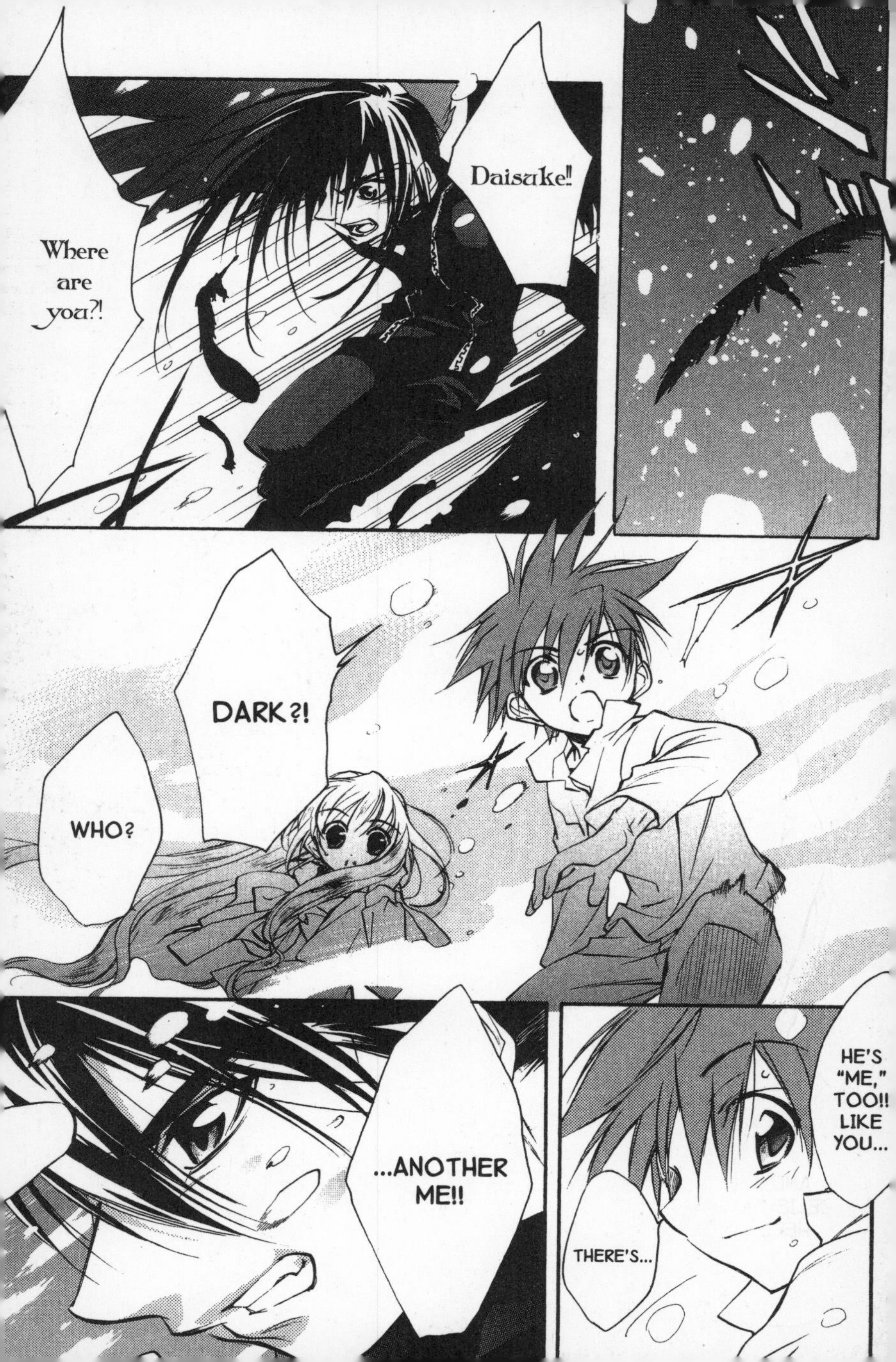
Daisuke!!
Where are you?!
DARK?!
WHO?
HE'S "ME," TOO!! LIKE YOU...
THERE'S...
...ANOTHER ME!!

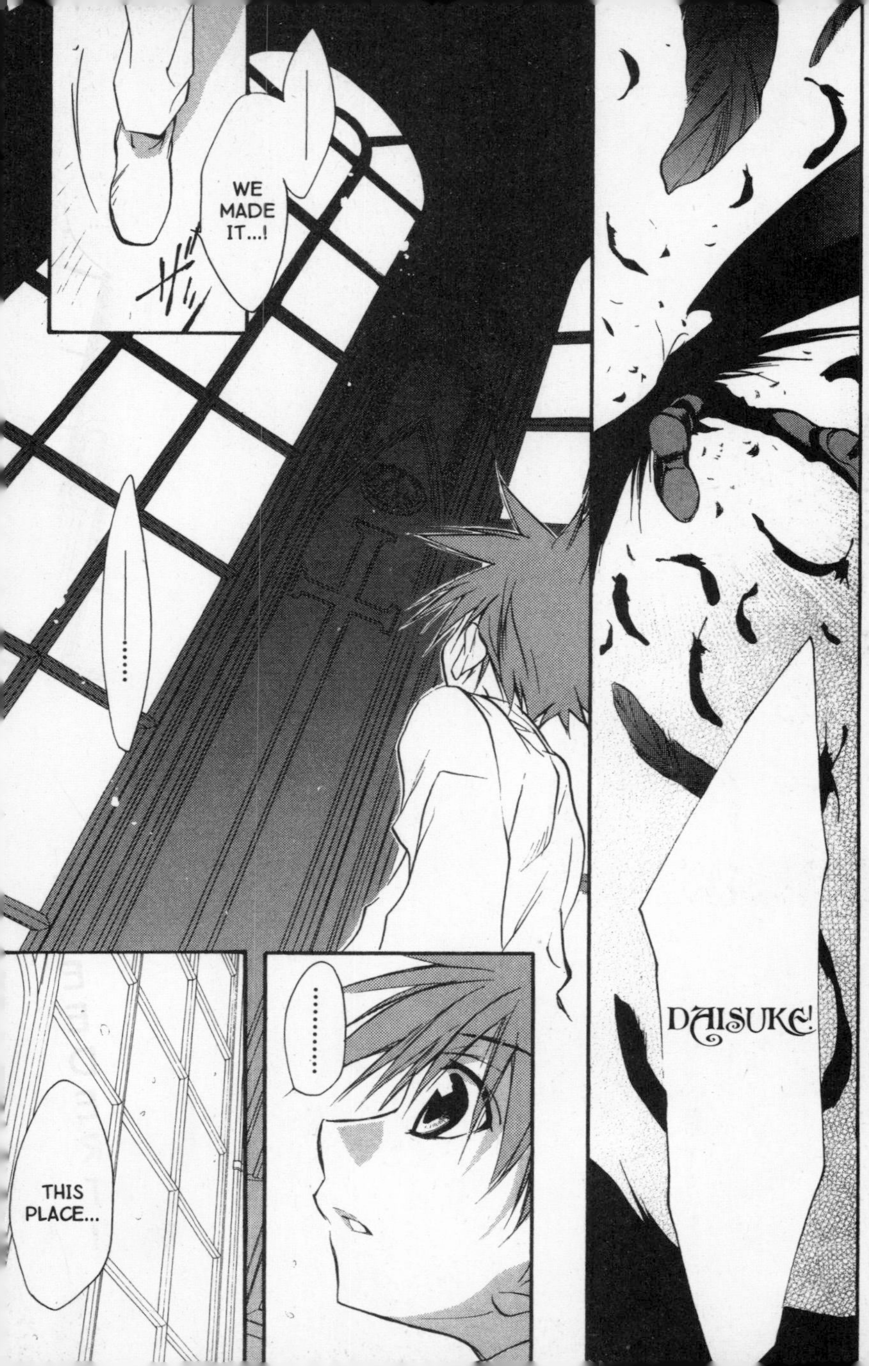
DAISUKE!
WE MADE IT...!
......
......
THIS PLACE...

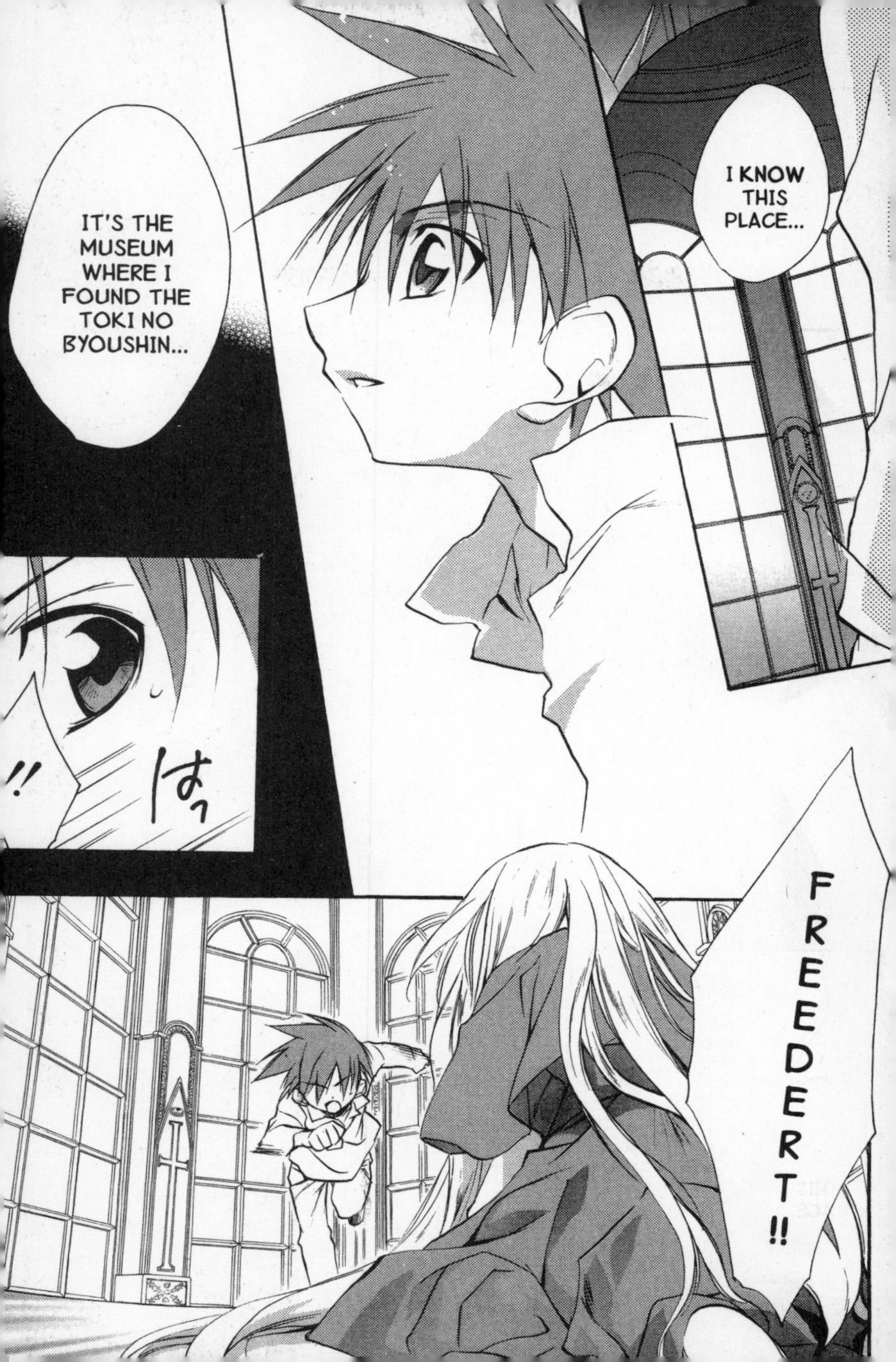
I KNOW THIS PLACE...
IT'S THE MUSEUM WHERE I FOUND THE TOKI NO BYOUSHIN...
!!
はっ
FREEDERT!!

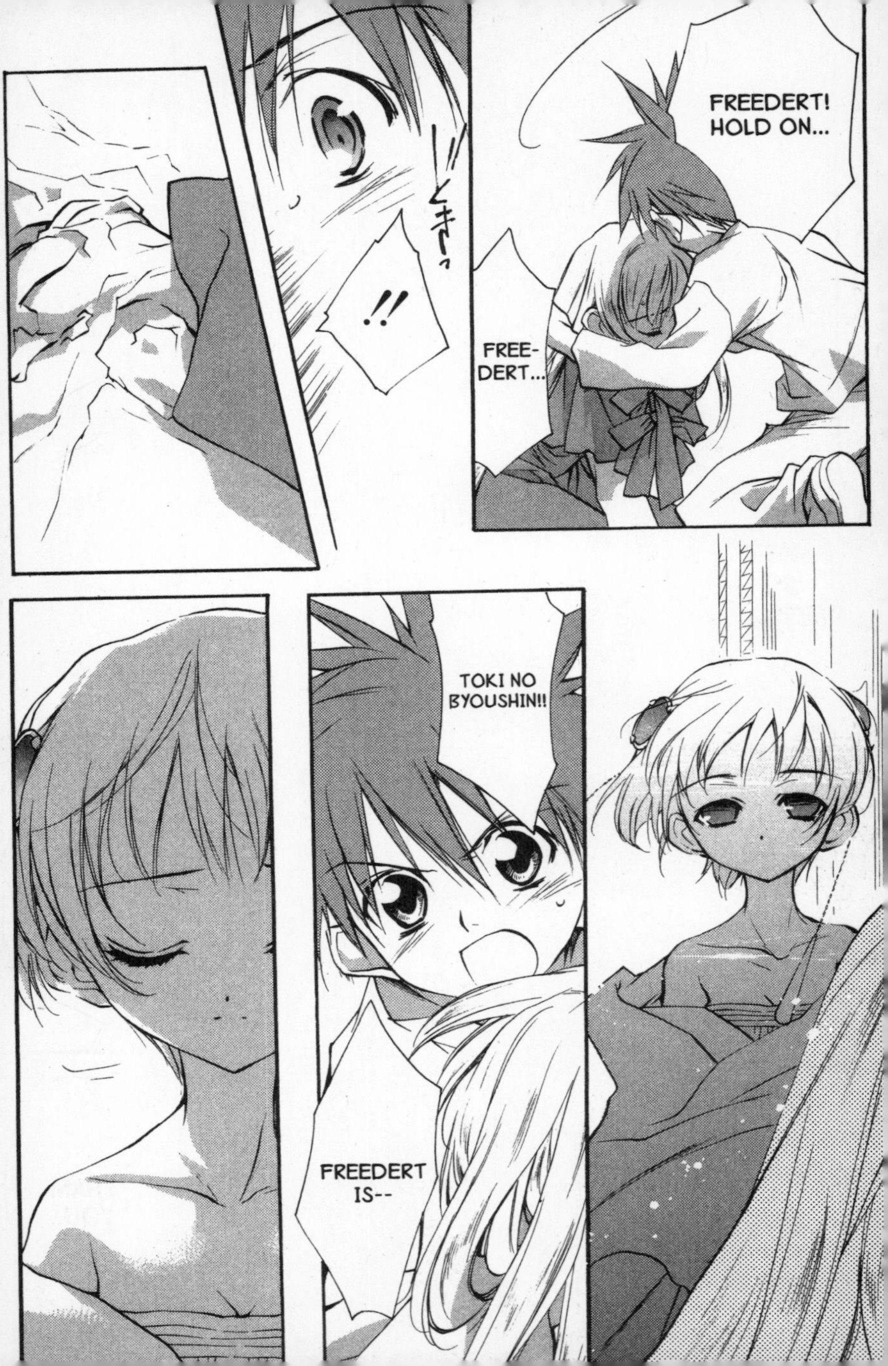
FREEDERT! HOLD ON...
FREE-DERT...
!!
TOKI NO BYOUSHIN!!
FREEDERT IS--

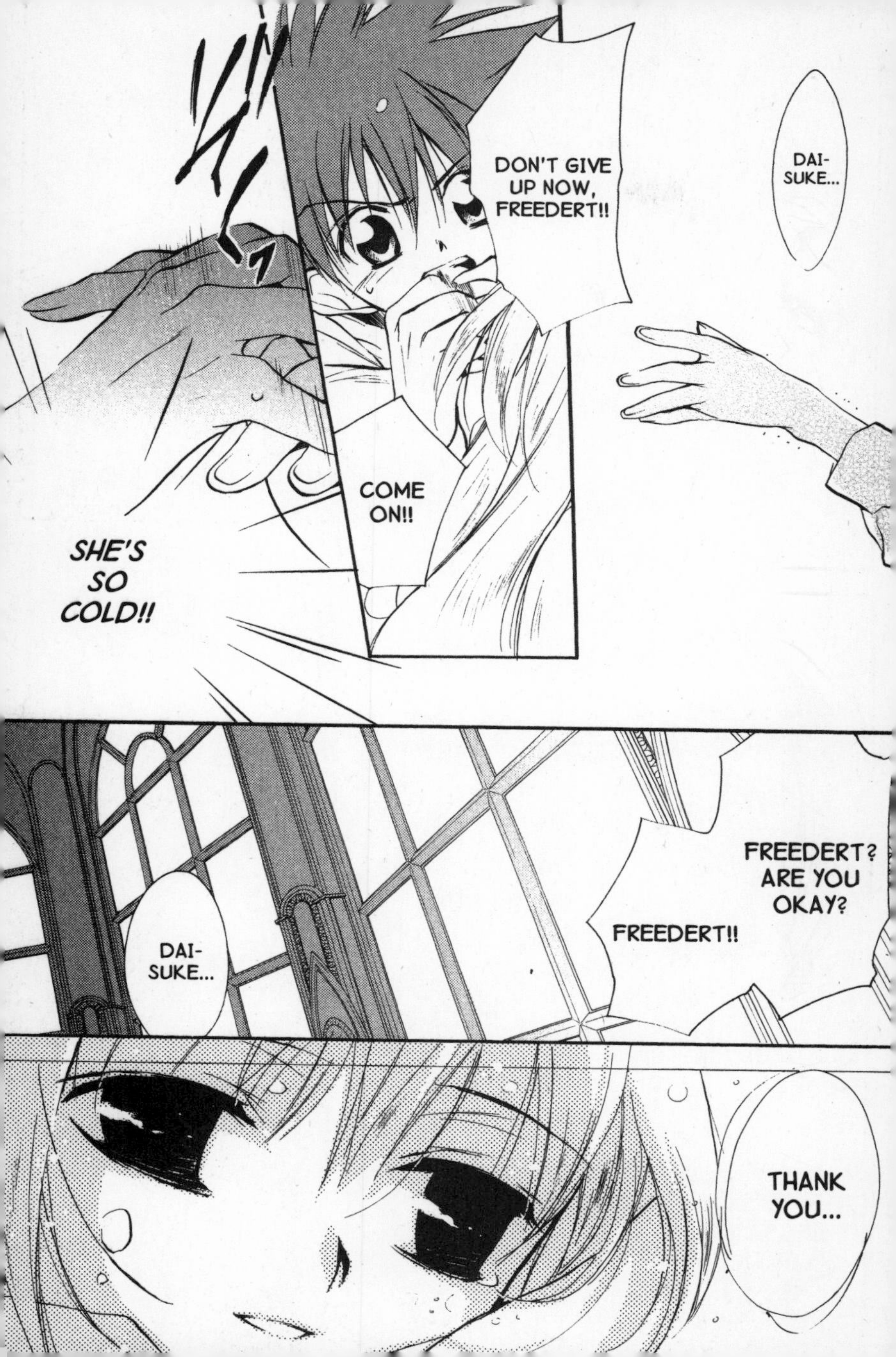
DAI-SUKE...
DON'T GIVE UP NOW, FREEDERT!!
COME ON!!
SHE'S SO COLD!!
FREEDERT? ARE YOU OKAY?
FREEDERT!!
DAI-SUKE...
THANK YOU...

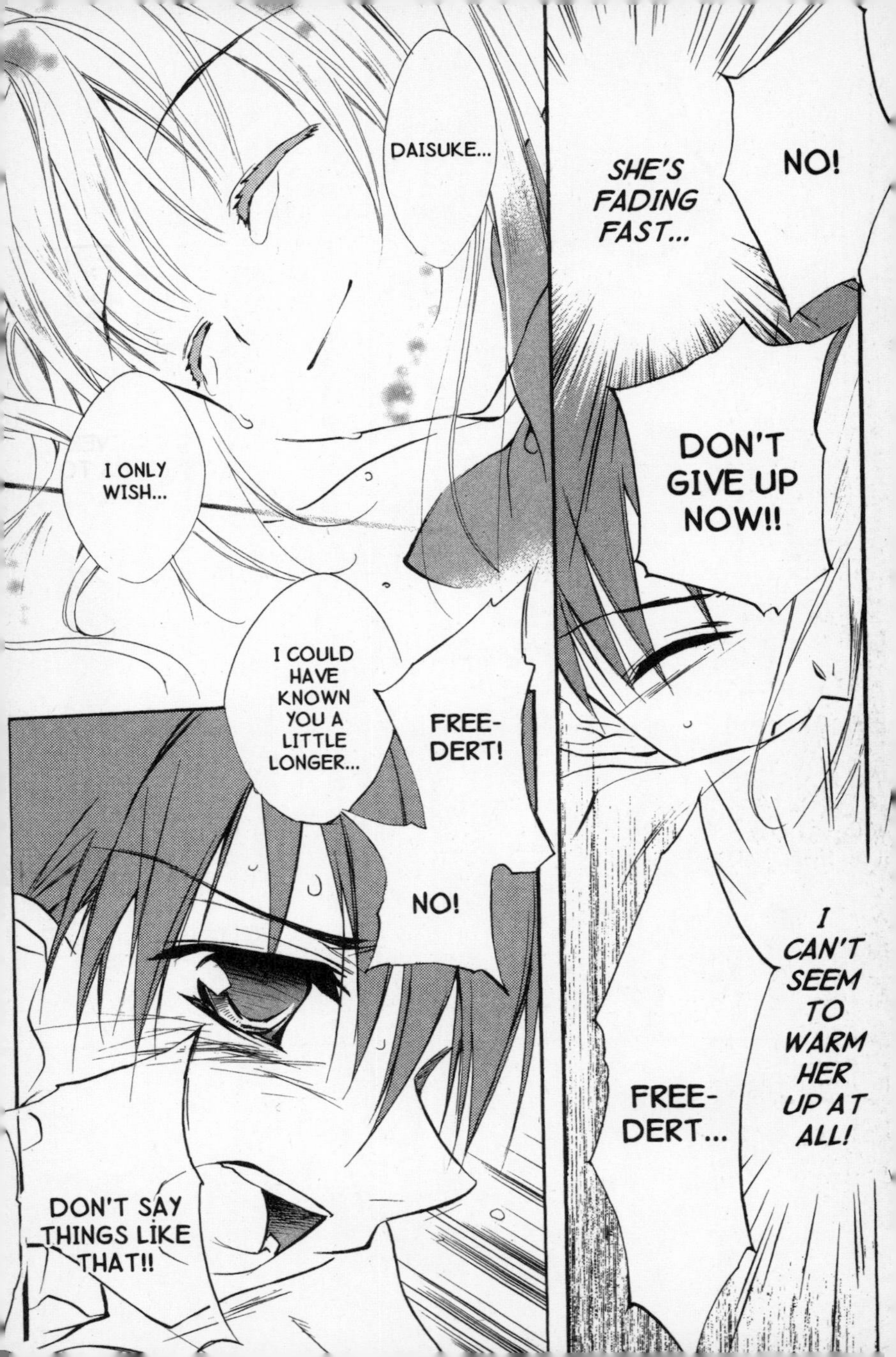
NO!
SHE'S FADING FAST...
DON'T GIVE UP NOW!!
I CAN'T SEEM TO WARM HER UP AT ALL!
FREE-DERT...
DAISUKE...
I ONLY WISH...
I COULD HAVE KNOWN YOU A LITTLE LONGER...
FREE-DERT!
NO!
DON'T SAY THINGS LIKE THAT!!

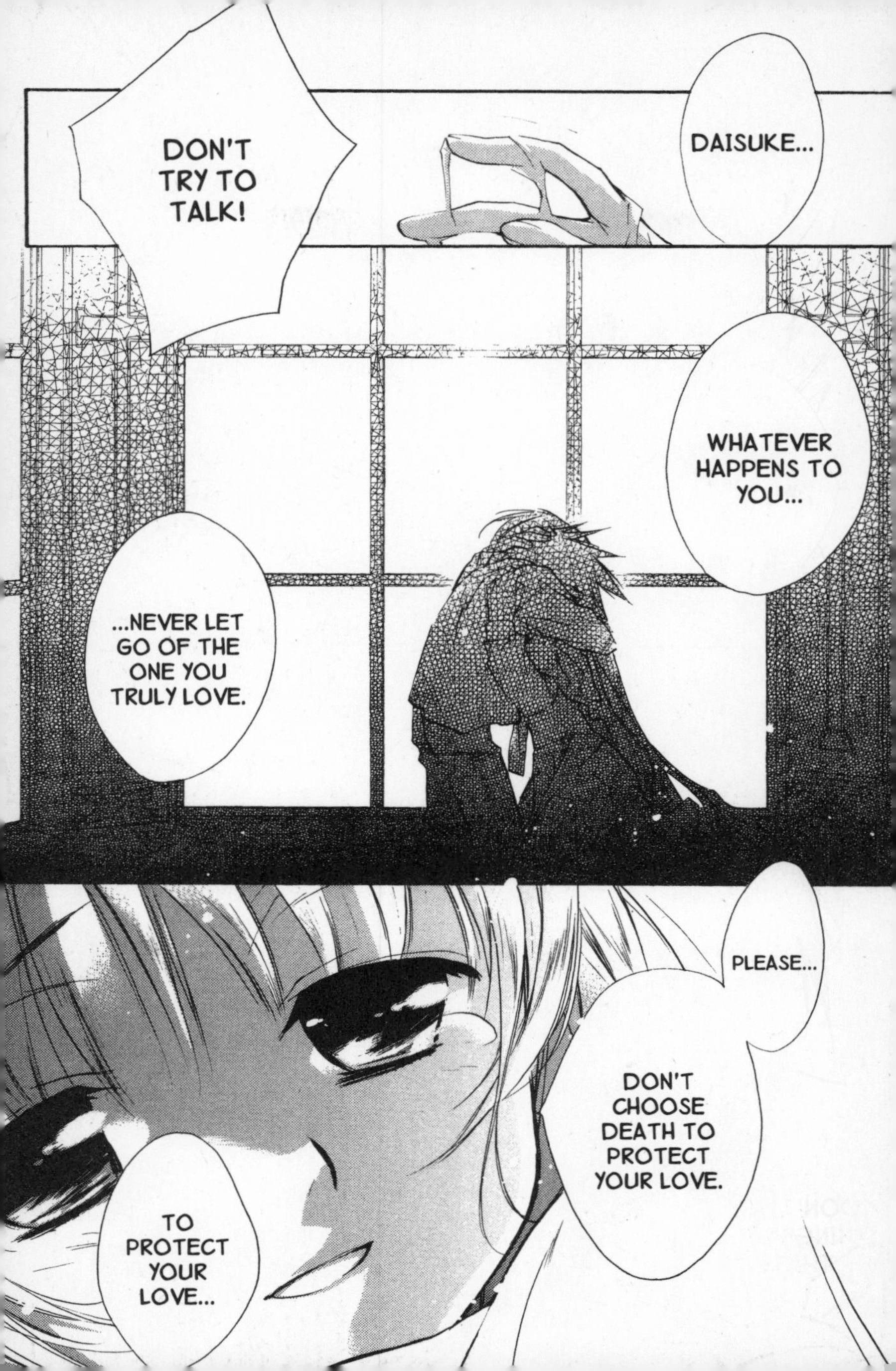
DAISUKE...
DON'T TRY TO TALK!
WHATEVER HAPPENS TO YOU...
...NEVER LET GO OF THE ONE YOU TRULY LOVE.
PLEASE...
DON'T CHOOSE DEATH TO PROTECT YOUR LOVE.
TO PROTECT YOUR LOVE...

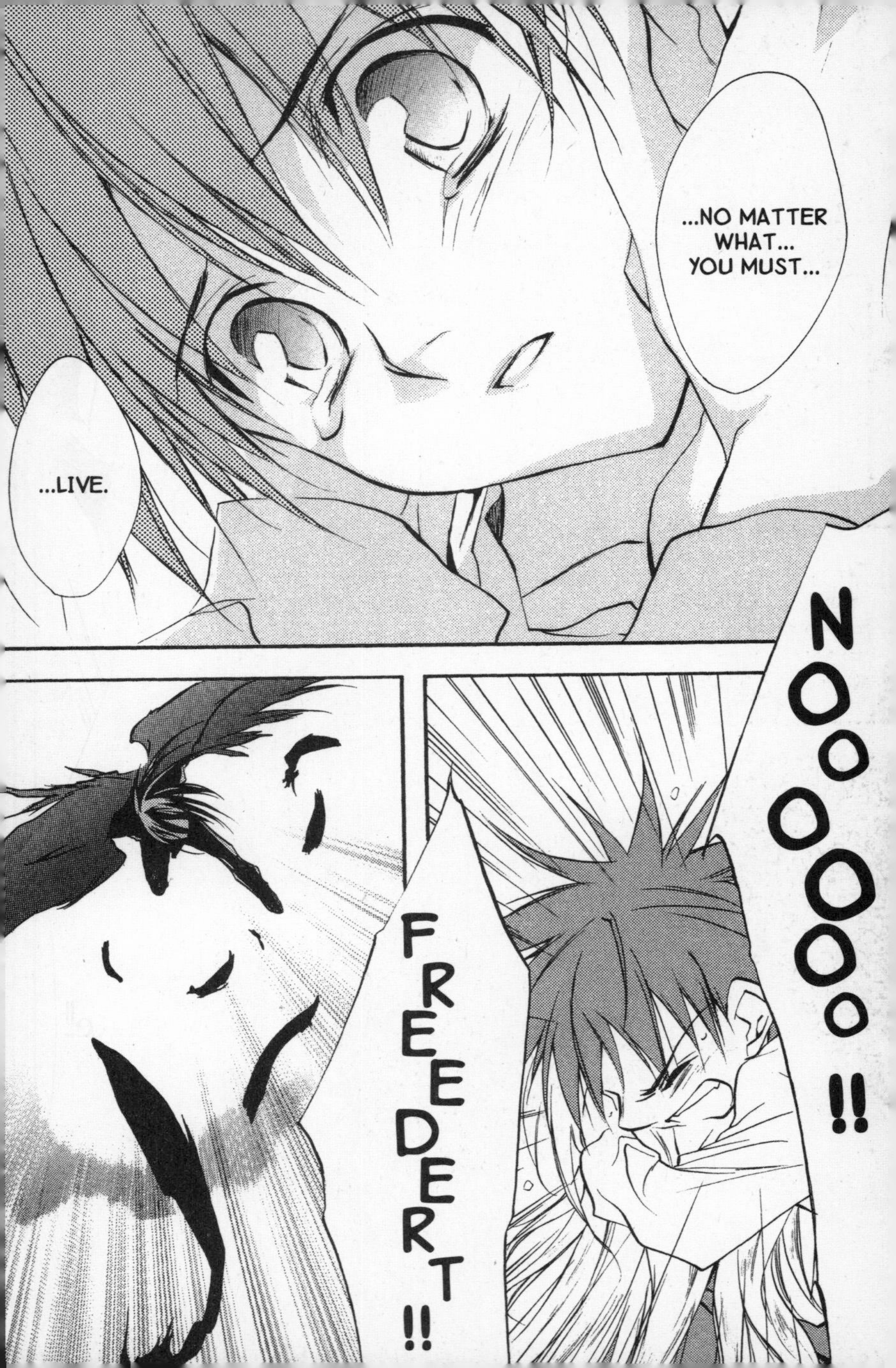
...NO MATTER WHAT... YOU MUST...
...LIVE.
NOOOOOO!!
FREEDERT!!

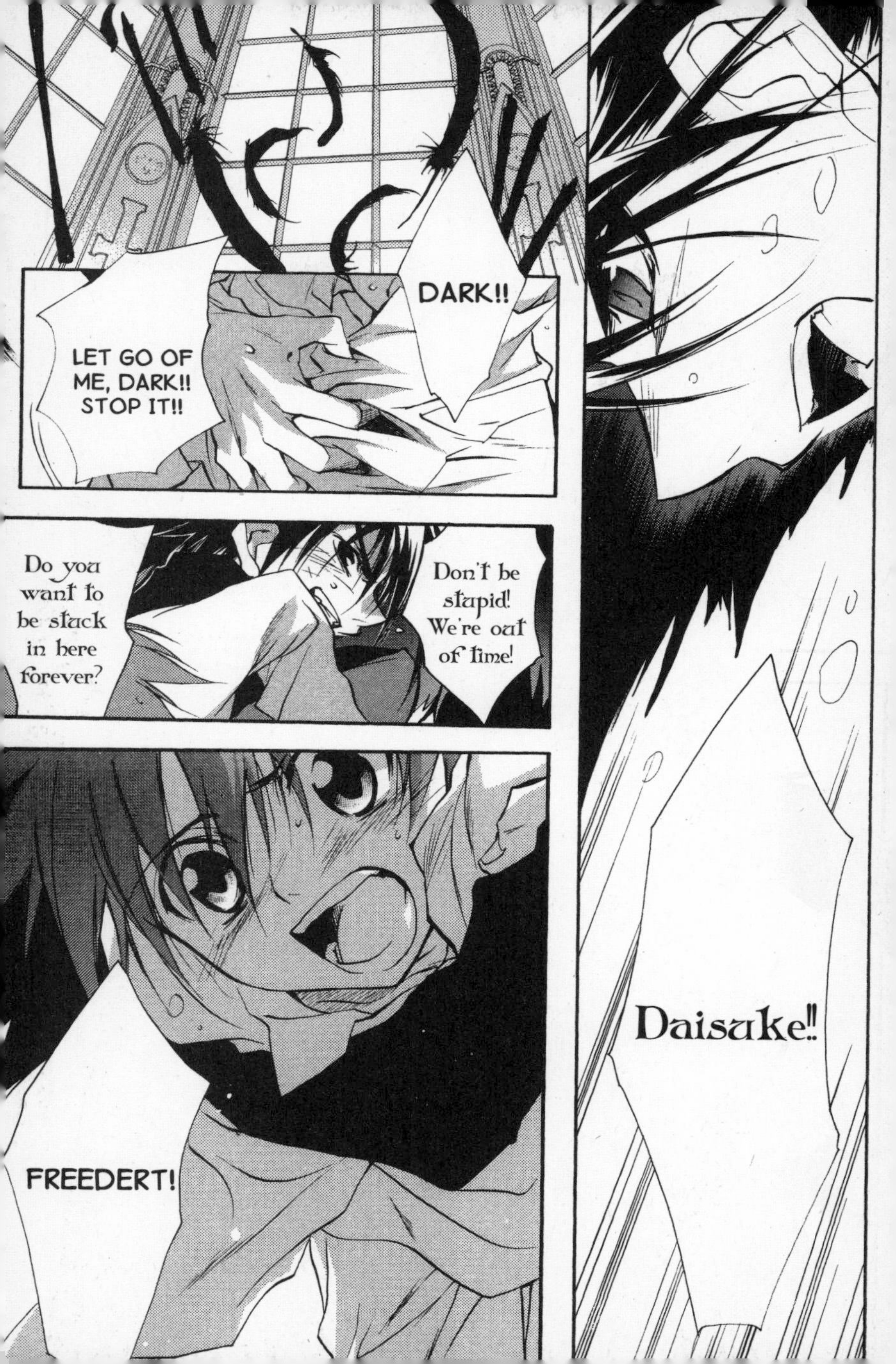
Daisuke!!
DARK!!
LET GO OF ME, DARK!! STOP IT!!
Don't be stupid! We're out of time!
Do you want to be stuck in here forever?
FREEDERT!

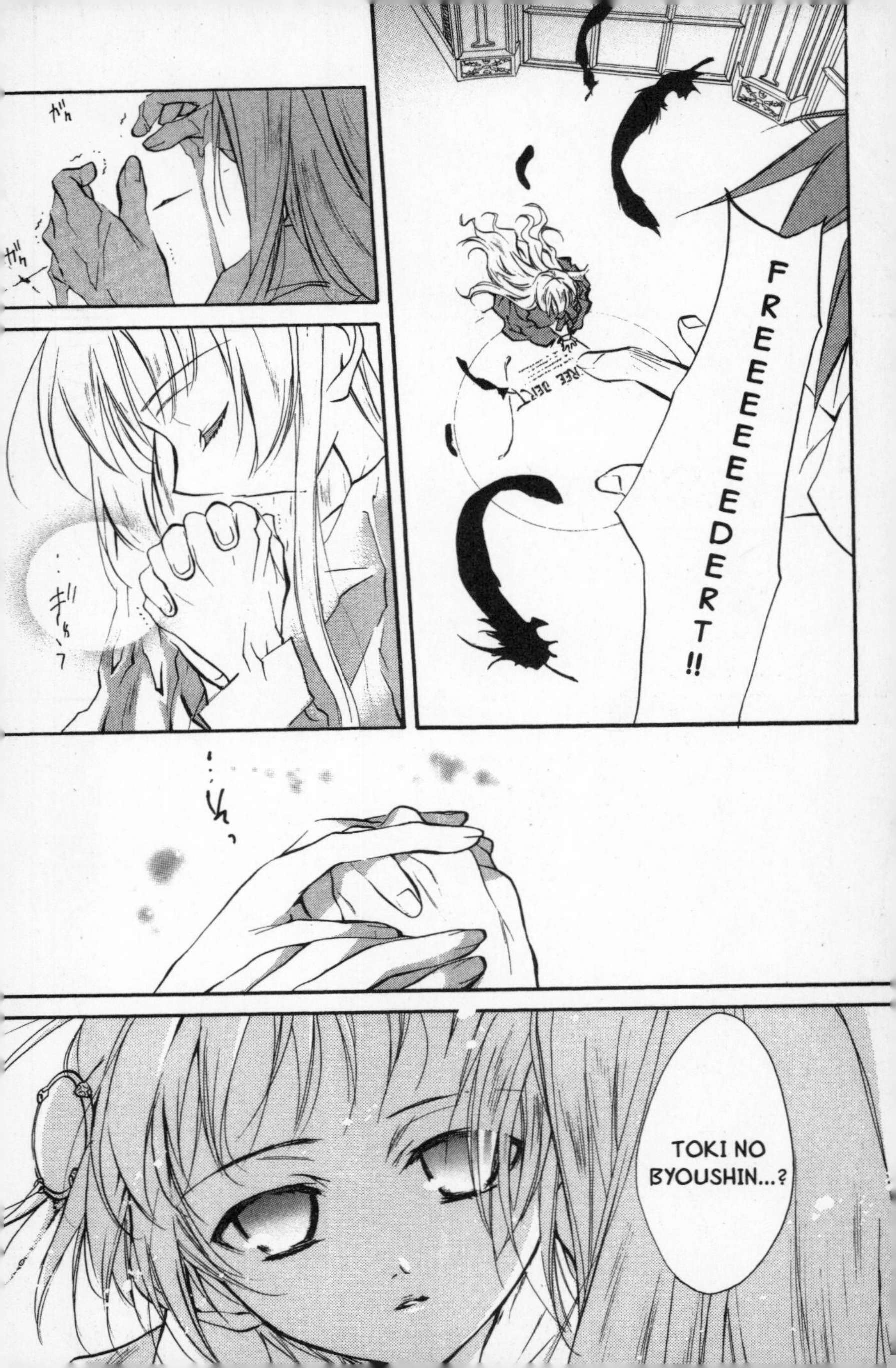
FREEEEEEDERT!!
TOKI NO BYOUSHIN...?

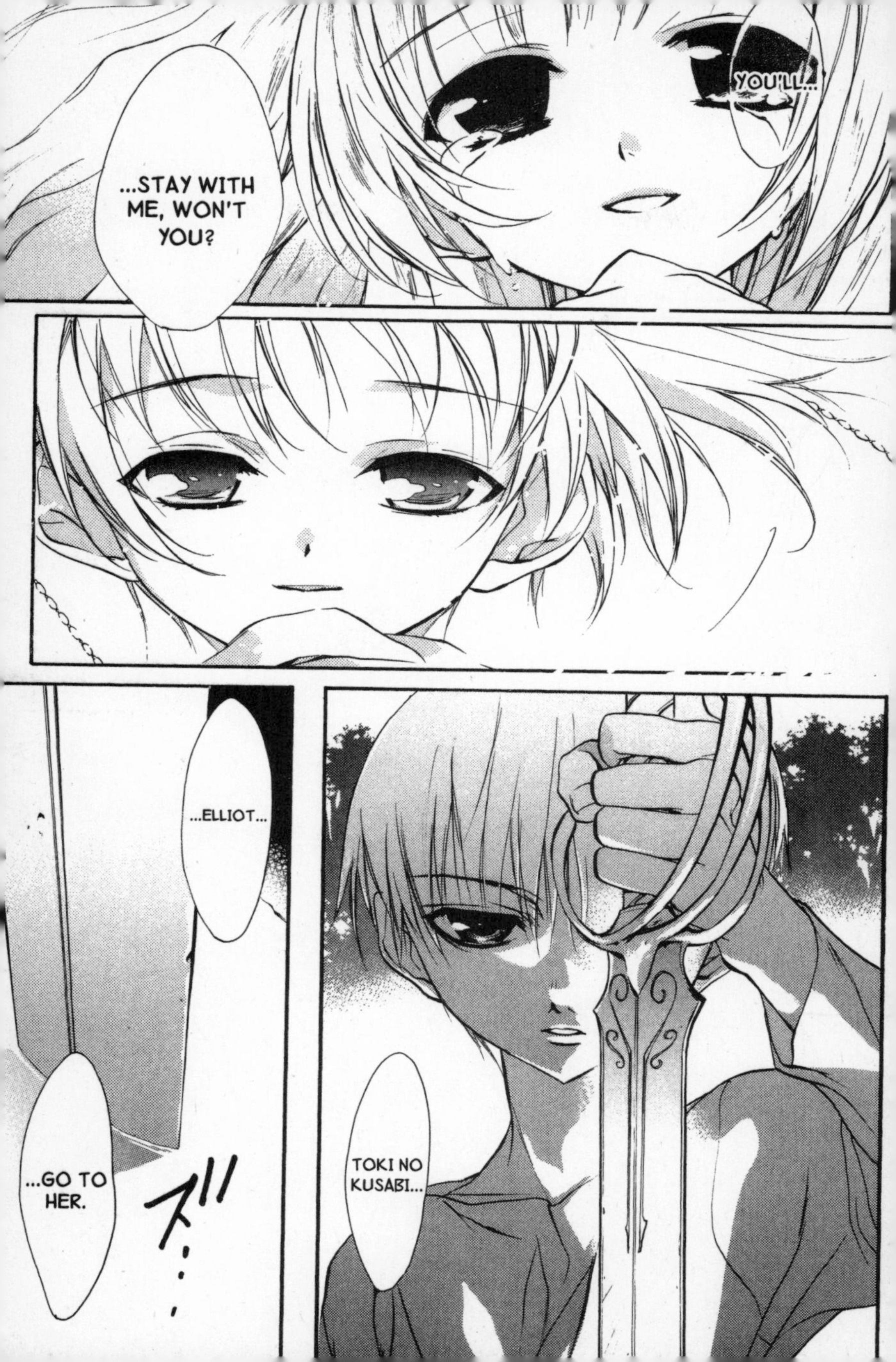
YOU'LL...
...STAY WITH ME, WON'T YOU?
TOKI NO KUSABI...
...ELLIOT...
...GO TO HER.
ズ…

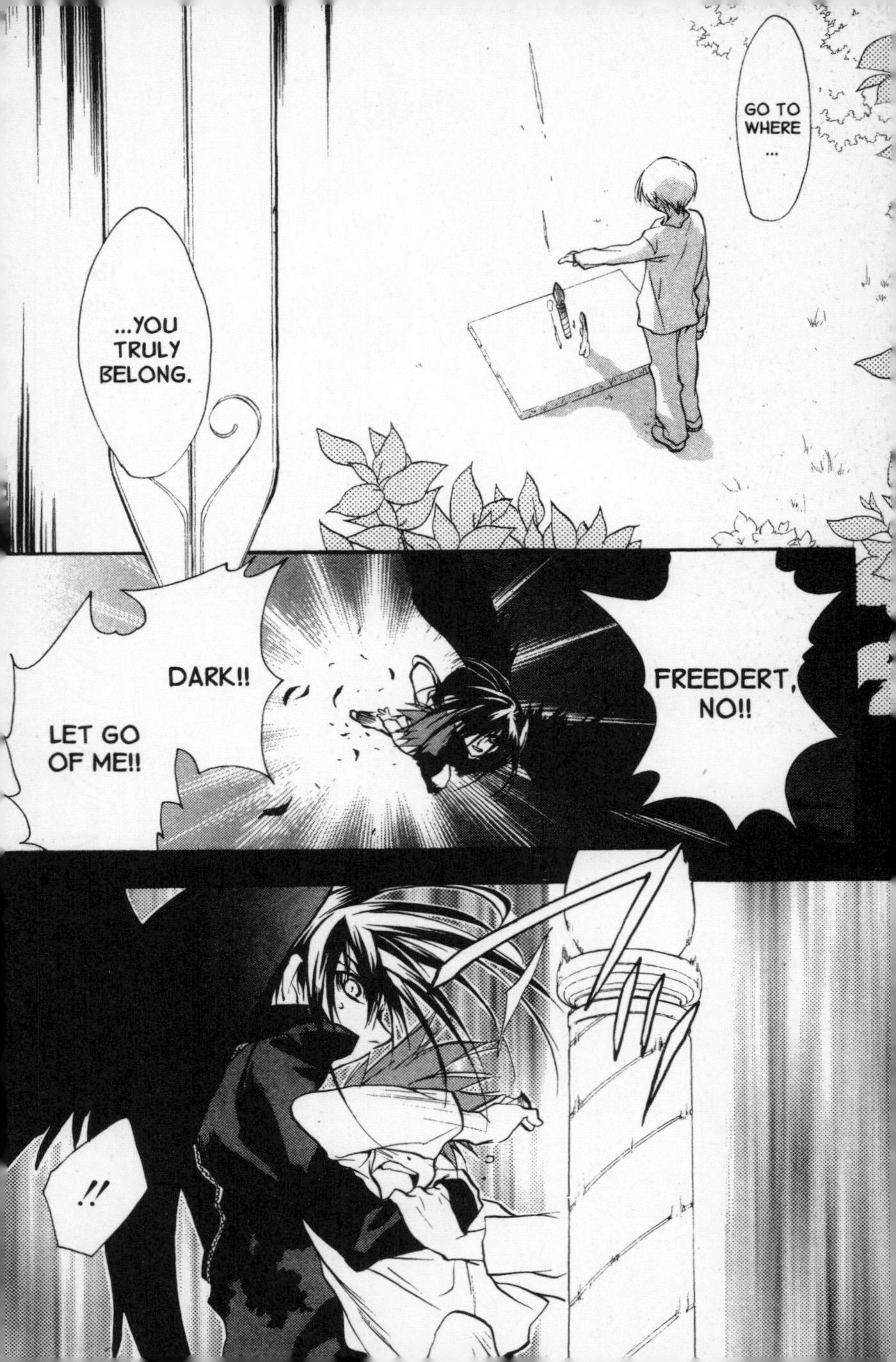
GO TO WHERE ...
...YOU TRULY BELONG.
FREEDERT, NO!!
DARK!!
LET GO OF ME!!
!!

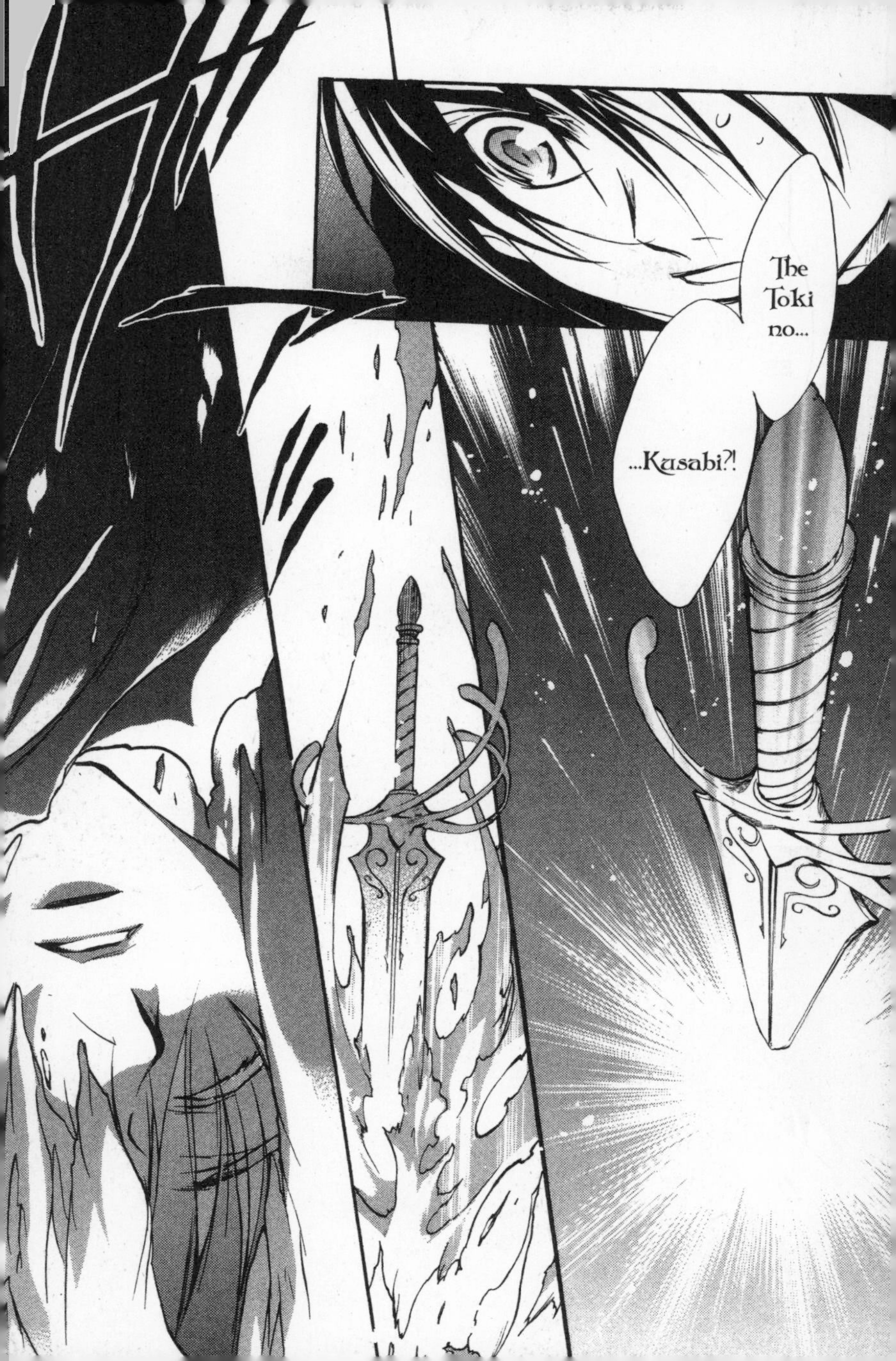
The Toki no...
...Kusabi?!

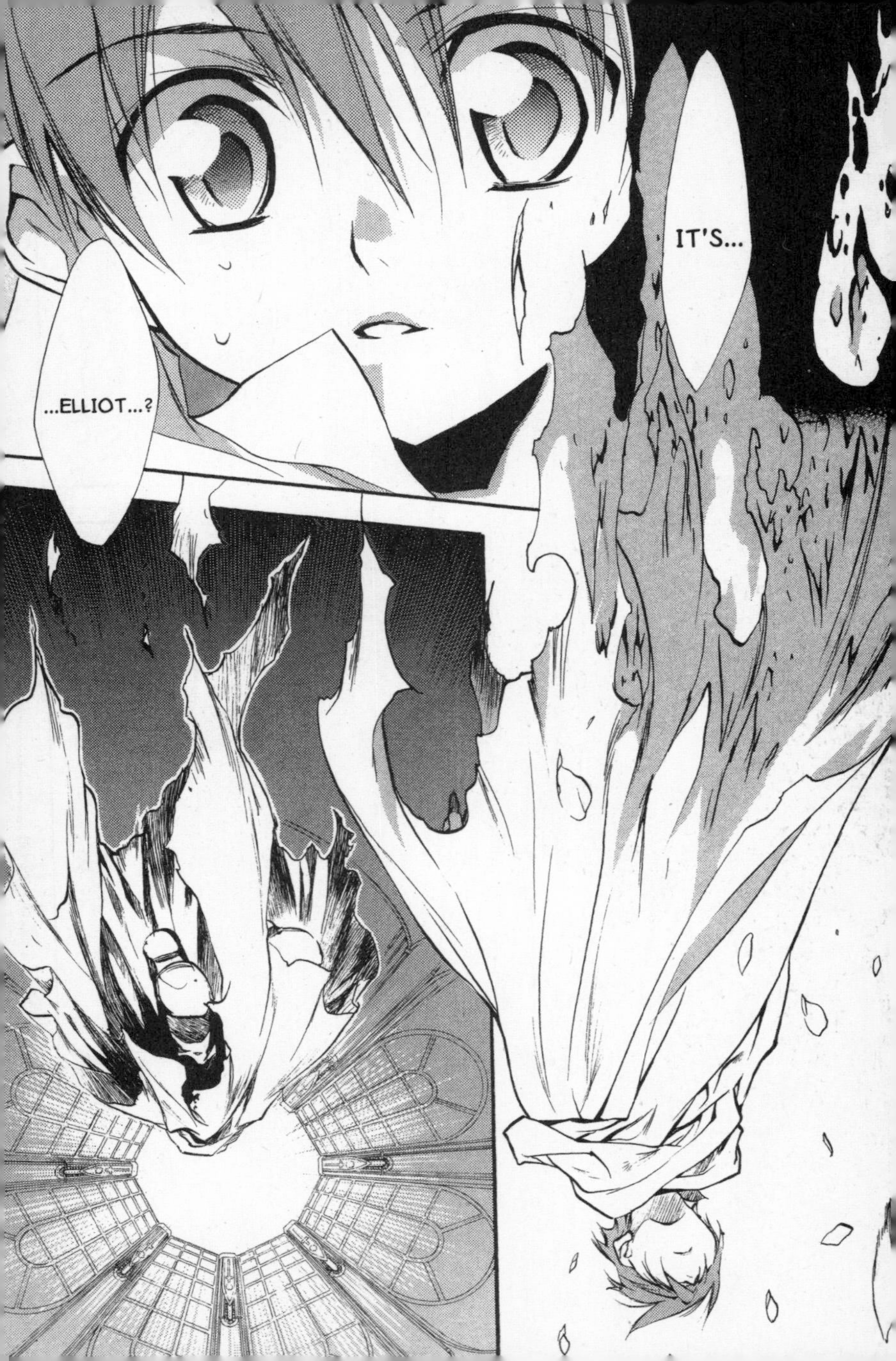
IT'S...
...ELLIOT...?

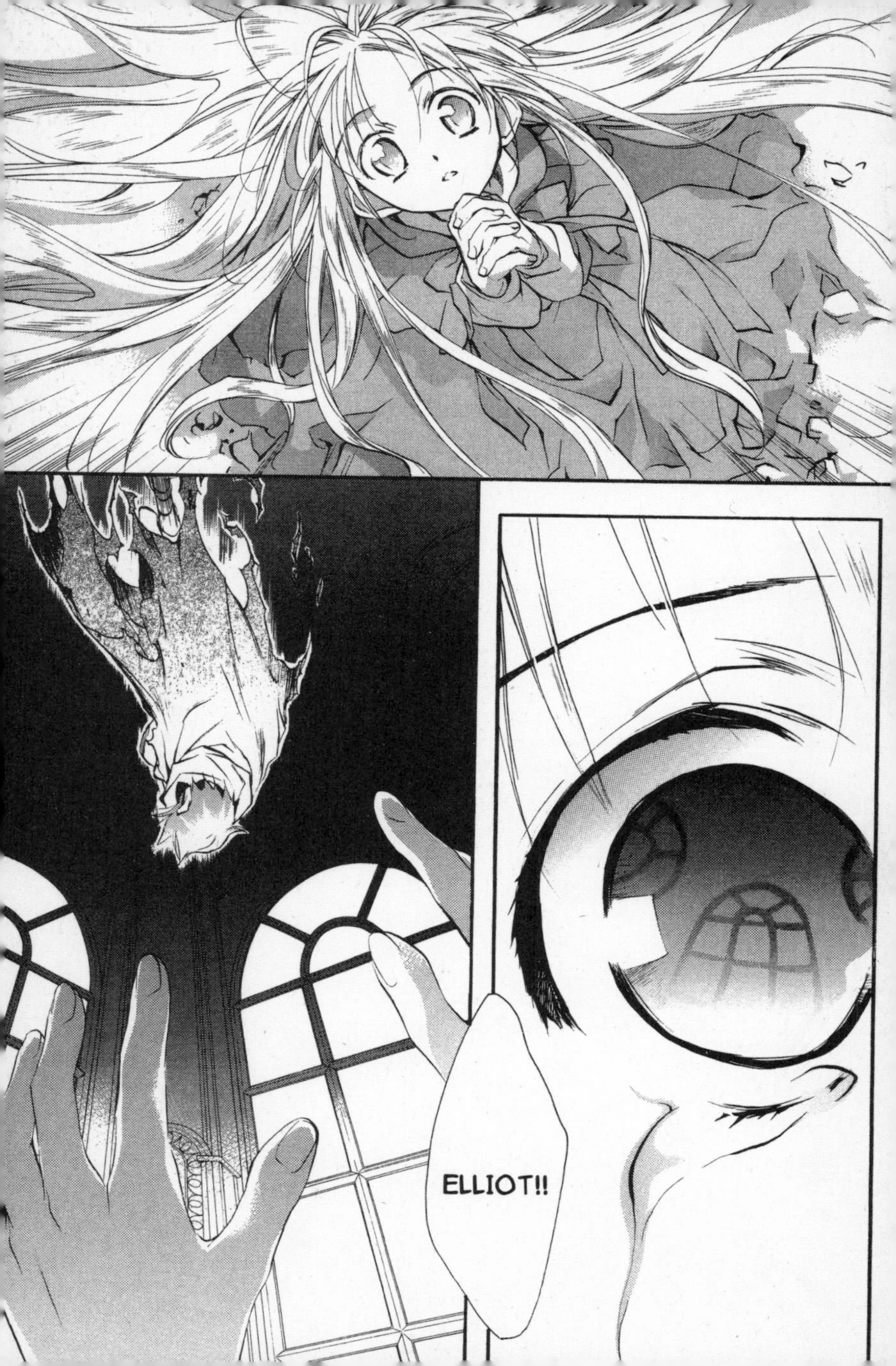
ELLIOT!!

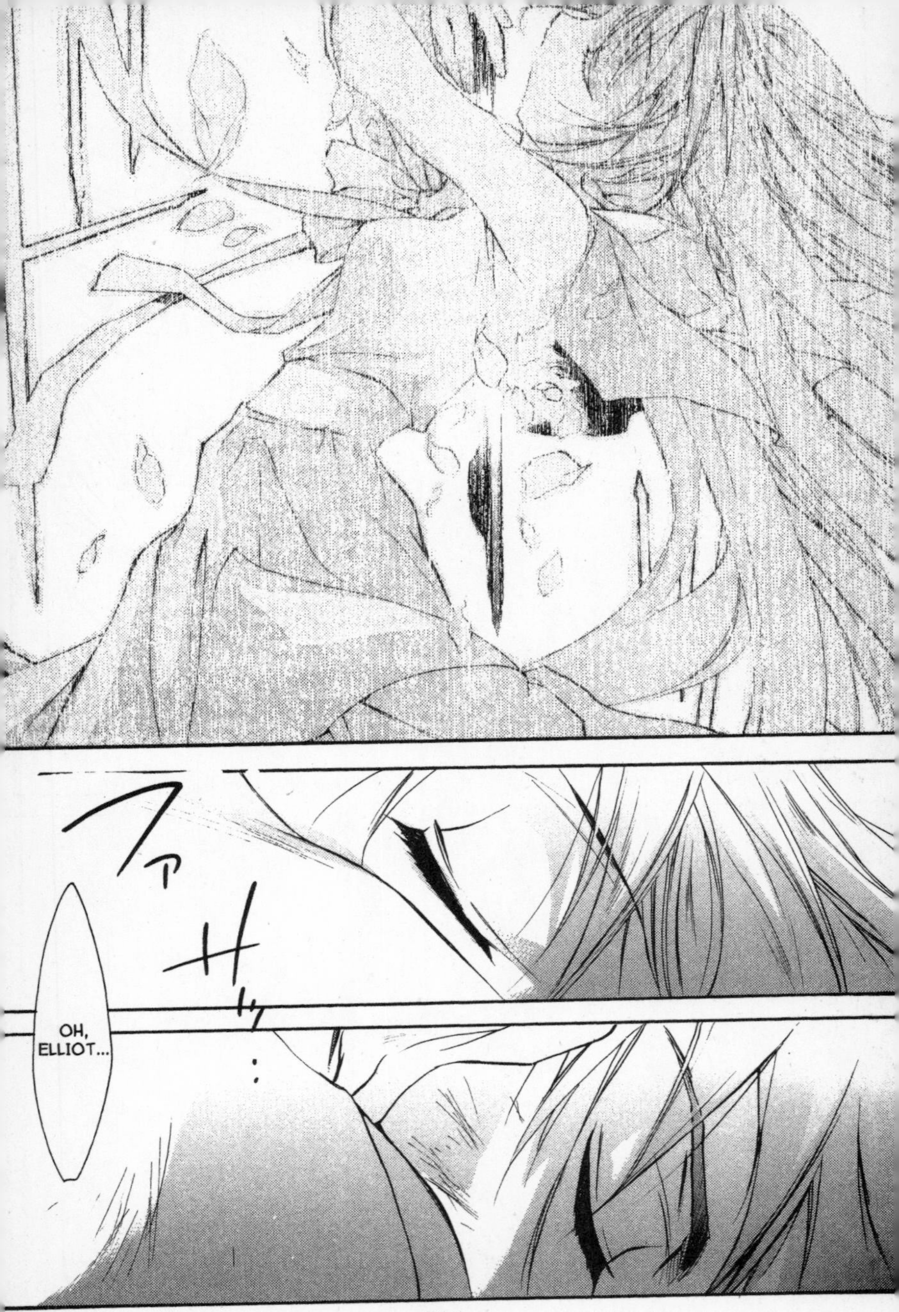
ファサッ
OH, ELLIOT...

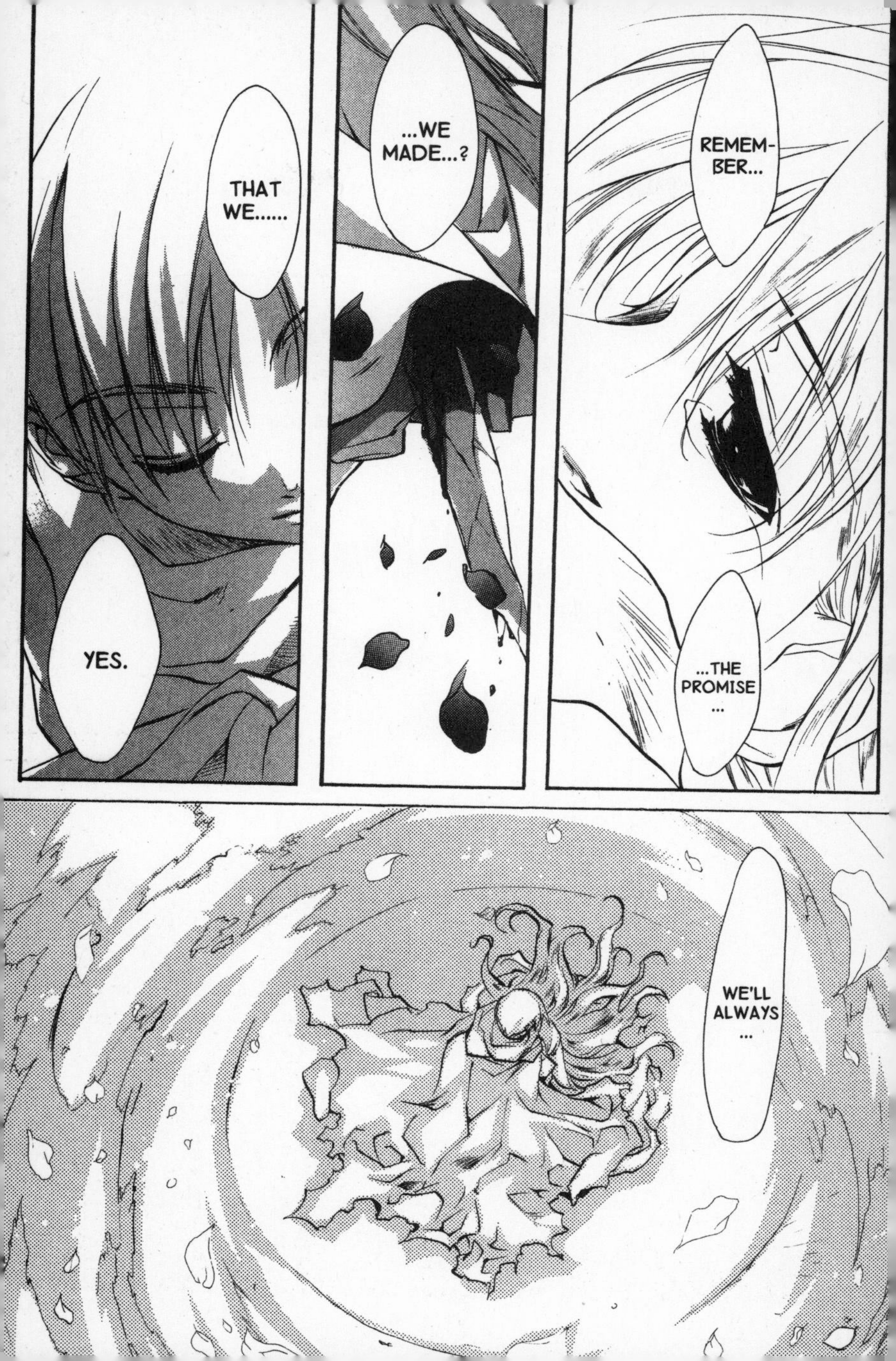
REMEMBER...
...THE PROMISE ...
...WE MADE...?
THAT WE......
YES.
WE'LL ALWAYS ...

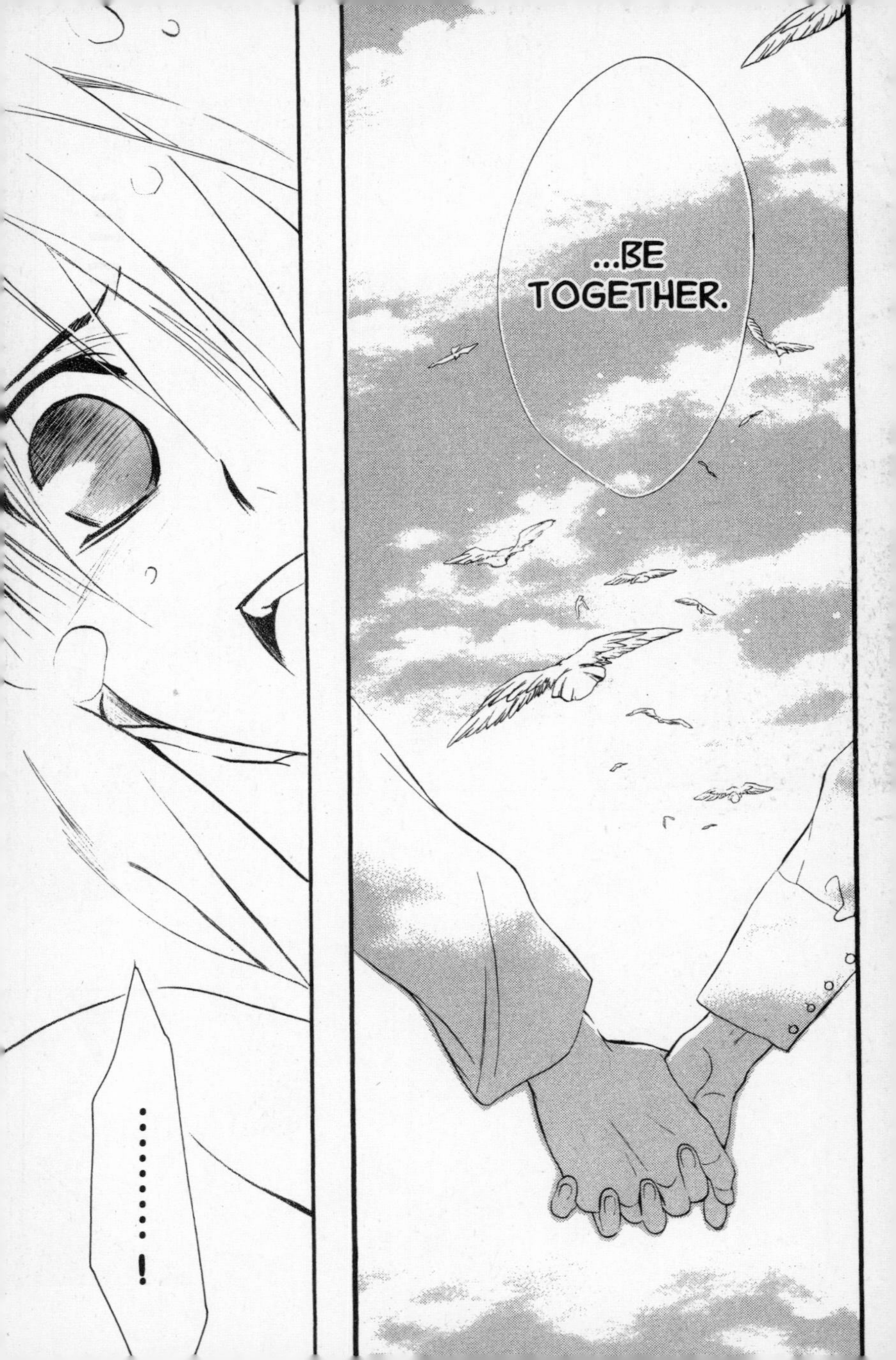
...BE TOGETHER.
..........!

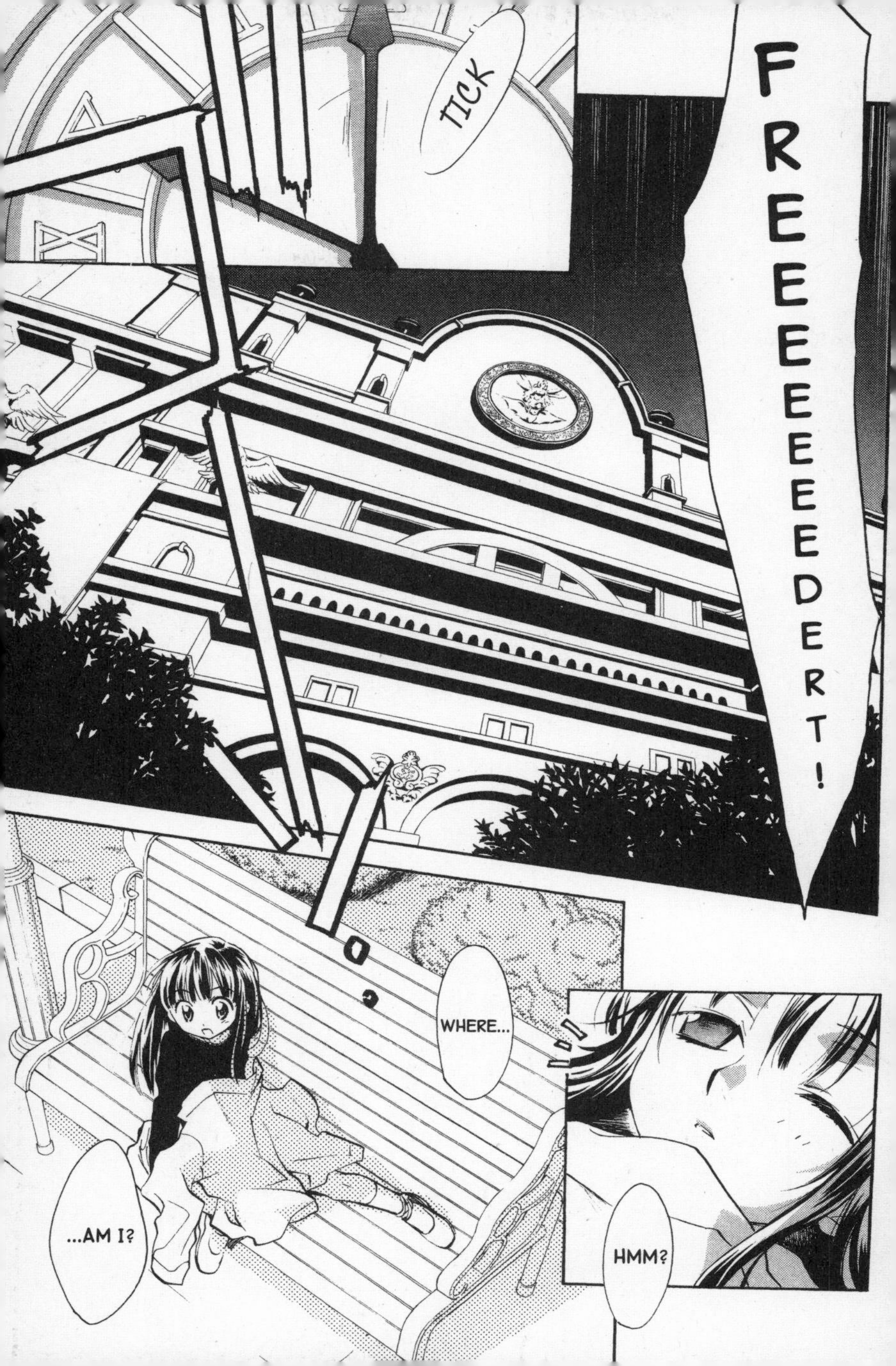
FREEEEEEDERT!
TICK
!
HMM?
WHERE...
...AM I?

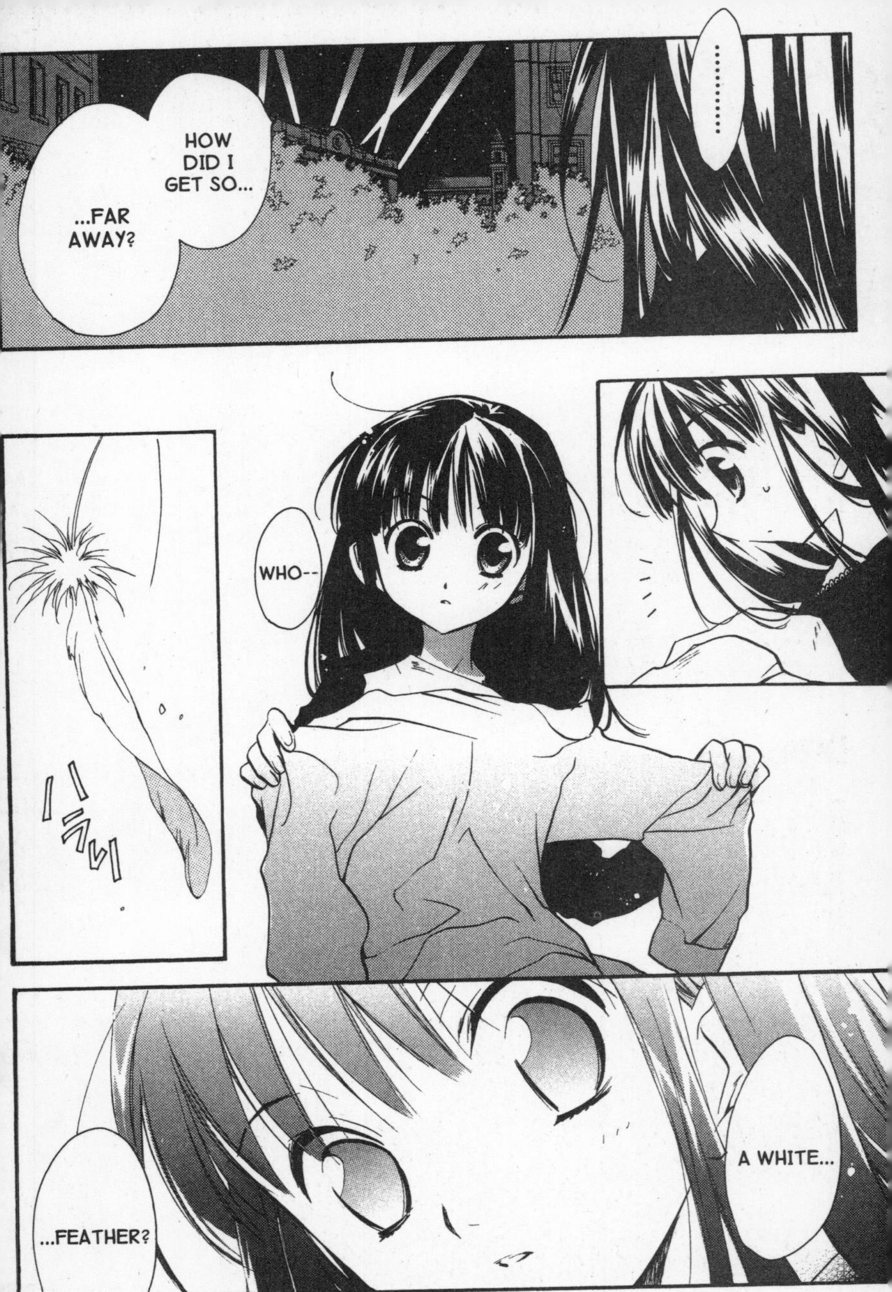
......
HOW DID I GET SO...
...FAR AWAY?
WHO--
A WHITE...
...FEATHER?

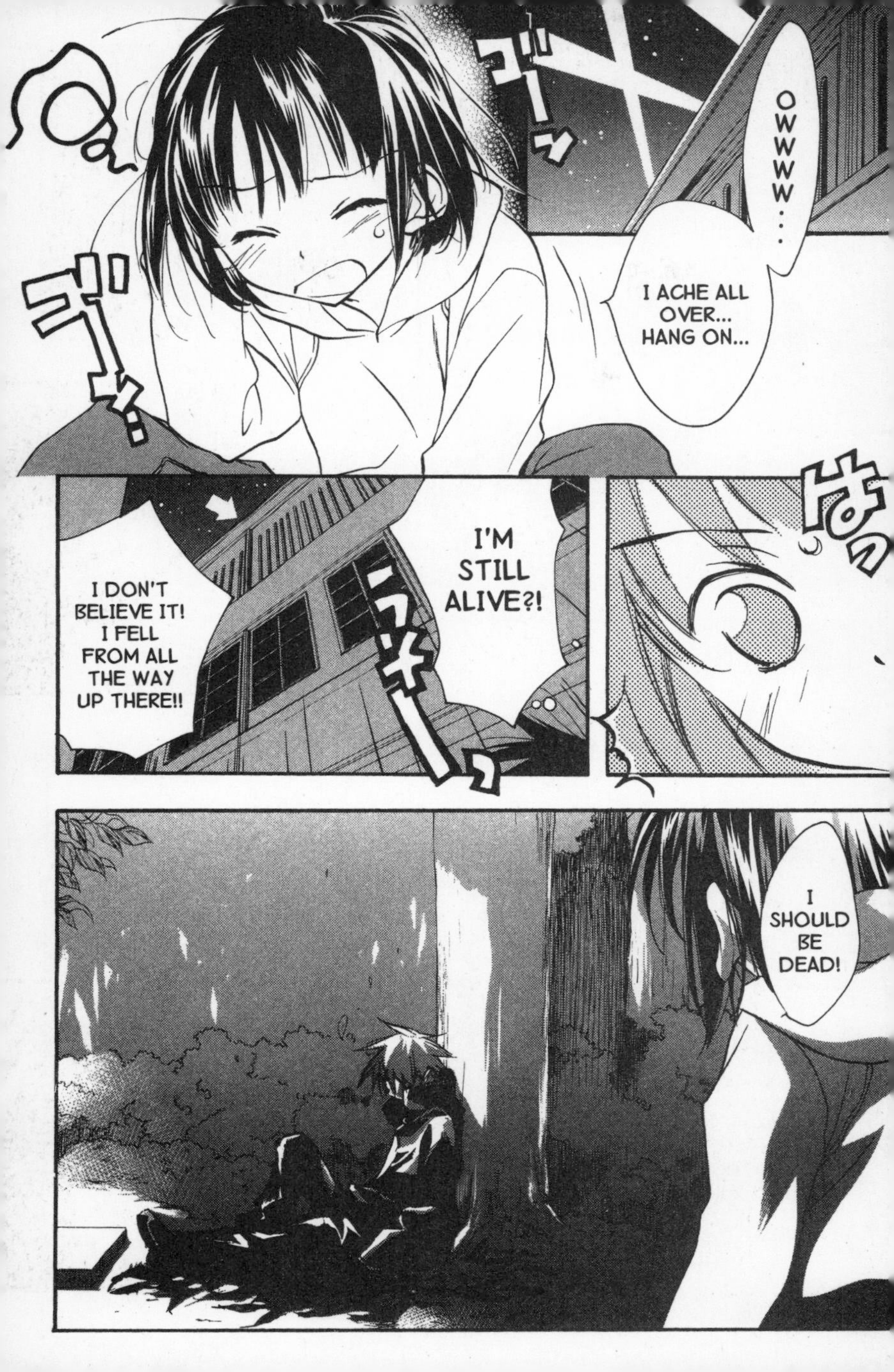
OWWWW...
I ACHE ALL OVER... HANG ON...
I'M STILL ALIVE?!
I DON'T BELIEVE IT! I FELL FROM ALL THE WAY UP THERE!!
I SHOULD BE DEAD!

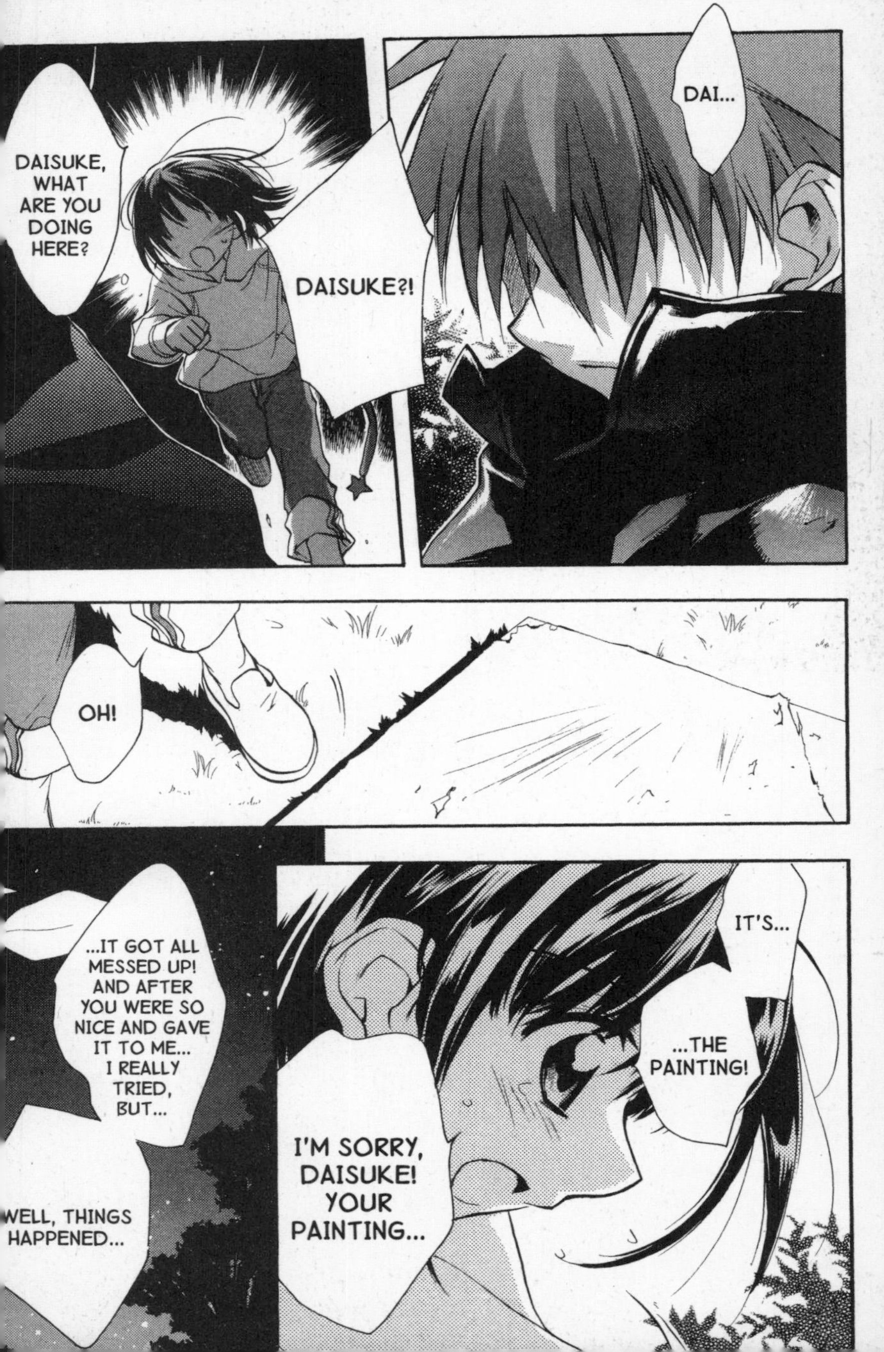
DAI...
DAISUKE?!
DAISUKE, WHAT ARE YOU DOING HERE?
OH!
IT'S...
...THE PAINTING!
I'M SORRY, DAISUKE! YOUR PAINTING...
...IT GOT ALL MESSED UP! AND AFTER YOU WERE SO NICE AND GAVE IT TO ME... I REALLY TRIED, BUT...
WELL, THINGS HAPPENED...

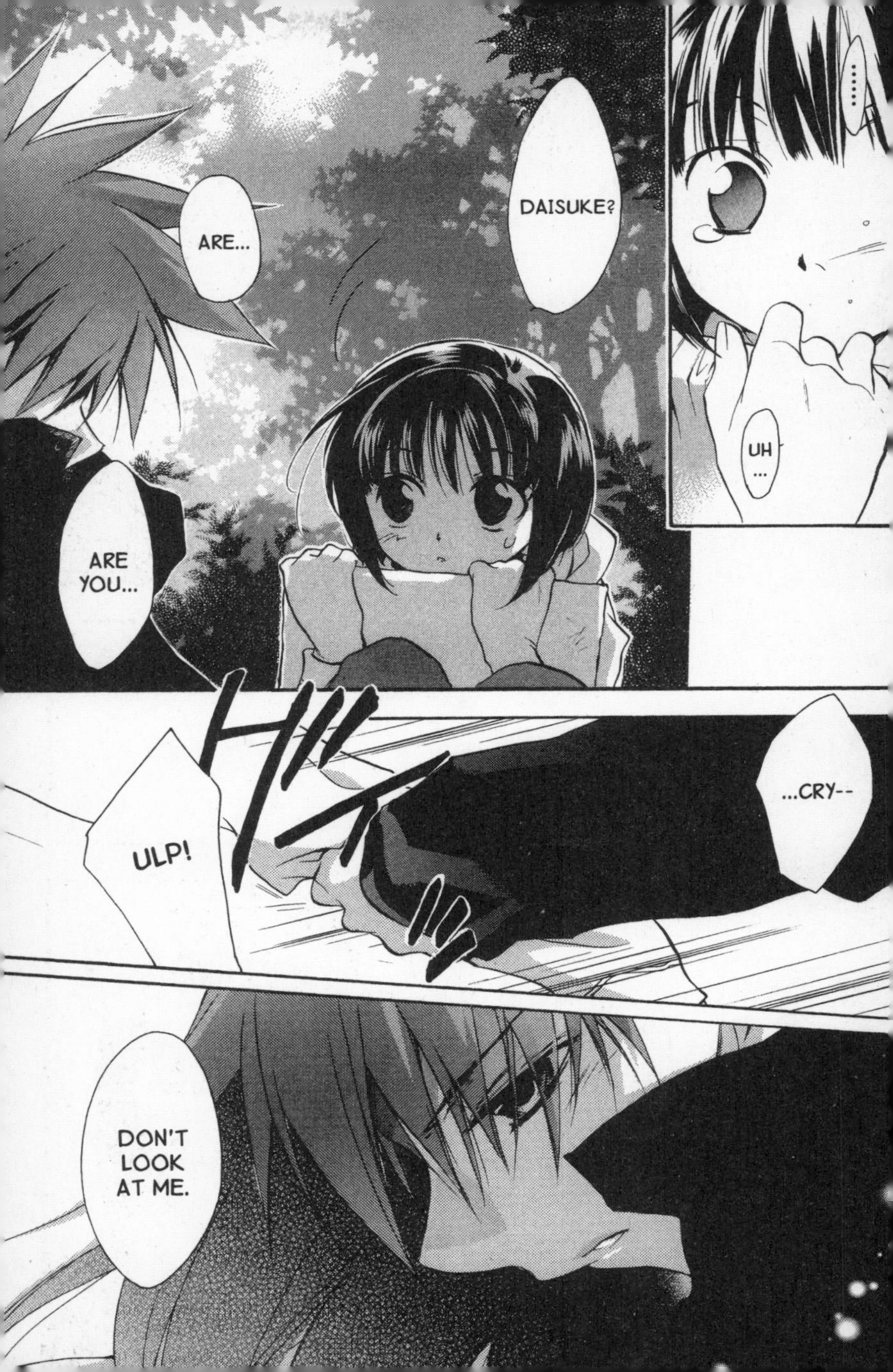

...
UH...
DAISUKE?
ARE...
ARE YOU...
...CRY--
ULP!
DON'T LOOK AT ME.

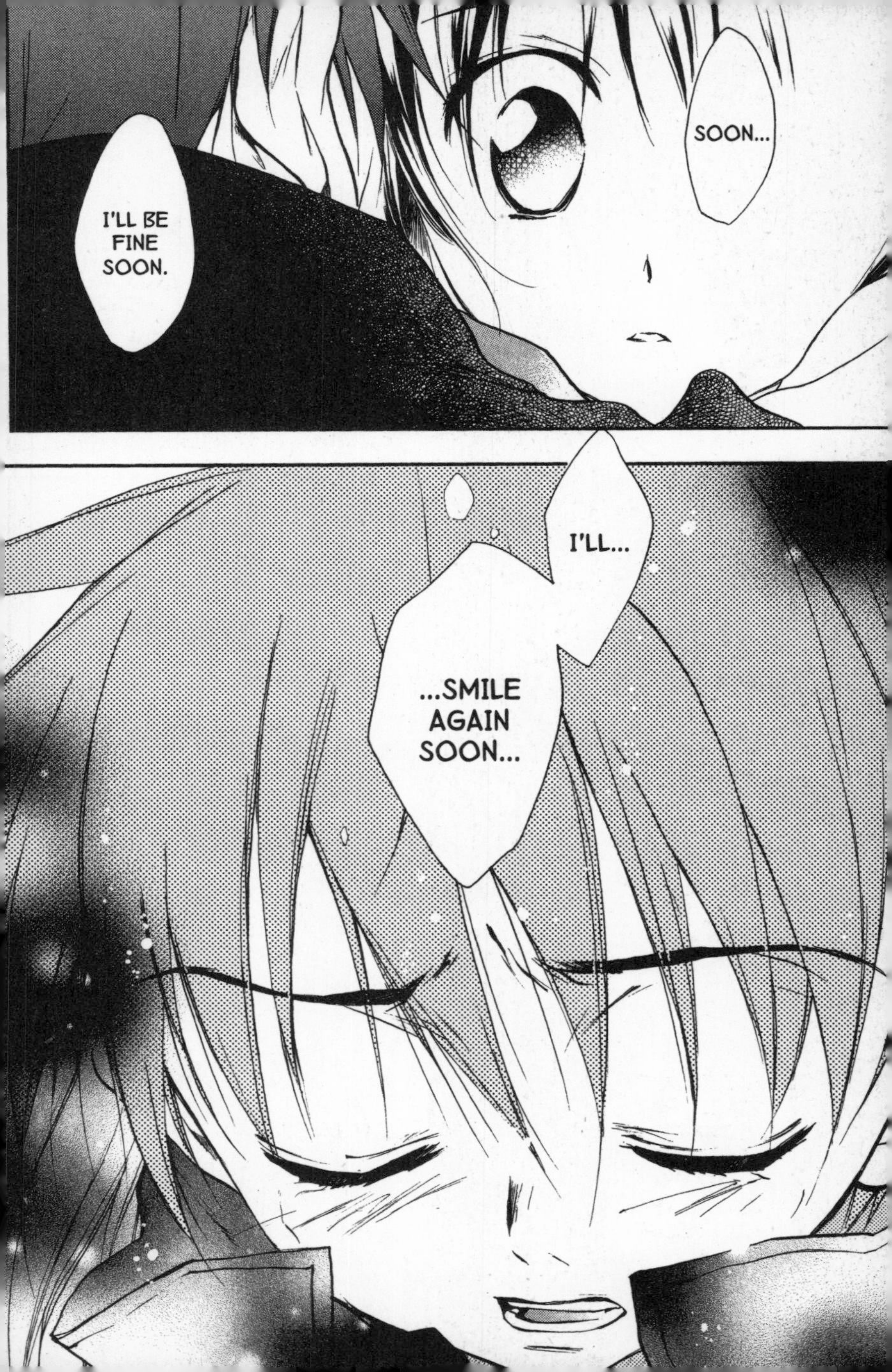
SOON...
I'LL BE FINE SOON.
I'LL...
...SMILE AGAIN SOON...

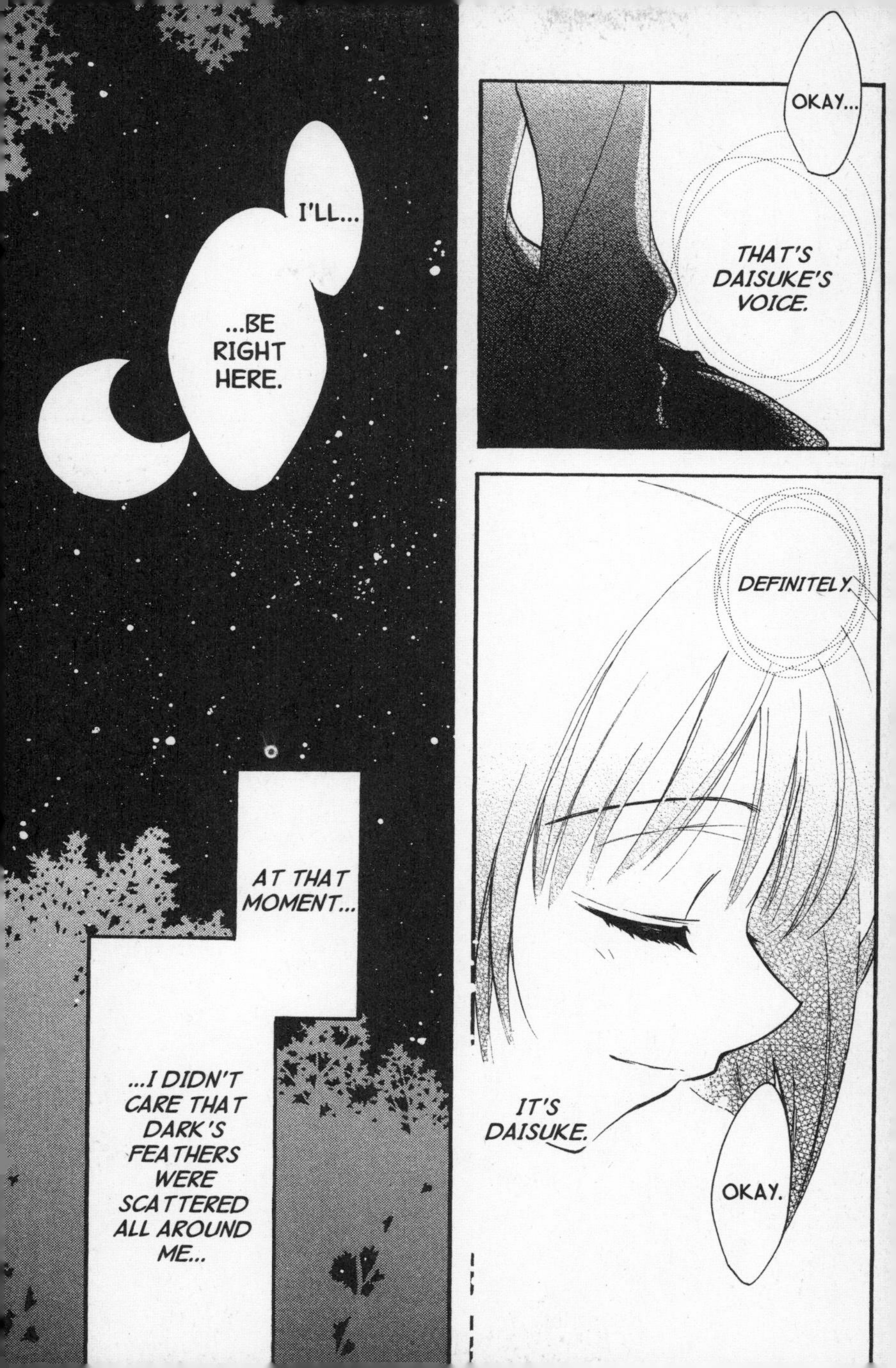
OKAY...
THAT'S DAISUKE'S VOICE.
DEFINITELY.
IT'S DAISUKE.
OKAY.
I'LL...
...BE RIGHT HERE.
AT THAT MOMENT...
...I DIDN'T CARE THAT DARK'S FEATHERS WERE SCATTERED ALL AROUND ME...

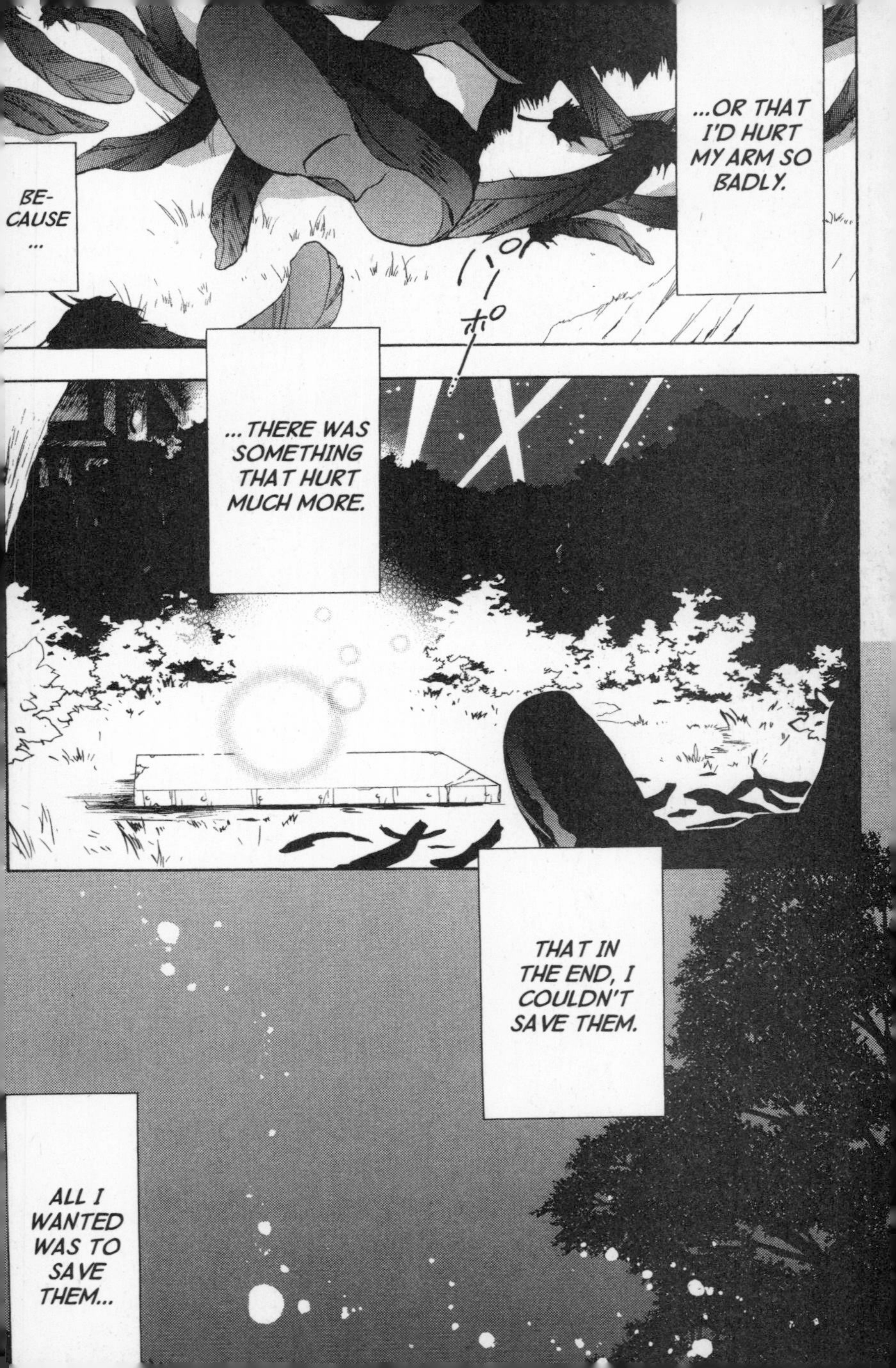
...OR THAT I'D HURT MY ARM SO BADLY.
BE-CAUSE ...
...THERE WAS SOMETHING THAT HURT MUCH MORE.
THAT IN THE END, I COULDN'T SAVE THEM.
ALL I WANTED WAS TO SAVE THEM...

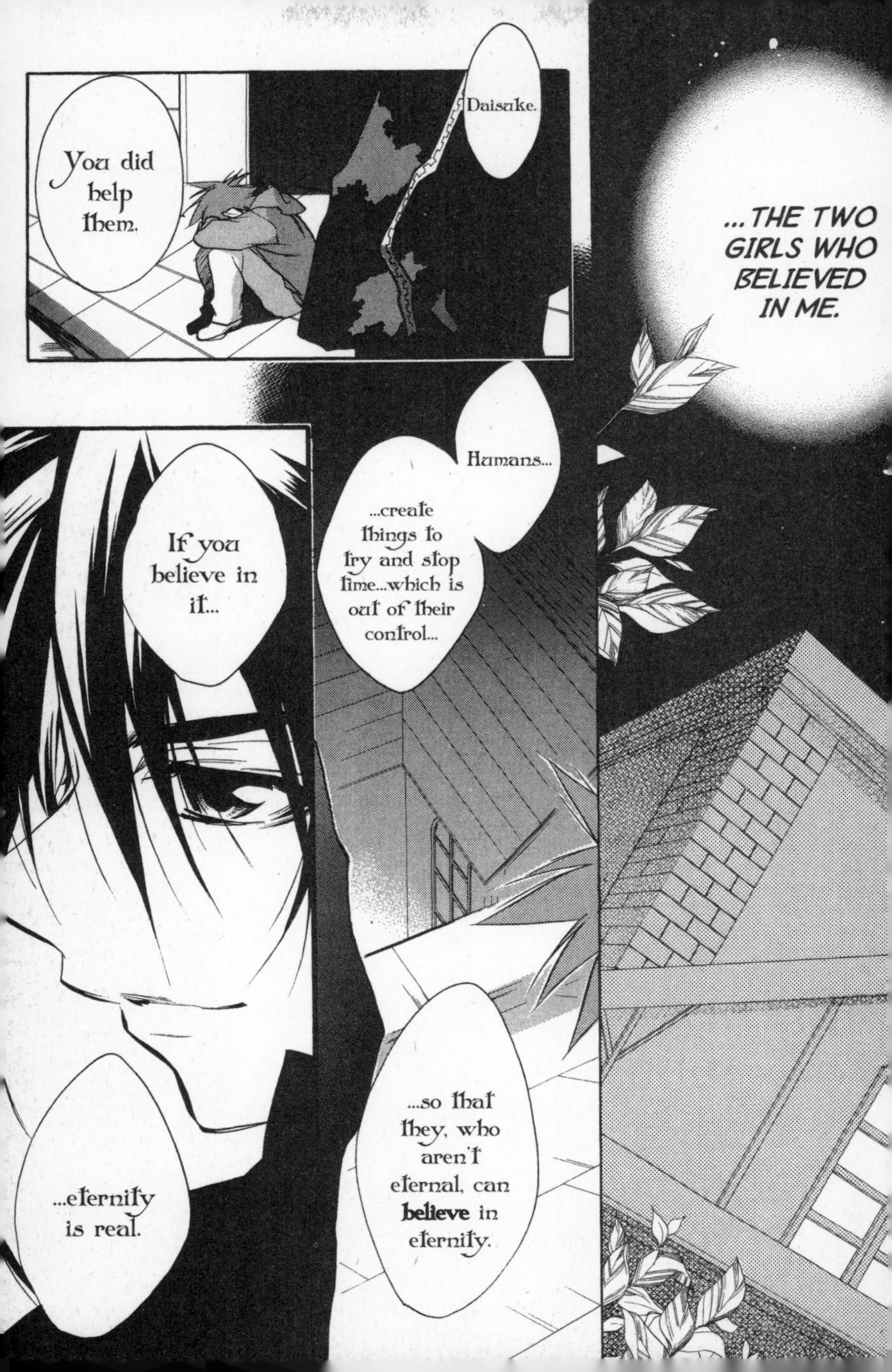
...THE TWO GIRLS WHO BELIEVED IN ME.
Daisuke.
You did help them.
Humans...
...create things to try and stop time...which is out of their control...
...so that they, who aren't eternal, can **believe** in eternity.
If you believe in it...
...eternity is real.

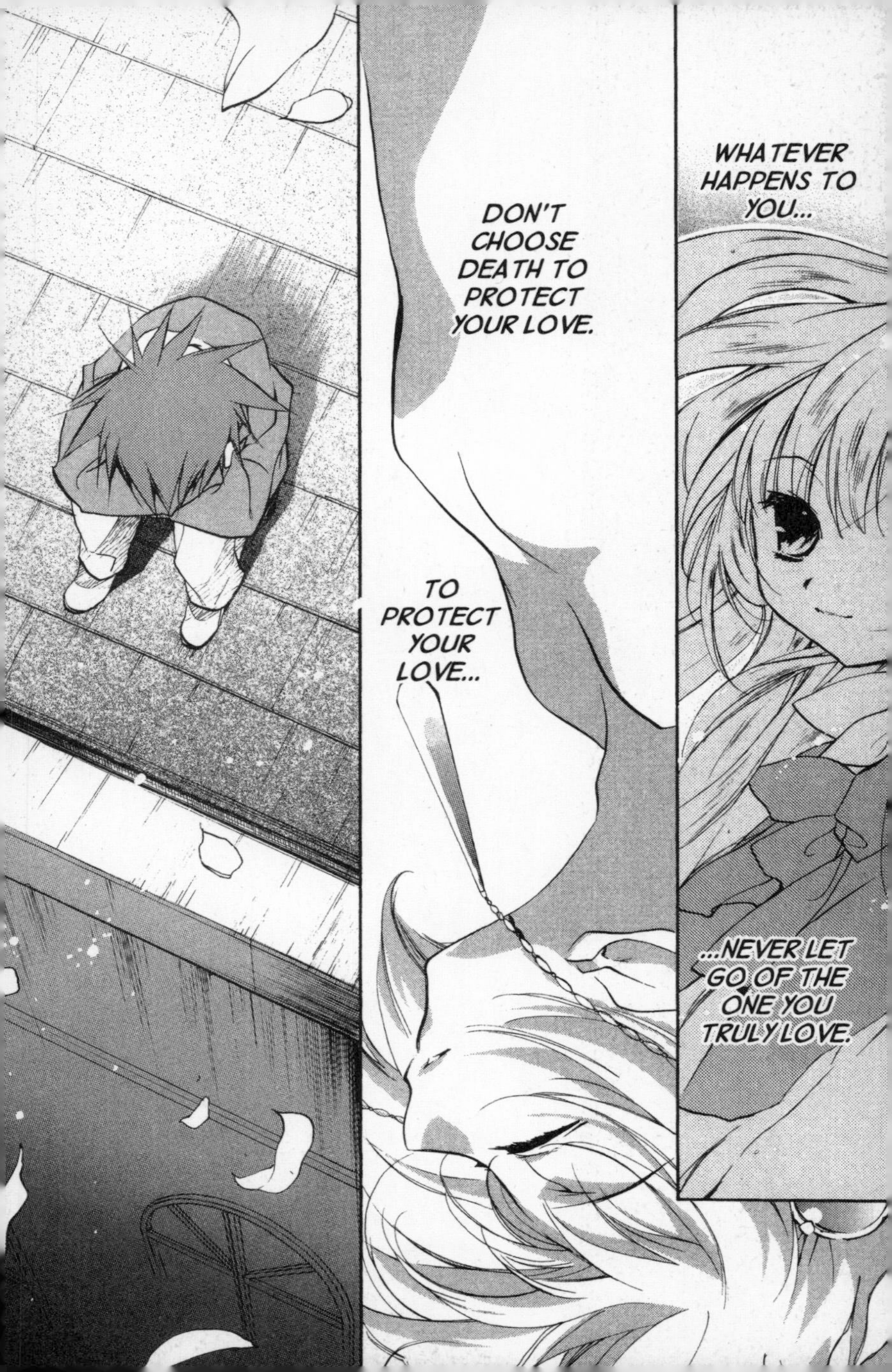
WHATEVER HAPPENS TO YOU...
...NEVER LET GO OF THE ONE YOU TRULY LOVE.
DON'T CHOOSE DEATH TO PROTECT YOUR LOVE.
TO PROTECT YOUR LOVE...

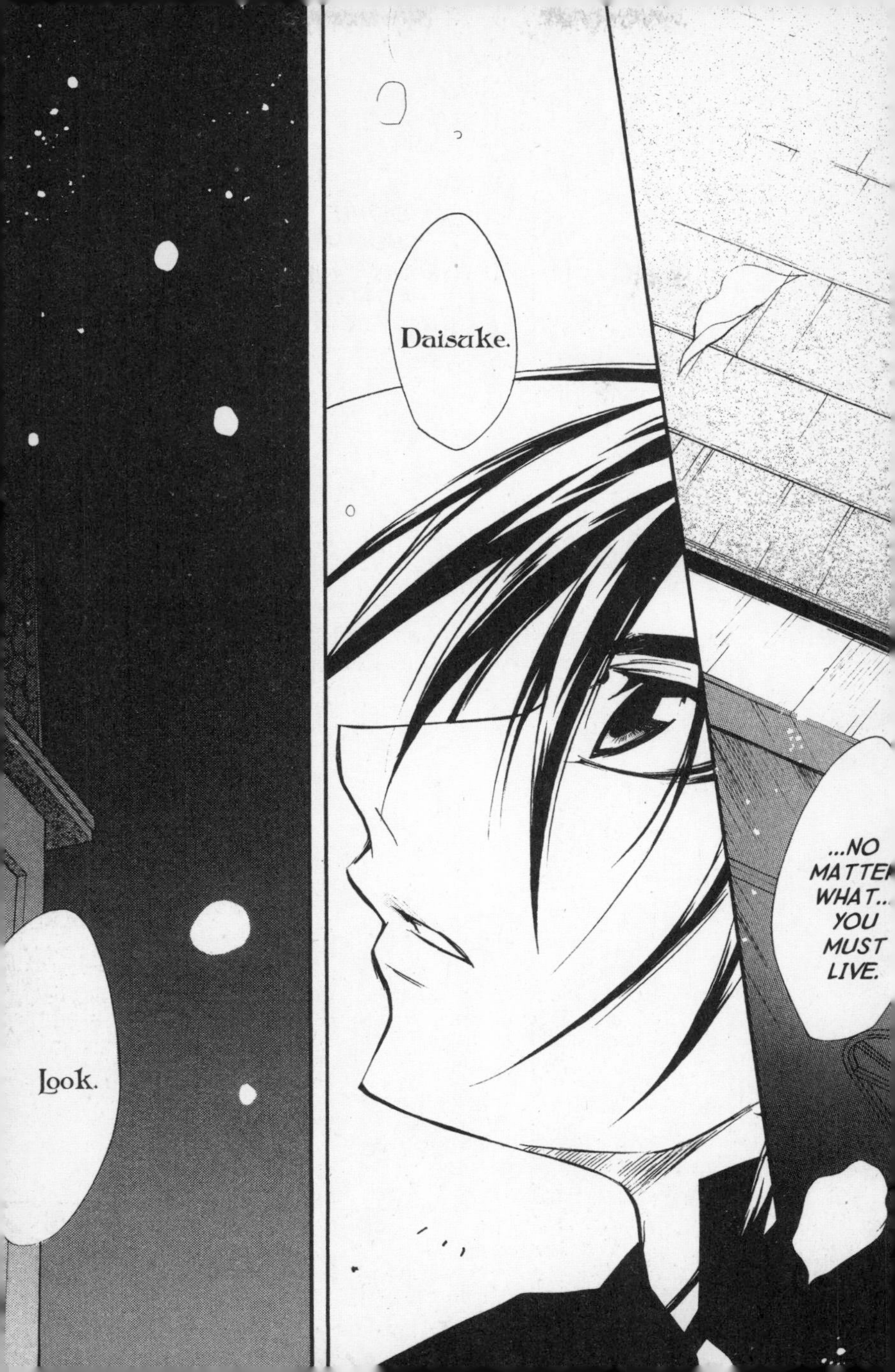
Daisuke.
...NO MATTER WHAT... YOU MUST LIVE.
Look.

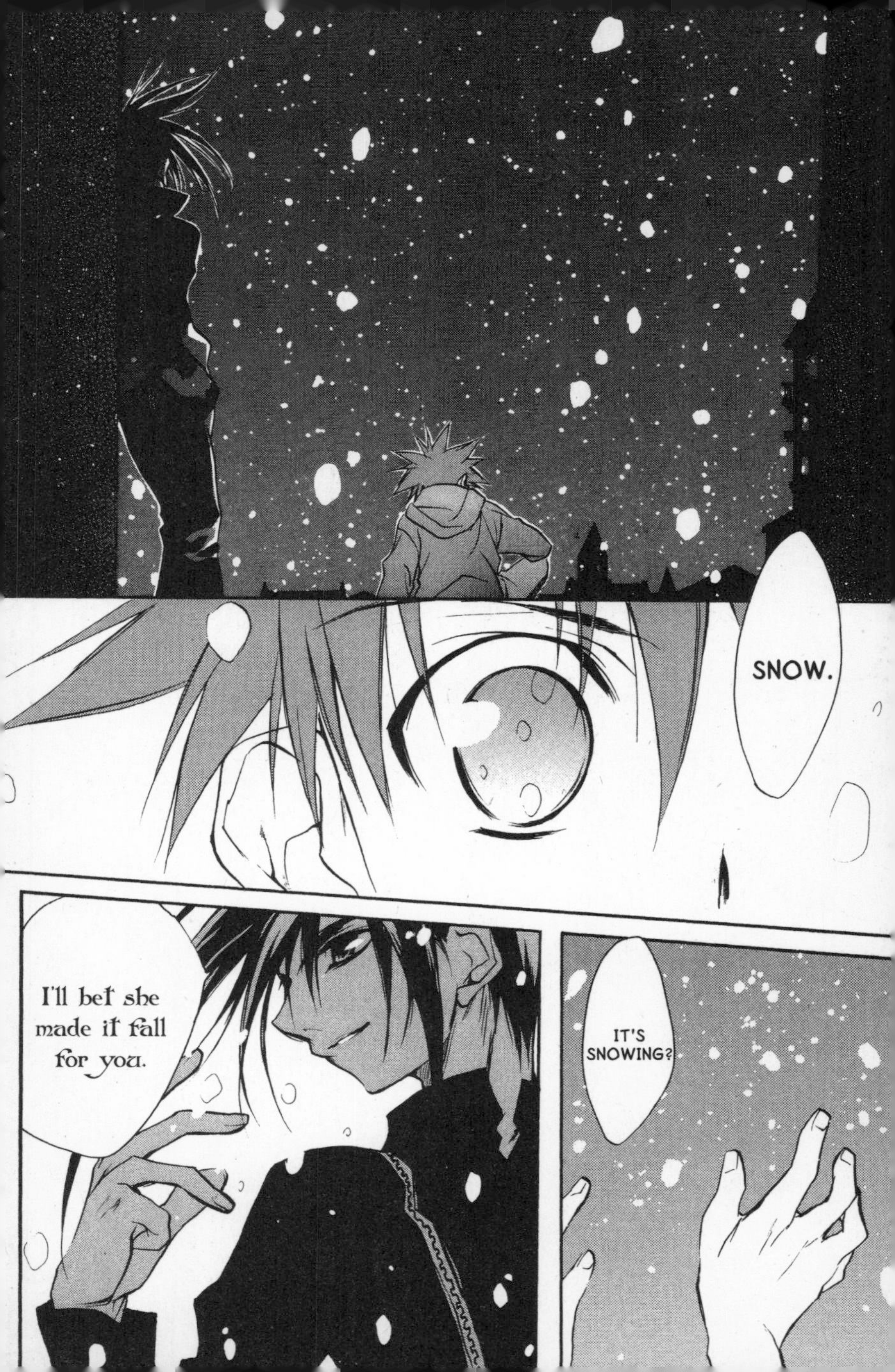
SNOW.
IT'S SNOWING?
I'll bet she made it fall for you.

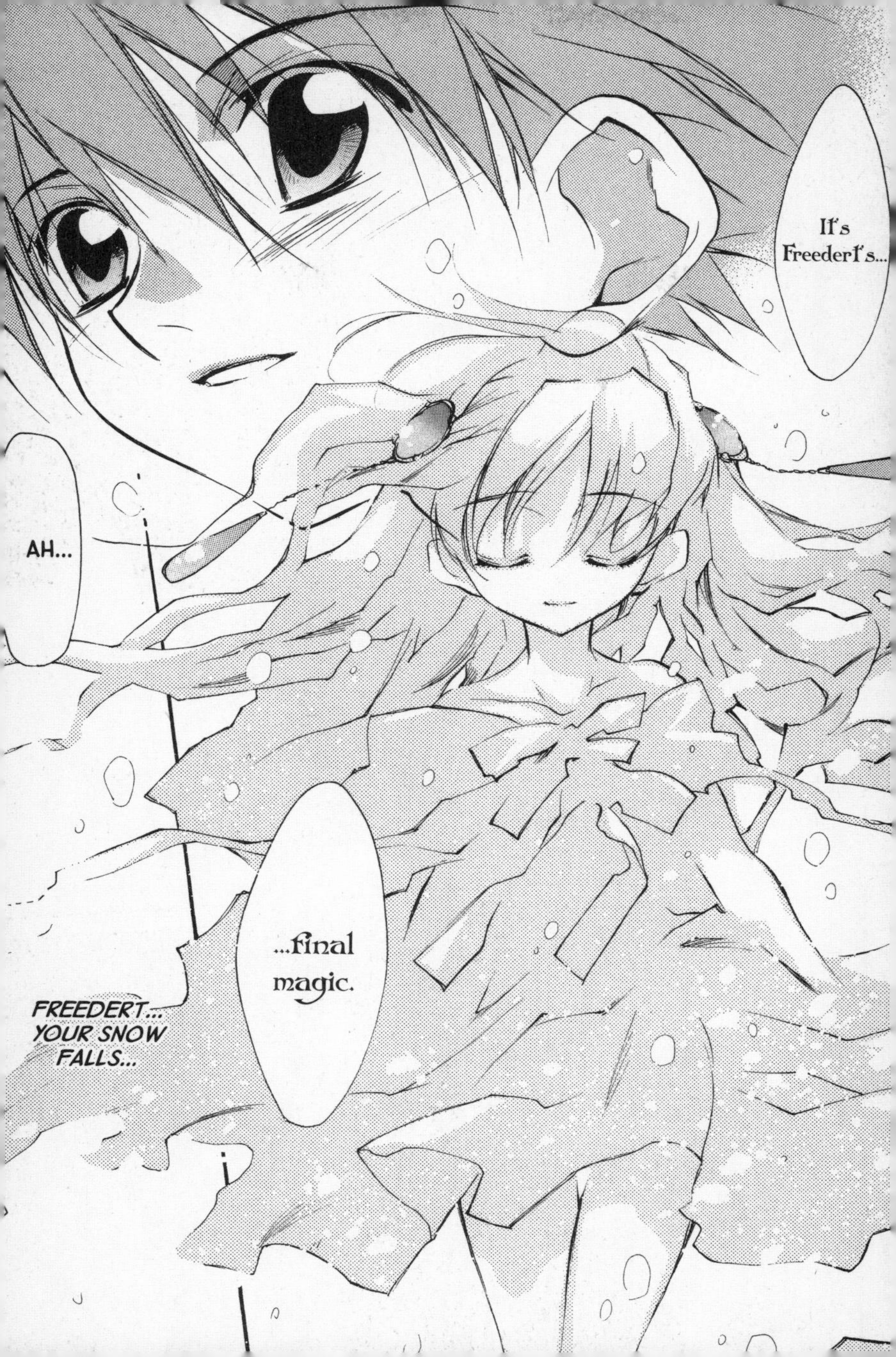
It's Freedert's...
...final magic.
AH...
FREEDERT... YOUR SNOW FALLS...

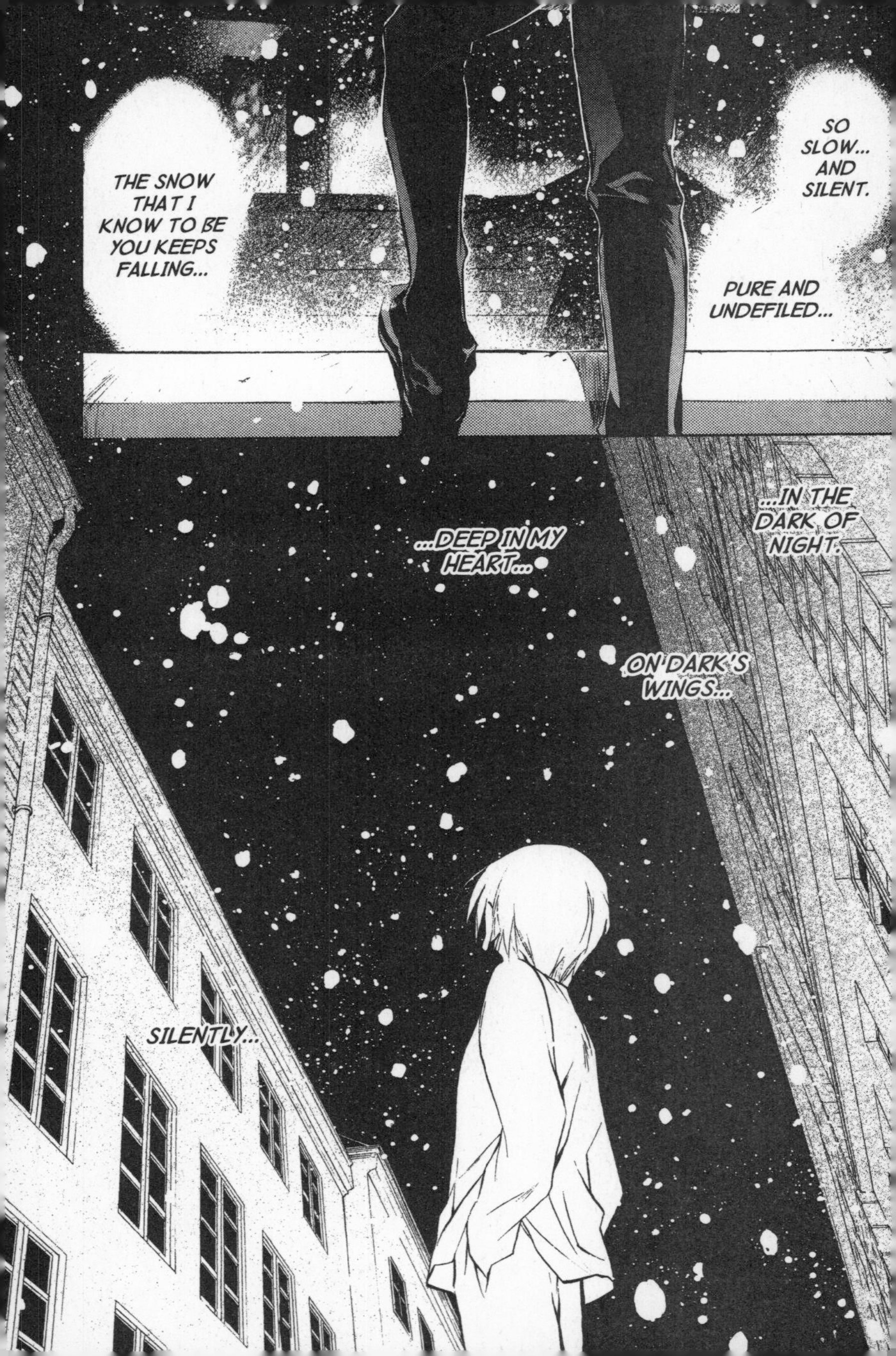
SO SLOW... AND SILENT.
PURE AND UNDEFILED...
THE SNOW THAT I KNOW TO BE YOU KEEPS FALLING...
...IN THE DARK OF NIGHT.
...DEEP IN MY HEART...
ON DARK'S WINGS...
SILENTLY...

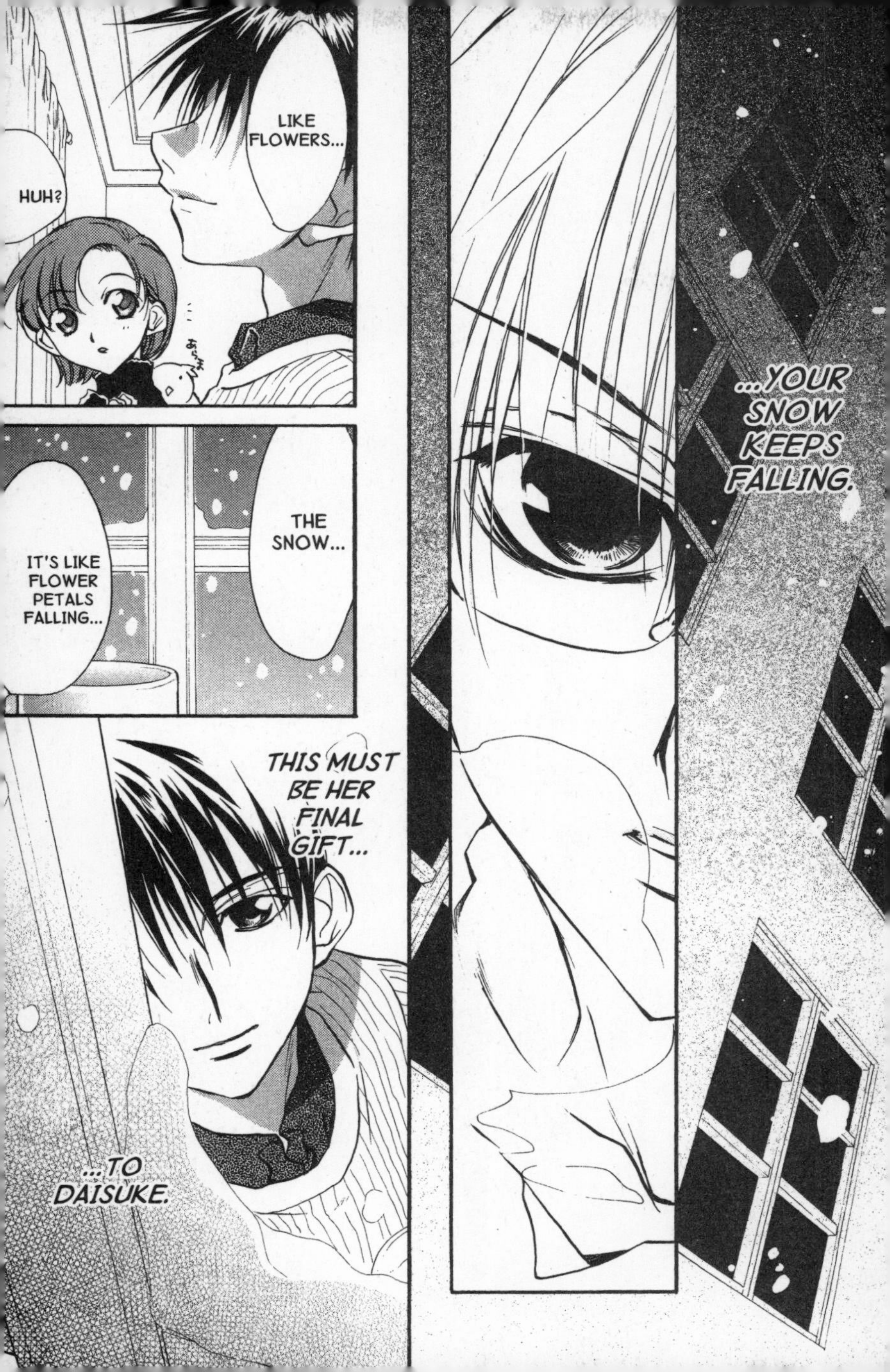
...YOUR SNOW KEEPS FALLING.
LIKE FLOWERS...
HUH?
THE SNOW...
IT'S LIKE FLOWER PETALS FALLING...
THIS MUST BE HER FINAL GIFT...
...TO DAISUKE.

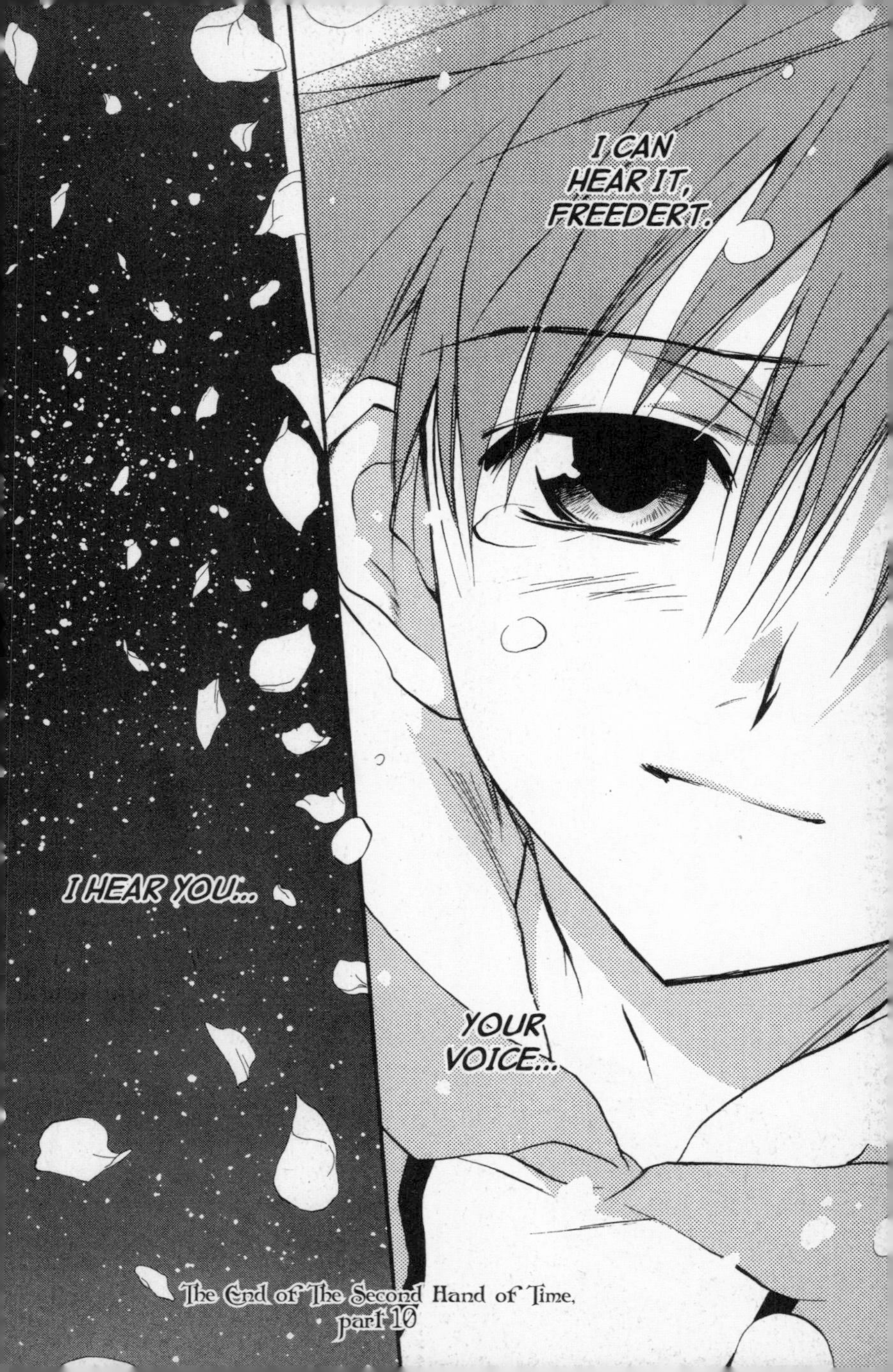
I CAN HEAR IT, FREEDERT.
I HEAR YOU...
YOUR VOICE...
The End of The Second Hand of Time, part 10

D•N•ANGEL
THINGS TO COME...

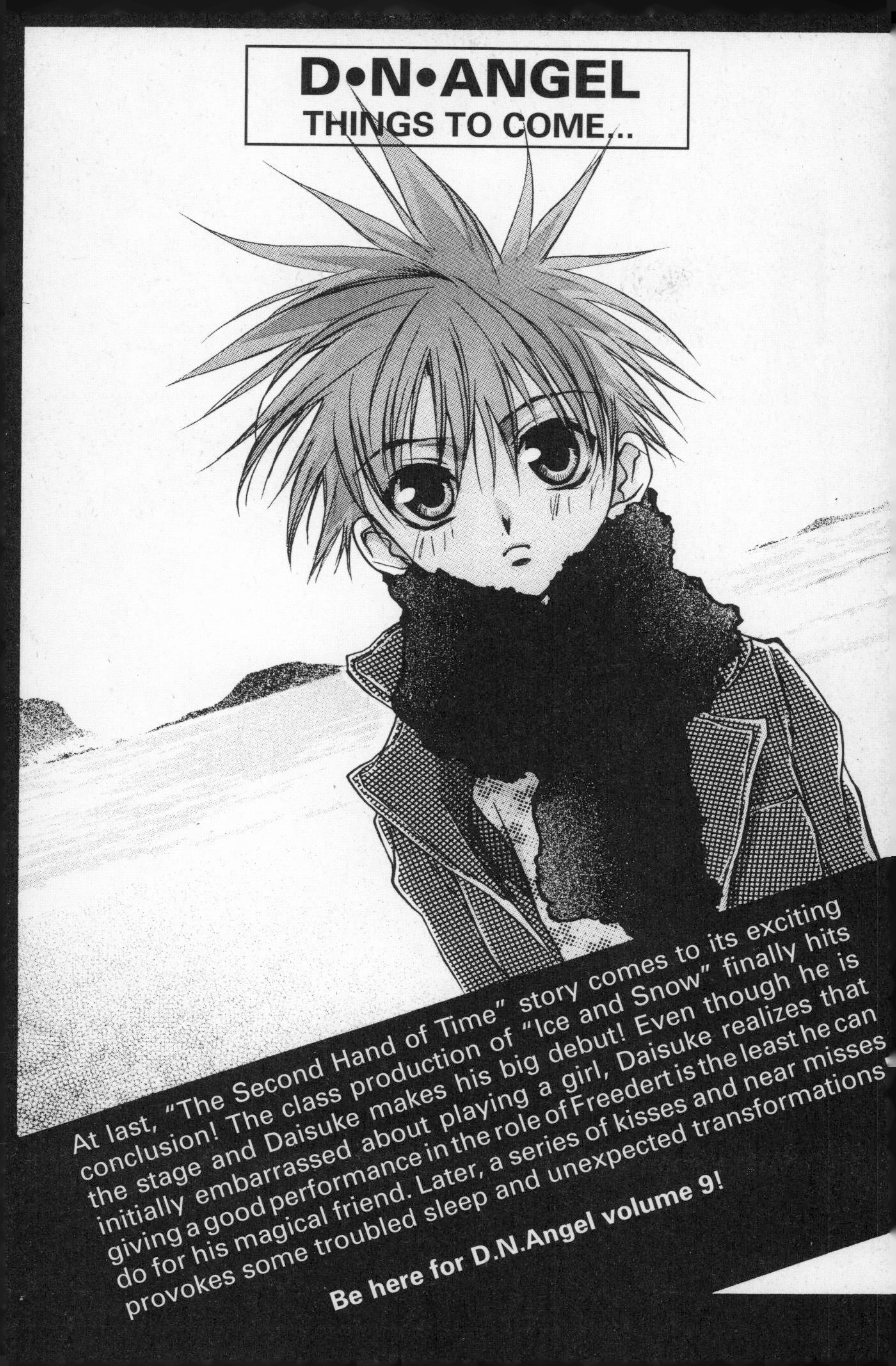

At last, "The Second Hand of Time" story comes to its exciting conclusion! The class production of "Ice and Snow" finally hits the stage and Daisuke makes his big debut! Even though he is initially embarrassed about playing a girl, Daisuke realizes that giving a good performance in the role of Freedert is the least he can do for his magical friend. Later, a series of kisses and near misses provokes some troubled sleep and unexpected transformations.

Be here for D.N.Angel volume 9!

TOKYOPOP SHOP

WWW.TOKYOPOP.COM/SHOP

HOT NEWS!

Check out the
TOKYOPOP SHOP!
The world's best
collection of manga in
English is now available
online in one place!

ARCANA

TOKYO MEW MEW A LA MODE

MBQ and other
hot titles are
available at
the store that
never closes!

MBQ

- LOOK FOR SPECIAL OFFERS
- PRE-ORDER UPCOMING RELEASES!
- COMPLETE YOUR COLLECTIONS

BECK: MONGOLIAN CHOP SQUAD

OT
OLDER TEEN
AGE 16+

ROCK IN MANGA!

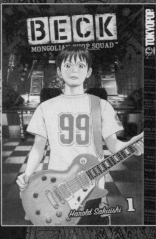

Yukio Tanaka is one boring guy with no hobbies, a weak taste in music and only a small vestige of a personality. But his life is forever changed when he meets Ryusuke Minami, an unpredictable rocker with a cool dog named Beck. Recently returned to Japan from America, Ryusuke inspires Yukio to get into music, and the two begin a journey through the world of rock 'n' roll dreams! With cameos of music's greatest stars—from John Lennon to David Bowie—and homages to supergroups such as Led Zeppelin and Nirvana, anyone who's anyone can make an appearance in *Beck*…even Beck himself! With action, music and gobs of comedy, *Beck* puts the rock in manga!

HAROLD SAKUISHI'S HIGHLY ADDICTIVE MANGA SERIES THAT SPAWNED A HIT ANIME HAS FINALLY REACHED THE STATES!

© Harold Sakuishi

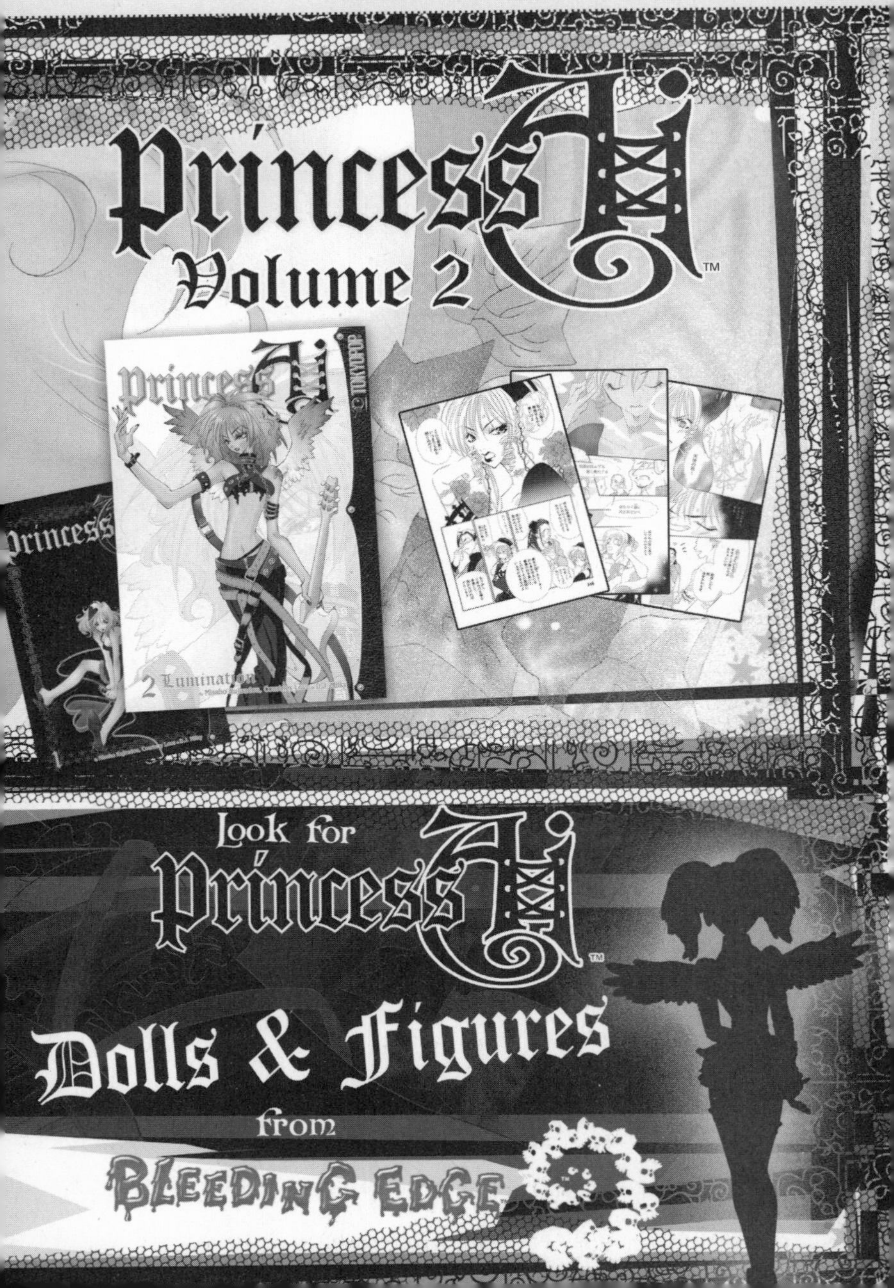
Princess Ai™
Volume 2
Princess Ai
TOKYOPOP
2 Lumination
Princess
Look for
Princess Ai™
Dolls & Figures
from
BLEEDING EDGE

A Diva Torn from Chaos
A Savior Doomed to Love

Volume 2
Lumination

Ai continues to search for her place in our world on the streets of Tokyo. Using her talent to support herself, Ai signs a contract with a top record label and begins her rise to stardom. But fame is unpredictable—as her talent blooms, all eyes are on Ai. When scandal surfaces, will she burn out in the spotlight of celebrity?

Preview the manga at:
www.TOKYOPOP.com/princessai

T
TEEN
AGE 13+

EDITORS' PICKS TOKYOPOP MANGA SUPPLEMENT

BY BUNJURO NAKAYAMA
AND BOW DITAMA

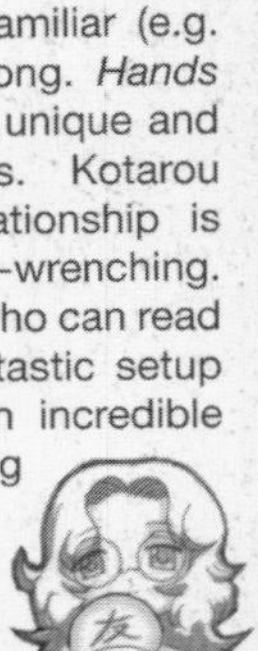

MAHOROMATIC: AUTOMATIC MAIDEN

Mahoro is a sweet, cute, female battle android who decides to go from mopping up alien invaders to mopping up after Suguru Misato, a teenaged orphan boy… and hilarity most definitely ensues. This series has great art and a slick story that easily switches from truly funny to downright heartwarming…but always with a large shadow looming over it. You see, only Mahoro knows that her days are quite literally numbered, and the end of each chapter lets you know exactly how much—or how little—time she has left!

~Rob Tokar, Sr. Editor

BY KASANE KATSUMOTO

HANDS OFF!

Cute boys with ESP who share a special bond… If you think this is familiar (e.g. *Legal Drug*), well, you're wrong. *Hands Off!* totally stands alone as a unique and thoroughly enjoyable series. Kotarou and Tatsuki's (platonic!) relationship is complex, fascinating and heart-wrenching. Throw in Yuuto, the playboy who can read auras, and you've got a fantastic setup for drama and comedy, with incredible themes of friendship running throughout. Don't be put off by Kotarou's danger-magnet status, either. The episodic stuff gradually changes, and the full arc of the characters' development is well worth waiting for.

~Lillian Diaz-Przybyl, Jr. Editor

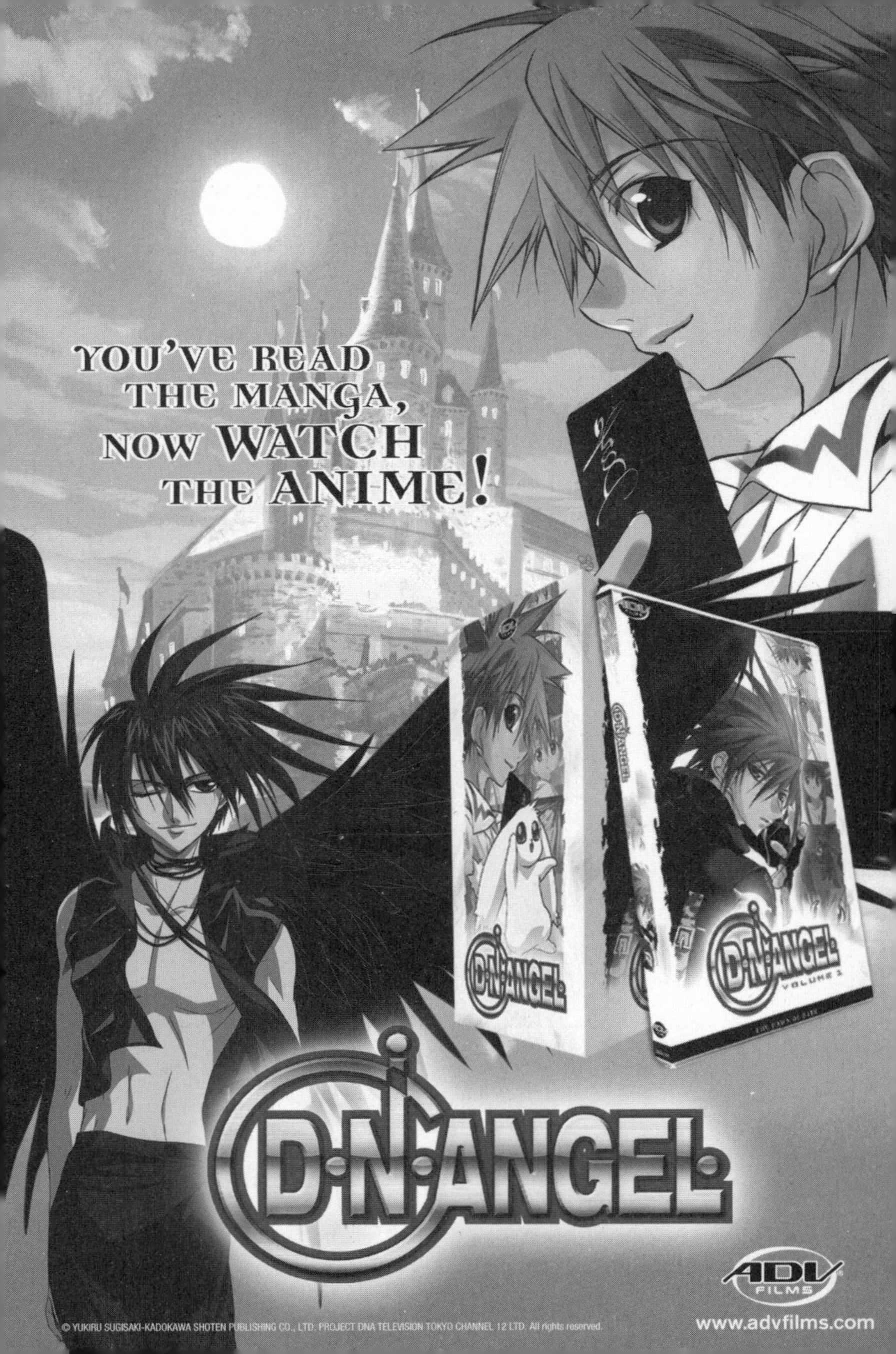

STOP!

This is the back of the book.
You wouldn't want to spoil a great ending!

This book is printed "manga-style," in the authentic Japanese right-to-left format. Since none of the artwork has been flipped or altered, readers get to experience the story just as the creator intended. You've been asking for it, so TOKYOPOP® delivered: authentic, hot-off-the-press, and far more fun!

DIRECTIONS

If this is your first time reading manga-style, here's a quick guide to help you understand how it works.

It's easy... just start in the top right panel and follow the numbers. Have fun, and look for more 100% authentic manga from TOKYOPOP®!